COMPENDIUM
OF THE SOCIAL DOCTRINE
OF THE CHURCH

PONTIFICAL COUNCIL
FOR JUSTICE AND PEACE

COMPENDIUM
OF THE SOCIAL DOCTRINE
OF THE CHURCH

LIBRERIA EDITRICE VATICANA

Canadian Conference of Catholic Bishops
Ottawa, Ontario

First Printing, January 2005, Reprint 2006
Printed in Canada

CCCB Publications
Canadian Conference of Catholic Bishops
2500 Don Reid Drive
Ottawa, Ontario K1H 2J2
www.cccbpublications.ca

ISBN: 0-88997-509-4

Legal deposit: National Library of Canada, Ottawa

184-469

TO HIS HOLINESS POPE JOHN PAUL II
MASTER OF SOCIAL DOCTRINE AND
EVANGELICAL WITNESS
TO JUSTICE AND PEACE

TABLE OF CONTENTS

INTRODUCTION
AN INTEGRAL AND SOLIDARY HUMANISM

PART ONE
CHAPTER ONE
GOD'S PLAN OF LOVE FOR HUMANITY

PART TWO

CHAPTER FIVE

THE FAMILY, THE VITAL CELL OF SOCIETY

CHAPTER SIX

HUMAN WORK

CHAPTER SEVEN

ECONOMIC LIFE

CHAPTER EIGHT

THE POLITICAL COMMUNITY

CHAPTER ELEVEN

THE PROMOTION OF PEACE

PART THREE

CHAPTER TWELVE

SOCIAL DOCTRINE AND ECCLESIAL ACTION

CONCLUSION
FOR A CIVILIZATION OF LOVE

SECRETARIAT OF STATE

From the Vatican, 29 June 2004

N. 559.332

Your Eminence,

Throughout the course of her history, and particularly in the last hundred years, the Church has never failed, in the words of Pope Leo XIII, to speak "the words that are hers" with regard to questions concerning life in society. Continuing to expound and update the rich patrimony of Catholic social doctrine, Pope John Paul II has for his part published three great Encyclicals — *Laborem Exercens, Sollicitudo Rei Socialis* and *Centesimus Annus* — that represent fundamental stages of Catholic thought in this area. For their part, numerous Bishops in every part of the world have contributed in recent times to a deeper understanding of the Church's social doctrine. Numerous scholars on every continent have done the same.

1.   It was therefore hoped that a compendium of all this material should be compiled, systematically presenting the foundations of Catholic social doctrine. It is commendable that the Pontifical Council for Justice and Peace has taken up this task, devoting intense efforts to this initiative in recent years.

I am pleased that the volume "Compendium of the Social Doctrine of the Church" has been published, sharing with you the joy of offering it to the faithful and to all people of good will, as food for human and spiritual growth, for individuals and communities alike.

2.   This work also shows the value of Catholic social doctrine as an instrument of evangelization (cf. *Centesimus Annus*, 54), because it places the human person and society in relationship with the light of the Gospel. The principles of the Church's social doctrine, which are based on the natural law, are then seen to be confirmed and strengthened, in the faith of the Church, by the Gospel of Christ.

In this light, men and women are invited above all to discover themselves as transcendent beings, in every dimension of their lives, including those related to social, economic and political contexts. Faith brings to fullness the meaning of the

---

His Eminence
Cardinal RENATO RAFFAELE MARTINO
President of the Pontifical Council for Justice and Peace
VATICAN CITY

family, which, founded on marriage between one man and one woman, constitutes the first and vital cell of society. It moreover sheds light on the dignity of work, which, as human activity destined to bring human beings to fulfilment, has priority over capital and confirms their rightful claim to share in the fruits that result from work.

3.   In the present text we can see the importance of moral values, founded on the natural law written on every human conscience; every human conscience is hence obliged to recognize and respect this law. Humanity today seeks greater justice in dealing with the vast phenomenon of globalization; it has a keen concern for ecology and a correct management of public affairs; it senses the need to safeguard national consciences, without losing sight however of the path of law and the awareness of the unity of the human family. The world of work, profoundly changed by the advances of modern technology, reveals extraordinary levels of quality, but unfortunately it must also acknowledge new forms of instability, exploitation and even slavery within the very societies that are considered affluent. In different areas of the planet the level of well-being continues to grow, but there is also a dangerous increase in the numbers of those who are becoming poor, and, for various reasons, the gap between less developed and rich countries is widening. The free market, an economic process with positive aspects, is nonetheless showing its limitations. On the other hand, the preferential love for the poor represents a fundamental choice for the Church, and she proposes it to all people of good will.

It is thus apparent that the Church cannot fail to make her voice heard concerning the "new things" (*res novae*) typical of the modern age, because it belongs to her to invite all people to do all they can to bring about an authentic civilization oriented ever more towards integral human development in solidarity.

4.   Contemporary cultural and social issues involve above all the lay faithful, who are called, as the Second Vatican Council reminds us, to deal with temporal affairs and order them according to God's will (cf. *Lumen Gentium*, 31). We can therefore easily understand the fundamental importance of the formation of the laity, so that the holiness of their lives and the strength of their witness will contribute to human progress. This document intends to help them in this daily mission.

Moreover, it is interesting to note how the many elements brought together here are shared by other Churches and Ecclesial Communities, as well as by other Religions. The text has been presented in such a way as to be useful not only from within (*ab intra*), that is among Catholics, but also from outside (*ab extra*). In fact, those who share the same Baptism with us, as well as the followers of other Religions and all people of good will, can find herein fruitful occasions for reflection and a common motivation for the integral development of every person and the whole person.

5.   The Holy Father, while hoping that the present document will help humanity in its active quest for the common good, invokes God's blessings on those who will take the time to reflect on the teachings of this publication. In expressing my

own personal good wishes for the success of this endeavour, I congratulate Your Eminence and your collaborators at the Pontifical Council of Justice and Peace for the important work carried out, and with sentiments of respect I remain

Yours sincerely in Christ,

Cardinal ANGELO SODANO

Secretary of State

PRESENTATION

I am pleased to present the *Compendium of the Social Doctrine of the Church*, which, according to the request received from the Holy Father, has been drawn up in order to give a concise but complete overview of the Church's social teaching.

Transforming social realities with the power of the Gospel, to which witness is borne by women and men faithful to Jesus Christ, has always been a challenge and it remains so today at the beginning of the third millennium of the Christian era. The proclamation of Jesus Christ, the "Good News" of salvation, love, justice and peace, is not readily received in today's world, devastated as it is by wars, poverty and injustices. For this very reason the men and women of our day have greater need than ever of the Gospel: of the faith that saves, of the hope that enlightens, of the charity that loves.

The Church is an expert in humanity, and anticipating with trust and with active involvement she continues to look towards the "new heavens" and the "new earth" (*2 Pet* 3:13), which she indicates to every person, in order to help people to live their lives in the dimension of authentic meaning. "*Gloria Dei vivens homo*": the human person who fully lives his or her dignity gives glory to God, who has given this dignity to men and women.

The reading of these pages is suggested above all in order to sustain and foster the activity of Christians in the social sector, especially the activity of the lay faithful to whom this area belongs in a particular way; the whole of their lives must be seen as a work of evangelization that produces fruit. Every believer must learn first of all to obey the Lord with the strength of faith, following the example of Saint Peter: "Master, we toiled all night and took nothing! But at your word I will let down the nets" (*Lk* 5:5). Every reader of "good will" will be able to understand the motives that prompt the Church to intervene with her doctrine in the social sector, an area which, at first glance, does not belong to the Church's competence, and these same readers will see the reasons for an encounter, for dialogue, for cooperation in serving the common good.

My predecessor, the late and venerable Cardinal François-Xavier Nguyên Van Thuân, guided with wisdom, constancy and far-sightedness the complex phase of the preparation of this document; his illness prevented him from bringing it to a conclusion with its publication. This work, entrusted to me and now offered to those who will read it, carries therefore the seal of a great witness to the Cross who remained *strong in faith* in the dark and terrible years of Vietnam. This witness will know of our gratitude for all his precious labour, undertaken with love and dedication, and he will bless those who stop to reflect on these pages.

I invoke the intercession of Saint Joseph, Guardian of the Redeemer and Husband of the Blessed Virgin Mary, Patron of the Universal Church and of

Work, so that this text will bear abundant fruit in the life of society as an instrument for the proclamation of the Gospel, for justice and for peace.

Vatican City, 2 April 2004, Memorial of Saint Francis of Paola.

Cardinal RENATO RAFFAELE MARTINO
President

+ GIAMPAOLO CREPALDI
Secretary

ABBREVIATIONS

a.	*in articulo*
AAS	*Acta Apostolicae Sedis*
ad 1um	*in responsione ad 1 argumentum*
ad 2um	*in responsione ad 2 argumentum et ita porro*
Ap. Exhort.	Apostolic Exhortation
Ap. Letter	Apostolic Letter
c.	*corpore articuli*
cf.	conferatur
ch.	chapter
d.	distinctio
DS	H. DENZINGER - A. SCHÖNMETZER, *Enchiridion Symbolorum definitionum et declarationum de rebus fidei et morum*
Ed. Leon.	SANCTI THOMAE AQUINATIS DOCTORIS ANGELICI *Opera omnia* iussu impensaque Leonis XIII P.M. edita
Enc. Letter	Encyclical Letter
ibid.	*ibidem*
PG	*Patrologia Graeca* (J. P. Migne)
PL	*Patrologia Latina* (J. P. Migne)
q.	*quaestio*
v.	verse
I	Prima Pars Summae Theologiae
I-II	Prima Secundae Partis Summae Theologiae
II-II	Secunda Secundae Partis Summae Theologiae
III	Tertia Pars Summae Theologiae

BIBLICAL ABBREVIATIONS

Acts	Acts of the Apostles		*2 Kg*	2 Kings
Am	Amos		*Lam*	Lamentations
Bar	Baruch		*Lev*	Leviticus
1 Chr	1 Chronicles		*Lk*	Luke
2 Chr	2 Chronicles		*1 Macc*	1 Maccabees
Col	Colossians		*2 Macc*	2 Maccabees
1 Cor	1 Corinthians		*Mal*	Malachi
2 Cor	2 Corinthians		*Mk*	Mark
Dan	Daniel		*Mt*	Matthew
Deut	Deuteronomy		*Mic*	Micah
Eccles	Ecclesiastes		*Nahum*	Nahum
Eph	Ephesians		*Neh*	Nehemiah
Esther	Esther		*Num*	Numbers
Ex	Exodus		*Ob*	Obadiah
Ezek	Ezekiel		*1 Pet*	1 Peter
Ezra	Ezra		*2 Pet*	2 Peter
Gal	Galatians		*Phil*	Philippians
Gen	Genesis		*Philem*	Philemon
Hab	Habakkuk		*Prov*	Proverbs
Hag	Haggai		*Ps*	Psalms
Heb	Hebrews		*Rev*	Revelation
Hos	Hosea		*Rom*	Romans
Is	Isaiah		*Ruth*	Ruth
Jas	James		*1 Sam*	1 Samuel
Jer	Jeremiah		*2 Sam*	2 Samuel
Job	Job		*Sir*	Sirach
Joel	Joel		*Song*	Song of Songs
Jn	John		*1 Thes*	1 Thessalonians
1 Jn	1 John		*2 Thes*	2 Thessalonians
2 Jn	2 John		*1 Tim*	1 Timothy
3 Jn	3 John		*2 Tim*	2 Timothy
Jon	Jonah		*Tit*	Titus
Josh	Joshua		*Tob*	Tobit
Jude	Jude		*Wis*	Wisdom
Jdg	Judges		*Zech*	Zechariah
Jdt	Judith		*Zeph*	Zapheniah
1 Kg	1 Kings			

COMPENDIUM
OF THE SOCIAL DOCTRINE
OF THE CHURCH

INTRODUCTION

AN INTEGRAL AND SOLIDARY HUMANISM

a. At the dawn of the Third Millennium

1. *The Church moves further into the Third Millennium of the Christian era as a pilgrim people, guided by Christ, the "great Shepherd"* (Heb 13:20). He is the "Holy Door" (cf. Jn 10:9) through which we passed during the Great Jubilee of the year 2000.[1] Jesus Christ is the Way, the Truth and the Life (cf. Jn 14:6): contemplating the Lord's face, we confirm our faith and our hope in him, the one Savior and goal of history.

The Church continues to speak to all people and all nations, for it is only in the name of Christ that salvation is given to men and women. Salvation, which the Lord Jesus obtained "at a price" (1 Cor 6:20; cf. 1 Pet 1:18-19), is achieved in the new life that awaits the righteous after death, but it also permeates this world in the realities of the economy and labor, of technology and communications, of society and politics, of the international community and the relations among cultures and peoples. "Jesus came to bring integral salvation, one which embraces the whole person and all mankind, and opens up the wondrous prospect of divine filiation."[2]

2. *At the dawn of this Third Millennium, the Church does not tire of proclaiming the Gospel that brings salvation and genuine freedom also to temporal realities.* She is mindful of the solemn exhortation given by Saint Paul to his disciple Timothy: "Preach the word, be urgent in season and out of season, convince, rebuke, and exhort, be unfailing in patience and in teaching. For the time is coming when people will not endure sound teaching, but having itching ears they will accumulate for themselves teachers to suit their own likings, and will turn away from listening to the truth and wander into myths. As for you, always be steady, endure suffering, do the work of an evangelist, fulfil your ministry" (2 Tim 4:2-5).

3. *To the people of our time, her travelling companions, the Church also offers her social doctrine.* In fact, when the Church "fulfils her mission of proclaiming the Gospel, she bears witness to man, in the name of Christ, to his dignity and his vocation to the communion of persons. She teaches him the demands of justice and peace in conformity with divine wisdom."[3] *This doctrine has its own profound unity, which flows from Faith in a whole and complete salvation, from Hope in a full-*

---

[1] Cf. John Paul II, Apostolic Letter *Novo Millennio Ineunte*, 1: AAS 93 (2001), 266.
[2] John Paul II, Encyclical Letter *Redemptoris Missio*, 11: AAS 83 (1991), 260.
[3] *Catechism of the Catholic Church*, 2419.

ness of justice, and from Love which makes all mankind truly brothers and sisters in Christ: it is the expression of God's love for the world, which he so loved "that he gave his only Son" (Jn 3:16). The new law of love embraces the entire human family and knows no limits, since the proclamation of the salvation wrought by Christ extends "to the ends of the earth" (Acts 1:8).

4.   *Discovering that they are loved by God, people come to understand their own transcendent dignity, they learn not to be satisfied with only themselves but to encounter their neighbor in a network of relationships that are ever more authentically human.* Men and women who are made "new" by the love of God are able to change the rules and the quality of relationships, transforming even social structures. They are people capable of bringing peace where there is conflict, of building and nurturing fraternal relationships where there is hatred, of seeking justice where there prevails the exploitation of man by man. Only love is capable of radically transforming the relationships that men maintain among themselves. This is the perspective that allows every person of good will to perceive the broad horizons of justice and human development in truth and goodness.

5.   *Love faces a vast field of work and the Church is eager to make her contribution with her social doctrine, which concerns the whole person and is addressed to all people.* So many needy brothers and sisters are waiting for help, so many who are oppressed are waiting for justice, so many who are unemployed are waiting for a job, so many peoples are waiting for respect. "How can it be that even today there are still people dying of hunger? Condemned to illiteracy? Lacking the most basic medical care? Without a roof over their head? The scenario of poverty can extend indefinitely, if in addition to its traditional forms we think of its newer patterns. These latter often affect financially affluent sectors and groups which are nevertheless threatened by despair at the lack of meaning in their lives, by drug addiction, by fear of abandonment in old age or sickness, by marginalization or social discrimination . . . And how can we remain indifferent to the prospect of an ecological crisis which is making vast areas of our planet uninhabitable and hostile to humanity? Or by the problems of peace, so often threatened by the spectre of catastrophic wars? Or by contempt for the fundamental human rights of so many people, especially children?"[4]

6.   *Christian love leads to denunciation, proposals and a commitment to cultural and social projects; it prompts positive activity that inspires all who sincerely have the good of man at heart to make their contribution.* Humanity is coming to understand ever more clearly that it is linked by one sole destiny that requires joint acceptance of responsibility, a responsibility inspired by an integral and shared humanism. It sees that this mutual destiny is often conditioned and even imposed by technological and economic factors, and it senses the need for a greater moral awareness that will guide its common journey. Marvelling at the many innovations of technology, the men and women of our day strongly desire that progress be directed towards the true good of the humanity, both of today and tomorrow.

---

[4]   John Paul II, Apostolic Letter *Novo Millennio Ineunte*, 50-51: AAS 93 (2001), 303-304.

b. The significance of this document

7. *The Christian knows that in the social doctrine of the Church can be found the principles for reflection, the criteria for judgment and the directives for action which are the starting point for the promotion of an integral and solidary humanism.* Making this doctrine known constitutes, therefore, a genuine pastoral priority, so that men and women will be enlightened by it and will be thus enabled to interpret today's reality and seek appropriate paths of action: "The teaching and spreading of her social doctrine are part of the Church's evangelizing mission."[5]

It is in this light that the publication of a document providing the fundamental elements of the social doctrine of the Church, showing the relationship between this doctrine and the new evangelization,[6] appeared to be so useful. The Pontifical Council for Justice and Peace, which has drawn up the present document and is fully responsible for its content, prepared the text in a broad-based consultation with its own Members and Consulters, with different Dicasteries of the Roman Curia, with the Bishops' Conferences of various countries, with individual Bishops and with experts on the issues addressed.

8. *This document intends to present in a complete and systematic manner, even if by means of an overview, the Church's social teaching, which is the fruit of careful Magisterial reflection and an expression of the Church's constant commitment in fidelity to the grace of salvation wrought in Christ and in loving concern for humanity's destiny.* Herein the most relevant theological, philosophical, moral, cultural and pastoral considerations of this teaching are systematically presented as they relate to *social questions*. In this way, witness is borne to the fruitfulness of the encounter between the Gospel and the problems that mankind encounters on its journey through history. In studying this Compendium, it is good to keep in mind that the citations of Magisterial texts are taken from documents of differing authority. Alongside council documents and encyclicals there are also papal addresses and documents drafted by offices of the Holy See. As one knows, but it seems to bear repeating, the reader should be aware that different levels of teaching authority are involved. The document limits itself to putting forth the fundamental elements of the Church's social doctrine, leaving to Episcopal Conferences the task of making the appropriate applications as required by the different local situations.[7]

9. *This document offers a complete overview of the fundamental framework of the doctrinal corpus of Catholic social teaching.* This overview allows us to address appropriately the social issues of our day, which must be considered as a whole, since they are characterized by an ever greater interconnectedness, influencing one another mutually and becoming increasingly a matter of concern for the entire human family. The exposition of the Church's social doctrine is meant to suggest a systematic approach for finding solutions to problems, so that discernment, judgment and

---

[5] John Paul II, Encyclical Letter *Sollicitudo Rei Socialis*, 41: AAS 80 (1988), 571-572.

[6] Cf. John Paul II, Post-Synodal Apostolic Exhortation *Ecclesia in America*, 54: AAS 91 (1999), 790.

[7] Cf. John Paul II, Post-Synodal Apostolic Exhortation *Ecclesia in America*, 54: AAS 91 (1999), 790; *Catechism of the Catholic Church*, 24.

decisions will correspond to reality, and so that solidarity and hope will have a greater impact on the complexities of current situations. These principles, in fact, are interrelated and shed light on one another mutually, insofar as they are an expression of Christian anthropology,[8] fruits of the revelation of God's love for the human person. *However, it must not be forgotten that the passing of time and the changing of social circumstances will require a constant updating of the reflections on the various issues raised here, in order to interpret the new signs of the times.*

10. *The document is presented as an instrument for the moral and pastoral discernment of the complex events that mark our time; as a guide to inspire, at the individual and collective levels, attitudes and choices that will permit all people to look to the future with greater trust and hope*; as an aid for the faithful concerning the Church's teaching in the area of social morality. From this there can spring new strategies suited to the demands of our time and in keeping with human needs and resources. But above all there can arise the motivation to rediscover the vocation proper to the different charisms within the Church that are destined to the evangelization of the social order, because *"all the members* of the Church are sharers in this secular dimension."[9] In short, the text is proposed as an incentive for dialogue with all who sincerely desire the good of mankind.

11. *This document is intended first of all for Bishops, who will determine the most suitable methods for making it known and for interpreting it correctly.* It is in fact part of the Bishops' *"munus docendi"* to teach that "worldly things and human institutions are ordered, according to the plan of God the Creator, towards people's salvation, and that they can therefore make no small contribution to the building up of the Body of Christ."[10] *Priests, men and women religious,* and, in general, *those responsible for formation* will find herein a guide for their teaching and a tool for their pastoral service. *The lay faithful,* who seek the Kingdom of God "by engaging in temporal affairs and directing them according to God's will,"[11] will find in it enlightenment for their own specific mission. *Christian communities* will be able to look to this document for assistance in analyzing situations objectively, in clarifying them in the light of the unchanging words of the Gospel, in drawing principles for reflection, criteria for judgment and guidelines for action.[12]

12. *This document is proposed also to the brethren of other Churches and Ecclesial Communities, to the followers of other religions, as well as to all people of good will who are committed to serving the common good*: may they receive it as the fruit of a universal human experience marked by countless signs of the presence of God's Spirit. It is a treasury of things old and new (cf. Mt 13:52), which the Church wishes to share, in thanksgiving to God, from whom comes "every good endow-

---

[8] Cf. John Paul II, Encyclical Letter *Centesimus Annus*, 55: AAS 83 (1991), 860.

[9] John Paul II, Post-Synodal Apostolic Exhortation *Christifideles Laici*, 15: AAS 81 (1989), 414.

[10] Second Vatican Ecumenical Council, Decree *Christus Dominus*, 12: AAS 58 (1966), 678.

[11] Second Vatican Ecumenical Council, Dogmatic Constitution *Lumen Gentium*, 31: AAS 57 (1965), 37.

[12] Cf. Paul VI, Apostolic Letter *Octogesima Adveniens*, 4: AAS 63 (1971), 403.

ment and ever perfect gift" (*Jas* 1:17). It is a sign of hope in the fact that religions and cultures today show openness to dialogue and sense the urgent need to join forces in promoting justice, fraternity, peace and the growth of the human person.

The Catholic Church joins her own commitment to that made in the social field by other Churches and Ecclesial Communities, whether at the level of doctrinal reflection or at the practical level. Together with them, the Catholic Church is convinced that from the common heritage of social teachings preserved by the living tradition of the people of God there will come motivations and orientations for an ever closer cooperation in the promotion of justice and peace.[13]

c. **At the service of the full truth about man**

13. *This document is an act of service on the part of the Church to the women and men of our time*, to whom she offers the legacy of her social doctrine, according to that style of dialogue by which God himself, in his only-begotten Son made man, "addresses men as his friends (cf. *Ex* 33:11; *Jn* 15:14-15) and moves among them (cf. *Bar* 3:38)."[14] Drawing inspiration from the Pastoral Constitution *Gaudium et Spes*, this document too places "man considered whole and entire, with body and soul, heart and conscience, mind and will" [15] as the key to its whole exposition. In this perspective, the Church is "inspired by no earthly ambition and seeks but one solitary goal: to carry forward the work of Christ himself under the lead of the befriending Spirit. For Christ entered this world to bear witness to the truth, to save and not to sit in judgment, to serve and not to be served."[16]

14. *By means of the present document, the Church intends to offer a contribution of truth to the question of man's place in nature and in human society, a question faced by civilizations and cultures in which expressions of human wisdom are found.* Rooted in a past that is often thousands of years old and manifesting themselves in forms of religion, philosophy and poetic genius of every time and of every people, these civilizations and cultures offer their own interpretation of the universe and of human society, and seek an understanding of existence and of the mystery that surrounds it. Who am I? Why is there pain, evil, death, despite all the progress that has been made? What is the value of so many accomplishments if the cost has been unbearable? What will there be after this life? These are the basic questions that characterize the course of human life.[17] In this regard, we can recall the admonition *"Know yourself,"* carved on the temple portal at Delphi, which testifies to the basic truth that man, called to be set apart from the rest of creation, is *man* precisely because in his essence he is oriented to *knowing himself.*

---

[13] Cf. Second Vatican Ecumenical Council, Pastoral Constitution *Gaudium et Spes*, 92: AAS 58 (1966), 1113-1114.

[14] Second Vatican Ecumenical Council, Dogmatic Constitution *Dei Verbum*, 2: AAS 58 (1966), 818.

[15] Second Vatican Ecumenical Council, Pastoral Constitution *Gaudium et Spes*, 3: AAS 58 (1966), 1026.

[16] Second Vatican Ecumenical Council, Pastoral Constitution *Gaudium et Spes*, 3: AAS 58 (1966), 1027.

[17] Cf. Second Vatican Ecumenical Council, Pastoral Constitution *Gaudium et Spes*, 10: AAS 58 (1966), 1032.

15.   *The direction that human existence, society and history will take depends largely on the answers given to the questions of man's place in nature and society; the purpose of the present document is to make a contribution to these answers.* The deepest meaning of human existence, in fact, is revealed in the free quest for that truth capable of giving direction and fullness to life. The aforementioned questions incessantly draw human intelligence and the human will to this quest. They are the highest expression of human nature, since they require a response that measures the depth of an individual's commitment to his own existence. Moreover, it is dealt here with *questions that are essentially religious*: "When the 'why of things' is investigated integrally with the search for the ultimate and exhaustive answer, then human reason reaches its apex and opens itself to religiousness. . . . [R]eligiousness represents the loftiest expression of the human person, because it is the culmination of his rational nature. It springs from man's profound aspiration for truth and is at the basis of the free and personal search he makes for the divine."[18]

16.   *The fundamental questions accompanying the human journey from the very beginning take on even greater significance in our own day, because of the enormity of the challenges, the novelty of the situations and the importance of the decisions facing modern generations.*
      The first of the great challenges facing humanity today is that of *the truth itself of the being who is man.* The boundary and relation between nature, technology and morality are issues that decisively summon personal and collective responsibility with regard to the attitudes to adopt concerning what human beings are, what they are able to accomplish and what they should be. A second challenge is found in *the understanding and management of pluralism and differences* at every level: in ways of thinking, moral choices, culture, religious affiliation, philosophy of human and social development. The third challenge is *globalization*, the significance of which is much wider and more profound than simple economic globalization, since history has witnessed the opening of a new era that concerns humanity's destiny.

17.   *The disciples of Jesus Christ feel that they are involved with these questions; they too carry them within their hearts and wish to commit themselves, together with all men and women, to the quest for the truth and the meaning of life lived both as individual persons and as a society. They contribute to this quest by their generous witness to the free and extraordinary gift that humanity has received:* God has spoken his Word to men and women throughout history; indeed he himself has entered history in order to enter into dialogue with humanity and to reveal to mankind his plan of salvation, justice and brotherhood. In Jesus Christ, his Son made man, God has freed us from sin and has shown us the path we are to walk and the goal towards which we are to strive.

d. **In the sign of solidarity, respect and love**

18.   *The Church journeys along the roads of history together with all of humanity.* She lives in the world, and although not of the world (cf. *Jn* 17:14-16) she is called to

---

[18] John Paul II, Address at General Audience (19 October 1983), 2: *L'Osservatore Romano*, English edition, 24 October 1983, p. 9.

serve the world according to her innermost vocation. This attitude, found also in the present document, is based on the deep conviction that just as it is important for the world to recognize the Church as a reality of history and a leaven in history, so too is it important for the Church to recognize what she has received from history and from the development of the human race.[19] The Second Vatican Council gave an eloquent demonstration of solidarity, respect and affection for the whole human family by engaging in dialogue with it about many problems, "bringing the light kindled from the Gospel and putting at the disposal of the human race the saving resources which the Church has received from her Founder under the promptings of the Holy Spirit. It is man himself who must be saved; it is human society which must be renewed."[20]

19. *The Church, the sign in history of God's love for mankind and of the vocation of the whole human race to unity as children of the one Father,[21] intends with this document on her social doctrine to propose to all men and women a humanism that is up to the standards of God's plan of love in history, an integral and solidary humanism* capable of creating a new social, economic and political order, founded on the dignity and freedom of every human person, to be brought about in peace, justice and solidarity. This humanism can become a reality if individual men and women and their communities are able to cultivate moral and social virtues in themselves and spread them in society. "Then, under the necessary help of divine grace, there will arise a generation of new men, the moulders of a new humanity."[22]

[19] Cf. Second Vatican Ecumenical Council, Pastoral Constitution *Gaudium et Spes*, 44: AAS 58 (1966), 1064.

[20] Second Vatican Ecumenical Council, Pastoral Constitution *Gaudium et Spes*, 3: AAS 58 (1966), 1026.

[21] Second Vatican Ecumenical Council, Dogmatic Constitution *Lumen Gentium*, 1: AAS 57 (1965), 5.

[22] Second Vatican Ecumenical Council, Pastoral Constitution *Gaudium et Spes*, 30: AAS 58 (1966), 1050.

PART ONE

"The theological dimension is needed both
for interpreting and for solving
present day problems in human society."

(*Centesimus Annus*, 55)

CHAPTER ONE

GOD'S PLAN OF LOVE FOR HUMANITY

I. GOD'S LIBERATING ACTION
IN THE HISTORY OF ISRAEL

a. God's gratuitous presence

20. *Every authentic religious experience, in all cultural traditions, leads to an intuition of the Mystery that, not infrequently, is able to recognize some aspect of God's face.* On the one hand, God is seen as the *origin of what exists*, as the presence that guarantees to men and women organized in a society the basic conditions of life, placing at their disposal the goods that are necessary. On the other hand, he appears as the *measure of what should be*, as the presence that challenges human action — both at the personal and at the social levels — regarding the use of those very goods in relation to other people. In every religious experience, therefore, importance attaches to the dimension of *gift* and *gratuitousness*, which is seen as an underlying element of the experience that the human beings have of their existence together with others in the world, as well as to the repercussions of this dimension on the human conscience, which senses that it is called to manage *responsibly and together with others* the gift received. Proof of this is found in the universal recognition of *the golden rule*, which expresses on the level of human relations the injunction addressed by the Mystery to men and women: "Whatever you wish that men should do to you, do so to them" (Mt 7:12).[23]

21. *Against the background of universal religious experience, in which humanity shares in different ways, God's progressive revelation of himself to the people of Israel stands out. This revelation responds to the human quest for the divine in an unexpected and surprising way, thanks to the historical manner — striking and penetrating — in which God's love for man is made concrete.* According to the Book of Exodus, the Lord speaks these words to Moses: "I have seen the affliction of my people who are in Egypt, and have heard their cry because of their taskmasters; I know their sufferings, and I have come down to deliver them out of the hand of the Egyptians, and to bring them up out of that land to a good and broad land, a land flowing with milk and honey" (Ex 3:7-8). The gratuitous presence of God — to which his very name alludes, the name he reveals to Moses, "*I am who I am*" (Ex 3:14) — is manifested in the freeing from slavery and in the promise. These become historical action, which is the origin of the manner in which the Lord's people collectively

---

[23] Cf. *Catechism of the Catholic Church*, 1789, 1970, 2510.

identify themselves, through the acquisition of *freedom* and the *land* that the Lord gives them.

22. *The gratuitousness of this historically efficacious divine action is constantly accompanied by the commitment to the covenant, proposed by God and accepted by Israel.* On Mount Sinai, God's initiative becomes concrete in the covenant with his people, to whom is given the *Decalogue of the commandments revealed by the Lord* (cf. *Ex* 19-24). The "ten commandments" (*Ex* 34:28; cf. *Deut* 4:13; 10:4) "express the implications of belonging to God through the establishment of the covenant. Moral existence is a response to the Lord's loving initiative. It is the acknowledgment and homage given to God and a worship of thanksgiving. It is cooperation with the plan God pursues in history."[24]

The Ten Commandments, *which constitute an extraordinary path of life and indicate the surest way for living in freedom from slavery to sin, contain a privileged expression of the natural law.* They "teach us the true humanity of man. They bring to light the essential duties, and therefore, indirectly, the fundamental rights inherent in the nature of the human person."[25] They describe universal human morality. In the Gospel, Jesus reminds the rich young man that the Ten Commandments (cf. *Mt* 19:18) "constitute the indispensable rules of all social life."[26]

23. *There comes from the Decalogue a commitment that concerns not only fidelity to the one true God, but also the social relations among the people of the Covenant.* These relations are regulated, in particular, by what has been called *the right of the poor*: "If there is among you a poor man, one of your brethren, . . . you shall not harden your heart or shut your hand against your poor brother, but you shall open your hand to him, and lend him sufficient for his need" (*Deut* 15:7-8). All of this applies also to strangers: "When a stranger sojourns with you in your land, you shall not do him wrong. The stranger who sojourns with you shall be to you as the native among you, and you shall love him as yourself; for you were strangers in the land of Egypt: I am the Lord your God" (*Lev* 19:33-34). The gift of freedom and the Promised Land, and the gift of the Covenant on Sinai and the Ten Commandments are therefore intimately linked to the practices which must regulate, in justice and solidarity, the development of Israelite society.

24. *Among the many norms which tend to give concrete expression to the style of gratuitousness and sharing in justice which God inspires, the law of the sabbatical year* (celebrated every seven years) *and that of the jubilee year* (celebrated every fifty years)[27] *stand out as important guidelines — unfortunately never fully put into effect historically — for the social and economic life of the people of Israel.* Besides requiring fields to lie fallow, these laws call for the cancellation of debts and a general release of persons and goods: everyone is free to return to his family of origin and to regain possession of his birthright.

---

[24] *Catechism of the Catholic Church*, 2062.
[25] *Catechism of the Catholic Church*, 2070.
[26] John Paul II, Encyclical Letter *Veritatis Splendor*, 97: AAS 85 (1993), 1209.
[27] These laws are found in *Ex* 23, *Deut* 15, *Lev* 25.

This legislation is designed to ensure that the salvific event of the Exodus and fideli-ty to the Covenant represents not only the founding principle of Israel's social, political and economic life, but also the principle for dealing with questions concerning economic poverty and social injustices. This principle is invoked in order to transform, con-tinuously and from within, the life of the people of the Covenant, so that this life will correspond to God's plan. To eliminate the discrimination and economic inequalities caused by socio-economic changes, every seven years the memory of the Exodus and the Covenant are translated into social and juridical terms, in order to bring the concepts of property, debts, loans and goods back to their deep-est meaning.

25. *The precepts of the sabbatical and jubilee years constitute a kind of social doctrine in miniature.*[28] They show how the principles of justice and social solidarity are inspired by the gratuitousness of the salvific event wrought by God, and that they do not have a merely corrective value for practices dominated by selfish interests and objectives, but must rather become, as a prophecy of the future, the norma-tive points of reference to which every generation in Israel must conform if it wishes to be faithful to its God.

These principles become the focus of the Prophets' preaching, which seeks to inter-nalize them. God's Spirit, poured into the human heart — the Prophets proclaim — will make these same sentiments of justice and solidarity, which reside in the Lord's heart, take root in you (cf. *Jer* 31:33 and *Ezek* 36:26-27). Then God's will, articulated in the *Decalogue* given on Sinai, will be able to take root creatively in man's innermost being. This *process of internalization* gives rise to greater depth and realism in social action, making possible the *progressive universalization of atti-tudes of justice and solidarity*, which the people of the Covenant are called to have towards all men and women of every people and nation.

b. **The principle of creation and God's gratuitous action**

26. *The reflection of the Prophets and that found in the Wisdom Literature, in coming to the formulation of the principle that all things were created by God, touch on the first manifestation and the source itself of God's plan for the whole of humanity.* In Israel's profession of faith, to affirm that God is Creator does not mean merely expressing a theoretical conviction, but also grasping the original extent of the Lord's gratu-itous and merciful action on behalf of man. In fact, God freely confers being and life on everything that exists. Man and woman, created in his image and likeness (cf. *Gen* 1:26-27), are for that very reason called to be the visible sign and the effective instrument of divine gratuitousness in the garden where God has placed them as cultivators and custodians of the goods of creation.

27. *It is in the free action of God the Creator that we find the very meaning of cre-ation, even if it has been distorted by the experience of sin.* In fact, the narrative of the first sin (cf. *Gen* 3:1-24) describes the permanent temptation and the disordered

---

[28] Cf. John Paul II, Apostolic Letter *Tertio Millennio Adveniente*, 13: AAS 87 (1995), 14.

situation in which humanity comes to find itself after the fall of its progenitors. Disobedience to God means hiding from his loving countenance and seeking to control one's life and action in the world. Breaking the relation of communion with God causes a rupture in the internal unity of the human person, in the relations of communion between man and woman and of the harmonious relations between mankind and other creatures.[29] It is in this original estrangement that are to be sought the deepest roots of all the evils that afflict social relations between people, of all the situations in economic and political life that attack the dignity of the person, that assail justice and solidarity.

II. JESUS CHRIST, THE FULFILLMENT OF THE FATHER'S PLAN OF LOVE

a. In Jesus Christ the decisive event of the history of God with mankind is fulfilled

28. *The benevolence and mercy that inspire God's actions and provide the key for understanding them become so very much closer to man that they take on the traits of the man Jesus, the Word made flesh.* In the Gospel of Saint Luke, Jesus describes his messianic ministry with the words of Isaiah which recall the prophetic significance of the jubilee: "The Spirit of the Lord is upon me, because he has anointed me to preach the good news to the poor. He has sent me to proclaim release to the captives and recovering of sight to the blind, to set at liberty those who are oppressed, to proclaim the acceptable year of the Lord" (*Lk* 4:18-19; cf. *Is* 61:1-2). *Jesus therefore places himself on the frontline of fulfillment, not only because he fulfils what was promised and what was awaited by Israel, but also in the deeper sense that in him the decisive event of the history of God with mankind is fulfilled.* He proclaims: "He who has seen me has seen the Father" (*Jn* 14:9). Jesus, in other words, is the tangible and definitive manifestation of how God acts towards men and women.

29. *The love that inspires Jesus' ministry among men is the love that he has experienced in his intimate union with the Father.* The New Testament allows us to enter deeply into the experience, that Jesus himself lives and communicates, the love of God his Father — "Abba" — and, therefore, it permits us to enter into the very heart of divine life. Jesus announces the liberating mercy of God to those whom he meets on his way, beginning with the poor, the marginalized, the sinners. He invites all to follow him because he is the first to obey God's plan of love, and he does so in a most singular way, as God's envoy in the world.

Jesus' self-awareness of being *the Son* is an expression of this primordial experience. The Son has been given everything, and freely so, by the Father: "All that the Father has is mine" (*Jn* 16:15). His in turn is the mission of making all men sharers in this gift and in this filial relationship: "No longer do I call you servants, for the servant does not know what his master is doing; but I have called you

---

[29] Cf. Second Vatican Ecumenical Council, Pastoral Constitution *Gaudium et Spes*, 13: AAS 58 (1966), 1035.

friends, for all that I have heard from my Father I have made known to you" (*Jn* 15:15).

For Jesus, recognizing the Father's love means modelling his actions on God's gratuitousness and mercy; it is these that generate new life. It means becoming — by his very existence — the example and pattern of this for his disciples. Jesus' followers are called to live *like him* and, after his Passover of death and resurrection, to live also *in him* and *by him*, thanks to the superabundant gift of the Holy Spirit, the Consoler, who internalizes Christ's own style of life in human hearts.

b. The revelation of Trinitarian love

30. *With the unceasing amazement of those who have experienced the inexpressible love of God (cf. Rom 8:26), the New Testament grasps, in the light of the full revelation of Trinitarian love offered by the Passover of Jesus Christ, the ultimate meaning of the Incarnation of the Son and his mission among men and women.* Saint Paul writes: "If God is for us, who is against us? He who did not spare his own Son but gave him up for us all, will he not also give us all things with him?" (*Rom* 8:31-32). Similar language is used also by Saint John: "In this is love, not that we loved God but that he loved us and sent his Son to be the expiation for our sins" (*1 Jn* 4:10).

31. *The Face of God, progressively revealed in the history of salvation, shines in its fullness in the Face of Jesus Christ crucified and risen from the dead. God is Trinity: Father, Son, and Holy Spirit; truly distinct and truly one, because God is an infinite communion of love.* God's gratuitous love for humanity is revealed, before anything else, as love springing from the Father, from whom everything draws its source; as the free communication that the Son makes of this love, giving himself anew to the Father and giving himself to mankind; as the ever new fruitfulness of divine love that the Holy Spirit pours forth into the hearts of men (cf. *Rom* 5:5).

By his words and deeds, and fully and definitively by his death and resurrection,[30] *Jesus reveals to humanity that God is Father and that we are all called by grace to become his children in the Spirit* (cf. *Rom* 8:15; *Gal* 4:6), *and therefore brothers and sisters among ourselves.* It is for this reason that the Church firmly believes that "the key, the centre and the purpose of the whole of man's history is to be found in her Lord and Master."[31]

32. *Meditating on the gratuitousness and superabundance of the Father's divine gift of the Son, which Jesus taught and bore witness to by giving his life for us, the Apostle John grasps its profound meaning and its most logical consequence.* "Beloved, if God so loves us, we also ought to love one another. No man has ever seen God; if we love one another, God abides in us and his love is perfected in us" (*1 Jn* 4:11-12). The reciprocity of love is required by the commandment that Jesus describes as "new" and as "his": "that you love one another; even as I have loved you, that you also

---

[30] Cf. Second Vatican Ecumenical Council, Dogmatic Constitution *Dei Verbum*, 4: AAS 58 (1966), 819.

[31] Second Vatican Ecumenical Council, Pastoral Constitution *Gaudium et Spes*, 10: AAS 58 (1966), 1033.

love one another" (*Jn* 13:34). The commandment of mutual love shows how to live in Christ the Trinitarian life within the Church, the Body of Christ, and how to transform history until it reaches its fulfilment in the heavenly Jerusalem.

33. *The commandment of mutual love, which represents the law of life for God's people,*[32] *must inspire, purify and elevate all human relationships in society and in politics.* "To be human means to be called to interpersonal communion,"[33] because the image and the likeness of the Trinitarian God are the basis of the whole of "*human 'ethos,'* which reaches its apex in the commandment of love."[34] The modern cultural, social, economic and political phenomenon of interdependence, which intensifies and makes particularly evident the bonds that unite the human family, accentuates once more, in the light of Revelation, "a new *model* of the *unity* of the human race, which must ultimately inspire our *solidarity*. This supreme *model of unity*, which is a reflection of the intimate life of God, one God in three Persons, is what we Christians mean by the word '*communion.*'"[35]

III. THE HUMAN PERSON IN GOD'S PLAN OF LOVE

a. **Trinitarian love, the origin and goal of the human person**

34. *The revelation in Christ of the mystery of God as Trinitarian love is at the same time the revelation of the vocation of the human person to love. This revelation sheds light on every aspect of the personal dignity and freedom of men and women, and on the depths of their social nature.* "Being a person in the image and likeness of God . . . involves existing in a relationship, in relation to the other 'I,'"[36] because God himself, one and triune, is the communion of the Father, of the Son and of the Holy Spirit.

In the communion of love that is God, and in which the Three Divine Persons mutually love one another and are the One God, the human person is called to discover the origin and goal of his existence and of history. The Council Fathers, in the Pastoral Constitution *Gaudium et Spes*, teach that "the Lord Jesus Christ, when praying to the Father 'that they may all be one . . . as we are one' (*Jn* 17:21-22), has opened up new horizons closed to human reason by implying that there is a certain parallel between the union existing among the divine Persons and the union of the children of God in truth and love. It follows, then, that if man is the only creature on earth that God has willed for its own sake, man can fully discover his true self only in a sincere giving of himself (cf. *Lk* 17:33)."[37]

35. *Christian revelation shines a new light on the identity, the vocation and the ultimate destiny of the human person and the human race.* Every person is created by God,

---

[32] Cf. Second Vatican Ecumenical Council, Dogmatic Constitution *Lumen Gentium*, 9: *AAS* 57 (1965), 12-14.

[33] John Paul II, Apostolic Letter *Mulieris Dignitatem*, 7: *AAS* 80 (1988), 1666.

[34] John Paul II, Apostolic Letter *Mulieris Dignitatem*, 7: *AAS* 80 (1988), 1665-1666.

[35] John Paul II, Encyclical Letter *Sollicitudo Rei Socialis*, 40: *AAS* 80 (1988), 569.

[36] John Paul II, Apostolic Letter *Mulieris Dignitatem*, 7: *AAS* 80 (1988), 1664.

[37] Second Vatican Ecumenical Council, Pastoral Constitution *Gaudium et Spes*, 24: *AAS* 58 (1966), 1045.

loved and saved in Jesus Christ, and fulfils himself by creating a network of multiple relationships of love, justice and solidarity with other persons while he goes about his various activities in the world. Human activity, when it aims at promoting the integral dignity and vocation of the person, the quality of living conditions and the meeting in solidarity of peoples and nations, is in accordance with the plan of God, who does not fail to show his love and providence to his children.

36. *The pages of the first book of Sacred Scripture, which describe the creation of man and woman in the image and likeness of God* (cf. Gen 1:26-27), *contain a fundamental teaching with regard to the identity and the vocation of the human person.* They tell us that the creation of man and woman is a free and gratuitous act of God; that man and woman, because they are free and intelligent, represent the "thou" created by God and that only in relationship with him can they discover and fulfil the authentic and complete meaning of their personal and social lives; that in their complementarities and reciprocity they are the image of Trinitarian Love in the created universe; that to them, as the culmination of creation, the Creator has entrusted the task of ordering created nature according to his design (cf. Gen 1:28).

37. *The Book of Genesis provides us with certain foundations of Christian anthropology*: the inalienable dignity of the human person, the roots and guarantee of which are found in God's design of creation; the constitutive social nature of human beings, the prototype of which is found in the original relationship between man and woman, the union of whom "constitutes the first form of communion between persons";[38] the meaning of human activity in the world, which is linked to the discovery and respect of the laws of nature that God has inscribed in the created universe, so that humanity may live in it and care for it in accordance with God's will. This vision of the human person, of society and of history is rooted in God and is ever more clearly seen when his plan of salvation becomes a reality.

b. Christian salvation: for all people and the whole person

38. *The salvation offered in its fullness to men in Jesus Christ by God the Father's initiative, and brought about and transmitted by the work of the Holy Spirit, is salvation for all people and of the whole person: it is universal and integral salvation.* It concerns the human person in all his dimensions: personal and social, spiritual and corporeal, historical and transcendent. It begins to be made a reality already in history, because what is created is good and willed by God, and because the Son of God became one of us.[39] Its completion, however, is in the future, when we shall be called, together with all creation (cf. *Rom* 8), to share in Christ's resurrection and in the eternal communion of life with the Father in the joy of the Holy Spirit. This out-

---

[38] Second Vatican Ecumenical Council, Pastoral Constitution *Gaudium et Spes*, 12: AAS 58 (1966), 1034.

[39] Cf. Second Vatican Ecumenical Council, Pastoral Constitution *Gaudium et Spes*, 22: AAS 58 (1966), 1043.

look shows quite clearly the error and deception of purely immanentistic visions of the meaning of history and in humanity's claims to self-salvation.

39. *The salvation offered by God to his children requires their free response and acceptance.* It is in this that faith consists, and it is through this that "man freely commits his entire self to God,"[40] responding to God's prior and superabundant love (cf. *1 Jn* 4:10) with concrete love for his brothers and sisters, and with steadfast hope because "he who promised is faithful" (*Heb* 10:23). In fact, the divine plan of salvation does not consign human creatures to a state of mere passivity or of lesser status in relation to their Creator, because their relationship to God, whom Jesus Christ reveals to us and in whom he freely makes us sharers by the working of the Holy Spirit, is that of a child to its parent: the very relationship that Jesus lives with the Father (cf. *Jn* 15-17; *Gal* 4:6-7).

40. *The universality and integrality of the salvation wrought by Christ makes indissoluble the link between the relationship that the person is called to have with God and the responsibility he has towards his neighbor in the concrete circumstances of history.* This is sensed, though not always without some confusion or misunderstanding, in humanity's universal quest for truth and meaning, and it becomes the cornerstone of God's covenant with Israel, as attested by the tablets of the Law and the preaching of the Prophets.

   This link finds a clear and precise expression in the teaching of Jesus Christ and is definitively confirmed by the supreme witness of the giving of his life, in obedience to the Father's will and out of love for his brothers and sisters. To the scribe who asks him "*Which commandment is the first of all?*" (*Mk* 12:28), Jesus answers: "*The first is: 'Hear, O Israel: the Lord our God, the Lord is one; and you shall love the Lord your God with all your heart, and with all your soul, and with all your mind, and with all your strength.' The second is this: 'You shall love your neighbor as yourself.' There is no other commandment greater than these*" (*Mk* 12:29-31).

   Inextricably linked in the human heart are the relationship with God — recognized as Creator and Father, the source and fulfilment of life and of salvation — and openness in concrete love towards man, who must be treated as another self, even if he is an enemy (cf. *Mt* 5:43-44). In man's inner dimension are rooted, in the final analysis, the commitment to justice and solidarity, to the building up of a social, economic and political life that corresponds to God's plan.

c. **The disciple of Christ as a new creation**

41. *Personal and social life, as well as human action in the world, is always threatened by sin.* Jesus Christ, however, "by suffering for us . . . not only gave us an example so that we might follow in His footsteps, but He also opened up a way. If we follow this path, life and death are made holy and acquire a new meaning."[41] Christ's

---

[40] Second Vatican Ecumenical Council, Dogmatic Constitution *Dei Verbum*, 5: *AAS* 58 (1966), 819.
[41] Second Vatican Ecumenical Council, Pastoral Constitution *Gaudium et Spes*, 22: *AAS* 58 (1966), 1043.

disciple adheres, in faith and through the sacraments, to Jesus' Paschal Mystery, so that his *old self*, with its evil inclinations, is crucified with Christ. As a new creation he is then enabled by grace to "walk in newness of life" (*Rom* 6:4). This "holds true not for Christians alone but also for all people of good will in whose hearts grace is active invisibly. For since Christ died for all, and since all men are in fact called to one and the same destiny, which is divine, we must hold that the Holy Spirit offers to all the possibility of being made partners, in a way known to God, in the Paschal Mystery."[42]

42. *The inner transformation of the human person, in his being progressively conformed to Christ, is the necessary prerequisite for a real transformation of his relationships with others.* "It is necessary, then, to appeal to the spiritual and moral capacities of the human person and to the permanent need for his inner conversion, so as to obtain social changes that will really serve him. The acknowledged priority of the conversion of heart in no way eliminates but on the contrary imposes the obligation of bringing the appropriate remedies to institutions and living conditions when they are an inducement to sin, so that they conform to the norms of justice and advance the good rather than hinder it."[43]

43. *It is not possible to love one's neighbor as oneself and to persevere in this conduct without the firm and constant determination to work for the good of all people and of each person, because we are all really responsible for everyone.*[44] According to the Council's teaching, "they also have a claim on our respect and charity that think and act differently from us in social, political and religious matters. In fact the more deeply we come to understand their ways of thinking through kindness and love, the more easily will we be able to enter into dialogue with them."[45] This path requires grace, which God offers to man in order to help him to overcome failings, to snatch him from the spiral of lies and violence, to sustain him and prompt him to restore with an ever new and ready spirit the network of authentic and honest relationships with his fellow men.[46]

44. *Even the relationship with the created universe and human activity aimed at tending it and transforming it, activity which is daily endangered by man's pride and his inordinate self-love, must be purified and perfected by the cross and resurrection of Christ.* "Redeemed by Christ and made a new creature by the Holy Spirit, man can, indeed he must, love the things of God's creation: it is from God that he has received them, and it is as flowing from God's hand that he looks upon them and reveres them. Man thanks his divine benefactor for all these things, he uses them and enjoys them in a spirit of poverty and freedom. Thus he is brought to a true

---

[42] Second Vatican Ecumenical Council, Pastoral Constitution *Gaudium et Spes*, 22: AAS 58 (1966), 1043.

[43] *Catechism of the Catholic Church*, 1888.

[44] Cf. John Paul II, Encyclical Letter *Sollicitudo Rei Socialis*, 38: AAS 80 (1988), 565-566.

[45] Second Vatican Ecumenical Council, Pastoral Constitution *Gaudium et Spes*, 28: AAS 58 (1966), 1048.

[46] Cf. *Catechism of the Catholic Church*, 1889.

possession of the world, as having nothing yet possessing everything: 'All [things] are yours; and you are Christ's; and Christ is God's' (1 Cor 3:22-23)."[47]

d. The transcendence of salvation and the autonomy of earthly realities

45. *Jesus Christ is the Son of God made man in whom and thanks to whom the world and man attain their authentic and full truth.* The mystery of God's being infinitely close to man — brought about in the Incarnation of Jesus Christ, who gave himself on the cross, abandoning himself to death — shows that *the more that human realities are seen in the light of God's plan and lived in communion with God, the more they are empowered and liberated in their distinctive identity and in the freedom that is proper to them.* Sharing in Christ's life of sonship, made possible by the Incarnation and the Paschal gift of the Spirit, far from being a mortification, has the effect of unleashing the authentic and independent traits and identity that characterize human beings in all their various expressions.

This perspective leads to *a correct approach to earthly realities and their autonomy,* which is strongly emphasized by the teaching of the Second Vatican Council: "If by the autonomy of earthly affairs we mean that created things and societies themselves enjoy their own laws and values which must be gradually deciphered, put to use and regulated by men, then it is entirely right to demand that autonomy. This . . . harmonizes also with the will of the Creator. For by the very circumstance of their having been created, all things are endowed with their own stability, truth, goodness, proper laws and order. Man must respect these as he isolates them by the appropriate methods of the individual sciences or arts."[48]

46. *There is no state of conflict between God and man, but a relationship of love in which the world and the fruits of human activity in the world are objects of mutual gift between the Father and his children, and among the children themselves, in Christ Jesus; in Christ and thanks to him the world and man attain their authentic and inherent meaning.* In a universal vision of God's love that embraces everything that exists, God himself is revealed to us in Christ as Father and giver of life, and man as the one who, in Christ, receives everything from God as gift, humbly and freely, and who truly possesses everything as his own when he knows and experiences everything as belonging to God, originating in God and moving towards God. In this regard, the Second Vatican Council teaches: "If the expression 'the autonomy of earthly affairs' is taken to mean that created things do not depend on God, and that man can use them without any reference to their Creator, anyone who acknowledges God will see how false such a meaning is. For without the Creator, the creature would disappear."[49]

---

[47] Second Vatican Ecumenical Council, Pastoral Constitution *Gaudium et Spes*, 37: AAS 58 (1966), 1055.

[48] Second Vatican Ecumenical Council, Pastoral Constitution *Gaudium et Spes*, 36: AAS 58 (1966), 1054; Second Vatican Ecumenical Council, Decree *Apostolicam Actuositatem*, 7: AAS 58 (1966), 843-844.

[49] Second Vatican Ecumenical Council, Pastoral Constitution *Gaudium et Spes*, 36: AAS 58 (1966), 1054.

47. *The human person, in himself and in his vocation, transcends the limits of the created universe, of society and of history: his ultimate end is God himself,*[50] *who has revealed himself to men in order to invite them and receive them into communion with himself.*[51] "Man cannot give himself to a purely human plan for reality, to an abstract ideal or to a false utopia. As a person, he can give himself to another person or to other persons, and ultimately to God, who is the author of his being and who alone can fully accept his gift."[52] For this reason, "a man is alienated if he refuses to transcend himself and to live the experience of self-giving and of the formation of an authentic human community oriented towards his final destiny, which is God. A society is alienated if its forms of social organization, production and consumption make it more difficult to offer this gift of self and to establish this solidarity between people."[53]

48. *The human person cannot and must not be manipulated by social, economic or political structures, because every person has the freedom to direct himself towards his ultimate end. On the other hand, every cultural, social, economic and political accomplishment, in which the social nature of the person and his activity of transforming the universe are brought about in history, must always be considered also in the context of its relative and provisional reality,* because "the form of this world is passing away" (*1 Cor* 7:31). We can speak here of an *eschatological relativity*, in the sense that man and the world are moving towards their end, which is the fulfilment of their destiny in God; we can also speak of a *theological relativity*, insofar as the gift of God, by which the definitive destiny of humanity and of creation will be attained, is infinitely greater than human possibilities and expectations. Any totalitarian vision of society and the State, and any purely intra-worldly ideology of progress are contrary to the integral truth of the human person and to God's plan in history.

IV. GOD'S PLAN AND THE MISSION OF THE CHURCH

a. The Church, sign and defender of the transcendence of the human person

49. *The Church, the community of those who have been brought together by the Risen Christ and who have set out to follow him, is "the sign and the safeguard of the transcendent dimension of the human person."*[54] She is "in Christ a kind of sacrament — a sign and instrument, that is, of communion with God and of unity among all men."[55] Her mission is that of proclaiming and communicating the salvation wrought in Jesus Christ, which he calls "the Kingdom of God" (*Mk* 1:15), that is, communion with God and among men. The goal of salvation, the Kingdom of

---

[50] Cf. *Catechism of the Catholic Church*, 2244.
[51] Cf. Second Vatican Ecumenical Council, Dogmatic Constitution *Dei Verbum*, 2: AAS 58 (1966), 818.
[52] John Paul II, Encyclical Letter *Centesimus Annus*, 41: AAS 83 (1991), 844.
[53] John Paul II, Encyclical Letter *Centesimus Annus*, 41: AAS 83 (1991), 844-845.
[54] Second Vatican Ecumenical Council, Pastoral Constitution *Gaudium et Spes*, 76: AAS 58 (1966), 1099.
[55] Second Vatican Ecumenical Council, Dogmatic Constitution *Lumen Gentium*, 1: AAS 57 (1965), 5.

God embraces all people and is fully realized beyond history, in God. The Church has received "the mission of proclaiming and establishing among all peoples the Kingdom of Christ and of God, and she is, on earth, the seed and the beginning of that Kingdom."[56]

50. *The Church places herself concretely at the service of the Kingdom of God above all by announcing and communicating the Gospel of salvation and by establishing new Christian communities.* Moreover, she "serves the Kingdom by spreading throughout the world the 'Gospel values' which are an expression of the Kingdom and which help people to accept God's plan. It is true that the inchoate reality of the Kingdom can also be found beyond the confines of the Church among peoples everywhere, to the extent that they live 'Gospel values' and are open to the working of the Spirit who breathes when and where he wills (cf. Jn 3:8). But it must immediately be added that this temporal dimension of the Kingdom remains incomplete unless it is related to the Kingdom of Christ present in the Church and straining towards eschatological fullness."[57] It follows from this, in particular, that *the Church is not to be confused with the political community and is not bound to any political system.*[58] In fact, the political community and the Church are *autonomous and independent* of each other in their own fields, and both are, even if under different titles, "devoted to the service of the personal and social vocation of the same human beings."[59] Indeed, it can be affirmed that the distinction between religion and politics and the principle of religious freedom constitute a specific achievement of Christianity and one of its fundamental historical and cultural contributions.

51. *According to the plan of God brought about in Christ, there corresponds to the identity and mission of the Church in the world "a saving and eschatological purpose which can be fully attained only in the next life."*[60] Precisely for this reason, the Church offers an original and irreplaceable contribution with the concern that impels her to make the family of mankind and its history more human, prompting her to place herself as a bulwark against every totalitarian temptation, as she shows man his integral and definitive vocation.[61]

By her preaching of the Gospel, the grace of the sacraments and the experience of fraternal communion, the Church "heals and elevates the dignity of the human person, . . . consolidates society and endows the daily activity of men with a deeper sense and meaning."[62] At the level of concrete historical dynamics, therefore, the coming of the Kingdom of God cannot be discerned in the per-

---

[56] Second Vatican Ecumenical Council, Dogmatic Constitution *Lumen Gentium*, 5: AAS 57 (1965), 8.

[57] John Paul II, Encyclical Letter *Redemptoris Missio*, 20: AAS 83 (1991), 267.

[58] Cf. Second Vatican Ecumenical Council, Pastoral Constitution *Gaudium et Spes*, 76: AAS 58 (1966), 1099; *Catechism of the Catholic Church*, 2245.

[59] Second Vatican Ecumenical Council, Pastoral Constitution *Gaudium et Spes*, 76: AAS 58 (1966), 1099.

[60] Second Vatican Ecumenical Council, Pastoral Constitution *Gaudium et Spes*, 40: AAS 58 (1966), 1058.

[61] Cf. *Catechism of the Catholic Church*, 2244.

[62] Second Vatican Ecumenical Council, Pastoral Constitution *Gaudium et Spes*, 40: AAS 58 (1966), 1058.

spective of a determined and definitive social, economic or political organization. Rather, it is seen in the development of a human social sense which for mankind is a leaven for attaining wholeness, justice and solidarity in openness to the Transcendent as a point of reference for one's own personal definitive fulfilment.

b. The Church, the Kingdom of God and the renewal of social relations

52. *God, in Christ, redeems not only the individual person but also the social relations existing between men.* As the Apostle Paul teaches, life in Christ makes the human person's identity and social sense — with their concrete consequences on the historical and social planes — emerge fully and in a new manner: "For in Christ Jesus you are all children of God, through faith. For as many of you as were baptized into Christ have put on Christ. There is neither Jew nor Greek, neither slave nor free, there is neither male nor female; for you are all one in Christ" (*Gal* 3:26-28). In this perspective, Church communities, brought together by the message of Jesus Christ and gathered in the Holy Spirit round the Risen Lord (cf. *Mt* 18:20, 28:19-20; *Lk* 24:46-49), offer themselves as places of communion, witness and mission, and as catalysts for the redemption and transformation of social relationships.

53. *The transformation of social relationships that responds to the demands of the Kingdom of God is not fixed within concrete boundaries once and for all. Rather, it is a task entrusted to the Christian community, which is to develop it and carry it out through reflection and practices inspired by the Gospel.* It is the same Spirit of the Lord, leading the people of God while simultaneously permeating the universe,[63] who from time to time inspires new and appropriate ways for humanity to exercise its creative responsibility.[64] This inspiration is given to the community of Christians who are a part of the world and of history, and who are therefore open to dialogue with all people of good will in the common quest for the seeds of truth and freedom sown in the vast field of humanity.[65] The dynamics of this renewal must be firmly anchored in the unchangeable principles of the natural law, inscribed by God the Creator in each of his creatures (cf. *Rom* 2:14-15), and bathed in eschatological light through Jesus Christ.

54. *Jesus Christ reveals to us that "God is love" (1 Jn 4:8) and he teaches us that "the fundamental law of human perfection, and consequently of the transformation of the world, is the new commandment of love.* He assures those who trust in the love of God that the way of love is open to all people and that the effort to establish a universal brotherhood will not be in vain."[66] This law is called to become the ulti-

---

[63] Cf. Second Vatican Ecumenical Council, *Gaudium et Spes*, 11: AAS 58 (1966), 1033.

[64] Cf. Paul VI, Apostolic Letter *Octogesima Adveniens*, 37: AAS 63 (1971), 426-427.

[65] Cf. John Paul II, Encyclical Letter *Redemptor Hominis*, 11: AAS 71 (1979), 276: "The Fathers of the Church rightly saw in the various religions as it were so many reflections of the one truth, 'seeds of the Word,' attesting that, though the routes taken may be different, there is but a single goal to which is directed the deepest aspiration of the human spirit."

[66] Second Vatican Ecumenical Council, Pastoral Constitution *Gaudium et Spes*, 38: AAS 58 (1966), 1055-1056.

mate measure and rule of every dynamic related to human relations. In short, it is the very mystery of God, Trinitarian Love, that is the basis of the meaning and value of the person, of social relations, of human activity in the world, insofar as humanity has received the revelation of this and a share in it through Christ in his Spirit.

55. *The transformation of the world is a fundamental requirement of our time also. To this need the Church's social Magisterium intends to offer the responses called for by the signs of the times, pointing above all to the mutual love between human beings, in the sight of God, as the most powerful instrument of change, on the personal and social levels.* Mutual love, in fact, sharing in the infinite love of God, is humanity's authentic purpose, both historical and transcendent. Therefore, "earthly progress must be carefully distinguished from the growth of Christ's kingdom. Nevertheless, to the extent that the former can contribute to the better ordering of human society, it is of vital concern to the kingdom of God."[67]

c. **New heavens and a new earth**

56. *God's promise and Jesus Christ's resurrection raise in Christians the well-founded hope that a new and eternal dwelling place is prepared for every human person, a new earth where justice abides* (cf. 2 Cor 5:1-2; 2 Pet 3:13). "Then, with death conquered, the children of God will be raised in Christ and what was sown in weakness and corruption will be clothed in incorruptibility: charity and its works will remain and all of creation, which God made for man, will be set free from its bondage to vanity."[68] This hope, rather than weaken, must instead strengthen concern for the work that is needed in the present reality.

57. *The good things — such as human dignity, brotherhood and freedom, all the good fruits of nature and of human enterprise — that in the Lord's Spirit and according to his command have spread throughout the earth, having been purified of every stain, illuminated and transfigured, belong to the Kingdom of truth and life, of holiness and grace, of justice, of love and of peace that Christ will present to the Father, and it is there that we shall once again find them.* The words of Christ in their solemn truth will then resound for all people: "Come, O blessed of my Father, inherit the kingdom prepared for you from the foundation of the world; for I was hungry and you gave me food, I was thirsty and you gave me drink, I was a stranger and you welcomed me, I was naked and you clothed me, I was sick and you visited me, I was in prison and you came to me . . . as you did it to one of the least of my brethren, you did it to me" (Mt 25:34-36,40).

58. *The complete fulfillment of the human person, achieved in Christ through the gift of the Spirit, develops in history and is mediated by personal relationships with other peo-*

---

[67] Second Vatican Ecumenical Council, Pastoral Constitution *Gaudium et Spes*, 39: AAS 58 (1966), 1057.

[68] Second Vatican Ecumenical Council, Pastoral Constitution *Gaudium et Spes*, 39: AAS 58 (1966), 1057.

ple, relationships that in turn reach perfection thanks to the commitment made to improve the world, in justice and peace. Human activity in history is of itself significant and effective for the definitive establishment of the Kingdom, although this remains a free gift of God, completely transcendent. Such activity, when it respects the objective order of temporal reality and is enlightened by truth and love, becomes an instrument for making justice and peace ever more fully and integrally present, and anticipates in our own day the promised Kingdom.

Conforming himself to Christ the Redeemer, man perceives himself as a creature willed by God and eternally chosen by him, called to grace and glory in all the fullness of the mystery in which he has become a sharer in Jesus Christ.[69] Being conformed to Christ and contemplating his face[70] instill in Christians an irrepressible longing for a foretaste in this world, in the context of human relationships, of what will be a reality in the definitive world to come; thus Christians strive to give food, drink, clothing, shelter, care, a welcome and company to the Lord who knocks at the door (cf. *Mt* 25:35-37).

d. Mary and her *"fiat"* in God's plan of love

59. *Heir to the hope of the righteous in Israel and first among the disciples of Jesus Christ is Mary, his Mother.* By her *"fiat"* to the plan of God's love (cf. *Lk* 1:38), in the name of all humanity, she accepts in history the One sent by the Father, the Savior of mankind. In her *Magnificat* she proclaims the advent of the Mystery of Salvation, the coming of the "Messiah of the poor" (cf. *Is* 11:4; 61:1). The God of the Covenant, whom the Virgin of Nazareth praises in song as her spirit rejoices, is the One who casts down the mighty from their thrones and raises up the lowly, fills the hungry with good things and sends the rich away empty, scatters the proud and shows mercy to those who fear him (cf. *Lk* 1:50-53).

Looking to the heart of Mary, to the depth of her faith expressed in the words of the *Magnificat*, Christ's disciples are called to renew ever more fully in themselves "the awareness that *the truth about God who saves*, the truth about God who is the source of every gift, *cannot be separated from the manifestation of his love of preference for the poor and humble*, that love which, celebrated in the *Magnificat*, is later expressed in the words and works of Jesus."[71] Mary is totally dependent upon God and completely directed towards him by the impetus of her faith. She is "the most perfect image of freedom and of the liberation of humanity and of the universe."[72]

---

[69] Cf. John Paul II, Encyclical Letter *Redemptor Hominis*, 13: AAS 71 (1979), 283-284.

[70] Cf. John Paul II, Apostolic Letter *Novo Millennio Ineunte*, 16-28: AAS 93 (2001), 276-285.

[71] John Paul II, Encyclical Letter *Redemptoris Mater*, 37: AAS 79 (1987), 410.

[72] Congregation for the Doctrine of the Faith, Instruction *Libertatis Conscientia*, 97: AAS 79 (1987), 597.

CHAPTER TWO

THE CHURCH'S MISSION AND SOCIAL DOCTRINE

I. EVANGELIZATION AND SOCIAL DOCTRINE

a. The Church, God's dwelling place with men and women

60. *The Church, sharing in mankind's joys and hopes, in its anxieties and sadness, stands with every man and woman* of every place and time, to bring them the good news of the Kingdom of God, which in Jesus Christ has come and continues to be present among them.[73] In the midst of mankind and in the world she is the sacrament of God's love and, therefore, of the most splendid hope, which inspires and sustains every authentic undertaking for and commitment to human liberation and advancement. The Church is present among mankind as God's tent of meeting, "God's dwelling place among men" (cf. *Rev* 21:3), so that man is not alone, lost or frightened in his task of making the world more human; thus men and women find support in the redeeming love of Christ. As minister of salvation, the Church is not in the abstract nor in a merely spiritual dimension, but in the context of the history and of the world in which man lives.[74] Here mankind is met by God's love and by the vocation to cooperate in the divine plan.

61. *Unique and unrepeatable in his individuality, every person is a being who is open to relationships with others in society.* Life together in society, in the network of relationships linking individuals, families and intermediate groups by encounter, communication and exchange, ensures a higher quality of living. The common good that people seek and attain in the formation of social communities is the guarantee of their personal, familial and associative good.[75] These are the reasons for which society originates and takes shape, with its array of structures, that is to say its political, economic, juridical and cultural constructs. To man, "as he is involved in a complex network of relationships within modern societies,"[76] the Church addresses her social doctrine. As an expert in humanity,[77] she is able to

---

[73] Cf. Second Vatican Ecumenical Council, Pastoral Constitution *Gaudium et Spes*, 1: AAS 58 (1966), 1025-1026.

[74] Cf. Second Vatican Ecumenical Council, Pastoral Constitution *Gaudium et Spes*, 40: AAS 58 (1966), 1057-1059; John Paul II, Encyclical Letter *Centesimus Annus*, 53-54: AAS 83 (1991), 859-860; John Paul II, Encyclical Letter *Sollicitudo Rei Socialis*, 1: AAS 80 (1988), 513-514.

[75] Cf. Second Vatican Ecumenical Council, Pastoral Constitution *Gaudium et Spes*, 32: AAS 58 (1966), 1051.

[76] John Paul II, Encyclical Letter *Centesimus Annus*, 54: AAS 83 (1991), 859.

[77] Cf. Paul VI, Encyclical Letter *Populorum Progressio*, 13: AAS 59 (1967), 263.

understand man in his vocation and aspirations, in his limits and misgivings, in his rights and duties, and to speak a word of life that reverberates in the historical and social circumstances of human existence.

b. Enriching and permeating society with the Gospel

62. *With her social teaching the Church seeks to proclaim the Gospel and make it present in the complex network of social relations.* It is not simply a matter of reaching out to man in society — man as the recipient of the proclamation of the Gospel — but of *enriching and permeating society itself with the Gospel.*[78] For the Church, therefore, tending to the needs of man means that she also involves society in her missionary and salvific work. The way people live together in society often determines the quality of life and therefore the conditions in which every man and woman understand themselves and make decisions concerning themselves and their vocation. For this reason, the Church is not indifferent to what is decided, brought about or experienced in society; she is attentive to the moral quality — that is, the authentically human and humanizing aspects — of social life. Society — and with it, politics, the economy, labor, law, culture — is not simply a secular and worldly reality, and therefore outside or foreign to the message and economy of salvation. Society in fact, with all that is accomplished within it, concerns man. Society is made up of men and women, who are "the primary and fundamental way for the Church."[79]

63. *By means of her social doctrine, the Church takes on the task of proclaiming what the Lord has entrusted to her. She makes the message of the freedom and redemption wrought by Christ, the Gospel of the Kingdom, present in human history.* In proclaiming the Gospel, the Church "bears witness to man, in the name of Christ, to his dignity and his vocation to the communion of persons. She teaches him the demands of justice and peace in conformity with divine wisdom."[80]

As the Gospel reverberating by means of the Church in the today of men and women,[81] *this social doctrine is a word that brings freedom.* This means that it has the effectiveness of truth and grace that comes from the Spirit of God, who penetrates hearts, predisposing them to thoughts and designs of love, justice, freedom and peace. Evangelizing the social sector, then, means infusing into the human heart the power of meaning and freedom found in the Gospel, in order to promote a society befitting mankind because it befits Christ: it means building a city of man that is more human because it is in greater conformity with the Kingdom of God.

64. *With her social doctrine not only does the Church not stray from her mission but she is rigorously faithful to it.* The redemption wrought by Christ and entrusted to

---

[78] Cf. Second Vatican Ecumenical Council, Pastoral Constitution *Gaudium et Spes*, 40: AAS 58 (1966), 1057-1059.

[79] John Paul II, Encyclical Letter *Redemptor Hominis*, 14: AAS 71 (1979), 284.

[80] *Catechism of the Catholic Church*, 2419.

[81] Cf. John Paul II, Homily at Pentecost for the First Centenary of *Rerum Novarum* (19 May 1991): AAS 84 (1992), 282.

the saving mission of the Church is certainly of the supernatural order. This dimension is not a delimitation of salvation but rather an *integral* expression of it.[82] The supernatural is not to be understood as an entity or a place that begins where the natural ends, but as the raising of the natural to a higher plane. In this way nothing of the created or the human order is foreign to or excluded from the supernatural or theological order of faith and grace, rather it is found within it, taken on and elevated by it. "In Jesus Christ the visible world which God created for man (cf. *Gen* 1:26-30) — the world that, when sin entered, 'was subjected to futility' (*Rom* 8:20; cf. *Rom* 8:19-22) — recovers again its original link with the divine source of Wisdom and Love. Indeed, 'God so loved the world that he gave his only Son' (*Jn* 3:16). As this link was broken in the man Adam, so in the Man Christ it was reforged (cf. *Rom* 5:12-21)."[83]

65. *Redemption begins with the Incarnation, by which the Son of God takes on all that is human, except sin, according to the solidarity established by the wisdom of the Divine Creator, and embraces everything in his gift of redeeming Love.* Man is touched by this Love in the fullness of his being: a being that is corporeal and spiritual, that is in a solidary relationship with others. The whole man — not a detached soul or a being closed within its own individuality, but a person and a society of persons — is involved in the salvific economy of the Gospel. As bearer of the Gospel's message of Incarnation and Redemption, the Church can follow no other path: with her social doctrine and the effective action that springs from it, not only does she not hide her face or tone down her mission, but she is faithful to Christ and shows herself to men and women as "the universal sacrament of salvation."[84] This is especially true in times such as the present, marked by increasing interdependence and globalization of social issues.

c. Social doctrine, evangelization and human promotion

66. *The Church's social doctrine is an integral part of her evangelizing ministry.* Nothing that concerns the community of men and women — situations and problems regarding justice, freedom, development, relations between peoples, peace — is foreign to evangelization, and evangelization would be incomplete if it did not take into account the mutual demands continually made by the Gospel and by the concrete, personal and social life of man.[85] Profound links exist between evangelization and human promotion: "These include links of an anthropological order, because the man who is to be evangelized is not an abstract being but is subject to social and economic questions. They also include links in the theological

---

[82] Cf. Paul VI, Apostolic Exhortation *Evangelii Nuntiandi* 9, 30: AAS 68 (1976), 10-11; John Paul II, *Address to the Third General Conference of Latin American Bishops,* Puebla, Mexico (28 January 1979), III/4-7: AAS 71 (1979), 199-204; Congregation for the Doctrine of the Faith, Instruction *Libertatis Conscientia*, 63-64, 80: AAS 79 (1987), 581-582, 590-591.

[83] John Paul II, Encyclical Letter *Redemptor Hominis*, 8: AAS 71 (1979), 270.

[84] Second Vatican Ecumenical Council, Dogmatic Constitution *Lumen Gentium*, 48: AAS 57 (1965), 53.

[85] Cf. Paul VI, Encyclical Letter *Evangelii Nuntiandi*, 29: AAS 68 (1976), 25.

order, since one cannot disassociate the plan of creation from the plan of Redemption. The latter plan touches the very concrete situations of injustice to be combated and of justice to be restored. They include links of the eminently evangelical order, which is that of charity: how in fact can one proclaim the new commandment without promoting in justice and in peace the true, authentic advancement of man?"[86]

67. *The Church's social doctrine "is itself a valid instrument of evangelization"*[87] *and is born of the always new meeting of the Gospel message and social life.* Understood in this way, this social doctrine is a distinctive way for the Church to carry out her ministry of the Word and her prophetic role.[88] "In effect, to teach and to spread her social doctrine pertains to the Church's evangelizing mission and is an essential part of the Christian message, since this doctrine points out the direct consequences of that message in the life of society and situates daily work and struggles for justice in the context of bearing witness to Christ the Savior."[89] This is not a marginal interest or activity, or one that is tacked on to the Church's mission, rather it is at the very heart of the Church's ministry of service: with her social doctrine the Church "proclaims God and his mystery of salvation in Christ to every human being, and for that very reason reveals man to himself."[90] This is a ministry that stems not only from proclamation but also from witness.

68. *The Church does not assume responsibility for every aspect of life in society, but speaks with the competence that is hers, which is that of proclaiming Christ the Redeemer:*[91] "Christ did not bequeath to the Church a mission in the political, economic or social order; the purpose he assigned to her was a religious one. But this religious mission can be the source of commitment, direction and vigor to establish and consolidate the community of men according to the law of God."[92] This means that the Church does not intervene in technical questions with her social doctrine, nor does she propose or establish systems or models of social organization.[93] This is not part of the mission entrusted to her by Christ. *The Church's competence comes from the Gospel:* from the message that sets man free, the message proclaimed and borne witness to by the Son of God made man.

d. The rights and duties of the Church

69. *With her social doctrine, the Church aims "at helping man on the path of salvation."*[94] This is her primary and sole purpose. There is no intention to usurp or

---

[86] Paul VI, Encyclical Letter *Evangelii Nuntiandi*, 31: AAS 68 (1976), 26.

[87] John Paul II, Encyclical Letter *Centesimus Annus*, 54: AAS 83 (1991), 860.

[88] Cf. John Paul II, Encyclical Letter *Sollicitudo Rei Socialis*, 41: AAS 80 (1988), 570-572.

[89] John Paul II, Encyclical Letter *Centesimus Annus*, 5: AAS 83 (1991), 799.

[90] John Paul II, Encyclical Letter *Centesimus Annus*, 54: AAS 83 (1991), 860.

[91] Cf. *Catechism of the Catholic Church*, 2420.

[92] Second Vatican Ecumenical Council, Pastoral Constitution *Gaudium et Spes*, 42: AAS 58 (1966), 1060.

[93] Cf. John Paul II, Encyclical Letter *Sollicitudo Rei Socialis*, 41: AAS 80 (1988), 570-572.

[94] John Paul II, Encyclical Letter *Centesimus Annus*, 54: AAS 83 (1991), 860.

invade the duties of others or to neglect her own; nor is there any thought of pursuing objectives that are foreign to her mission. This mission serves to give an overall shape to *the Church's right and at the same time her duty* to develop a social doctrine of her own and to influence society and societal structures with it by means of the responsibility and tasks to which it gives rise.

70. *The Church has the right to be a teacher for mankind, a teacher of the truth of faith: the truth not only of dogmas but also of the morals whose source lies in human nature itself and in the Gospel.*[95] The word of the Gospel, in fact, is not only to be heard but is also to be observed and put into practice (cf. Mt 7:24; Lk 6:46-47; Jn 14:21,23-24; Jas 1:22). Consistency in behavior shows what one truly believes and is not limited only to things strictly church-related or spiritual but involves men and women in the entirety of their life experience and in the context of all their responsibilities. However worldly these responsibilities may be, their subject remains man, that is, the human being whom God calls, by means of the Church, to participate in his gift of salvation.

Men and women must respond to the gift of salvation not with a partial, abstract or merely verbal acceptance, but with the whole of their lives — in every relationship that defines life — so as not to neglect anything, leaving it in a profane and worldly realm where it is irrelevant or foreign to salvation. For this reason the Church's social doctrine is not a privilege for her, nor a digression, a convenience or interference: *it is her right to proclaim the Gospel in the context of society*, to make the liberating word of the Gospel resound in the complex worlds of production, labor, business, finance, trade, politics, law, culture, social communications, where men and women live.

71. *This right of the Church is at the same time a duty, because she cannot forsake this responsibility without denying herself and her fidelity to Christ:* "Woe to me if I do not preach the Gospel!" (1 Cor 9:16). The warning that St. Paul addresses to himself rings in the Church's conscience as a call to walk all paths of evangelization, not only those that lead to individual consciences but also those that wind their way into public institutions: on the one hand, religion must not be restricted "to the purely private sphere,"[96] on the other, the Christian message must not be relegated to a purely other-worldly salvation incapable of shedding light on our earthly existence.[97]

Because of the public relevance of the Gospel and faith, because of the corrupting effects of injustice, that is, of sin, the Church cannot remain indifferent to social matters:[98] "To the Church belongs the right always and everywhere to announce moral principles, including those pertaining to the social order, and to make judg-

---

[95] Cf. Second Vatican Ecumenical Council, Declaration *Dignitatis Humanae*, 14: AAS 58 (1966), 940; John Paul II, Encyclical Letter *Veritatis Splendor*, 27, 64, 110: AAS 85 (1993), 1154-1155, 1183-1184, 1219-1220.

[96] John Paul II, *Message to the Secretary-General of the United Nations, on the occasion of the thirtieth anniversary of the Universal Declaration of Human Rights* (2 December 1978): *Insegnamenti di Giovanni Paolo II*, I (1978), 261.

[97] Cf. John Paul II, Encyclical Letter *Centesimus Annus*, 5: AAS 83 (1991), 799.

[98] Cf. Paul VI, Apostolic Exhortation *Evangelii Nuntiandi*, 34: AAS 68 (1976), 28.

ments on any human affairs to the extent that they are required by the fundamental rights of the human person or the salvation of souls."[99]

II. THE NATURE OF THE CHURCH'S SOCIAL DOCTRINE

a. Knowledge illuminated by faith

72. *The Church's social doctrine was not initially thought of as an organic system but was formed over the course of time, through the numerous interventions of the Magisterium on social issues.* The fact that it came about in this manner makes it understandable that certain changes may have taken place with regard to its nature, method and epistemological structure. With significant allusions already being made in *Laborem Exercens*,[100] a decisive clarification in this regard was made in the Encyclical *Sollicitudo Rei Socialis*: the Church's social doctrine "belongs to the field, not of *ideology*, but of *theology* and particularly of moral theology."[101] It cannot be defined according to socio-economic parameters. It is not an ideological or pragmatic system intended to define and generate economic, political and social relationships, but is a *category unto itself*. It is "the *accurate formulation* of the results of a careful reflection on the complex realities of human existence, in society and in the international order, in the light of faith and of the Church's tradition. Its main aim is to *interpret* these realities, determining their conformity with or divergence from the lines of the Gospel teaching on man and his vocation, a vocation which is at once earthly and transcendent; its aim is thus to *guide* Christian behavior."[102]

73. *The Church's social doctrine is therefore of a theological nature, specifically theological-moral,* "since it is a doctrine aimed at *guiding people's behavior*."[103] "This teaching . . . is to be found at the crossroads where Christian life and conscience come into contact with the real world. [It] is seen in the efforts of individuals, families, people involved in cultural and social life, as well as politicians and statesmen to give it a concrete form and application in history."[104] In fact, this social doctrine reflects three levels of theological-moral teaching: the *foundational* level of motivations; the *directive* level of norms for life in society; the *deliberative* level of consciences, called to mediate objective and general norms in concrete and particular social situations. These three levels implicitly define also the proper method and specific epistemological structure of the social doctrine of the Church.

74. *The Church's social doctrine finds its essential foundation in biblical revelation and in the tradition of the Church.* From this source, which comes from above, it draws inspiration and light to understand, judge and guide human experience and his-

---

[99]   *Code of Canon Law*, canon 747, § 2.
[100] Cf. John Paul II, Encyclical Letter *Laborem Exercens*, 3: AAS 73 (1981), 583-584.
[101] John Paul II, Encyclical Letter *Sollicitudo Rei Socialis*, 41: AAS 80 (1988), 571.
[102] John Paul II, Encyclical Letter *Sollicitudo Rei Socialis*, 41: AAS 80 (1988), 571.
[103] John Paul II, Encyclical Letter *Sollicitudo Rei Socialis*, 41: AAS 80 (1988), 572.
[104] John Paul II, Encyclical Letter *Centesimus Annus*, 59: AAS 83 (1991), 864-865.

tory. Before anything else and above everything else is God's plan for the created world and, in particular, for the life and destiny of men and women, called to Trinitarian communion.

Faith, which receives the divine word and puts it into practice, effectively interacts with reason. The understanding of faith, especially faith leading to practical action, is structured by reason and makes use of every contribution that reason has to offer. Social doctrine too, insofar as it is knowledge applied to the circumstantial and historical aspects of praxis, brings *"fides et ratio"*[105] together and is an eloquent expression of that rich relationship.

75. *Faith and reason represent the two cognitive paths of the Church's social doctrine: Revelation and human nature.* The "knowing" of faith understands and directs the life of men and women according to the light of the historical-salvific mystery, God's revelation and gift of himself to us in Christ. This understanding of faith includes reason, by means of which — insofar as possible — it unravels and comprehends revealed truth and integrates it with the truth of human nature, found in the divine plan expressed in creation.[106] This is the *integral truth* of the human person as a spiritual and corporeal being, in relationship with God, with other human beings and with other creatures.[107]

Being centred on the mystery of Christ, moreover, does not weaken or exclude the role of reason and hence does not deprive the Church's social doctrine of rationality or, therefore, of universal applicability. Since the mystery of Christ illuminates the mystery of man, it gives fullness of meaning to human dignity and to the ethical requirements which defend it. The Church's social doctrine is *knowledge enlightened by faith*, which, as such, is the expression of a greater capacity for knowledge. It explains to all people the truths that it affirms and the duties that it demands; it can be accepted and shared by all.

b. In friendly dialogue with all branches of knowledge

76. *The Church's social doctrine avails itself of contributions from all branches of knowledge, whatever their source, and has an important interdisciplinary dimension.* "In order better to incarnate the one truth about man in different and constantly changing social, economic and political contexts, this teaching enters into dialogue with the various disciplines concerned with man. It assimilates what these disciplines have to contribute."[108] The social doctrine makes use of the significant contributions of philosophy as well as the descriptive contributions of the human sciences.

77. *Above all, the contribution of philosophy is essential. This contribution has already been seen in the appeal to human nature as a source and to reason as the cognitive path*

---

[105] Cf. John Paul II, Encyclical Letter *Fides et Ratio: AAS* 91 (1999), 5-88.
[106] Cf. Second Vatican Ecumenical Council, Declaration *Dignitatis Humanae*, 14: *AAS* 58 (1966), 940.
[107] Cf. John Paul II, Encyclical Letter *Veritatis Splendor*, 13, 50, 79: *AAS* 85 (1993), 1143-1144, 1173-1174, 1197.
[108] John Paul II, Encyclical Letter *Centesimus Annus*, 59: *AAS* 83 (1991), 864.

of faith itself. By means of reason, the Church's social doctrine espouses philosophy in its own internal logic, in other words, in the argumentation that is proper to it.

Affirming that the Church's social doctrine is part of theology rather than philosophy does not imply a disowning or underestimation of the role or contribution of philosophy. In fact, philosophy is a suitable and indispensable instrument for arriving at a correct understanding of the basic concepts of the Church's social doctrine, concepts such as the person, society, freedom, conscience, ethics, law, justice, the common good, solidarity, subsidiarity, the State. This understanding is such that it inspires harmonious living in society. It is philosophy once more that shows the reasonableness and acceptability of shining the light of the Gospel on society, and that inspires in every mind and conscience openness and assent to the truth.

78. *A significant contribution to the Church's social doctrine comes also from human sciences and the social sciences.*[109] *In view of that particular part of the truth that it may reveal, no branch of knowledge is excluded.* The Church recognizes and receives everything that contributes to the understanding of man in the ever broader, more fluid and more complex network of his social relationships. She is aware of the fact that a profound understanding of man does not come from theology alone, without the contributions of many branches of knowledge to which theology itself refers.

This attentive and constant openness to other branches of knowledge makes the Church's social doctrine reliable, concrete and relevant. Thanks to the sciences, the Church can gain a more precise understanding of man in society, speak to the men and women of her own day in a more convincing manner and more effectively fulfill her task of incarnating in the conscience and social responsibility of our time, the word of God and the faith from which social doctrine flows.[110]

This interdisciplinary dialogue also challenges the sciences to grasp the perspectives of meaning, value and commitment that the Church's social doctrine reveals and to "open themselves to a broader horizon, aimed at serving the individual person who is acknowledged and loved in the fullness of his or her vocation."[111]

c. An expression of the Church's ministry of teaching

79. *The social doctrine belongs to the Church because the Church is the subject that formulates it, disseminates it and teaches it.* It is not a prerogative of a certain component of the ecclesial body but of the entire community; it is the expression of the way that the Church understands society and of her position regarding social structures and changes. The whole of the Church community — priests, religious

---

[109] In this regard, the foundation of the Pontifical Academy of Social Sciences is significant; in the *motu proprio* establishing the Academy one reads: "Social science research can effectively contribute to improving human relations, as has been shown by the progress achieved in various sectors of society especially during the century now drawing to a close. This is why the Church, ever concerned for man's true good, has turned with growing interest to this field of scientific research in order to obtain concrete information for fulfilling the duties of her Magisterium": John Paul II, Motu Proprio *Socialium Scientiarum* (1 January 1994): AAS 86 (1994), 209.

[110] Cf. John Paul II, Encyclical Letter *Centesimus Annus*, 54: AAS 83 (1991), 860.

[111] John Paul II, Encyclical Letter *Centesimus Annus*, 59: AAS 83 (1991), 864.

and laity — participates in the formulation of this social doctrine, each according to the different tasks, charisms and ministries found within her.

These many and varied contributions — which are themselves expressions of the "supernatural appreciation of the faith (sensus fidei) of the whole people"[112] *— are taken up, interpreted and formed into a unified whole by the Magisterium, which promulgates the social teaching as Church doctrine.* To the Church's Magisterium belongs those who have received the *"munus docendi,"* or the ministry of teaching in the areas of faith and morals with the authority received from Christ. The Church's social doctrine is not only the thought or work of qualified persons, but is the thought of the Church, insofar as it is the work of the Magisterium, which teaches with the authority that Christ conferred on the Apostles and their successors: the Pope and the Bishops in communion with him.[113]

80. *In the Church's social doctrine the Magisterium is at work in all its various components and expressions.* Of primary importance is the universal Magisterium of the Pope and the Council: this is the Magisterium that determines the direction and gives marks of the development of this social doctrine. This doctrine in turn is integrated into the Magisterium of the Bishops who, in the concrete and particular situations of the many different local circumstances, give precise definition to this teaching, translating it and putting it into practice.[114] The social teaching of the Bishops offers valid contributions and impetus to the Magisterium of the Roman Pontiff. In this way, there is a circulating at work that in fact expresses the collegiality of the Church's Pastors united to the Pope in the Church's social teaching. The doctrinal body that emerges includes and integrates in this fashion the universal teaching of the Popes and the particular teaching of the Bishops.

Insofar as it is part of Church's moral teaching, the Church's social doctrine has the same dignity and authority as her moral teaching. It is *authentic Magisterium,* which obligates the faithful to adhere to it.[115] The doctrinal weight of the different teachings and the assent required are determined by the nature of the particular teachings, by their level of independence from contingent and variable elements, and by the frequency with which they are invoked.[116]

d. For a society reconciled in justice and love

81. *The object of the Church's social doctrine is essentially the same that constitutes the reason for its existence: the human person called to salvation, and as such entrusted by Christ to the Church's care and responsibility.*[117] By means of her social doctrine, the Church shows her concern for human life in society, aware that the quality of

---

[112] Second Vatican Ecumenical Council, Dogmatic Constitution *Lumen Gentium,* 12: AAS 57 (1965), 16.

[113] Cf. *Catechism of the Catholic Church,* 2034.

[114] Cf. Paul VI, Apostolic Letter *Octogesima Adveniens,* 3-5: AAS 63 (1971), 402-405.

[115] Cf. *Catechism of the Catholic Church,* 2037.

[116] Cf. Congregation for the Doctrine of the Faith, Instruction *Donum Veritatis,* 16-17, 23: AAS 82 (1990), 1557-1558, 1559-1560.

[117] Cf. John Paul II, Encyclical Letter *Centesimus Annus,* 53: AAS 83 (1991), 859.

social life — that is, of the relationships of justice and love that form the fabric of society — depends in a decisive manner on the protection and promotion of the human person, for whom every community comes into existence. In fact, at play in society are the dignity and rights of the person, and peace in the relationships between persons and between communities of persons. These are goods that the social community must pursue and guarantee. In this perspective, the Church's social doctrine has the task of *proclamation*, but also of *denunciation*.

In the first place it is the proclamation of what the Church possesses as proper to herself: "a view of man and of human affairs in their totality."[118] This is done not only on the level of principles but also in practice. The Church's social doctrine, in fact, offers not only meaning, value and criteria of judgment, but also the norms and directives of action that arise from these.[119] With her social doctrine the Church does not attempt to structure or organize society, but to appeal to, guide and form consciences.

This social doctrine also entails a duty to denounce, when sin is present: the sin of injustice and violence that in different ways moves through society and is embodied in it.[120] By denunciation, the Church's social doctrine becomes judge and defender of unrecognized and violated rights, especially those of the poor, the least and the weak.[121] The more these rights are ignored or trampled, the greater becomes the extent of violence and injustice, involving entire categories of people and large geographical areas of the world, thus giving rise to *social questions*, that is, to abuses and imbalances that lead to social upheaval. A large part of the Church's social teaching is solicited and determined by important social questions, to which *social justice* is the proper answer.

82. *The intent of the Church's social doctrine is of the religious and moral order.*[122] *Religious* because the Church's evangelizing and salvific mission embraces man "in the full truth of his existence, of his personal being and also of his community and social being."[123] *Moral* because the Church aims at a "complete form of human-

---

[118] Paul VI, Encyclical Letter *Populorum Progressio*, 13: AAS 59 (1967), 264.

[119] Cf. Paul VI, Apostolic Letter *Octogesima Adveniens*, 4: AAS 63 (1971), 403-404; John Paul II, Encyclical Letter *Sollicitudo Rei Socialis*, 41: AAS 80 (1988), 570-572; *Catechism of the Catholic Church*, 2423; Congregation for the Doctrine of the Faith, Instruction *Libertatis Conscientia*, 72: AAS 79 (1987), 586.

[120] Cf. Second Vatican Ecumenical Council, Pastoral Constitution *Gaudium et Spes*, 25: AAS 58 (1966), 1045-1046.

[121] Cf. Second Vatican Ecumenical Council, Pastoral Constitution *Gaudium et Spes*, 76: AAS 58 (1966), 1099-1100; Pius XII, Radio Message for the fiftieth anniversary of *Rerum Novarum*: AAS 33 (1941), 196-197.

[122] Cf. Pius XI, Encyclical Letter *Quadragesimo Anno*: AAS 23 (1931), 190; Pius XII, Radio Message for the fiftieth anniversary of *Rerum Novarum*: AAS 23 (1931), 196-197; Second Vatican Ecumenical Council, Pastoral Constitution *Gaudium et Spes*, 42: AAS 58 (1966), 1079; John Paul II, Encyclical Letter *Sollicitudo Rei Socialis*, 41: AAS 80 (1988), 570-572; John Paul II, Encyclical Letter *Centesimus Annus*, 53: AAS 83 (1991), 859; Congregation for the Doctrine of the Faith, Instruction *Libertatis Conscientia*, 72: AAS 79 (1987), 585-586.

[123] John Paul II, Encyclical Letter *Redemptor Hominis*, 14: AAS 71 (1979), 284; cf. John Paul II, Address to the Third General Conference of Latin American Bishops, Puebla, Mexico (28 January 1979), III/2: AAS 71 (1979), 199.

ism,"[124] that is to say, at the "liberation from everything that oppresses man"[125] and "the development of the whole man and of all men."[126] The Church's social doctrine indicates the path to follow for a society reconciled and in harmony through justice and love, a society that anticipates in history, in a preparatory and prefigurative manner, the "new heavens and a new earth in which righteousness dwells" (2 Pet 3:13).

e. A message for the sons and daughters of the Church and for humanity

83. *The first recipient of the Church's social doctrine is the Church community in its entire membership, because everyone has social responsibilities that must be fulfilled.* The conscience is called by this social teaching to recognize and fulfil the obligations of justice and charity in society. This doctrine is a light of moral truth that inspires appropriate responses according to the vocation and ministry of each Christian. In the tasks of evangelization, that is to say, of teaching, catechesis and formation that the Church's social doctrine inspires, it is addressed to every Christian, each according to the competence, charisms, office and mission of proclamation that is proper to each one.[127]

This social doctrine implies as well responsibilities regarding the building, organization and functioning of society, that is to say, political, economic and administrative obligations — obligations of a secular nature — which belong to the lay faithful, not to priests or religious.[128] These responsibilities belong to the laity in a distinctive manner, by reason of the *secular condition* of their state of life, and of the *secular nature* of their vocation.[129] By fulfilling these responsibilities, the lay faithful put the Church's social teaching into action and thus fulfil the Church's secular mission.[130]

84. *Besides being destined primarily and specifically to the sons and daughters of the Church, her social doctrine also has a universal destination.* The light of the Gospel that the Church's social doctrine shines on society illuminates all men and women, and every conscience and mind is in a position to grasp the human depths of meaning and values expressed in it and the potential of humanity and humanization contained in its norms of action. It is to all people — in the name of mankind, of human dignity which is one and unique, and of humanity's care and promotion of society — to everyone in the name of the one God, Creator and ultimate end of man, that the Church's social doctrine is addressed.[131] *This social doc-*

---

[124] Paul VI, Encyclical Letter *Populorum Progressio*, 42: AAS 59 (1967), 278.

[125] Paul VI, Apostolic Exhortation *Evangelii Nuntiandi*, 9: AAS 68 (1976), 10.

[126] Paul VI, Encyclical Letter *Populorum Progressio*, 42: AAS 59 (1967), 278.

[127] Cf. *Catechism of the Catholic Church*, 2039.

[128] Cf. *Catechism of the Catholic Church*, 2442.

[129] Cf. John Paul II, Post-Synodal Apostolic Exhortation *Christifideles Laici*, 15: AAS 81 (1989), 413; Second Vatican Ecumenical Council, Dogmatic Constitution *Lumen Gentium*, 31: AAS 57 (1965), 37.

[130] Cf. Second Vatican Ecumenical Council, Pastoral Constitution *Gaudium et Spes*, 43: AAS 58 (1966), 1061-1064; Paul VI, Encyclical Letter *Populorum Progressio*, 81: AAS 59 (1967), 296-297.

[131] Cf. John XXIII, Encyclical Letter *Mater et Magistra*: AAS 53 (1961), 453.

trine is a teaching explicitly addressed to all people of good will,[132] and in fact is heard by members of other Churches and Ecclesial Communities, by followers of other religious traditions and by people who belong to no religious group.

f. Under the sign of continuity and renewal

85. *Guided by the perennial light of the Gospel and ever attentive to evolution of society, the Church's social doctrine is characterized by continuity and renewal.*[133]

It shows above all the *continuity* of a teaching that refers to the universal values drawn from Revelation and human nature. For this reason the Church's social doctrine does not depend on the different cultures, ideologies or opinions; it is a *constant* teaching that "remains identical in its fundamental inspiration, in its 'principles of reflection,' in its 'criteria of judgment,' in its basic 'directives for action,' and above all in its vital link with the Gospel of the Lord."[134] This is the foundational and permanent nucleus of the Church's social doctrine, by which it moves through history without being conditioned by history or running the risk of fading away.

On the other hand, in its constant turning to history and in engaging the events taking place, *the Church's social doctrine shows a capacity for continuous renewal.* Standing firm in its principles does not make it a rigid teaching system, but a Magisterium capable of opening itself to *new things*, without having its nature altered by them.[135] It is a teaching that is "subject to the necessary and opportune adaptations suggested by the changes in historical conditions and by the unceasing flow of the events which are the setting of the life of people and society."[136]

86. *The Church's social doctrine is presented as a "work site" where the work is always in progress, where perennial truth penetrates and permeates new circumstances, indicating paths of justice and peace.* Faith does not presume to confine changeable social and political realities within a closed framework.[137] Rather, the contrary is true: faith is the leaven of innovation and creativity. The teaching that constantly takes this as its starting point "develops through reflection applied to the changing situations of this world, under the driving force of the Gospel as the source of renewal."[138]

Mother and Teacher, the Church does not close herself off nor retreat within herself but is always open, reaching out to and turned towards man, whose destiny of salvation is her reason for being. She is in the midst of men and women as the living

---

[132] Beginning with the Encyclical *Pacem in Terris* of John XXIII, the recipient is expressly identified in this manner in the initial address of such documents.

[133] Cf. John Paul II, Encyclical Letter *Sollicitudo Rei Socialis*, 3: AAS 80 (1988), 515; Pius XII, Address to Participants in a Convention of the Catholic Action movement (29 April 1945), in *Discorsi e Radiomessaggi di Pio XII*, vol. VII, 37-38; John Paul II, Address at the international symposium "From *Rerum Novarum* to *Laborem Exercens*: towards the year 2000" (3 April 1982): *Insegnamenti di Giovanni Paolo II*, V, 1 (1982), 1095-1096.

[134] John Paul II, Encyclical Letter *Sollicitudo Rei Socialis*, 3: AAS 80 (1988), 515.

[135] Cf. Congregation for the Doctrine of the Faith, Instruction *Libertatis Conscientia*, 72: AAS 79 (1987), 585-586.

[136] John Paul II, Encyclical Letter *Sollicitudo Rei Socialis*, 3: AAS 80 (1988), 515.

[137] Cf. John Paul II, Encyclical Letter *Centesimus Annus*, 46: AAS 83 (1991), 850-851.

[138] Paul VI, Apostolic Letter *Octogesima Adveniens*, 42: AAS 63 (1971), 431.

icon of the Good Shepherd, who goes in search of and finds man where he is, in the existential and historical circumstances of his life. It is there that the Church becomes for man a point of contact with the Gospel, with the message of liberation and reconciliation, of justice and peace.

III. THE CHURCH'S SOCIAL DOCTRINE IN OUR TIME: HISTORICAL NOTES

a. The beginning of a new path

87. The term "social doctrine" goes back to Pope Pius XI[139] and designates the doctrinal "corpus" concerning issues relevant to society which, from the Encyclical Letter *Rerum Novarum*[140] of Pope Leo XIII, developed in the Church through the Magisterium of the Roman Pontiffs and the Bishops in communion with them.[141] The Church's concern for social matters certainly did not begin with that document, for the Church has never failed to show interest in society. Nonetheless, the Encyclical Letter *Rerum Novarum* marks the beginning of a new path. Grafting itself onto a tradition hundreds of years old, it signals a new beginning and a singular development of the Church's teaching in the area of social matters.[142]

In her continuous attention to men and women living in society, the Church has accumulated a rich doctrinal heritage. This has its roots in Sacred Scripture, especially the Gospels and the apostolic writings, and takes on shape and body beginning from the Fathers of the Church and the great Doctors of the Middle Ages, constituting a doctrine in which, even without explicit and direct Magisterial pronouncements, the Church gradually came to recognize her competence.

88. *In the nineteenth century, events of an economic nature produced a dramatic social, political and cultural impact.* Events connected with the Industrial Revolution profoundly changed centuries-old societal structures, raising serious problems of justice and posing the first great social question — *the labor question* — prompted by the conflict between capital and labor. In this context, the Church felt the need to become involved and intervene in a new way: the *res novae* ("new things") brought about by these events represented a challenge to her teaching and motivated her special pastoral concern for masses of people. A new discernment of the situation was needed, a discernment capable of finding appropriate solutions to unfamiliar and unexplored problems.

---

[139] Cf. Pius XI, Encyclical Letter *Quadragesimo Anno*: AAS 23 (1931), 179; Pius XII, in his Radio Message for the fiftieth anniversary of *Rerum Novarum*: AAS 33 (1941), 197, speaks of "Catholic social doctrine" and, in the Encyclical Letter *Menti Nostrae* of 23 September 1950: AAS 42 (1950), 657, of "the Church's social doctrine." John XXIII retains the expression "the Church's social doctrine" (Encyclical Letter *Mater et Magistra*: AAS 53 [1961], 453; Encyclical Letter *Pacem in Terris*: AAS 55 [1963], 300-301) and also uses "Christian social doctrine" (Encyclical Letter *Mater et Magistra*: AAS 53 [1961], 453) or even "Catholic social doctrine" (Encyclical Letter *Mater et Magistra*: AAS 53 [1961], 454).

[140] Cf. Leo XIII, Encyclical Letter *Rerum Novarum*: Acta Leonis XIII, 11 (1892), 97-144.

[141] Cf. John Paul II, Encyclical Letter *Laborem Exercens*, 3: AAS 73 (1981), 583-584; John Paul II, Encyclical Letter *Sollicitudo Rei Socialis*, 1: AAS 80 (1988), 513-514.

[142] Cf. *Catechism of the Catholic Church*, 2421.

b. From *Rerum Novarum* to our own day

89. *In response to the first great social question, Pope Leo XIII promulgated the first social encyclical, Rerum Novarum.*[143] This Encyclical examines the condition of salaried workers, which was particularly distressing for industrial laborers who languished in inhumane misery. The *labor question* is dealt with according to its true dimensions. It is explored in all its social and political expressions so that a proper evaluation may be made in the light of the doctrinal principles founded on Revelation and on natural law and morality.

Rerum Novarum lists errors that give rise to social ills, excludes socialism as a remedy and expounds with precision and in contemporary terms "the Catholic doctrine on work, the right to property, the principle of collaboration instead of class struggle as the fundamental means for social change, the rights of the weak, the dignity of the poor and the obligations of the rich, the perfecting of justice through charity, on the right to form professional associations."[144]

Rerum Novarum became the document inspiring Christian activity in the social sphere and the point of reference for this activity.[145] The Encyclical's central theme is the just ordering of society, in view of which there is the obligation to identify criteria of judgment that will help to evaluate existing socio-political systems and to suggest lines of action for their appropriate transformation.

90. *Rerum Novarum* dealt with the *labor question* using a methodology that would become "*a lasting paradigm*" [146] for successive developments in the Church's social doctrine. The principles affirmed by Pope Leo XIII would be taken up again and studied more deeply in successive social encyclicals. The whole of the Church's social doctrine can be seen as an updating, a deeper analysis and an expansion of the original nucleus of principles presented in *Rerum Novarum*. With this courageous and farsighted text, Pope Leo XIII "gave the Church 'citizenship status' as it were, amid the changing realities of public life"[147] and made an "incisive statement"[148] which became "a permanent element of the Church's social teaching."[149] He affirmed that serious social problems "could be solved only by cooperation between all forces"[150] and added that, "in regard to the Church, her cooperation will never be found lacking."[151]

---

[143] Cf. Leo XIII, Encyclical Letter *Rerum Novarum: Acta Leonis XIII*, 11 (1892), 97-144.

[144] Congregation for Catholic Education, *Guidelines for the Study and Teaching of the Church's Social Doctrine in the Formation of Priests*, 20, Vatican Polyglot Press, Rome 1988, p. 24.

[145] Cf. Pius XI, Encyclical Letter *Quadragesimo Anno*, 39 *AAS* 23 (1931), 189; Pius XII, Radio Message for the fiftieth anniversary of *Rerum Novarum: AAS* 33 (1941), 198.

[146] John Paul II, Encyclical Letter *Centesimus Annus*, 5: *AAS* 83 (1991), 799.

[147] John Paul II, Encyclical Letter *Centesimus Annus*, 5: *AAS* 83 (1991), 799.

[148] John Paul II, Encyclical Letter *Centesimus Annus*, 56: *AAS* 83 (1991), 862.

[149] John Paul II, Encyclical Letter *Centesimus Annus*, 60: *AAS* 83 (1991), 865.

[150] John Paul II, Encyclical Letter *Centesimus Annus*, 60: *AAS* 83 (1991), 865.

[151] Leo XIII, Encyclical Letter *Rerum Novarum: Acta Leonis XIII*, 11 (1892), 143; cf. John Paul II, Encyclical Letter *Centesimus Annus*, 56: *AAS* 83 (1991), 862.

91. At the beginning of the 1930s, following the grave economic crisis of 1929, Pope Pius XI published the Encyclical *Quadragesimo Anno*,[152] commemorating the fortieth anniversary of *Rerum Novarum*. The Pope reread the past in the light of the economic and social situation in which the expansion of the influence of financial groups, both nationally and internationally, was added to the effects of industrialization. It was the post-war period, during which totalitarian regimes were being imposed in Europe even as the class struggle was becoming more bitter. The Encyclical warns about the failure to respect the freedom to form associations and stresses the principles of solidarity and cooperation in order to overcome social contradictions. The relationships between capital and labor must be characterized by cooperation.[153]

Quadragesimo Anno confirms the principle that salaries should be proportional not only to the needs of the worker but also to those of the worker's family. The State, in its relations with the private sector, should apply the *principle of subsidiarity*, a principle that will become a permanent element of the Church's social doctrine. The Encyclical rejects liberalism, understood as unlimited competition between economic forces, and reconfirms the value of private property, recalling its social function. In a society in need of being rebuilt from its economic foundations, a society which itself becomes completely "the question" to deal with, "Pius XI felt the duty and the responsibility to promote a greater awareness, a more precise interpretation and an urgent application of the moral law governing human relations . . . with the intent of overcoming the conflict between classes and arriving at a new social order based on justice and charity."[154]

92. *Pope Pius XI did not fail to raise his voice against the totalitarian regimes that were being imposed in Europe during his pontificate.* Already on 29 June 1931 he had protested against the abuse of power by the totalitarian fascist regime in Italy with the Encyclical *Non Abbiamo Bisogno*.[155] He published the Encyclical *Mit Brennender Sorge*, on the situation of the Catholic Church under the German *Reich*, on 14 March 1937.[156] The text of *Mit Brennender Sorge* was read from the pulpit of every Catholic Church in Germany, after having been distributed in the greatest of secrecy. The Encyclical came out after years of abuse and violence, and it had been expressly requested from Pope Pius XI by the German Bishops after the *Reich* had implemented ever more coercive and repressive measures in 1936, particularly with regard to young people, who were required to enrol as members of the Hitler Youth Movement. The Pope spoke directly to priests, religious and lay faithful, giving them encouragement and calling them to resistance until such time that a true peace between Church and State would be restored. In 1938, with the spreading of anti-Semitism, Pope Pius XI affirmed: "Spiritually we are all Semites."[157]

---

[152] Cf. Pius XI, Encyclical Letter *Quadragesimo Anno*: AAS 23 (1931), 177-228.

[153] Cf. Pius XI, Encyclical Letter *Quadragesimo Anno*: AAS 23 (1931), 186-189.

[154] Congregation for Catholic Education, *Guidelines for the Study and Teaching of the Church's Social Doctrine in the Formation of Priests*, 21, Vatican Polyglot Press, Rome 1988, p. 24.

[155] Cf. Pius XI, Encyclical Letter *Non Abbiamo Bisogno*: AAS 23 (1931), 285-312.

[156] The official German text can be found in AAS 29 (1937), 145-167.

[157] Pius XI, Address to Belgian Radio Journalists (6 September 1938), in John Paul II, Address to international leaders of the Anti-Defamation League of B'nai B'rith (22 March 1984): *L'Osservatore Romano*, English edition, 26 March 1984, pp. 8, 11.

With the Encyclical Letter *Divini Redemptoris*,[158] on atheistic communism and Christian social doctrine, Pope Pius XI offered a systematic criticism of communism, describing it as *"intrinsically perverse,"*[159] and indicated that the principal means for correcting the evils perpetrated by it could be found in the renewal of Christian life, the practice of evangelical charity, the fulfilment of the duties of justice at both the interpersonal and social levels in relation to the common good, and the institutionalization of professional and interprofessional groups.

93. In the *Christmas Radio Messages* of Pope Pius XII,[160] together with other important interventions in social matters, Magisterial reflection on a new social order guided by morality and law, and focusing on justice and peace, become deeper. His pontificate covered the terrible years of the Second World War and the difficult years of reconstruction. He published no social encyclicals but in many different contexts he constantly showed his concern for the international order, which had been badly shaken. "During the war and the post-war period, for many people of all continents and for millions of believers and nonbelievers, the social teaching of Pope Pius XII represented the voice of universal conscience. . . . With his moral authority and prestige, Pope Pius XII brought the light of Christian wisdom to countless men of every category and social level."[161]
    One of the characteristics of Pope Pius XII's interventions is the importance he gave to the relationship between morality and law. He insisted on the notion of natural law as the soul of the system to be established on both the national and the international levels. Another important aspect of Pope Pius XII's teaching was his attention to the professional and business classes, called to work together in a special way for the attainment of the common good. "Due to his sensitivity and intelligence in grasping the 'signs of the times,' Pope Pius XII can be considered the immediate precursor of Vatican Council II and of the social teaching of the Popes who followed him."[162]

94. The 1960s bring promising prospects: recovery after the devastation of the war, the beginning of decolonization, and the first timid signs of a *thaw* in the relations between the American and Soviet blocs. This is the context within which

---

[158] The official Latin text can be found in *AAS* 29 (1937), 65-106.

[159] Cf. Pius XI, Encyclical Letter *Divini Redemptoris*: *AAS* 29 (1937), 130.

[160] Cf. Pius XII, Christmas Radio Messages: on peace and the international order, 1939, *AAS* 32 (1940), 5-13; 1940, *AAS* 33 (1941), 5-14; 1941, *AAS* 34 (1942), 10-21; 1945, *AAS* 38 (1946), 15-25; 1946, *AAS* 39 (1947), 7-17; 1948, *AAS* 41 (1949), 8-16; 1950, *AAS* 43 (1951), 49-59; 1951, *AAS* 44 (1952), 5-15; 1954, *AAS* 47 (1955), 15-28; 1955, *AAS* 48 (1956), 26-41; on the order within nations, 1942, *AAS* 35 (1943), 9-24; on democracy, 1944, *AAS* 37 (1945), 10-23; on the function of Christian civilization, 1 September 1944, *AAS* 36 (1944), 249-258; on making a return to God in generosity and brotherhood, 1947, *AAS* 40 (1948), 8-16; on the year of the great return and of great forgiveness, 1949, *AAS* 42 (1950), 121-133; on the depersonalization of man, 1952, *AAS* 45 (1953), 33-46; on the role of progress in technology and peace among peoples, 1953, *AAS* 46 (1954), 5-16.

[161] Congregation for Catholic Education, *Guidelines for the Study and Teaching of the Church's Social Doctrine in the Formation of Priests*, 22, Vatican Polyglot Press, Rome 1988, p. 25.

[162] Congregation for Catholic Education, *Guidelines for the Study and Teaching of the Church's Social Doctrine in the Formation of Priests*, 22, Vatican Polyglot Press, Rome 1988, p. 25.

Blessed Pope John XXIII reads deeply into the "signs of the times."[163] *The social question is becoming universal and involves all countries*: together with the labor question and the Industrial Revolution, there come to the fore problems of agriculture, of developing regions, of increasing populations, and those concerning the need for global economic cooperation. Inequalities that in the past were experienced within nations are now becoming international and make the dramatic situation of the Third World ever more evident.

Blessed Pope John XXIII, in his Encyclical *Mater et Magistra*,[164] "aims at updating the already known documents, and at taking a further step forward in the process of involving the whole Christian community."[165] The key words in the Encyclical are *community* and *socialization*:[166] *the Church is called in truth, justice and love to cooperate in building with all men and women an authentic communion.* In this way economic growth will not be limited to satisfying men's needs, but it will also promote their dignity.

95. With the Encyclical *Pacem in Terris*,[167] Blessed Pope John XXIII brings to the forefront the problem of peace in an era marked by nuclear proliferation. Moreover, *Pacem in Terris* contains one of the first in-depth reflections on rights on the part of the Church; it is the Encyclical of peace and human dignity. It continues and completes the discussion presented in *Mater et Magistra*, and, continuing in the direction indicated by Pope Leo XIII, it emphasizes the importance of the cooperation of all men and women. It is the first time that a Church document is addressed also to "all men of good will,"[168] who are called to a great task: "to establish with truth, justice, love and freedom new methods of relationships in human society."[169] *Pacem in Terris* dwells on the public authority of the world community, called to "tackle and solve problems of an economic, social, political or cultural character which are posed by the universal common good."[170] On the tenth anniversary of *Pacem in Terris*, Cardinal Maurice Roy, the President of the Pontifical Commission for Justice and Peace, sent Pope Paul VI a letter together with a document with a series of reflections on the different possibilities afforded by the teaching contained in Pope John XXIII's Encyclical for shedding light on the new problems connected with the promotion of peace.[171]

96. The Pastoral Constitution *Gaudium et Spes*[172] of the Second Vatican Council is a significant response of the Church to the expectations of the contemporary

---

[163] Cf. John XXIII, Encyclical Letter *Pacem in Terris*: AAS 55 (1963), 267-269, 278-279, 291, 295-296.

[164] Cf. John XXIII, Encyclical Letter *Mater et Magistra*: AAS 53 (1961), 401-464.

[165] Congregation for Catholic Education, *Guidelines for the Study and Teaching of the Church's Social Doctrine in the Formation of Priests*, 23, Vatican Polyglot Press, Rome 1988, p. 26.

[166] Cf. John XXIII Encyclical Letter *Mater et Magistra*: AAS 53 (1961), 415-418.

[167] Cf. John XXIII, Encyclical Letter *Pacem in Terris*: AAS 55 (1963), 257-304.

[168] John XXIII, Encyclical Letter *Pacem in Terris*, Title: AAS 55 (1963), 257.

[169] John XXIII, Encyclical Letter *Pacem in Terris*: AAS 55 (1963), 301.

[170] Cf. John XXIII, Encyclical Letter *Pacem in Terris*: AAS 55 (1963), 294.

[171] Cf. Cardinal Maurice Roy, Letter to Paul VI and Document on the occasion of the tenth anniversary of *Pacem in Terris*, *L'Osservatore Romano*, English edition, 19 April 1973, pp. 1-8.

[172] Cf. Second Vatican Ecumenical Council, Pastoral Constitution *Gaudium et Spes*: AAS 58 (1966), 1025-1120.

world. In this Constitution, "in harmony with the ecclesiological renewal, a new concept of how to be a community of believers and people of God are reflected. It aroused new interest regarding the doctrine contained in the preceding documents on the witness and life of Christians, as authentic ways of making the presence of God in the world visible."[173] *Gaudium et Spes* presents the face of a Church that "cherishes a feeling of deep solidarity with the human race and its history,"[174] that travels the same journey as all mankind and shares the same earthly lot with the world, but which at the same time "is to be a leaven and, as it were, the soul of human society in its renewal by Christ and transformation into the family of God."[175]

Gaudium et Spes presents in a systematic manner the themes of culture, of economic and social life, of marriage and the family, of the political community, of peace and the community of peoples, in the light of a Christian anthropological outlook and of the Church's mission. Everything is considered from the starting point of the person and with a view to the person, "the only creature that God willed for its own sake."[176] Society, its structures and development must be oriented towards "the progress of the human person."[177] For the first time, the Magisterium of the Church, at its highest level, speaks at great length about the different temporal aspects of Christian life: "It must be recognized that the attention given by the Constitution to social, psychological, political, economic, moral and religious changes has increasingly stimulated . . . the Church's pastoral concern for men's problems and dialogue with the world."[178]

97. Another very important document of the Second Vatican Council in the corpus of the Church's social doctrine is the Declaration *Dignitatis Humanae*,[179] in which *the right to religious freedom* is clearly proclaimed. The document presents the theme in two chapters. The first, of a general character, affirms that religious freedom is based on the dignity of the human person and that it must be sanctioned as a civil right in the legal order of society. The second chapter deals with the theme in the light of Revelation and clarifies its pastoral implications, pointing out that it is a right that concerns not only people as individuals but also the different communities of people.

---

[173] Congregation for Catholic Education, *Guidelines for the Study and Teaching of the Church's Social Doctrine in the Formation of Priests*, 24, Vatican Polyglot Press, Rome 1988, p. 28.

[174] Second Vatican Ecumenical Council, Pastoral Constitution *Gaudium et Spes*, 1: AAS 58 (1966), 1026.

[175] Second Vatican Ecumenical Council, Pastoral Constitution *Gaudium et Spes*, 40: AAS 58 (1966), 1058.

[176] Second Vatican Ecumenical Council, Pastoral Constitution *Gaudium et Spes*, 24: AAS 58 (1966), 1045.

[177] Second Vatican Ecumenical Council, Pastoral Constitution *Gaudium et Spes*, 25: AAS 58 (1966), 1045.

[178] Congregation for Catholic Education, *Guidelines for the Study and Teaching of the Church's Social Doctrine in the Formation of Priests*, 24, Vatican Polyglot Press, Rome 1988, p. 29.

[179] Cf. Second Vatican Ecumenical Council, Declaration *Dignitatis Humanae*: AAS 58 (1966), 929-946.

98. "Development is the new name for peace,"[180] Pope Paul VI solemnly proclaims in his Encyclical *Populorum Progressio*,[181] which may be considered a development of the chapter on economic and social life in *Gaudium et Spes*, even while it introduces some significant new elements. In particular, it presents the outlines of an integral development of man and of a development in solidarity with all humanity: "These two topics are to be considered the axes around which the Encyclical is structured. In wishing to convince its receivers of the urgent need for action in solidarity, the Pope presents development as 'the transition from less humane conditions to those which are more humane' and indicates its characteristics."[182] This *transition* is not limited to merely economic or technological dimensions, but implies for each person the acquisition of culture, the respect of the dignity of others, the acknowledgment of "the highest good, the recognition of God Himself, the author and end of these blessings."[183] Development that benefits everyone responds to the demands of justice on a global scale that guarantees worldwide peace and makes it possible to achieve a "complete humanism"[184] guided by spiritual values.

99. In this regard, in 1967, Pope Paul VI establishes the Pontifical Commission "*Iustitia et Pax*," thus fulfilling the wishes of the Council Fathers who considered it "most opportune that an organism of the Universal Church be set up in order that both the justice and love of Christ toward the poor might be developed everywhere. The role of such an organism would be to stimulate the Catholic community to promote progress in needy regions and international social justice."[185] By initiative of Pope Paul VI, beginning in 1968, the Church celebrates the first day of the year as the *World Day of Peace*. This same Pontiff started the tradition of writing annual Messages that deal with the theme chosen for each *World Day of Peace*. These Messages expand and enrich the corpus of the Church's social doctrine.

100. At the beginning of the 1970s, in a climate of turbulence and strong ideological controversy, Pope Paul VI returns to the social teaching of Pope Leo XIII and updates it, on the occasion of the eightieth anniversary of *Rerum Novarum*, with his Apostolic Letter *Octogesima Adveniens*.[186] The Pope reflects on post-industrial society with all of its complex problems, noting the inadequacy of ideologies in responding to these challenges: urbanization, the condition of young people, the condition of women, unemployment, discrimination, emigration, population growth, the influence of the means of social communications, the ecological problem.

---

[180] Paul VI, Encyclical Letter *Populorum Progressio*, 76-80: AAS 59 (1967), 294-296.
[181] Cf. Paul VI, Encyclical Letter *Populorum Progressio*: AAS 59 (1967), 257-299.
[182] Congregation for Catholic Education, *Guidelines for the Study and Teaching of the Church's Social Doctrine in the Formation of Priests*, 25, Vatican Polyglot Press, Rome 1988, p. 29.
[183] Paul VI, Encyclical Letter *Populorum Progressio*, 21: AAS 59 (1967), 267.
[184] Paul VI, Encyclical Letter *Populorum Progressio*, 42: AAS 59 (1967), 278.
[185] Second Vatican Ecumenical Council, Pastoral Constitution *Gaudium et Spes*, 90: AAS 58 (1966), 1112.
[186] Cf. Paul VI, Apostolic Letter *Octogesima Adveniens*: AAS 63 (1971), 401-441.

101. Ninety years after *Rerum Novarum*, Pope John Paul II devoted the Encyclical *Laborem Exercens* [187] to *work*, the fundamental good of the human person, the primary element of economic activity and the key to the entire social question. *Laborem Exercens* outlines a spirituality and ethic of work in the context of a profound theological and philosophical reflection. Work must not be understood only in the objective and material sense, but one must keep in mind its subjective dimension, insofar as it is always an expression of the person. Besides being a decisive paradigm for social life, work has all the dignity of being a context in which the person's natural and supernatural vocation must find fulfilment.

102. With the Encyclical *Sollicitudo Rei Socialis*,[188] Pope John Paul II commemorates the twentieth anniversary of *Populorum Progressio* and deals once more with the theme of development along two fundamental lines: "on one hand, the dramatic situation of the modern world, under the aspect of the failed development of the Third World, and on the other, the meaning of, conditions and requirements for a development worthy of man."[189] The Encyclical presents differences between progress and development, and insists that "true development cannot be limited to the multiplication of goods and service — to what one possesses — but must contribute to the fullness of the 'being' of man. In this way the moral nature of real development is meant to be shown clearly."[190] Pope John Paul II, alluding to the motto of the pontificate of Pope Pius XII, "*opus iustitiae pax*" (peace is the fruit of justice), comments: "Today, one could say, with the same exactness and the same power of biblical inspiration (cf. *Is* 32:17; *Jas* 3:18), *opus solidaritatis pax* (peace is the fruit of solidarity)."[191]

103. On the hundredth anniversary of *Rerum Novarum*, Pope John Paul II promulgates his third social encyclical, *Centesimus Annus*,[192] whence emerges the doctrinal continuity of a hundred years of the Church's social Magisterium. Taking up anew one of the fundamental principles of the Christian view of social and political organization, which had been the central theme of the previous Encyclical, the Pope writes: "What we nowadays call the principle of solidarity . . . is frequently stated by Pope Leo XIII, who uses the term 'friendship' . . . Pope Pius XI refers to it with the equally meaningful term 'social charity.' Pope Paul VI, expanding the concept to cover the many modern aspects of the social question, speaks of a 'civilization of love.'"[193] Pope John Paul II demonstrates how the Church's social teaching moves along the axis of reciprocity between God and man: recognizing God in every person and every person in God is the condition of authentic

---

[187] Cf. John Paul II, Encyclical Letter *Laborem Exercens*: AAS 73 (1981), 577-647.
[188] Cf. John Paul II, Encyclical Letter *Sollicitudo Rei Socialis*: AAS 80 (1988), 513-586.
[189] Congregation for Catholic Education, *Guidelines for the Study and Teaching of the Church's Social Doctrine in the Formation of Priests*, 26, Vatican Polyglot Press, Rome 1988, p. 32.
[190] Congregation for Catholic Education, *Guidelines for the Study and Teaching of the Church's Social Doctrine in the Formation of Priests*, 26, Vatican Polyglot Press, Rome 1988, p. 32.
[191] John Paul II, Encyclical Letter *Sollicitudo Rei Socialis*, 39: AAS 80 (1988), 568.
[192] Cf. John Paul II, Encyclical Letter *Centesimus Annus*: AAS 83 (1991), 793-867.
[193] John Paul II, Encyclical Letter *Centesimus Annus*, 10: AAS 83 (1991), 805.

human development. The articulate and in-depth analysis of the "new things," and particularly of the great breakthrough of 1989 with the collapse of the Soviet system, shows appreciation for democracy and the free economy, in the context of an indispensable solidarity.

c. In the light and under the impulse of the Gospel

104. *The documents referred to here constitute the milestones of the path travelled by the Church's social doctrine from the time of Pope Leo XIII to our own day.* This brief summary would become much longer if we considered all the interventions motivated, other than by a specific theme, by "the pastoral concern to present to the entire Christian community and to all men of good will the fundamental principles, universal criteria and guidelines suitable for suggesting basic choices and coherent practice for every concrete situation."[194]

In the formulation and teaching of this social doctrine, the Church has been, and continues to be, prompted not by theoretical motivation but by pastoral concerns. She is spurred on by the repercussions that social upheavals have on people, on multitudes of men and women, on human dignity itself, in contexts where "man painstakingly searches for a better world, without working with equal zeal for the betterment of his own spirit."[195] For these reasons, this social doctrine has arisen and developed an "updated doctrinal 'corpus' . . . [that] builds up gradually, as the Church, in the fullness of the word revealed by Christ Jesus and with the assistance of the Holy Spirit (cf. *Jn* 14:16,26; 16:13-15), reads events as they unfold in the course of history."[196]

---

[194] Congregation for Catholic Education, *Guidelines for the Study and Teaching of the Church's Social Doctrine in the Formation of Priests*, 27, Vatican Polyglot Press, Rome 1988, p. 33.

[195] Second Vatican Ecumenical Council, Pastoral Constitution *Gaudium et Spes*, 4: AAS 58 (1966), 1028.

[196] John Paul II, Encyclical Letter *Sollicitudo Rei Socialis*, 1: AAS 80 (1988), 514; cf. *Catechism of the Catholic Church*, 2422.

CHAPTER THREE

THE HUMAN PERSON AND HUMAN RIGHTS

I. SOCIAL DOCTRINE
AND THE PERSONALIST PRINCIPLE

105. *The Church sees in men and women, in every person, the living image of God himself. This image finds, and must always find anew, an ever deeper and fuller unfolding of itself in the mystery of Christ, the Perfect Image of God, the One who reveals God to man and man to himself.* It is to these men and women, who have received an incomparable and inalienable dignity from God himself, that the Church speaks, rendering to them the highest and most singular service, constantly reminding them of their lofty vocation so that they may always be mindful of it and worthy of it. Christ, the Son of God, "by his incarnation has united himself in some fashion with every person";[197] for this reason the Church recognizes as her fundamental duty the task of seeing that this union is continuously brought about and renewed. In Christ the Lord, the Church indicates and strives to be the first to embark upon the path of the human person,[198] and she invites all people to recognize in everyone — near and far, known and unknown, and above all in the poor and the suffering — a brother or sister "for whom Christ died" (*1 Cor* 8:11; *Rom* 14:15).[199]

106. *All of social life is an expression of its unmistakable protagonist: the human person.* The Church has many times and in many ways been the authoritative advocate of this understanding, recognizing and affirming the centrality of the human person in every sector and expression of society: "Human society is therefore the object of the social teaching of the Church since she is neither outside nor over and above socially united men, but exists exclusively in them and, therefore, for them."[200] This important awareness is expressed in the affirmation that "far from being the object or passive element of social life" the human person "is rather, and must always remain, its subject, foundation and goal."[201] The origin of social life is therefore found in the human person, and society cannot refuse to recognize its active and responsible subject; every expression of society must be directed towards the human person.

---

[197] Second Vatican Ecumenical Council, Pastoral Constitution *Gaudium et Spes*, 22: AAS 58 (1966), 1042.

[198] Cf. John Paul II, Encyclical Letter *Redemptor Hominis*, 14: AAS 71 (1979), 284.

[199] Cf. *Catechism of the Catholic Church*, 1931.

[200] Congregation for Catholic Education, *Guidelines for the Study and Teaching of the Church's Social Doctrine in the Formation of Priests*, 35, Vatican Polyglot Press, Rome 1988, p. 39.

[201] Pius XII, Radio Message of 24 December 1944, 5: AAS 37 (1945), 12.

107. *Men and women, in the concrete circumstances of history, represent the heart and soul of Catholic social thought.*[202] *The whole of the Church's social doctrine, in fact, develops from the principle that affirms the inviolable dignity of the human person.*[203] In her manifold expressions of this knowledge, the Church has striven above all to defend human dignity in the face of every attempt to redimension or distort its image; moreover she has often denounced the many violations of human dignity. History attests that it is from the fabric of social relationships that there arise some of the best possibilities for ennobling the human person, but it is also there that lie in wait the most loathsome rejections of human dignity.

II. THE HUMAN PERSON AS THE "IMAGO DEI"

a. Creatures in the image of God

108. *The fundamental message of Sacred Scripture proclaims that the human person is a creature of God* (cf. Ps 139:14-18), *and sees in his being in the image of God the element that characterizes and distinguishes him:* "God created man in his own image, in the image of God he created him; male and female he created them" (Gen 1:27). God places the human creature at the centre and summit of the created order. Man (in Hebrew, "*adam*") is formed from the earth ("*adamah*") and God blows into his nostrils the breath of life (cf. Gen 2:7). Therefore, "being in the image of God the human individual possesses the dignity of a person, who is not just something, but someone. He is capable of self-knowledge, of self-possession and of freely giving himself and entering into communion with other persons. Further, he is called by grace to a covenant with his Creator, to offer him a response of faith and love that no other creature can give in his stead."[204]

109. *The likeness with God shows that the essence and existence of man are constitutively related to God in the most profound manner.*[205] This is a relationship that exists in itself, it is therefore not something that comes afterwards and is not added from the outside. The whole of man's life is a quest and a search for God. This relationship with God can be ignored or even forgotten or dismissed, but it can never be eliminated. Indeed, among all the world's visible creatures, only man has a "capacity for God" ("*homo est Dei capax*").[206] The human being is a personal being created by God to be in relationship with him; man finds life and self-expression only in relationship, and tends naturally to God.[207]

[202] Cf. John Paul II, Encyclical Letter *Centesimus Annus*, 11: AAS 83 (1991), 807.
[203] Cf. John XXIII, Encyclical Letter *Mater et Magistra*: AAS 53 (1961), 453, 459.
[204] *Catechism of the Catholic Church*, 357.
[205] Cf. *Catechism of the Catholic Church*, 356, 358.
[206] *Catechism of the Catholic Church*, title of Chapter 1, Section 1, Part 1; cf. Second Vatican Ecumenical Council, Pastoral Constitution *Gaudium et Spes*, 12: AAS 58 (1966), 1034; John Paul II, Encyclical Letter *Evangelium Vitae*, 34: AAS 87 (1995), 440.
[207] Cf. John Paul II, Encyclical Letter *Evangelium Vitae*, 35: AAS 87 (1995), 440-441; *Catechism of the Catholic Church*, 1721.

110. *The relationship between God and man is reflected in the relational and social dimension of human nature.* Man, in fact, is not a solitary being, but "a social being, and unless he relates himself to others he can neither live nor develop his potential."[208] In this regard the fact that God created *human beings as man and woman* (cf. *Gen* 1:27) is significant:[209] "How very significant is the dissatisfaction which marks man's life in Eden as long as his sole point of reference is the world of plants and animals (cf. *Gen* 2:20). Only the appearance of the woman, a being who is flesh of his flesh and bone of his bones (cf. *Gen* 2:23), and in whom the spirit of God the Creator is also alive, can satisfy the need for interpersonal dialogue, so vital for human existence. In one's neighbor, whether man or woman, there is a reflection of God himself, the definitive goal and fulfilment of every person."[210]

111. *Man and woman have the same dignity and are of equal value,*[211] *not only because they are both, in their differences, created in the image of God, but even more profoundly because the dynamic of reciprocity that gives life to the "we" in the human couple, is an image of God.*[212] In a relationship of mutual communion, man and woman fulfil themselves in a profound way, rediscovering themselves as persons through the sincere gift of themselves.[213] Their covenant of union is presented in Sacred Scripture as an image of the Covenant of God with man (cf. *Hos* 1-3; *Is* 54; *Eph* 5:21-33) and, at the same time, as a service to life.[214] Indeed, the human couple can participate in God's act of creation: "God blessed them, and God said to them, 'Be fruitful and multiply, and fill the earth and subdue it' " (*Gen* 1:28).

112. *Man and woman are in relationship with others above all as those to whom the lives of others have been entrusted.*[215] "For your lifeblood I will surely require a reckoning, . . . I will require it . . . of man [and] of every man's brother" (*Gen* 9:5), God tells Noah after the flood. In this perspective, the relationship with God requires that *the life of man be considered sacred and inviolable.*[216] The fifth commandment, "Thou shalt not kill" (*Ex* 20:13; *Deut* 5:17), has validity because God alone is Lord of life and death.[217] The respect owed to the inviolability and integrity of physical life finds its climax in the positive commandment: "You shall love your neighbor as yourself" (*Lev* 19:18), by which Jesus enjoins the obligation to tend to the needs of one's neighbor (cf. *Mt* 22:37-40; *Mk* 12:29-31; *Lk* 10:27-28).

---

[208] Second Vatican Ecumenical Council, Pastoral Constitution *Gaudium et Spes*, 12: AAS 58 (1966), 1034.

[209] Cf. *Catechism of the Catholic Church*, 369.

[210] John Paul II, Encyclical Letter *Evangelium Vitae*, 35: AAS 87 (1995), 440.

[211] Cf. *Catechism of the Catholic Church*, 2334.

[212] Cf. *Catechism of the Catholic Church*, 371.

[213] Cf. John Paul II, Letter to Families *Gratissimam Sane*, 6, 8, 14, 16, 19-20: AAS 86 (1994), 873-874, 876-878, 899-903, 910-919.

[214] Cf. Second Vatican Ecumenical Council, Pastoral Constitution *Gaudium et Spes*, 50-51: AAS 58 (1966), 1070-1072.

[215] Cf. John Paul II, Encyclical Letter *Evangelium Vitae*, 19: AAS 87 (1995), 421-422.

[216] Cf. *Catechism of the Catholic Church*, 2258.

[217] Cf. Second Vatican Ecumenical Council, Pastoral Constitution *Gaudium et Spes*, 27: AAS 58 (1966), 1047-1048; *Catechism of the Catholic Church*, 2259-2261.

113. *With this specific vocation to life, man and woman find themselves also in the presence of all the other creatures. They can and are obliged to put them at their own service and to enjoy them, but their dominion over the world requires the exercise of responsibility, it is not a freedom of arbitrary and selfish exploitation.* All of creation in fact has value and is "good" (cf. *Gen* 1:4,10,12,18,21,25) in the sight of God, who is its author. Man must discover and respect its value. This is a marvellous challenge to his intellect, which should lift him up as on wings[218] towards the contemplation of the truth of all God's creatures, that is, the contemplation of what God sees as *good* in them. The Book of Genesis teaches that human dominion over the world consists in *naming things* (cf. *Gen* 2:19-20). In giving things their names, man must recognize them for what they are and establish with each of them a relationship of responsibility.[219]

114. *Man is also in relationship with himself and is able to reflect on himself.* Sacred Scripture speaks in this regard about the *heart of man*. The heart designates man's inner spirituality, what distinguishes him from every other creature. God "has made everything beautiful in its time; also he has put eternity into man's mind, yet so that he cannot find out what God has done from the beginning to the end" (*Eccles* 3:11). In the end, the heart indicates the spiritual faculties which most properly belong to man, which are his prerogatives insofar as he is created in the image of his Creator: reason, the discernment of good and evil, free will.[220] When he listens to the deep aspirations of his heart, no person can fail to make his own the words of truth expressed by Saint Augustine: "You have made us for yourself, O Lord, and our hearts are restless until they rest in you."[221]

b. The tragedy of sin

115. *This marvellous vision of man's creation by God is inseparable from the tragic appearance of original sin.* With a clear affirmation the Apostle Paul sums up the account of man's fall contained in the first pages of the Bible: "Sin came into the world through one man and death through sin" (*Rom* 5:12). Man, against God's prohibition, allows himself to be seduced by the serpent and stretches out his hand to the tree of life, falling prey to death. By this gesture, man tries to break through his limits as a creature, challenging God, his sole Lord and the source of his life. It is a sin of disobedience (cf. *Rom* 5:19) that separates man from God.[222]

From revelation we know that Adam, the first man, transgresses God's commandment and loses the holiness and justice in which he was made, holiness and justice which were received not only for himself but for all of humanity: "By yielding to the tempter, Adam and Eve committed a *personal sin*, but this sin affected *the human nature* that they would then transmit *in a fallen state*. It is a sin which will be transmitted

---

[218] Cf. John Paul II, Encyclical Letter *Fides et Ratio*, proem: *AAS* 91 (1999), 5.
[219] Cf. *Catechism of the Catholic Church*, 373.
[220] Cf. John Paul II, Encyclical Letter *Evangelium Vitae*, 34: *AAS* 87 (1995), 438-440.
[221] Saint Augustine, *Confessions*, I, 1: PL 32, 661: "Tu excitas, ut laudare te delectet; quia fecisti nos ad te, et inquietum est cor nostrum, donec requiescat in te."
[222] Cf. *Catechism of the Catholic Church*, 1850.

by propagation to all mankind, that is, by the transmission of a human nature deprived of original holiness and justice."[223]

116. *At the root of personal and social divisions, which in differing degrees offend the value and dignity of the human person, there is a wound which is present in man's inmost self.* "In the light of faith we call it sin: beginning with original sin, which all of us bear from birth as an inheritance from our first parents, to the sin which each one of us commits when we abuse our own freedom."[224] The consequences of sin, insofar as it is an act of separation from God, are alienation, that is, the separation of man not only from God but also from himself, from other men and from the world around him. "Man's rupture with God leads tragically to divisions between brothers. In the description of the 'first sin,' the rupture with Yahweh simultaneously breaks the bond of friendship that had united the human family. Thus the subsequent pages of *Genesis* show us the man and the woman as it were pointing an accusing finger at each other (cf. *Gen.* 3:12). Later we have brother hating brother and finally taking his brother's life (cf. *Gen* 4:2-16). According to the Babel story, the result of sin is the shattering of the human family, already begun with the first sin and now reaching its most extreme form on the social level."[225] Reflecting on the mystery of sin, we cannot fail to take into consideration this tragic connection between cause and effect.

117. *The mystery of sin is composed of a twofold wound, which the sinner opens in his own side and in the relationship with his neighbor. That is why we can speak of personal and social sin.* Every sin is *personal* under a certain aspect; under another, every sin is *social*, insofar as and because it also has social consequences. In its true sense, sin is always an *act of the person*, because it is the free act of an individual person and not properly speaking of a group or community. The character of social sin can unquestionably be ascribed to every sin, taking into account the fact that "by virtue of human solidarity which is as mysterious and intangible as it is real and concrete, each individual's sin in some way affects others."[226] It is not, however, legitimate or acceptable to understand social sin in a way that, more or less consciously, leads to a weakening or the virtual cancellation of the personal component by admitting only social guilt and responsibility. At the bottom of every situation of sin there is always the individual who sins.

118. *Certain sins, moreover, constitute by their very object a direct assault on one's neighbor. Such sins in particular are known as social sins.* Social sin is every sin committed against the justice due in relations between individuals, between the indi-

---

223 *Catechism of the Catholic Church*, 404.

224 John Paul II, Apostolic Exhortation *Reconciliatio et Paenitentia*, 2: AAS 77 (1985), 188; cf. *Catechism of the Catholic Church*, 1849.

225 John Paul II, Apostolic Exhortation *Reconciliatio et Paenitentia*, 15: AAS 77 (1985), 212-213.

226 John Paul II, Apostolic Exhortation *Reconciliatio et Paenitentia*, 16: AAS 77 (1985), 214. The text explains moreover that there is a *law of descent*, which is a kind of *communion of sin*, in which a soul that lowers itself through sin drags down with it the Church and, in some way, the entire world; to this law there corresponds a *law of ascent*, the profound and magnificent mystery of the *communion of saints*, thanks to which every soul that rises above itself also raises the world.

vidual and the community, and also between the community and the individual. Social too is every sin against the rights of the human person, starting with the right to life, including that of life in the womb, and every sin against the physical integrity of the individual; every sin against the freedom of others, especially against the supreme freedom to believe in God and worship him; and every sin against the dignity and honor of one's neighbor. Every sin against the common good and its demands, in the whole broad area of rights and duties of citizens, is also social sin. In the end, social sin is that sin that "refers to the relationships between the various human communities. These relationships are not always in accordance with the plan of God, who intends that there be justice in the world and freedom and peace between individuals, groups and peoples."[227]

119. *The consequences of sin perpetuate the structures of sin. These are rooted in personal sin and, therefore, are always connected to concrete acts of the individuals who commit them, consolidate them and make it difficult to remove them.* It is thus that they grow stronger, spread and become sources of other sins, conditioning human conduct.[228] These are obstacles and conditioning that go well beyond the actions and brief life span of the individual and interfere also in the process of the development of peoples, the delay and slow pace of which must be judged in this light.[229] The actions and attitudes opposed to the will of God and the good of neighbor, as well as the structures arising from such behavior, appear to fall into two categories today: "on the one hand, the all-consuming desire for profit, and on the other, the thirst for power, with the intention of imposing one's will upon others. In order to characterize better each of these attitudes, one can add the expression: 'at any price.'"[230]

c. The universality of sin and the universality of salvation

120. *The doctrine of original sin, which teaches the universality of sin, has an important foundation:* "If we say we have no sin, we deceive ourselves, and the truth is not in us" (*1 Jn* 1:8). This doctrine encourages men and women not to remain in guilt and not to take guilt lightly, continuously seeking scapegoats in other people and justification in the environment, in heredity, in institutions, in structures and in relationships. This is a teaching that unmasks such deceptions.

The doctrine of the universality of sin, however, must not be separated from the consciousness of the universality of salvation in Jesus Christ. If it is so separated it engenders a false anxiety of sin and a pessimistic view of the world and life, which leads to contempt of the cultural and civil accomplishments of mankind.

121. *Christian realism sees the abysses of sin, but in the light of the hope, greater than any evil, given by Jesus Christ's act of redemption, in which sin and death are destroyed* (cf. *Rom* 5:18-21; *1 Cor* 15:56-57): "In him God reconciled man to himself."[231] It

---

[227] John Paul II, Apostolic Exhortation *Reconciliatio et Paenitentia*, 16: AAS 77 (1985), 216.
[228] Cf. *Catechism of the Catholic Church*, 1869.
[229] Cf. John Paul II, Encyclical Letter *Sollicitudo Rei Socialis*, 36: AAS 80 (1988), 561-563.
[230] John Paul II, Encyclical Letter *Sollicitudo Rei Socialis*, 37: AAS 80 (1988), 563.
[231] John Paul II, Apostolic Exhortation *Reconciliatio et Paenitentia*, 10: AAS 77 (1965), 205.

is Christ, the image of God (cf. *2 Cor* 4:4; *Col* 1:15), who enlightens fully and brings to completion the image and likeness of God in man. The Word that became man in Jesus Christ has always been mankind's life and light, the light that enlightens every person (cf. *Jn* 1:4,9). God desires in the one mediator Jesus Christ, his Son, the salvation of all men and women (cf. *1 Tim* 2:4-5). Jesus is at the same time the Son of God and the new Adam, that is, the new man (cf. *1 Cor* 15:47-49; *Rom* 5:14): "Christ the new Adam, in the very revelation of the mystery of the Father and of his love, fully reveals man to himself and brings to light his most high calling."[232] In him we are, by God, "predestined to be conformed to the image of his Son, in order that he might be the first-born among many brethren" (*Rom* 8:29).

122. *The new reality that Jesus Christ gives us is not grafted onto human nature nor is it added from outside: it is rather that reality of communion with the Trinitarian God to which men and women have always been oriented in the depths of their being, thanks to their creaturely likeness to God.* But this is also a reality that people cannot attain by their own forces alone. Through the Spirit of Jesus Christ, the incarnate Son of God, in whom this reality of communion has already been brought about in a singular manner, men and women are received as children of God (cf. *Rom* 8:14-17; *Gal* 4:4-7). By means of Christ, we share in the nature of God, who gives us infinitely more "than all that we ask or think" (*Eph* 3:20). What mankind has already received is nothing more than a token or a "guarantee" (*2 Cor* 1:22; *Eph* 1:14) of what it will receive in its fullness only in the presence of God, seen "face to face" (*1 Cor* 13:12), that is, a guarantee of eternal life: "And this is eternal life, that they know you the only true God, and Jesus Christ whom you have sent" (*Jn* 17:3).

123. *The universality of this hope also includes, besides the men and women of all peoples, heaven and earth*: "Shower, O heavens, from above, and let the skies rain down righteousness; let the earth open, that salvation may sprout forth, and let it cause righteousness to spring up also; I the Lord have created it" (*Is* 45:8). According to the New Testament, all creation, together indeed with all humanity, awaits the Redeemer: subjected to futility, creation reaches out full of hope, with groans and birth pangs, longing to be freed from decay (cf. *Rom* 8:18-22).

III. THE MANY ASPECTS OF THE HUMAN PERSON

124. *Prizing highly the marvellous biblical message, the Church's social doctrine stops to dwell above all on the principal and indispensable dimensions of the human person. Thus it is able to grasp the most significant facets of the mystery and dignity of human beings.* In the past there has been no lack of various reductionist conceptions of the human person, many of which are still dramatically present on the stage of modern history. These are ideological in character or are simply the result of widespread forms of custom or thought concerning mankind, human life and human destiny. The com-

---

[232] Second Vatican Ecumenical Council, Pastoral Constitution *Gaudium et Spes*, 22: AAS 58 (1966), 1042.

mon denominator among these is the attempt to make the image of man unclear by emphasizing only one of his characteristics at the expense of all the others.[233]

125. *The human person may never be thought of only as an absolute individual being, built up by himself and on himself, as if his characteristic traits depended on no one else but himself. Nor can the person be thought of as a mere cell of an organism that is inclined at most to grant it recognition in its functional role within the overall system.* Reductionist conceptions of the full truth of men and women have already been the object of the Church's social concern many times, and she has not failed to raise her voice against these, as against other drastically reductive perspectives, taking care to proclaim instead that "individuals do not feel themselves isolated units, like grains of sand, but united by the very force of their nature and by their internal destiny, into an organic, harmonious mutual relationship."[234] She has affirmed instead that man cannot be understood "simply as an element, a molecule within the social organism,"[235] and is therefore attentive that the affirmation of the primacy of the person is not seen as corresponding to an individualistic or mass vision.

126. *Christian faith, while inviting that whatever is good and worthy of man should be sought out wherever it may be found (cf. 1 Thes 5:21), "is above and is sometimes opposed to the ideologies,* in that it recognizes God, who is transcendent and the Creator, and who, through all the levels of creation, calls on man as endowed with responsibility and freedom."[236]

The Church's social doctrine strives to indicate the different dimensions of the mystery of man, who must be approached "in the full truth of his existence, of his personal being and also of his community and social being,"[237] with special attention so that the value of the human person may be readily perceived.

A. THE UNITY OF THE PERSON

127. *Man was created by God in unity of body and soul.*[238] "The spiritual and immortal soul is the principle of unity of the human being, whereby it exists as a whole — *corpore et anima unus* — as a person. These definitions not only point out that the body, which has been promised the resurrection, will also share in glory. They also remind us that reason and free will are linked with all the bodily and sense faculties. *The person, including the body, is completely entrusted to himself, and it is in the unity of body and soul that the person is the subject of his own moral acts.*"[239]

128. *Through his corporeality man unites in himself elements of the material world;* these "reach their summit through him, and through him raise their voice in free

[233] Cf. Paul VI, Apostolic Letter *Octogesima Adveniens*, 26-39: AAS 63 (1971), 420-428.
[234] Pius XII, Encyclical Letter *Summi Pontificatus*: AAS 31 (1939), 463.
[235] John Paul II, Encyclical Letter *Centesimus Annus*, 13: AAS 83 (1991), 809.
[236] Paul VI, Apostolic Letter *Octogesima Adveniens*, 27: AAS 63 (1971), 421.
[237] John Paul II, Encyclical Letter *Redemptor Hominis*, 14: AAS 71 (1979), 284.
[238] Cf. Fourth Lateran Ecumenical Council, Chapter 1, *De Fide Catholica*: DS 800, p. 259; First Vatican Ecumenical Council, *Dei Filius*, c. 1: *De Deo rerum omnium Creatore*: DS 3002, p. 587; First Vatican Ecumenical Council, canons 2, 5: DS 3022, 3025, pp. 592, 593.
[239] John Paul II, Encyclical Letter *Veritatis Splendor*, 48: AAS 85 (1993), 1172.

praise of the Creator."[240] This dimension makes it possible for man to be part of the material world, but not as in a prison or in exile. It is not proper to despise bodily life; rather "man . . . is obliged to regard his body as good and honorable since God has created it and will raise it up on the last day."[241] Because of this bodily dimension, however, following the wound of sin, man experiences the rebellion of his body and the perverse inclinations of his heart; he must always keep careful watch over these lest he become enslaved to them and become a victim of a purely earthly vision of life.

Through his spirituality man moves beyond the realm of mere things and plunges into the innermost structure of reality. When he enters into his own heart, that is, when he reflects on his destiny, he discovers that he is superior to the material world because of his unique dignity as one who converses with God, under whose gaze he makes decisions about his life. In his inner life he recognizes that the person has "a spiritual and immortal soul" and he knows that the person is not merely "a speck of nature or a nameless constituent of the city of man."[242]

129. *Therefore, man has two different characteristics: he is a material being, linked to this world by his body, and he is a spiritual being, open to transcendence* and to the discovery of "more penetrating truths," thanks to his intellect, by which "he shares in the light of the divine mind."[243] The Church affirms: "The unity of soul and body is so profound that one has to consider the soul to be the 'form' of the body: i.e., it is because of its spiritual soul that the body made of matter becomes a living, human body; spirit and matter, in man, are not two natures united, but rather their union forms a single nature."[244] Neither the spiritualism that despises the reality of the body nor the materialism that considers the spirit a mere manifestation of the material do justice to the complex nature, to the totality or to the unity of the human being.

B. Opening to Transcendence and Uniqueness of the Person

a. **Open to transcendence**

130. *Openness to transcendence belongs to the human person: man is open to the infinite and to all created beings.* He is open above all to the infinite — God — because with his intellect and will he raises himself above all the created order and above himself, he becomes independent from creatures, is free in relation to created things and tends towards total truth and the absolute good. He is open also to others, to the men and women of the world, because only insofar as he under-

---

[240] Second Vatican Ecumenical Council, Pastoral Constitution *Gaudium et Spes*, 14: AAS 58 (1966), 1035; cf. *Catechism of the Catholic Church*, 364.

[241] Second Vatican Ecumenical Council, Pastoral Constitution *Gaudium et Spes*, 14: AAS 58 (1966), 1035.

[242] Second Vatican Ecumenical Council, Pastoral Constitution *Gaudium et Spes*, 14: AAS 58 (1966), 1036; cf. *Catechism of the Catholic Church*, 363, 1703.

[243] Second Vatican Ecumenical Council, Pastoral Constitution *Gaudium et Spes*, 15: AAS 58 (1966), 1036.

[244] *Catechism of the Catholic Church*, 365.

stands himself in reference to a "thou" can he say "I." He comes out of himself, from the self-centred preservation of his own life, to enter into a relationship of dialogue and communion with others.

The human person is open to the fullness of being, to the unlimited horizon of being. He has in himself the ability to transcend the individual particular objects that he knows, thanks effectively to his openness to unlimited being. In a certain sense the human soul is — because of its cognitive dimension — all things: "all immaterial things enjoy a certain infiniteness, insofar as they embrace everything, or because it is a question of the essence of a spiritual reality that functions as a model and likeness of everything, as is the case with God, or because it has a likeness to everything or is 'in act' like the Angels or 'in potential' like souls."[245]

b. Unique and unrepeatable

131. *Man exists as a unique and unrepeatable being, he exists as an "I" capable of self-understanding, self-possession and self-determination.* The human person is an intelligent and conscious being, capable of reflecting on himself and therefore of being aware of himself and his actions. However, it is not intellect, consciousness and freedom that define the person, rather it is the person who is the basis of the acts of intellect, consciousness and freedom. These acts can even be absent, for even without them man does not cease to be a person.

The human person, must always be understood in his unrepeatable and inviolable uniqueness. In fact, man exists above all as a *subjective entity*, as a centre of *consciousness* and *freedom*, whose unique life experiences, comparable to those of no one else, underlie the inadmissibility of any attempt to reduce his status by forcing him into preconceived categories or power systems, whether ideological or otherwise. This entails above all the requirement not only of simple *respect* on the part of others, especially political and social institutions and their leaders with regard to every man and woman on the earth, but even more, this means that the primary commitment of each person towards others, and particularly of these same institutions, must be for the promotion and integral development of the person.

c. Respect for human dignity

132. *A just society can become a reality only when it is based on the respect of the transcendent dignity of the human person. The person represents the ultimate end of society, by which it is ordered to the person:* "Hence, the social order and its development must invariably work to the benefit of the human person, since the order of things is to be subordinate to the order of persons, and not the other way around."[246] Respect

---

[245] Saint Thomas Aquinas, *Commentum in tertium librum Sententiarum*, d. 27, q. 1, a. 4: "Ex utraque autem parte res immateriales infinitatem habent quodammodo, quia sunt quodammodo omnia, sive inquantum essentia rei immaterialis est exemplar et similitudo omnium, sicut in Deo accidit, sive quia habet similitudinem omnium vel actu vel potentia, sicut accidit in Angelis et animabus"; cf. Saint Thomas Aquinas, *Summa Theologiae*, I, q. 75, a. 5: Ed. Leon. 5, 201-203.

[246] Second Vatican Ecumenical Council, Pastoral Constitution *Gaudium et Spes*, 26: AAS 58 (1966), 1046-1047.

for human dignity can in no way be separated from obedience to this principle. It is necessary to "consider every neighbor without exception as another self, taking into account first of all his life and the means necessary for living it with dignity."[247] Every political, economic, social, scientific and cultural programme must be inspired by the awareness of the primacy of each human being over society.[248]

133. *In no case, therefore, is the human person to be manipulated for ends that are foreign to his own development,* which can find complete fulfilment only in God and his plan of salvation: in fact, man in his interiority transcends the universe and is the only creature willed by God for itself.[249] For this reason neither his life nor the development of his thought, nor his good, nor those who are part of his personal and social activities can be subjected to unjust restrictions in the exercise of their rights and freedom.

The person cannot be a means for carrying out economic, social or political projects imposed by some authority, even in the name of an alleged progress of the civil community as a whole or of other persons, either in the present or the future. It is therefore necessary that public authorities keep careful watch so that restrictions placed on freedom or any onus placed on personal activity will never become harmful to personal dignity, thus guaranteeing the effective practicability of human rights. All this, once more, is based on the vision of man as a *person*, that is to say, as an *active* and *responsible* subject of his own growth process, together with the community to which he belongs.

134. *Authentic social changes are effective and lasting only to the extent that they are based on resolute changes in personal conduct.* An authentic moralization of social life will never be possible unless it starts with people and has people as its point of reference: indeed, "living a moral life bears witness to the dignity of the person."[250] It is obviously the task of people to develop those moral attitudes that are fundamental for any society that truly wishes to be human (justice, honesty, truthfulness, etc.), and which in no way can simply be expected of others or delegated to institutions. It is the task of everyone, and in a special way of those who hold various forms of political, judicial or professional responsibility with regard to others, to be the watchful conscience of society and the first to bear witness to civil social conditions that are worthy of human beings.

C. THE FREEDOM OF THE HUMAN PERSON

a. The value and limits of freedom

135. *Man can turn to good only in freedom, which God has given to him as one of the highest signs of his image:*[251] "For God has willed that man remain 'under the con-

---

[247] Second Vatican Ecumenical Council, Pastoral Constitution *Gaudium et Spes*, 27: AAS 58 (1966), 1047.
[248] Cf. *Catechism of the Catholic Church*, 2235.
[249] Cf. Second Vatican Ecumenical Council, Pastoral Constitution *Gaudium et Spes*, 24: AAS 58 (1966), 1045; *Catechism of the Catholic Church*, 27, 356 and 358.
[250] *Catechism of the Catholic Church*, 1706.
[251] Cf. *Catechism of the Catholic Church*, 1705.

trol of his own decisions' (Sir 15:14), so that he can seek his Creator spontaneously, and come freely to utter and blissful perfection through loyalty to Him.
Hence man's dignity demands that he act according to a knowing and free choice
that is personally motivated and prompted from within, neither under blind internal impulse nor by mere external pressure."[252]

Man rightly appreciates freedom and strives for it passionately: rightly does he
desire and must form and guide, by his own free initiative, his personal and social
life, accepting personal responsibility for it.[253] In fact, freedom not only allows man
suitably to modify the state of things outside of himself, but it also determines the
growth of his being as a person through choices consistent with the true good.[254]
In this way man generates himself, he is *father* of his own being,[255] he constructs
the social order.[256]

136. *Freedom is not contrary to man's dependence as a creature on God.*[257] *Revelation
teaches that the power to decide good and evil does not belong to man but to God alone*
(cf. Gen 2:16-17). "Man is certainly free, inasmuch as he can understand and
accept God's commands. And he possesses an extremely far-reaching freedom,
since he can eat 'of every tree of the garden'. But his freedom is not unlimited: it
must halt before the 'tree of the knowledge of good and evil,' for it is called to
accept the moral law given by God. In fact, human freedom finds its authentic
and complete fulfilment precisely in the acceptance of that law."[258]

137. *The proper exercise of personal freedom requires specific conditions of an economic, social, juridic, political and cultural order* that "are too often disregarded or violated. Such situations of blindness and injustice injure the moral life and involve
the strong as well as the weak in the temptation to sin against charity. By deviat-
ing from the moral law man violates his own freedom, becomes imprisoned within himself, disrupts neighborly fellowship and rebels against divine truth."[259]
Removing injustices promotes human freedom and dignity: nonetheless, "the first
thing to be done is to appeal to the spiritual and moral capacities of the individual and to the permanent need for inner conversion, if one is to achieve the economic and social changes that will truly be at the service of man."[260]

b. The bond uniting freedom with truth and the natural law

138. *In the exercise of their freedom, men and women perform morally good acts that
are constructive for the person and for society when they are obedient to truth, that is,*

---

[252] Second Vatican Ecumenical Council, Pastoral Constitution *Gaudium et Spes*, 17: AAS 58 (1966),
    1037; cf. *Catechism of the Catholic Church*, 1730-1732.
[253] Cf. John Paul II, Encyclical Letter *Veritatis Splendor*, 34: AAS 85 (1993), 1160-1161; Second
    Vatican Ecumenical Council, Pastoral Constitution *Gaudium et Spes*, 17: AAS 58 (1966), 1038.
[254] Cf. *Catechism of the Catholic Church*, 1733.
[255] Cf. Gregory of Nyssa, *De Vita Moysis*, II, 2-3: PG 44, 327B-328B: "unde fit, ut nos ipsi patres
    quodammodo simus nostri . . . vitii ac virtutis ratione fingentes."
[256] Cf. John Paul II, Encyclical Letter *Centesimus Annus*, 13: AAS 83 (1991), 809-810.
[257] Cf. *Catechism of the Catholic Church*, 1706.
[258] John Paul II, Encyclical Letter *Veritatis Splendor*, 35: AAS 85 (1993), 1161-1162.
[259] *Catechism of the Catholic Church*, 1740.
[260] Congregation for the Doctrine of the Faith, Instruction *Libertatis Conscientia*, 75: AAS 79
    (1987), 587.

when they do not presume to be the creators and absolute masters of truth or of ethical norms.[261] Freedom in fact does not have "its absolute and unconditional origin . . . in itself, but in the life within which it is situated and which represents for it, at one and the same time, both a limitation and a possibility. Human freedom belongs to us as creatures; it is a freedom which is given as a gift, one to be received like a seed and to be cultivated responsibly."[262] When the contrary is the case, freedom dies, destroying man and society.[263]

139. *The truth concerning good and evil is recognized in a practical and concrete manner by the judgment of conscience, which leads to the acceptance of responsibility for the good accomplished and the evil committed.* "Consequently *in the practical judgment of conscience,* which imposes on the person the obligation to perform a given act, *the link between freedom and truth is made manifest.* Precisely for this reason conscience expresses itself in acts of 'judgment' which reflect the truth about the good, and not in arbitrary 'decisions'. The maturity and responsibility of these judgments — and, when all is said and done, of the individual who is their subject — are not measured by the liberation of the conscience from objective truth, in favor of an alleged autonomy in personal decisions, but, on the contrary, by an insistent search for truth and by allowing oneself to be guided by that truth in one's actions."[264]

140. *The exercise of freedom implies a reference to a natural moral law, of a universal character, that precedes and unites all rights and duties.*[265] The natural law "is nothing other than the light of intellect infused within us by God. Thanks to this, we know what must be done and what must be avoided. This light or this law has been given by God to creation."[266] It consists in the participation in his eternal law, which is identified with God himself.[267] This law is called "natural" because the reason that promulgates it is proper to human nature. It is universal, it extends to all people insofar as it is established by reason. In its principal precepts, the divine and natural law is presented in the Decalogue and indicates the primary and essential norms regulating moral life.[268] Its central focus is the act of aspiring and submitting to God, the source and judge of everything that is good, and also the act of seeing others as equal to oneself. The natural law expresses the dignity of the person and lays the foundations of the person's fundamental duties.[269]

---

[261] Cf. *Catechism of the Catholic Church*, 1749-1756.

[262] John Paul II, Encyclical Letter *Veritatis Splendor*, 86: AAS 85 (1993), 1201.

[263] Cf. John Paul II, Encyclical Letter *Veritatis Splendor*, 44, 99: AAS 85 (1993), 1168-1169, 1210-1211.

[264] John Paul II, Encyclical Letter *Veritatis Splendor*, 61: AAS 85 (1993), 1181-1182.

[265] Cf. Encyclical Letter *Veritatis Splendor*, 50: AAS 85 (1993), 1173-1174.

[266] Saint Thomas Aquinas, *In Duo Praecepta Caritatis et in Decem Legis Praecepta Expositio*, c. 1: "Nunc autem de scientia operandorum intendimus: ad quam tractandan quadruplex lex invenitur. Prima dicitur lex naturae; et haec nihil aliud est nisi lumen intellectum insitum nobis a Deo, per quod cognoscimus quid agendum et quid vitandum. Hoc lumen et hanc legem dedit Deus homini in creatione": Divi Thomae Aquinatis, Doctoris Angelici, *Opuscola Theologica*, vol. II: *De re spirituali*, cura et studio P. Fr. Raymundi Spiazzi, O.P., Marietti ed., Taurini - Romae 1954, p. 245.

[267] Cf. Saint Thomas Aquinas, *Summa Theologiae*, I-II, q. 91, a. 2, c: Ed. Leon. 7, 154: "participatio legis aeternae in rationali creatura lex naturalis dicitur."

[268] Cf. *Catechism of the Catholic Church*, 1955.

[269] Cf. *Catechism of the Catholic Church*, 1956.

141. *In the diversity of cultures, the natural law unites peoples, enjoining common principles.* Although its application may require adaptations to the many different conditions of life according to place, time and circumstances,[270] it remains *immutable* "under the flux of ideas and customs and supports their progress . . . Even when it is rejected in its very principles, it cannot be destroyed or removed from the heart of man. It always rises again in the life of individuals and societies."[271]

Its precepts, however, are not clearly and immediately perceived by everyone. Religious and moral truths can be known "by everyone with facility, with firm certainty and without the admixture of error"[272] only with the help of Grace and Revelation. The natural law offers a foundation prepared by God for the revealed law and Grace, in full harmony with the work of the Spirit.[273]

142. *The natural law, which is the law of God, cannot be annulled by human sinfulness.*[274] It lays the indispensable moral foundation for building the human community and for establishing the civil law that draws its consequences of a concrete and contingent nature from the principles of the natural law.[275] If the perception of the universality of the moral law is dimmed, people cannot build a true and lasting communion with others, because when a correspondence between truth and good is lacking, "whether culpably or not, our acts damage the communion of persons, to the detriment of each."[276] Only freedom rooted in a common nature, in fact, can make all men responsible and enable them to justify public morality. Those who proclaim themselves to be the sole measure of realities and of truth cannot live peacefully in society with their fellow men and cooperate with them.[277]

143. *Freedom mysteriously tends to betray the openness to truth and human goodness, and too often it prefers evil and being selfishly closed off, raising itself to the status of a divinity that creates good and evil*: "Although he was made by God in a state of holiness, from the very onset of his history man abused his liberty, at the urging of the Evil One. Man set himself against God and sought to attain his goal apart from God . . . Often refusing to acknowledge God as his beginning, man has disrupted also his proper relationship to his own ultimate goal as well as his whole relationship toward himself and others and all created things."[278] *Human freedom needs therefore to be liberated.* Christ, by the power of his Paschal Mystery, frees man from

---

[270] Cf. *Catechism of the Catholic Church*, 1957.
[271] *Catechism of the Catholic Church*, 1958.
[272] First Vatican Ecumenical Council, *Dei Filius*, c. 2: DS 3005, p. 588; cf. Pius XII, Encyclical Letter *Humani Generis*: AAS 42 (1950), 562.
[273] Cf. *Catechism of the Catholic Church*, 1960.
[274] Cf. Saint Augustine, *Confessions*, 2, 4, 9: PL 32, 678: "Furtum certe punit lex tua, Domine, et lex scripta in cordibus hominum, quam ne ipsa quidem delet iniquitas."
[275] Cf. *Catechism of the Catholic Church*, 1959.
[276] John Paul II, Encyclical Letter *Veritatis Splendor*, 51: AAS 85 (1993), 1175.
[277] Cf. John Paul II, Encyclical Letter *Evangelium Vitae*, 19-20: AAS 87 (1995), 421-424.
[278] Second Vatican Ecumenical Council, Pastoral Constitution *Gaudium et Spes*, 13: AAS 58 (1966), 1034-1035.

his disordered love of self,[279] which is the source of his contempt for his neighbor and of those relationships marked by domination of others. Christ shows us that freedom attains its fulfilment in the gift of self.[280] By his sacrifice on the cross, Jesus places man once more in communion with God and his neighbor.

D. THE EQUAL DIGNITY OF ALL PEOPLE

144. *"God shows no partiality"* (Acts 10:34; cf. *Rom* 2:11; *Gal* 2:6; *Eph* 6:9), *since all people have the same dignity as creatures made in his image and likeness.*[281] The Incarnation of the Son of God shows the equality of all people with regard to dignity: "There is neither Jew nor Greek, there is neither slave nor free, there is neither male nor female; for you are all one in Christ Jesus" (*Gal* 3:28; cf. *Rom* 10:12; *1 Cor* 12:13, *Col* 3:11).

Since something of the glory of God shines on the face of every person, the dignity of every person before God is the basis of the dignity of man before other men.[282] Moreover, this is the ultimate foundation of the radical equality and brotherhood among all people, regardless of their race, nation, sex, origin, culture, or class.

145. *Only the recognition of human dignity can make possible the common and personal growth of everyone* (cf. *Jas* 2:1-9). To stimulate this kind of growth it is necessary in particular to help the least, effectively ensuring conditions of equal opportunity for men and women and guaranteeing an objective equality between the different social classes before the law.[283]

Also in relations between peoples and States, conditions of equality and parity are prerequisites for the authentic progress of the international community.[284] Despite the steps taken in this direction, it must not forget that there still exist many inequalities and forms of dependence.[285]

Together with equality in the recognition of the dignity of each person and of every people there must also be an awareness that it will be possible to safeguard and promote human dignity only if this is done as a community, by the whole of humanity. Only through the mutual action of individuals and peoples sincerely concerned for the good of all men and women can a genuine universal brotherhood be attained;[286]

---

[279] Cf. *Catechism of the Catholic Church*, 1741.

[280] Cf. John Paul II, Encyclical Letter *Veritatis Splendor*, 87: AAS 85 (1993), 1202-1203.

[281] Cf. *Catechism of the Catholic Church*, 1934.

[282] Cf. Second Vatican Ecumenical Council, Pastoral Constitution *Gaudium et Spes*, 29: AAS 58 (1966), 1048-1049.

[283] Cf. Paul VI, Encyclical Letter *Octogesima Adveniens*, 16: AAS 63 (1971), 413.

[284] Cf. John XXIII, Encyclical Letter *Pacem in Terris*, 47-48: AAS 55 (1963), 279-281; Paul VI, Address to the General Assembly of the United Nations (4 October 1965), 5: AAS 57 (1965), 881; John Paul II, Address to the Fiftieth General Assembly of the United Nations (5 October 1995), 13: *L'Osservatore Romano*, English edition, 11 October 1995, p. 9-10.

[285] Cf. Second Vatican Ecumenical Council, Pastoral Constitution *Gaudium et Spes*, 84: AAS 58 (1966), 1107-1108.

[286] Cf. Paul VI, Address to the General Assembly of the United Nations, 5: AAS 57 (1965), 881; Paul VI, Encyclical Letter *Populorum Progressio*, 43-44: AAS 59 (1967), 278-279.

otherwise, the persistence of conditions of serious disparity and inequality will make us all poorer.

146. *"Male" and "female" differentiate two individuals of equal dignity, which does not however reflect a static equality, because the specificity of the female is different from the specificity of the male, and this difference in equality is enriching and indispensable for the harmony of life in society*: "The condition that will assure the rightful presence of woman in the Church and in society is a more penetrating and accurate consideration of the anthropological foundation for masculinity and femininity with the intent of clarifying woman's personal identity in relation to man, that is, a diversity yet mutual complementarily, not only as it concerns roles to be held and functions to be performed, but also, and more deeply, as it concerns her make-up and meaning as a person."[287]

147. *Woman is the complement of man, as man is the complement of woman: man and woman complete each other mutually, not only from a physical and psychological point of view, but also ontologically.* It is only because of the duality of "male" and "female" that the "human" being becomes a full reality. It is the "unity of the two,"[288] or in other words a relational "uni-duality," that allows each person to experience the interpersonal and reciprocal relationship as a gift that at the same time is a mission: "to this 'unity of the two' God has entrusted not only the work of procreation and family life, but the creation of history itself."[289] "The woman is 'a helper' for the man, just as the man is 'a helper' for the woman!":[290] in the encounter of man and woman a unitary conception of the human person is brought about, based not on the logic of self-centredness and self-affirmation, but on that of love and solidarity.

148. *Persons with disabilities are fully human subjects, with rights and duties*: "in spite of the limitations and sufferings affecting their bodies and faculties, they point up more clearly the dignity and greatness of man."[291] Since persons with disabilities are subjects with all their rights, they are to be helped to participate in every dimension of family and social life at every level accessible to them and according to their possibilities.

The rights of persons with disabilities need to be promoted with effective and appropriate measures: "It would be radically unworthy of man, and a denial of our common humanity, to admit to the life of the community, and thus admit to work, only those who are fully functional. To do so would be to practice a serious form of discrimination, that of the strong and healthy against the weak and sick."[292] Great attention must be paid not only to the physical and psychological work con-

---

[287] John Paul II, Post-Synodal Apostolic Exhortation *Christifideles Laici*, 50: AAS 81 (1989), 489.

[288] John Paul II, Apostolic Letter *Mulieris Dignitatem*, 11: AAS 80 (1988), 1678.

[289] John Paul II, Letter to Women, 8: AAS 87 (1995), 808.

[290] John Paul II, Sunday Angelus (9 July 1995): *L'Osservatore Romano*, English edition, 12 July 1995, p. 1; cf. Congregation for the Doctrine of the Faith, *Letter to the Bishops of the Catholic Church on the Collaboration of Men and Women in the Church and in the World*: *L'Osservatore Romano*, English edition, 11/18 August 2004, pp. 5-8.

[291] John Paul II, Encyclical Letter *Laborem Exercens*, 22: AAS 73 (1981), 634.

[292] John Paul II, Encyclical Letter *Laborem Exercens*, 22: AAS 73 (1981), 634.

ditions, to a just wage, to the possibility of promotion and the elimination of obstacles, but also to the affective and sexual dimensions of persons with disabilities: "They too need to love and to be loved, they need tenderness, closeness and intimacy,"[293] according to their capacities and with respect for the moral order, which is the same for the non-handicapped and the handicapped alike.

E. THE SOCIAL NATURE OF HUMAN BEINGS

149. *The human person is essentially a social being* [294] *because God, who created humanity, willed it so.*[295] Human nature, in fact, reveals itself as a nature of a being who responds to his own needs. This is based on a *relational subjectivity*, that is, in the manner of a free and responsible being who recognizes the necessity of integrating himself in cooperation with his fellow human beings, and who is *capable of communion* with them on the level of knowledge and love. "A *society* is a group of persons bound together organically by a principle of unity that goes beyond each one of them. As an assembly that is at once visible and spiritual, a society endures through time: it gathers up the past and prepares for the future."[296]

It is therefore necessary to stress that community life is a natural characteristic that distinguishes man from the rest of earthly creatures. Social activity carries in itself a particular sign of man and of humanity that of a person at work within a community of persons: this is the sign that determines man's interior traits and in a sense constitutes his very nature.[297] This relational characteristic takes on, in the light of faith, a more profound and enduring meaning. Made in the image and likeness of God (cf. Gen 1:26), and made visible in the universe in order to live in society (cf. Gen 2:20,23) and exercise dominion over the earth (cf. Gen 1:26,28-30), the human person is for this reason called from the very beginning to life in society: "God did not create man as a 'solitary being' but wished him to be a 'social being'. Social life therefore is not exterior to man: he can only grow and realize his vocation in relation with others."[298]

150. *The social nature of human beings does not automatically lead to communion among persons, to the gift of self.* Because of pride and selfishness, man discovers in

---

[293] John Paul II, Message for the International Symposium on the Dignity and Rights of the Mentally Disabled Person, 5 January 2004, 5: *L'Osservatore Romano*, English edition, 21 January 2004, p. 6.

[294] Cf. Second Vatican Ecumenical Council, Pastoral Constitution *Gaudium et Spes*, 12: AAS 58 (1966), 1034; *Catechism of the Catholic Church*, 1879.

[295] Cf. Pius XII, Radio Message of 24 December 1942, 6: AAS 35 (1943), 11-12; John XXIII, Encyclical Letter *Pacem in Terris*: AAS 55 (1963), 264-265.

[296] *Catechism of the Catholic Church*, 1880.

[297] The natural social disposition of men and women also makes it evident that the origin of society is not found in a "contract" or "agreement," but in human nature itself; and from this arises the possibility of freely creating different agreements of association. It must not be forgotten that the ideologies of the social contract are based on a false anthropology; consequently, their results cannot be — and in fact they have not been — profitable for society or for people. The Magisterium has declared such opinions as openly absurd and entirely disastrous: cf. Leo XIII, Encyclical Letter *Libertas Praestantissimum*: *Acta Leonis XIII*, 8 (1889), 226-227.

[298] Congregation for the Doctrine of the Faith, Instruction *Libertatis Conscientia*, 32: AAS 79 (1987), 567.

himself the seeds of asocial behavior, impulses leading him to close himself within his own individuality and to dominate his neighbor.[299] Every society worthy of the name can be sure that it stands in the truth when all of its members, thanks to their ability to know what is good, are able to pursue it for themselves and for others. It is out of love for one's own good and for that of others that people come together in stable groups with the purpose of attaining a common good. The different human societies also must establish among themselves relationships of solidarity, communication and cooperation, in the service of man and the common good.[300]

151. *The social nature of human beings is not uniform but is expressed in many different ways.* In fact, the common good depends on a healthy *social pluralism.* The different components of society are called to build a unified and harmonious whole, within which it is possible for each element to preserve and develop its own characteristics and autonomy. Some components — such as the family, the civil community and the religious community — respond more immediately to the intimate nature of man, while others come about more on a voluntary basis. "To promote the participation of the greatest number in the life of a society, the creation of voluntary associations and institutions must be encouraged 'on both national and international levels, which relate to economic and social goals, to cultural and recreational activities, to sport, to various professions, and to political affairs'. This *'socialization'* also expresses the natural tendency for the sake of attaining objectives that exceed individual capacities. It develops the qualities of the person, especially the sense of initiative and responsibility, and helps guarantee his rights."[301]

IV. HUMAN RIGHTS

a. The value of human rights

152. *The movement towards the identification and proclamation of human rights is one of the most significant attempts to respond effectively to the inescapable demands of human dignity.*[302] The Church sees in these rights the extraordinary opportunity that our modern times offer, through the affirmation of these rights, for more effectively recognizing human dignity and universally promoting it as a characteristic inscribed by God the Creator in his creature.[303] The Church's Magisterium has not

---

[299] Cf. Second Vatican Ecumenical Council, Pastoral Constitution *Gaudium et Spes*, 25: AAS 58 (1966), 1045-1046.

[300] Cf. John Paul II, Encyclical Letter *Sollicitudo Rei Socialis*, 26: AAS 80 (1988), 544-547; Second Vatican Ecumenical Council, Pastoral Constitution *Gaudium et Spes*, 76: AAS 58 (1966), 1099-1100.

[301] *Catechism of the Catholic Church*, 1882.

[302] Cf. Second Vatican Ecumenical Council, Declaration *Dignitatis Humanae*, 1: AAS 58 (1966), 929-930.

[303] Cf. Second Vatican Ecumenical Council, Pastoral Constitution *Gaudium et Spes*, 41: AAS 58 (1966), 1059-1060; Congregation for Catholic Education, *Guidelines for the Study and Teaching of the Church's Social Doctrine in the Formation of Priests*, 32, Vatican Polyglot Press, Rome 1988, pp. 36-37.

failed to note the positive value of the *Universal Declaration of Human Rights*, adopted by the United Nations on 10 December 1948, which Pope John Paul II defined as "a true milestone on the path of humanity's moral progress."[304]

153. *In fact, the roots of human rights are to be found in the dignity that belongs to each human being.*[305] This dignity, inherent in human life and equal in every person, is perceived and understood first of all by reason. The natural foundation of rights appears all the more solid when, in light of the supernatural, it is considered that human dignity, after having been given by God and having been profoundly wounded by sin, was taken on and redeemed by Jesus Christ in his incarnation, death and resurrection.[306]

The ultimate source of human rights is not found in the mere will of human beings,[307] *in the reality of the State, in public powers, but in man himself and in God his Creator.* These rights are "universal, inviolable, inalienable."[308] *Universal* because they are present in all human beings, without exception of time, place or subject. *Inviolable* insofar as "they are inherent in the human person and in human dignity"[309] and because "it would be vain to proclaim rights, if at the same time everything were not done to ensure the duty of respecting them by all people, everywhere, and for all people."[310] *Inalienable* insofar as "no one can legitimately deprive another person, whoever they may be, of these rights, since this would do violence to their nature."[311]

154. *Human rights are to be defended not only individually but also as a whole: protecting them only partially would imply a kind of failure to recognize them.* They correspond to the demands of human dignity and entail, in the first place, the fulfilment of the essential needs of the person in the material and spiritual spheres. "These rights apply to every stage of life and to every political, social, economic and cultural situation. Together they form a single whole, directed unambiguously towards the promotion of every aspect of the good of both the person and society . . . The integral promotion of every category of human rights is the true guarantee of full respect for each individual right."[312] Universality and indivisibility are distinctive characteristics of human rights: they are "two guiding principles which at the same

---

[304] John Paul II, Address to the 34th General Assembly of the United Nations (2 October 1979), 7: AAS 71 (1979), 1147-1148; for John Paul II, this *Declaration* "remains one of the highest expressions of the human conscience of our time": Address to the Fiftieth General Assembly of the United Nations (5 October 1995), 2: *L'Osservatore Romano*, English edition, 11 October 1995, p. 8.

[305] Cf. Second Vatican Ecumenical Council, Pastoral Constitution *Gaudium et Spes*, 27: AAS 58 (1966), 1047-1048; *Catechism of the Catholic Church*, 1930.

[306] Cf. John XIII, Encyclical Letter *Pacem in Terris*: AAS 55 (1963), 259; Second Vatican Ecumenical Council, Pastoral Constitution *Gaudium et Spes*, 22: AAS 58 (1966), 1079.

[307] Cf. John XXIII, Encyclical Letter *Pacem in Terris*: AAS 55 (1963), 278-279.

[308] John XXIII, Encyclical Letter *Pacem in Terris*: AAS 55 (1963), 259.

[309] John Paul II, Message for the 1999 World Day of Peace, 3: AAS 91 (1999), 379.

[310] Paul VI, Message to the International Conference on Human Rights, Teheran (15 April 1968): *L'Osservatore Romano*, English edition, 2 May 1968, p. 4.

[311] John Paul II, Message for the 1999 World Day of Peace, 3: AAS 91 (1999), 379.

[312] John Paul II, Message for the 1999 World Day of Peace, 3: AAS 91 (1999), 379.

time demand that human rights be rooted in each culture and that their juridical profile be strengthened so as to ensure that they are fully observed."[313]

b. The specification of rights

155. *The teachings of Pope John XXIII,*[314] *the Second Vatican Council,*[315] *and Pope Paul VI* [316] have given abundant indication of the concept of human rights as articulated by the Magisterium. Pope John Paul II has drawn up a list of them in the Encyclical *Centesimus Annus:* "the right to life, an integral part of which is the right of the child to develop in the mother's womb from the moment of conception; the right to *live in* a united family and in a moral environment conducive to the growth of the child's personality; the right to develop one's intelligence and *freedom* in seeking and knowing the *truth*; the right to share in the work which makes wise use of the earth's material resources, and to derive from that work the means to support oneself and one's dependents; and the right *freely to establish* a family, to have and to rear children through the responsible exercise of one's sexuality. In a certain sense, the source and synthesis of these rights is religious *freedom*, understood as the right to live in the truth of one's faith and in conformity with one's transcendent dignity as a person."[317]

The first right presented in this list is the right to life, from conception to its natural end,[318] which is the condition for the exercise of all other rights and, in particular, implies the illicitness of every form of procured abortion and of euthanasia.[319] *Emphasis is given to the paramount value of the right to religious freedom:* "all men are to be immune from coercion on the part of individuals or of social groups and of any human power, in such wise that no one is to be forced to act in a manner contrary to his own beliefs, whether privately or publicly, whether alone or in association with others, within due limits."[320] The respect of this right is an indicative sign of "man's authentic progress in any regime, in any society, system or milieu."[321]

c. Rights and duties

156. *Inextricably connected to the topic of rights is the issue of the duties falling to men and women*, which is given appropriate emphasis in the interventions of the Magis-

---

[313] John Paul II, Message for the 1998 World Day of Peace, 2: AAS 90 (1998), 149.

[314] Cf. John XXIII, Encyclical Letter *Pacem in Terris*: AAS 55 (1963), 259-264.

[315] Cf. Second Vatican Ecumenical Council, Pastoral Constitution *Gaudium et Spes*, 26: AAS 58 (1966), 1046-1047.

[316] Cf. Paul VI, Address to the General Assembly of the United Nations (4 October 1965), 6: AAS 57 (1965), 883-884; Paul VI, Message to the Bishops Gathered for the Synod (26 October 1974): AAS 66 (1974), 631-639.

[317] John Paul II, Encyclical Letter *Centesimus Annus*, 47: AAS 83 (1991), 851-852; cf. also Address to the 34th General Assembly of the United Nations (2 October 1979), 13: AAS 71 (1979) 1152-1153.

[318] Cf. John Paul II, Encyclical Letter *Evangelium Vitae*, 2: AAS 87 (1995), 402.

[319] Cf. Second Vatican Ecumenical Council, Pastoral Constitution *Gaudium et Spes*, 27: AAS 58 (1966), 1047-1048; John Paul II, Encyclical Letter *Veritatis Splendor*, 80: AAS 85 (1993), 1197-1198; John Paul II, Encyclical Letter *Evangelium Vitae*, 7-28: AAS 87 (1995), 408-433.

[320] Second Vatican Ecumenical Council, Declaration *Dignitatis Humanae*, 2: AAS 58 (1966), 930-931.

[321] John Paul II, Encyclical Letter *Redemptor Hominis*, 17: AAS 71 (1979), 300.

terium. The mutual complementarities between rights and duties — they are indissolubly linked — are recalled several times, above all in the human person who possesses them.[322] This bond also has a social dimension: "in human society to one man's right there corresponds a duty in all other persons: the duty, namely, of acknowledging and respecting the right in question."[323] *The Magisterium underlines the contradiction inherent in affirming rights without acknowledging corresponding responsibilities.* "Those, therefore, who claim their own rights, yet altogether forget or neglect to carry out their respective duties, are people who build with one hand and destroy with the other."[324]

d. Rights of peoples and nations

157. *The field of human rights has expanded to include the rights of peoples and nations*[325]: in fact, "what is true for the individual is also true for peoples."[326] The Magisterium points out that international law "rests upon the principle of equal respect for States, for each people's right to self-determination and for their free cooperation in view of the higher common good of humanity."[327] Peace is founded not only on respect for human rights but also on respect for the rights of peoples, in particular the right to independence.[328]

The rights of nations are nothing but "'human rights' fostered at the specific level of community life."[329] A nation has a "fundamental right to existence," to "its own language and culture, through which a people expresses and promotes . . . its fundamental spiritual 'sovereignty,'" to "shape its life according to its own traditions, excluding, of course, every abuse of basic human rights and in particular the oppression of minorities," to "build its future by providing an appropriate education for the younger generation."[330] The international order requires a *balance between particularity and universality*, which all nations are called to bring about, for their primary duty is to live in a posture of peace, respect and solidarity with other nations.

e. Filling in the gap between the letter and the spirit

158. *The solemn proclamation of human rights is contradicted by a painful reality of violations*, wars and violence of every kind, in the first place, genocides and mass

[322] Cf. John XXIII, Encyclical Letter *Pacem in Terris*: AAS 55 (1963), 259-264; Second Vatican Ecumenical Council, Pastoral Constitution *Gaudium et Spes*, 26: AAS 58 (1966), 1046-1047.
[323] John XXIII, Encyclical Letter *Pacem in Terris*: AAS 55 (1963), 264.
[324] John XXIII, Encyclical Letter *Pacem in Terris*: AAS 55 (1963), 264.
[325] Cf. John Paul II, Encyclical Letter *Sollicitudo Rei Socialis*, 33: AAS 80 (1988), 557-559; John Paul II, Encyclical Letter *Centesimus Annus*, 21: AAS 83 (1991), 818-819.
[326] John Paul II, Letter on the occasion of the fiftieth anniversary of the outbreak of the Second World War, 8: *L'Osservatore Romano*, English edition, 4 September 1989, p. 2.
[327] John Paul II, Letter on the occasion of the fiftieth anniversary of the outbreak of the Second World War, 8: *L'Osservatore Romano*, English edition, 4 September 1989, p. 2.
[328] Cf. John Paul II, Address to the Diplomatic Corps (9 January 1988), 7-8: *L'Osservatore Romano*, English edition, 25 January 1988, p. 7.
[329] John Paul II, Address to the Fiftieth General Assembly of the United Nations (5 October 1995), 8: *L'Osservatore Romano*, English edition, 11 October 1995, p. 9.
[330] John Paul II, Address to the Fiftieth General Assembly of the United Nations (5 October 1995), 8: *L'Osservatore Romano*, English edition, 11 October 1995, p. 9.

deportations, the spreading on a virtual worldwide dimension of ever new forms of slavery such as trafficking in human beings, child soldiers, the exploitation of workers, illegal drug trafficking, prostitution. "Even in countries with democratic forms of government, these rights are not always fully respected."[331]

Unfortunately, there is a gap between the "letter" and the "spirit" of human rights,[332] which can often be attributed to a merely formal recognition of these rights. The Church's social doctrine, in consideration of the privilege accorded by the Gospel to the poor, repeats over and over that "the more fortunate should *renounce* some of their rights so as to place their goods more generously at the service of others" and that an excessive affirmation of equality "can give rise to an individualism in which each one claims his own rights without wishing to be answerable for the common good."[333]

159. *The Church, aware that her essentially religious mission includes the defence and promotion of human rights,*[334] "holds in high esteem the dynamic approach of today which is everywhere fostering these rights."[335] The Church profoundly experiences the need to respect justice[336] and human rights[337] within her own ranks.

This pastoral commitment develops in a twofold direction: in the proclamation of the Christian foundations of human rights and in the denunciation of the violations of these rights.[338] In any event, "*proclamation* is always more important than *denunciation*, and the latter cannot ignore the former, which gives it true solidity and the force of higher motivation."[339] For greater effectiveness, this commitment is open to ecumenical cooperation, to dialogue with other religions, to all appropriate contacts with other organizations, governmental and non-governmental, at the national and international levels. The Church trusts above all in the help of the Lord and his Spirit who, poured forth into human hearts, is the surest guarantee for respecting justice and human rights, and for contributing to peace. "The promotion of justice and peace and the penetration of all spheres of human society with the light and the leaven of the Gospel have always been the object of the Church's efforts in fulfilment of the Lord's command."[340]

---

[331] John Paul II, Encyclical Letter *Centesimus Annus*, 47: AAS 83 (1991), 852.

[332] Cf. John Paul II, Encyclical Letter *Redemptor Hominis*, 17: AAS 71 (1979), 295-300.

[333] Paul VI, Encyclical Letter *Octogesima Adveniens*, 23: AAS 63 (1971), 418.

[334] Cf. John Paul II, Encyclical Letter *Centesimus Annus*, 54: AAS 83 (1991), 859-860.

[335] Second Vatican Ecumenical Council, Pastoral Constitution *Gaudium et Spes*, 41: AAS 58 (1966), 1060.

[336] Cf. John Paul II, Address to Officials and Advocates of the Tribunal of the Roman Rota (17 February 1979), 4: *Insegnamenti di Giovanni Paolo II*, II, 1 (1979), 413-414.

[337] Cf. *Code of Canon Law*, canons 208-223.

[338] Cf. Pontifical Commission "Iustitia et Pax," *The Church and Human Rights*, 70-90, Vatican City 1975, pp. 45-54.

[339] John Paul II, Encyclical Letter *Sollecitudo Rei Socialis*, 41: AAS 80 (1988), 572.

[340] Paul VI, Motu Proprio *Iustitiam et Pacem* (10 December 1976): *L'Osservatore Romano*, 23 December 1976, p. 10.

CHAPTER FOUR

PRINCIPLES OF THE CHURCH'S SOCIAL DOCTRINE

I. MEANING AND UNITY

160. *The permanent principles of the Church's social doctrine*[341] *constitute the very heart of Catholic social teaching.* These are the principles of: *the dignity of the human person*, which has already been dealt with in the preceding chapter, and which is the foundation of all the other principles and content of the Church's social doctrine;[342] *the common good; subsidiarity;* and *solidarity.* These principles, the expression of the whole truth about man known by reason and faith, are born of "the encounter of the Gospel message and of its demands summarized in the supreme commandment of love of God and neighbor in justice with the problems emanating from the life of society."[343] In the course of history and with the light of the Spirit, the Church has wisely reflected within her own tradition of faith and has been able to provide an ever more accurate foundation and shape to these principles, progressively explaining them in the attempt to respond coherently to the demands of the times and to the continuous developments of social life.

161. *These are principles of a general and fundamental character, since they concern the reality of society in its entirety*: from close and immediate relationships to those mediated by politics, economics and law; from relationships among communities and groups to relations between peoples and nations. Because of their *permanence in time* and their *universality of meaning*, the Church presents them as the primary and fundamental perameters of reference for interpreting and evaluating social phenomena, which is the necessary source for working out the criteria for the discernment and orientation of social interactions in every area.

162. *The principles of the Church's social doctrine must be appreciated in their unity, interrelatedness and articulation.* This requirement is rooted in the meaning that the Church herself attributes to her social doctrine, as a unified doctrinal corpus that interprets modern social realities in a systematic manner.[344] Examining each of these principles individually must not lead to using them only in part or in an

---

[341] Cf. Congregation for Catholic Education, *Guidelines for the Study and Teaching of the Church's Social Doctrine in the Formation of Priests*, 29-42, Vatican Polyglot Press, Rome 1988, pp. 35-43.

[342] Cf. John XXIII, Encyclical Letter *Mater et Magistra: AAS* 53 (1961), 453.

[343] Congregation for the Doctrine of the Faith, Instruction *Libertatis Conscientia*, 72: *AAS* 79 (1987), 585.

[344] Cf. John Paul II, Encyclical Letter *Sollicitudo Rei Socialis*, 1 *AAS* 80 (1988), 513-514.

erroneous manner, which would be the case if they were to be invoked in a disjointed and unconnected way with respect to each of the others. A deep theoretical understanding and the actual application of even just one of these social principles clearly shows the reciprocity, complementarities and interconnectedness that is part of their structure. These fundamental principles of the Church's social doctrine, moreover, represent much more than a permanent legacy of reflection, which is also an essential part of the Christian message, since they indicate the paths possible for building a good, authentic and renewed social life.[345]

163. *The principles of the social doctrine, in their entirety, constitute that primary articulation of the truth of society by which every conscience is challenged and invited to interact with every other conscience in truth, in responsibility shared fully with all people and also regarding all people.* In fact, man cannot avoid the *question of freedom and of the meaning of life in society*, since society is a reality that is neither external nor foreign to his being.

These principles have a profoundly moral significance because they refer to the ultimate and organizational foundations of life in society. To understand them completely it is necessary to act in accordance with them, following the path of development that they indicate for a life worthy of man. The ethical requirement inherent in these pre-eminent social principles concerns both the personal behavior of individuals — in that they are the first and indispensable responsible subjects of social life at every level — and at the same time institutions represented by laws, customary norms and civil constructs, because of their capacity to influence and condition the choices of many people over a long period of time. In fact, these principles remind us that the origins of a society existing in history are found in the interconnectedness of the freedoms of all the persons who interact within it, contributing by means of their choices either to build it up or to impoverish it.

II. THE PRINCIPLE OF THE COMMON GOOD

a. Meaning and primary implications

164. *The principle of the common good, to which every aspect of social life must be related if it is to attain its fullest meaning, stems from the dignity, unity and equality of all people.* According to its primary and broadly accepted sense, *the common good* indicates "the sum total of social conditions which allow people, either as groups or as individuals, to reach their fulfilment more fully and more easily."[346]

The common good does not consist in the simple sum of the particular goods of each subject of a social entity. Belonging to everyone and to each person, it is and remains "common," because it is indivisible and because only together is it possible to

---

[345] Cf. Congregation for Catholic Education, *Guidelines for the Study and Teaching of the Church's Social Doctrine in the Formation of Priests*, 47, Vatican Polyglot Press, Rome 1988, p. 47.

[346] Second Vatican Ecumenical Council, *Gaudium et Spes*, 26: AAS 58 (1966), 1046; cf. *Catechism of the Catholic Church*, 1905-1912; John XXIII, Encyclical Letter *Mater et Magistra*: AAS 53 (1961), 417-421; John XXIII, Encyclical Letter *Pacem in Terris*: AAS 55 (1963), 272-273; Paul VI, Apostolic Letter *Octogesima Adveniens*, 46: AAS 63 (1971), 433-435.

attain it, increase it and safeguard its effectiveness, with regard also to the future. Just as the moral actions of an individual are accomplished in doing what is good, so too the actions of a society attain their full stature when they bring about the common good. The common good, in fact, can be understood as the social and community dimension of the moral good.

165. *A society that wishes and intends to remain at the service of the human being at every level is a society that has the common good — the good of all people and of the whole person*[347] *— as its primary goal. The human person cannot find fulfilment in himself, that is, apart from the fact that he exists "with" others and "for" others.* This truth does not simply require that he live with others at various levels of social life, but that he seek unceasingly — in actual practice and not merely at the level of ideas — the good, that is, the meaning and truth, found in existing forms of social life. No expression of social life — from the family to intermediate social groups, associations, enterprises of an economic nature, cities, regions, States, up to the community of peoples and nations — can escape the issue of its own common good, in that this is a constitutive element of its significance and the authentic reason for its very existence.[348]

b. Responsibility of everyone for the common good

166. *The demands of the common good are dependent on the social conditions of each historical period and are strictly connected to respect for and the integral promotion of the person and his fundamental rights.*[349] These demands concern above all the commitment to peace, the organization of the State's powers, a sound juridical system, the protection of the environment, and the provision of essential services to all, some of which are at the same time human rights: food, housing, work, education and access to culture, transportation, basic health care, the freedom of communication and expression, and the protection of religious freedom.[350] Nor must one forget the contribution that every nation is required in duty to make towards a true worldwide cooperation for the common good of the whole of humanity and for future generations also.[351]

167. *The common good therefore involves all members of society, no one is exempt from cooperating, according to each one's possibilities, in attaining it and developing it.*[352] The common good must be served in its fullness, not according to reductionist visions that are subordinated by certain people to their advantages; own rather it is to be based on a logic that leads to the assumption of greater responsibility. The com-

---

[347] Cf. *Catechism of the Catholic Church*, 1912.
[348] Cf. John XXIII, Encyclical Letter *Pacem in Terris*: AAS 55 (1963), 272.
[349] Cf. *Catechism of the Catholic Church*, 1907.
[350] Cf. Second Vatican Ecumenical Council, Pastoral Constitution *Gaudium et Spes*, 26: AAS 58 (1966), 1046-1047.
[351] Cf. John XXIII, Encyclical Letter *Mater et Magistra*: AAS 53 (1961), 421.
[352] Cf. John XXIII, Encyclical Letter *Mater et Magistra*: AAS 53 (1961), 417; Paul VI, Apostolic Letter *Octogesima Adveniens*, 46: AAS 63 (1971), 433-435; *Catechism of the Catholic Church*, 1913.

mon good corresponds to the highest of human instincts,[353] but it is a good that is very difficult to attain because it requires the constant ability and effort to seek the good of others as though it were one's own good.

Everyone also has the right to enjoy the conditions of social life that are brought about by the quest for the common good. The teaching of Pope Pius XI is still relevant: "the distribution of created goods, which, as every discerning person knows, is laboring today under the gravest evils due to the huge disparity between the few exceedingly rich and the unnumbered propertyless, must be effectively called back to and brought into conformity with the norms of the common good, that is, social justice."[354]

c. Tasks of the political community

168. *The responsibility for attaining the common good, besides falling to individual persons, belongs also to the State, since the common good is the reason that the political authority exists.*[355] The State, in fact, must guarantee the coherency, unity and organization of the civil society of which it is an expression,[356] in order that the common good may be attained with the contribution of every citizen. The individual person, the family or intermediate groups are not able to achieve their full development by themselves for living a truly human life. Hence the necessity of political institutions, the purpose of which is to make available to persons the necessary material, cultural, moral and spiritual goods. The goal of life in society is in fact the historically attainable common good.[357]

169. *To ensure the common good, the government of each country has the specific duty to harmonize the different sectoral interests with the requirements of justice.*[358] The proper reconciling of the particular goods of groups and those of individuals is, in fact, one of the most delicate tasks of public authority. Moreover, it must not be forgotten that in the democratic State, where decisions are usually made by the majority of representatives elected by the people, those responsible for government are required to interpret the common good of their country not only according to the guidelines of the majority but also according to the effective good of all the members of the community, including the minority.

---

[353] Saint Thomas Aquinas places "knowledge of the truth about God" and "life in society" at the highest and most specific level of man's "*inclinationes naturales*" (*Summa Theologiae*, I-II, q. 94, a. 2: Ed. Leon. 7, 170: "Secundum igitur ordinem inclinationum naturalium est ordo praeceptorum legis naturae . . . Tertio modo inest homini inclinatio ad bonum secundum naturam rationis, quae est sibi propria; sicut homo habet naturalem inclinationem ad hoc quod veritatem cognoscat de Deo, et ad hoc quod in societate vivat").

[354] Pius XI, Encyclical Letter *Quadragesimo Anno: AAS* 23 (1931), 197.

[355] Cf. *Catechism of the Catholic Church*, 1910.

[356] Cf. Second Vatican Ecumenical Council, Pastoral Constitution *Gaudium et Spes*, 74: *AAS* 58 (1966), 1095-1097; John Paul II, Encyclical Letter *Redemptor Hominis*, 17: *AAS* 71 (1979), 295-300.

[357] Cf. Leo XIII, Encyclical Letter *Rerum Novarum: Acta Leonis XIII*, 11 (1892), 133-135; Pius XII, Radio Message for the fiftieth anniversary of *Rerum Novarum: AAS* 33 (1941), 200.

[358] Cf. *Catechism of the Catholic Church*, 1908.

170. *The common good of society is not an end in itself; it has value only in reference to attaining the ultimate ends of the person and the universal common good of the whole of creation.* God is the ultimate end of his creatures and for no reason may the common good be deprived of its transcendent dimension, which moves beyond the historical dimension while at the same time fulfilling it.[359] This perspective reaches its fullness by virtue of faith in Jesus' Passover, which sheds clear light on the attainment of humanity's true common good. Our history — the personal and collective effort to elevate the human condition — begins and ends in Jesus: thanks to him, by means of him and in light of him every reality, including human society, can be brought to its Supreme Good, to its fulfilment. A purely historical and materialistic vision would end up transforming the common good into a simple *socio-economic well-being*, without any transcendental goal, that is, without its most intimate reason for existing.

III. THE UNIVERSAL DESTINATION OF GOODS

a. Origin and meaning

171. *Among the numerous implications of the common good, immediate significance is taken on by the principle of the universal destination of goods*: "God destined the earth and all it contains for all men and all peoples so that all created things would be shared fairly by all mankind under the guidance of justice tempered by charity."[360] This principle is based on the fact that "the original source of all that is good is the very act of God, who created both the earth and man, and who gave the earth to man so that he might have dominion over it by his work and enjoy its fruits (*Gen* 1:28-29). God gave the earth to the whole human race for the sustenance of all its members, without excluding or favoring anyone. This is *the foundation of the universal destination of the earth's goods*. The earth, by reason of its fruitfulness and its capacity to satisfy human needs, is God's first gift for the sustenance of human life."[361] The human person cannot do without the material goods that correspond to his primary needs and constitute the basic conditions for his existence; these goods are absolutely indispensable if he is to feed himself, grow, communicate, associate with others, and attain the highest purposes to which he is called.[362]

172. *The universal right to use the goods of the earth is based on the principle of the universal destination of goods.* Each person must have access to the level of well-being necessary for his full development. The right to the common use of goods is the "first principle of the whole ethical and social order"[363] and "the characteristic

---

[359] Cf. John Paul II, Encyclical Letter *Centesimus Annus*, 41: AAS 83 (1991), 843-845.
[360] Second Vatican Ecumenical Council, Pastoral Constitution *Gaudium et Spes*, 69: AAS 58 (1966), 1090.
[361] John Paul II, Encyclical Letter *Centesimus Annus*, 31: AAS 83 (1991), 831.
[362] Cf. Pius XII, Radio Message for the fiftieth anniversary of *Rerum Novarum*: AAS 33 (1941), 199-200.
[363] John Paul II, Encyclical Letter *Laborem Exercens*, 19: AAS 73 (1981), 525.

principle of Christian social doctrine."[364] For this reason the Church feels bound in duty to specify the nature and characteristics of this principle. It is first of all a *natural* right, inscribed in human nature and not merely a positive right connected with changing historical circumstances; moreover it is an "inherent" [365] right. It is innate in individual persons, in every person, and has *priority* with regard to any human intervention concerning goods, to any legal system concerning the same, to any economic or social system or method: "All other rights, whatever they are, including property rights and the right of free trade must be subordinated to this norm [the universal destination of goods]; they must not hinder it, but must rather expedite its application. It must be considered a serious and urgent social obligation to refer these rights to their original purpose."[366]

173. *Putting the principal of the universal destination of goods into concrete practice, according to the different cultural and social contexts, means that methods, limits and objects must be precisely defined.* Universal destination and utilization of goods do not mean that everything is at the disposal of each person or of all people, or that the same object may be useful or belong to each person or all people. If it is true that everyone is born with the right to use the goods of the earth, it is likewise true that, in order to ensure that this right is exercised in an equitable and orderly fashion, regulated interventions are necessary, interventions that are the result of national and international agreements, and a juridical order that adjudicates and specifies the exercise of this right.

174. *The principle of the universal destination of goods is an invitation to develop an economic vision inspired by moral values that permit people not to lose sight of the origin or purpose of these goods, so as to bring about a world of fairness and solidarity,* in which the creation of wealth can take on a positive function. Wealth, in effect, presents this possibility in the many different forms in which it can find expression as the result of a process of production that works with the available technological and economic resources, both natural and derived. This result is guided by resourcefulness, planning and labor, and used as a means for promoting the well-being of all men and all peoples and for preventing their exclusion and exploitation.

175. *The universal destination of goods requires a common effort to obtain for every person and for all peoples the conditions necessary for integral development, so that everyone can contribute to making a more humane world,* "in which each individual can give and receive, and in which the progress of some will no longer be an obstacle to the development of others, nor a pretext for their enslavement."[367] This principle corresponds to the call made unceasingly by the Gospel to people and societies of all times, tempted as they always are by the desire to possess, temptations which the Lord Jesus chose to undergo (cf. *Mk* 1:12-13; *Mt* 4:1-11; *Lk* 4:1-13) in order to teach us how to overcome them with his grace.

[364] John Paul II, Encyclical Letter *Sollicitudo Rei Socialis*, 42: AAS 80 (1988), 573.
[365] Pius XII, Radio Message for the fiftieth anniversary of *Rerum Novarum*: AAS 33 (1941), 199.
[366] Paul VI, Encyclical Letter *Populorum Progressio*, 22: AAS 59 (1967), 268.
[367] Congregation for the Doctrine of the Faith, *Libertatis Conscientia*, 90: AAS 79 (1987), 594.

b. The universal destination of goods and private property

176. *By means of work and making use of the gift of intelligence, people are able to exercise dominion over the earth and make it a fitting home*: "In this way, he makes part of the earth his own, precisely the part which he has acquired through work; *this is the origin of individual property*."[368] Private property and other forms of private ownership of goods "assure a person a highly necessary sphere for the exercise of his personal and family autonomy and ought to be considered as an extension of human freedom . . . stimulating exercise of responsibility, it constitutes one of the conditions for civil liberty."[369] Private property is an essential element of an authentically social and democratic economic policy, and it is the guarantee of a correct social order. *The Church's social doctrine requires that ownership of goods be equally accessible to all,*[370] so that all may become, at least in some measure, owners, and it excludes recourse to forms of "common and promiscuous dominion."[371]

177. *Christian tradition has never recognized the right to private property as absolute and untouchable*: "On the contrary, it has always understood this right within the broader context of the right common to all to use the goods of the whole of creation: the right to private property is subordinated to the right to common use, to the fact that goods are meant for everyone."[372] The principle of the universal destination of goods is an affirmation both of God's full and perennial lordship over every reality and of the requirement that the goods of creation remain ever destined to the development of the whole person and of all humanity.[373] This principle is not opposed to the right to private property [374] but indicates the need to regulate it. *Private property, in fact, regardless of the concrete forms of the regulations and juridical norms relative to it, is in its essence only an instrument for respecting the principle of the universal destination of goods; in the final analysis, therefore, it is not an end but a means.*[375]

178. *The Church's social teaching moreover calls for recognition of the social function of any form of private ownership*[376] that clearly refers to its necessary relation to the common good.[377] Man "should regard the external things that he legitimately

---

[368] John Paul II, Encyclical Letter *Centesimus Annus*, 31: AAS 83 (1991), 832.

[369] Second Vatican Ecumenical Council, Pastoral Constitution *Gaudium et Spes*, 71: AAS 58 (1966), 1092-1093; cf. Leo XIII, Encyclical Letter *Rerum Novarum*: Acta Leonis XIII, 11 (1892), 103-104; Pius XII, Radio Message for the fiftieth anniversary of *Rerum Novarum*: AAS 33 (1941), 199; Pius XII, Radio Message of 24 December 1942: AAS 35 (1943), 17; Pius XII, Radio Message of 1 September 1944: AAS 36 (1944), 253; John XXIII, Encyclical Letter *Mater et Magistra*: AAS 53 (1961), 428-429.

[370] Cf. John Paul II, Encyclical Letter *Centesimus Annus*, 6: AAS 83 (1991), 800-801.

[371] Leo XIII, Encyclical Letter *Rerum Novarum*: Acta Leonis XIII, 11 (1892), 102.

[372] John Paul II, Encyclical Letter *Laborem Exercens*, 14: AAS 73 (1981), 613.

[373] Cf. Second Vatican Ecumenical Council, Pastoral Constitution *Gaudium et Spes*, 69: AAS 58 (1966), 1090-1092; *Catechism of the Catholic Church*, 2402-2406.

[374] Cf. Leo XIII, Encyclical Letter *Rerum Novarum*: Acta Leonis XIII, 11 (1892), 102.

[375] Cf. Paul VI, Encyclical Letter *Populorum Progressio*, 22-23: AAS 59 (1967), 268-269.

[376] Cf. John XXIII, Encyclical Letter *Mater et Magistra*: AAS 53 (1961), 430-431; John Paul II, Address to the Third General Conference of Latin American Bishops, Puebla, Mexico (28 January 1979), III/4: AAS 71 (1979), 199-201.

[377] Cf. Pius XI, Encyclical Letter *Quadragesimo Anno*: AAS 23 (1931), 191-192, 193-194, 196-197.

possesses not only as his own but also as common in the sense that they should be able to benefit not only him but also others."[378] *The universal destination of goods entails obligations on how goods are to be used by their legitimate owners.* Individual persons may not use their resources without considering the effects that this use will have, rather they must act in a way that benefits not only themselves and their family but also the common good. From this there arises the duty on the part of owners not to let the goods in their possession go idle and to channel them to productive activity, even entrusting them to others who are desirous and capable of putting them to use in production.

179. *The present historical period has placed at the disposal of society new goods that were completely unknown until recent times. This calls for a fresh reading of the principle of the universal destination of the goods of the earth and makes it necessary to extend this principle so that it includes the latest developments brought about by economic and technological progress.* The ownership of these new goods — the results of knowledge, technology and know-how — becomes ever more decisive, because "the wealth of the industrialized nations is based much more on this kind of ownership than on natural resources."[379]

New technological and scientific knowledge must be placed at the service of mankind's primary needs, gradually increasing humanity's common patrimony. Putting the principle of the universal destination of goods into full effect therefore requires action at the international level and planned programmes on the part of all countries. "It is necessary to break down the barriers and monopolies which leave so many countries on the margins of development, and to provide all individuals and nations with the basic conditions which will enable them to share in development."[380]

180. *If forms of property unknown in the past take on significant importance in the process of economic and social development, nonetheless, traditional forms of property must not be forgotten. Individual property is not the only legitimate form of ownership. The ancient form of community property also has a particular importance;* though it can be found in economically advanced countries, it is particularly characteristic of the social structure of many indigenous peoples. This is a form of property that has such a profound impact on the economic, cultural and political life of those peoples that it constitutes a fundamental element of their survival and well-being. The defence and appreciation of community property must not exclude, however, an awareness of the fact that this type of property also is destined to evolve. If actions were taken only to preserve its present form, there would be the risk of tying it to the past and in this way compromising it.[381]

An *equitable distribution of land remains ever critical, especially in developing countries and in countries that have recently changed from systems based on collectivi-*

---

[378] Second Vatican Ecumenical Council, Pastoral Constitution *Gaudium et Spes*, 69: AAS 58 (1966), 1090.
[379] John Paul II, Encyclical Letter *Centesimus Annus*, 32: AAS 83 (1991), 832.
[380] John Paul II, Encyclical Letter *Centesimus Annus*, 35: AAS 83 (1991), 837.
[381] Cf. Second Vatican Ecumenical Council, Pastoral Constitution *Gaudium et Spes*, 69: AAS 58 (1966), 1090-1092.

ties or colonization.[382] In rural areas, the possibility of acquiring land through opportunities offered by labor and credit markets is a necessary condition for access to other goods and services. Besides constituting an effective means for safeguarding the environment, this possibility represents a system of social security that can be put in place also in those countries with a weak administrative structure.

181. *To the subjects, whether individuals or communities, that exercise ownership of various types of property accrue a series of objective advantages:* better living conditions, security for the future, and a greater number of options from which to choose. *On the other hand, property may also bring a series of deceptive promises that are a source of temptation.* Those people and societies that go so far as to absolutize the role of property end up experiencing the bitterest type of slavery. In fact, there is no category of possession that can be considered indifferent with regard to the influence that it may have both on individuals and on institutions. Owners who heedlessly idolize their goods (cf. Mt 6:24, 19:21-26; Lk 16:13) become owned and enslaved by them.[383] Only by recognizing that these goods are dependent on God the Creator and then directing their use to the common good, is it possible to give material goods their proper function as useful tools for the growth of individuals and peoples.

c. **The universal destination of goods and the preferential option for the poor**

182. *The principle of the universal destination of goods requires that the poor, the marginalized and in all cases those whose living conditions interfere with their proper growth should be the focus of particular concern. To this end, the preferential option for the poor should be reaffirmed in all its force.*[384] "This is an option, or a *special form* of primacy in the exercise of Christian charity, to which the whole tradition of the Church bears witness. It affects the life of each Christian inasmuch as he or she seeks to imitate the life of Christ, but it applies equally to our *social responsibilities* and hence to our manner of living, and to the logical decisions to be made concerning the ownership and use of goods. Today, furthermore, given the worldwide dimension which the social question has assumed, this love of preference for the poor, and the decisions which it inspires in us, cannot but embrace the immense multitudes of the hungry, the needy, the homeless, those without health care and, above all, those without hope of a better future."[385]

---

[382] Cf. Pontifical Council for Justice and Peace, *Towards a Better Distribution of Land. The Challenge of Agrarian Reform* (23 November 1997), 27-31: Libreria Editrice Vaticana, Vatican City 1997, pp. 28-31.

[383] Cf. John Paul II, Encyclical Letter *Sollicitudo Rei Socialis*, 27-34, 37: AAS 80 (1988), 547-560, 563-564; John Paul II, Encyclical Letter *Centesimus Annus*, 41: AAS 83 (1991), 843-845.

[384] Cf. John Paul II, Address to the Third General Conference of Latin American Bishops, Puebla, Mexico (28 January 1979), I/8: AAS 71 (1979), 194-195.

[385] John Paul II, Encyclical Letter *Sollicitudo Rei Socialis*, 42: AAS 80 (1988), 572-573; cf. John Paul II, Encyclical Letter *Evangelium Vitae*, 32: AAS 87 (1995), 436-437; John Paul II, Apostolic Letter *Tertio Millennio Adveniente*, 51: AAS 87 (1995), 36; John Paul II, Apostolic Letter *Novo Millennio Ineunte*, 49-50: AAS 93 (2001), 302-303.

183. *Human misery is a clear sign of man's natural condition of frailty and of his need for salvation.*[386] Christ the Savior showed compassion in this regard, identifying himself with the "least" among men (cf. Mt 25:40,45). "It is by what they have done for the poor that Jesus Christ will recognize his chosen ones. When 'the poor have the good news preached to them' (Mt 11:5), it is a sign of Christ's presence."[387]

Jesus says: "You always have the poor with you, but you will not always have me" (Mt 26:11; cf. Mk 14:7; Jn 12:8). He makes this statement not to contrast the attention due to him with service of the poor. Christian realism, while appreciating on the one hand the praiseworthy efforts being made to defeat poverty, is cautious on the other hand regarding ideological positions and Messianistic beliefs that sustain the illusion that it is possible to eliminate the problem of poverty completely from this world. This will happen only upon Christ's return, when he will be with us once more, for ever. In the meantime, *the poor remain entrusted to us and it is this responsibility upon which we shall be judged at the end of time* (cf. Mt 25:31-46): "Our Lord warns us that we shall be separated from him if we fail to meet the serious needs of the poor and the little ones who are his brethren."[388]

184. *The Church's love for the poor is inspired by the Gospel of the Beatitudes, by the poverty of Jesus and by his attention to the poor. This love concerns material poverty and also the numerous forms of cultural and religious poverty.*[389] The Church, "since her origin and in spite of the failing of many of her members, has not ceased to work for their relief, defence and liberation through numerous works of charity which remain indispensable always and everywhere."[390] Prompted by the Gospel injunction, "You have received without paying, give without pay" (Mt 10:8), the Church teaches that one should assist one's fellow man in his various needs and fills the human community with countless *works of corporal and spiritual mercy*. "Among all these, giving alms to the poor is one of the chief witnesses to fraternal charity: it is also a work of justice pleasing to God,"[391] even if the practice of charity is not limited to alms-giving but implies addressing the social and political dimensions of the problem of poverty. In her teaching the Church constantly returns to this relationship between charity and justice: "When we attend to the needs of those in want, we give them what is theirs, not ours. More than performing works of mercy, we are paying a debt of justice."[392] The Council Fathers strongly recommended that this duty be fulfilled correctly, remembering that "what is already due in justice is not to be offered as a gift of charity."[393] Love for the poor is certainly "incompatible with immoderate love of riches or their selfish use"[394] (cf. Jas 5:1-6).

[386] Cf. *Catechism of the Catholic Church*, 2448.
[387] *Catechism of the Catholic Church*, 2443.
[388] *Catechism of the Catholic Church*, 1033.
[389] Cf. *Catechism of the Catholic Church*, 2444.
[390] *Catechism of the Catholic Church*, 2448.
[391] *Catechism of the Catholic Church*, 2447.
[392] Saint Gregory the Great, *Regula Pastoralis*, 3, 21: PL 77, 87: "Nam cum qualibet necessaria indigentibus ministramus, sua illis reddimus, non nostra largimur; iustitiae potius debitum soluimus, quam misericordiae opera implemus."
[393] Second Vatican Ecumenical Council, Decree *Apostolicam Actuositatem*, 8: AAS 58 (1966), 845; cf. *Catechism of the Catholic Church*, 2446.
[394] *Catechism of the Catholic Church*, 2445.

IV. THE PRINCIPLE OF SUBSIDIARITY

a. **Origin and meaning**

185. *Subsidiarity is among the most constant and characteristic directives of the Church's social doctrine* and has been present since the first great social encyclical.[395] It is impossible to promote the dignity of the person without showing concern for the family, groups, associations, local territorial realities; in short, for that aggregate of economic, social, cultural, sports-oriented, recreational, professional and political expressions to which people spontaneously give life and which make it possible for them to achieve effective social growth.[396] This is the realm of *civil society*, understood as the sum of the relationships between individuals and intermediate social groupings, which are the first relationships to arise and which come about thanks to "the creative subjectivity of the citizen."[397] This network of relationships strengthens the social fabric and constitutes the basis of a true community of persons, making possible the recognition of higher forms of social activity.[398]

186. *The necessity of defending and promoting the original expressions of social life is emphasized by the Church in the Encyclical* Quadragesimo Anno, *in which the principle of subsidiarity is indicated as a most important principle of "social philosophy."* "Just as it is gravely wrong to take from individuals what they can accomplish by their own initiative and industry and give it to the community, so also it is an injustice and at the same time a grave evil and disturbance of right order to assign to a greater and higher association what lesser and subordinate organizations can do. For every social activity ought of its very nature to furnish help to the members of the body social, and never destroy and absorb them."[399]

On the basis of this principle, all societies of a superior order must adopt attitudes of help ("subsidium") — therefore of support, promotion, development — with respect to lower-order societies. In this way, intermediate social entities can properly perform the functions that fall to them without being required to hand them over unjustly to other social entities of a higher level, by which they would end up being absorbed and substituted, in the end seeing themselves denied their dignity and essential place.

Subsidiarity, understood *in the positive sense* as economic, institutional or juridical assistance offered to lesser social entities, entails a corresponding series

---

[395] Cf. Leo XIII, Encyclical Letter *Rerum Novarum*: *Acta Leonis XIII*, 11 (1892), 101-102, 123.

[396] Cf. *Catechism of the Catholic Church*, 1882.

[397] John Paul II, Encyclical Letter *Sollicitudo Rei Socialis*, 15: AAS 80 (1988), 529; cf. Pius XI, Encyclical Letter *Quadragesimo Anno*: AAS 23 (1931), 203; John XXIII, Encyclical Letter *Mater et Magistra*: AAS 53 (1961), 439; Second Vatican Ecumenical Council, Pastoral Constitution *Gaudium et Spes*, 65: AAS 58 (1966), 1086-1087; Congregation for the Doctrine of the Faith, Instruction *Libertatis Conscientia*, 73, 85-86: AAS 79 (1987), 586, 592-593; John Paul II, Encyclical Letter *Centesimus Annus*, 48: AAS 83 (1991), 852-854; *Catechism of the Catholic Church*, 1883-1885.

[398] Cf. John Paul II, Encyclical Letter *Centesimus Annus*, 49: AAS 83 (1991), 854-856; John Paul II, Encyclical Letter *Sollicitudo Rei Socialis*, 15: AAS 80 (1988), 528-530.

[399] Pius XI, Encyclical Letter *Quadragesimo Anno*: AAS 23 (1931), 203; cf. John Paul II, Encyclical Letter *Centesimus Annus*, 48: AAS 83 (1991), 852-854; *Catechism of the Catholic Church*, 1883.

of *negative* implications that require the State to refrain from anything that would de facto restrict the existential space of the smaller essential cells of society. Their initiative, freedom and responsibility must not be supplanted.

b. Concrete indications

187. *The principle of subsidiarity protects people from abuses by higher-level social authority and calls on these same authorities to help individuals and intermediate groups to fulfil their duties. This principle is imperative because every person, family and inter-mediate group has something original to offer to the community.* Experience shows that the denial of subsidiarity, or its limitation in the name of an alleged democratization or equality of all members of society, limits and sometimes even destroys the spirit of freedom and initiative.

The principle of subsidiarity is opposed to certain forms of centralization, bureaucratization, and welfare assistance and to the unjustified and excessive presence of the State in public mechanisms. "By intervening directly and depriving society of its responsibility, the Social Assistance State leads to a loss of human energies and an inordinate increase of public agencies, which are dominated more by bureaucratic ways of thinking than by concern for serving their clients, and which are accompanied by an enormous increase in spending."[400] An absent or insufficient recognition of private initiative — in economic matters also — and the failure to recognize its public function, contribute to the undermining of the principle of subsidiarity, as monopolies do as well.

In order for the principle of subsidiarity to be put into practice there is a *corresponding need* for: respect and effective promotion of the human person and the family; ever greater appreciation of associations and intermediate organizations in their fundamental choices and in those that cannot be delegated to or exercised by others; the encouragement of private initiative so that every social entity remains at the service of the common good, each with its own distinctive characteristics; the presence of pluralism in society and due representation of its vital components; safeguarding human rights and the rights of minorities; bringing about bureaucratic and administrative decentralization; striking a balance between the public and private spheres, with the resulting recognition of the *social* function of the private sphere; appropriate methods for making citizens more responsible in actively "being a part" of the political and social reality of their country.

188. *Various circumstances may make it advisable that the State step in to supply certain functions.*[401] One may think, for example, of situations in which it is necessary for the State itself to stimulate the economy because it is impossible for civil society to support initiatives on its own. One may also envision the reality of serious social imbalance or injustice where only the intervention of the public authority can create conditions of greater equality, justice and peace. In light of the prin-

---

[400] John Paul II, Encyclical Letter *Centesimus Annus*, 48: AAS 83 (1991), 854.
[401] Cf. John Paul II, Encyclical Letter *Centesimus Annus*, 48: AAS 83 (1991), 852-854.

ciple of subsidiarity, however, this institutional substitution must not continue any longer than is absolutely necessary, since justification for such intervention is found only in the *exceptional nature* of the situation. In any case, the common good correctly understood, the demands of which will never in any way be contrary to the defence and promotion of the primacy of the person and the way this is expressed in society, must remain the criteria for making decisions concerning the application of the principle of subsidiarity.

V. PARTICIPATION

a. Meaning and value

189. *The characteristic implication of subsidiarity is participation,*[402] *which is expressed essentially in a series of activities by means of which the citizen, either as an individual or in association with others, whether directly or through representation, contributes to the cultural, economic, political and social life of the civil community to which he belongs.*[403] *Participation is a duty to be fulfilled consciously by all, with responsibility and with a view to the common good.*[404]

This cannot be confined or restricted to only a certain area of social life, given its importance for growth — above all human growth — in areas such as the world of work and economic activity, especially in their internal dynamics; [405] in the sectors of information and culture; and, more than anything else, in the fields of social and political life even at the highest levels. The cooperation of all peoples and the building of an international community in a framework of solidarity depends on this latter area.[406] In this perspective it becomes absolutely necessary to encourage participation above all of the most disadvantaged, as well as the occasional rotation of political leaders in order to forestall the establishment of hidden privileges. Moreover, strong moral pressure is needed, so that the administration of public life will be the result of the shared responsibility of each individual with regard to the common good.

b. Participation and democracy

190. *Participation in community life is not only one of the greatest aspirations of the citizen, called to exercise freely and responsibly his civic role with and for others,*[407] *but is also one of the pillars of all democratic orders and one of the major guarantees of the*

---

[402] Cf. Paul VI, Apostolic Letter *Octogesima Adveniens*, 22, 46: AAS 63 (1971), 417, 433-435; Congregation for Catholic Education, *Guidelines for the Study and Teaching of the Church's Social Doctrine in the Formation of Priests*, 40, Vatican Polyglot Press, Rome 1988, pp. 41-42.

[403] Cf. Second Vatican Ecumenical Council, Pastoral Constitution *Gaudium et Spes*, 75: AAS 58 (1966), 1097-1099.

[404] Cf. *Catechism of the Catholic Church*, 1913-1917.

[405] Cf. John XXIII, Encyclical Letter *Mater et Magistra*: AAS 53 (1961), 423-425; John Paul II, Encyclical Letter *Laborem Exercens*, 14: AAS 73 (1981), 612-616; John Paul II, Encyclical Letter *Centesimus Annus*, 35: AAS 83 (1991), 836-838.

[406] Cf. John Paul II, Encyclical Letter *Sollicitudo Rei Socialis*, 44-45: AAS 80 (1988), 575-578.

[407] Cf. John XXIII, Encyclical Letter *Pacem in Terris*: AAS 55 (1963), 278.

permanence of the democratic system. Democratic government, in fact, is defined first of all by the assignment of powers and functions on the part of the people, exercised in their name, in their regard and on their behalf. It is therefore clearly evident that *every democracy must be participative.*[408] This means that the different subjects of civil community at every level must be informed, listened to and involved in the exercise of the carried-out functions.

191. *Participation can be achieved in all the different relationships between the citizen and institutions: to this end, particular attention must be given to the historical and social contexts in which such participation can truly be brought about.* The overcoming of cultural, juridical and social obstacles that often constitutes real barriers to the *shared participation* of citizens in the destiny of their communities' calls for work in the areas of information and education.[409] In this regard, all those attitudes that encourage in citizens an inadequate or incorrect practice of participation or that cause widespread disaffection with everything connected with the sphere of social and political life are a source of concern and deserve careful consideration. For example, one thinks of attempts by certain citizens to "make deals" with institutions in order to obtain more advantageous conditions for themselves, as though these institutions were at the service of their selfish needs; or of the practice of citizens to limit their participation to the electoral process, in many cases reaching the point where they even abstain from voting.[410]

In the area of participation, a further *source of concern is found in those countries ruled by totalitarian or dictatorial regimes*, where the fundamental right to participate in public life is denied at its origin, since it is considered a threat to the State itself.[411] In some countries where this right is only formally proclaimed while in reality it cannot be concretely exercised while, in still other countries the burgeoning bureaucracy *de facto* denies citizens the possibility of taking active part in social and political life.[412]

VI. THE PRINCIPLE OF SOLIDARITY

a. Meaning and value

192. *Solidarity highlights in a particular way the intrinsic social nature of the human person, the equality of all in dignity and rights and the common path of individuals and peoples towards an ever more committed unity.* Never before has there been such a widespread awareness of the *bond of interdependence between individuals and peoples,*

---

[408] Cf. John Paul II, Encyclical Letter *Centesimus Annus*, 46: AAS 83 (1991), 850-851.

[409] Cf. *Catechism of the Catholic Church*, 1917.

[410] Cf. Second Vatican Ecumenical Council, Pastoral Constitution *Gaudium et Spes*, 30-31: AAS 58 (1966), 1049-1050; John Paul II, Encyclical Letter *Centesimus Annus*, 47: AAS 83 (1991), 851-852.

[411] Cf. John Paul II, Encyclical Letter *Centesimus Annus*, 44-45: AAS 83 (1991), 848-849.

[412] Cf. John Paul II, Encyclical Letter *Sollicitudo Rei Socialis*, 15: AAS 80 (1988), 528-530; Pius XII, Christmas Radio Message of 24 December 1952: AAS 45 (1953), 37; Paul VI, Apostolic Letter *Octogesima Adveniens*, 47: AAS 63 (1971), 435-437.

which is found at every level.[413] The very rapid expansion in ways and means of communication "in real time," such as those offered by information technology, the extraordinary advances in computer technology, the increased volume of commerce and information exchange all bear witness to the fact that, for the first time since the beginning of human history, it is now possible — at least technically — to establish relationships between people who are separated by great distances and are unknown to each other.

In the presence of the phenomenon of interdependence and its constant expansion, however, there persist in every part of the world stark inequalities between developed and developing countries, inequalities stoked also by various forms of exploitation, oppression and corruption that have a negative influence on the internal and international life of many States. The acceleration of interdependence between persons and peoples needs to be accompanied by equally intense efforts on the ethical-social plane, in order to avoid the dangerous consequences of perpetrating injustice on a global scale. This would have very negative repercussions even in the very countries that are presently more advantaged.[414]

b. Solidarity as a social principle and a moral virtue

193. The new relationships of interdependence between individuals and peoples, which are de facto forms of solidarity, have to be transformed into relationships tending towards genuine ethical-social solidarity. This is a moral requirement inherent within all human relationships. Solidarity is seen therefore under two complementary aspects: that of a social principle[415] and that of a moral virtue.[416]

Solidarity must be seen above all in its value as a moral virtue that determines the order of institutions. On the basis of this principle the "structures of sin"[417] that dominate relationships between individuals and peoples must be overcome. They must be purified and transformed into structures of solidarity through the creation or appropriate modification of laws, market regulations, and juridical systems.

Solidarity is also an authentic moral virtue, not a "feeling of vague compassion or shallow distress at the misfortunes of so many people, both near and far. On the contrary, it is a firm and persevering determination to commit oneself to the common good. That is to say to the good of all and of each individual, because we are all really responsible for all."[418] Solidarity rises to the rank of fundamental social virtue since it places itself in the sphere of justice. It is a virtue directed par excellence to the common good, and is found in "a commitment to the good of one's neighbor

---

[413] There can be associated to the concept of interdependence the classical theme of socialization, repeatedly examined by the Church's social doctrine; cf. John XXIII, Encyclical Letter Mater et Magistra: AAS 53 (1961), 415-417; Second Vatican Ecumenical Council, Pastoral Constitution Gaudium et Spes, 42: AAS 58 (1966), 1060-1061; John Paul II, Encyclical Letter Laborem Exercens, 14-15: AAS 73 (1981), 612-618.

[414] Cf. John Paul II, Encyclical Letter Sollicitudo Rei Socialis, 11-22: AAS 80 (1988), 525-540.

[415] Cf. Catechism of the Catholic Church, 1939-1941.

[416] Cf. Catechism of the Catholic Church, 1942.

[417] John Paul II, Encyclical Letter Sollicitudo Rei Socialis, 36, 37: AAS 80 (1988), 561-564; cf. John Paul II, Apostolic Exhortation Reconciliatio et Paenitentia, 16: AAS 77 (1985), 213-217.

[418] John Paul II, Encyclical Letter Sollicitudo Rei Socialis, 38: AAS 80 (1988), 565-566.

with the readiness, in the Gospel sense, to 'lose oneself' for the sake of the other instead of exploiting him, and to 'serve him' instead of oppressing him for one's own advantage (cf. *Mt* 10:40-42, 20:25; *Mk* 10:42-45; *Lk* 22:25-27)."[419]

c. Solidarity and the common growth of mankind

194. *The message of the Church's social doctrine regarding solidarity clearly shows that there exists an intimate bond between solidarity and the common good, between solidarity and the universal destination of goods, between solidarity and equality among men and peoples, between solidarity and peace in the world.*[420] The term "solidarity," widely used by the Magisterium,[421] expresses in summary fashion the need to recognize in the composite ties that unite men and social groups among themselves, the space given to human freedom for common growth in which all share and in which they participate. The commitment to this goal is translated into the positive contribution of seeing that nothing is lacking in the common cause and also of seeking points of possible agreement where attitudes of separation and fragmentation prevail. It translates into the willingness to give oneself for the good of one's neighbor, beyond any individual or particular interest.[422]

195. *The principle of solidarity requires that men and women of our day cultivate a greater awareness that they are debtors of the society of which they have become part.* They are debtors because of those conditions that make human existence livable, and because of the indivisible and indispensable legacy constituted by culture, sci-

[419] John Paul II, Encyclical Letter *Sollicitudo Rei Socialis*, 38: AAS 80 (1988), 566; cf. John Paul II, Encyclical Letter *Laborem Exercens*, 8: AAS 73 (1981), 594-598; John Paul II, Encyclical Letter *Centesimus Annus*, 57: AAS 83 (1991), 862-863.

[420] Cf. John Paul II, Encyclical Letter *Sollicitudo Rei Socialis*, 17, 39, 45: AAS 80 (1988), 532-533, 566-568, 577-578. International solidarity too is required by the moral order; peace in the world depends in large part on this: cf. Second Vatican Ecumenical Council, Pastoral Constitution *Gaudium et Spes*, 83-86: AAS 58 (1966), 1107-1110; Paul VI, Encyclical Letter *Populorum Progressio*, 48: AAS 59 (1967), 281; Pontifical Commission "Iustitia et Pax," *At the Service of the Human Community: an Ethical Approach to the International Debt Question* (27 December 1986), I, 1, Vatican Polyglot Press, Vatican City 1986, p. 11; *Catechism of the Catholic Church*, 1941, 2438.

[421] Solidarity, though not yet with that explicit name, is one of the basic principles of *Rerum Novarum* (cf. John XXIII, Encyclical Letter *Mater et Magistra*: AAS 53 [1961], 407). "What we nowadays call the principle of solidarity . . . is frequently stated by Pope Leo XIII, who uses the term 'friendship,' a concept already found in Greek philosophy. Pope Pius XI refers to it with the equally meaningful term 'social charity'. Pope Paul VI, expanding the concept to cover the many modern aspects of the social question, speaks of a 'civilization of love'" (John Paul II, Encyclical Letter *Centesimus Annus*, 10: AAS 83 [1991], 805). Solidarity is one of the basic principles of the entire social teaching of the Church (cf. Congregation for the Doctrine of the Faith, Instruction *Libertatis Conscientia*, 73: AAS 79 [1987], 586). Starting with Pius XII (cf. Encyclical Letter *Summi Pontificatus*: AAS 31 [1939], 426-427), the term *solidarity* is used ever more frequently and with ever broader meaning: from that of "law" in the same encyclical to that of "principle" (cf. John XXIII, Encyclical Letter *Mater et Magistra*: AAS 53 [1961], 407), that of "duty" (cf. Paul VI, Encyclical Letter *Populorum Progressio*, 17, 48: AAS 59 [1967], 265-266, 281) and that of "value" (cf. John Paul II, Encyclical Letter *Sollicitudo Rei Socialis*, 38: AAS 80 [1988], 564-566), and finally that of "virtue" (cf. John Paul II, Encyclical Letter *Sollicitudo Rei Socialis*, 38, 40: AAS 80 [1988], 564-566, 568-569).

[422] Cf. Congregation for Catholic Education, *Guidelines for the Study and Teaching of the Church's Social Doctrine in the Formation of Priests*, 38, Vatican Polyglot Press, Rome 1988, pp. 40-41.

entific and technical knowledge, material and immaterial goods and by all that the human condition has produced. A similar debt must be recognized in the various forms of social interaction, so that humanity's journey will not be interrupted but remain open to present and future generations, all of them called together to share the same gift in solidarity.

d. Solidarity in the life and message of Jesus Christ

196. *The unsurpassed apex of the perspective indicated here is the life of Jesus of Nazareth, the New Man, who is one with humanity even to the point of "death on a cross" (Phil 2:8).* In him it is always possible to recognize the living sign of that measureless and transcendent love of *God-with-us*, who takes on the infirmities of his people, walks with them, saves them and makes them one.[423] In him and thanks to him, life in society too, despite all its contradictions and ambiguities, can be rediscovered as a place of life and hope, in that it is a sign of grace that is continuously offered to all and because it is an invitation to ever higher and more involved forms of sharing.

Jesus of Nazareth makes the connection between solidarity and charity shine brightly before all, illuminating the entire meaning of this connection:[424] *"In the light of faith, solidarity seeks to go beyond itself, to take on the specifically Christian dimensions of total gratuity, forgiveness and reconciliation. One's neighbor is then not only a human being with his or her own rights and a fundamental equality with everyone else, but becomes the living image of God the Father, redeemed by the blood of Jesus Christ and placed under the permanent action of the Holy Spirit. One's neighbor must therefore be loved, even if an enemy, with the same love with which the Lord loves him or her; and for that person's sake one must be ready for sacrifice, even the ultimate one: to lay down one's life for the brethren (cf. 1 Jn 3:16)."*[425]

VII. THE FUNDAMENTAL VALUES OF SOCIAL LIFE

a. The relationship between principles and values

197. *Besides the principles that must guide the building of a society worthy of man, the Church's social doctrine also indicates fundamental values.* The relationship between principles and values is undoubtedly one of reciprocity, in that social values are an expression of appreciation to be attributed to those specific aspects of moral good that these principles foster, serving as points of reference for the proper structuring and ordered leading of life in society. These values require, therefore, both the

---

[423] Cf. Second Vatican Ecumenical Council, Pastoral Constitution *Gaudium et Spes*, 32: AAS 58 (1966), 1051.

[424] Cf. John Paul II, Encyclical Letter *Sollicitudo Rei Socialis*, 40: AAS 80 (1988), 568: "*Solidarity* is undoubtedly a *Christian virtue*. In what has been said so far it has been possible to identify many points of contact between solidarity and *charity*, which is the distinguishing mark of Christ's disciples (cf. *Jn* 13:35)."

[425] John Paul II, Encyclical Letter *Sollicitudo Rei Socialis*, 40: AAS 80 (1988), 569.

practice of the fundamental principles of social life and the personal exercise of virtue, hence of those moral attitudes that correspond to these very values.[426]

All social values are inherent in the dignity of the human person, whose authentic development they foster. Essentially, these values are: truth, freedom, justice, love.[427] Putting them into practice is the sure and necessary way of obtaining personal perfection and a more human social existence. They constitute the indispensable point of reference for public authorities, called to carry out "substantial reforms of economic, political, cultural and technological structures and the necessary changes in institutions."[428] Respect for the legitimate autonomy of earthly realities prompts the Church not to claim specific competence of a technical or temporal order,[429] but it does not prevent her from intervening to show how, in the different choices made by men and women, these values are either affirmed or denied.[430]

b. **Truth**

198. *Men and women have the specific duty to move always towards the truth, to respect it and bear responsible witness to it.*[431] *Living in the truth* has special significance in social relationships. In fact, when the coexistence of human beings within a community is founded on truth, it is ordered and fruitful, and it corresponds to their dignity as persons.[432] The more people and social groups strive to resolve social problems according to the truth, the more they distance themselves from abuses and act in accordance with the objective demands of morality.

Modern times call for an intensive educational effort[433] *and a corresponding commitment on the part of all so that the quest for truth* cannot be ascribed to the sum of different opinions, nor to one or another of these opinions — will be encouraged in every sector and will prevail over every attempt to relativize its demands or to offend it.[434] This is an issue that involves the world of public communications and that of the economy in a particular way. In these areas, the unscrupulous use of

---

[426] Cf. *Catechism of the Catholic Church*, 1886.

[427] Cf. Second Vatican Ecumenical Council, Pastoral Constitution *Gaudium et Spes*, 26: AAS 58 (1966), 1046-1047; John XXIII, Encyclical Letter *Pacem in Terris*: AAS 55 (1963), 265-266.

[428] Congregation for Catholic Education, *Guidelines for the Study and Teaching of the Church's Social Doctrine in the Formation of Priests*, 43, Vatican Polyglot Press, Rome 1988, p. 44.

[429] Cf. Second Vatican Ecumenical Council, Pastoral Constitution *Gaudium et Spes*, 36: AAS 58 (1966), 1053-1054.

[430] Cf. Second Vatican Ecumenical Council, Pastoral Constitution *Gaudium et Spes*, 1: AAS 58 (1966), 1025-1026; Paul VI, Encyclical Letter *Populorum Progressio*, 13: AAS 59 (1967), 263-264.

[431] Cf. *Catechism of the Catholic Church*, 2467.

[432] Cf. John XXIII, Encyclical Letter *Pacem in Terris*: AAS 55 (1963), 265-266, 281.

[433] Cf. Second Vatican Ecumenical Council, Pastoral Constitution *Gaudium et Spes*, 61: AAS 58 (1966), 1081-1082; Paul VI, Encyclical Letter *Populorum Progressio*, 35, 40: AAS 59 (1967), 274-275, 277; John Paul II, Encyclical Letter *Sollicitudo Rei Socialis*, 44: AAS 80 (1988), 575-577. For social reform, "the primary task, which will affect the success of all the others, belongs to the order of education": Congregation for the Doctrine of the Faith, Instruction *Libertatis Conscientia*, 99: AAS 79 (1987), 599.

[434] Cf. Second Vatican Ecumenical Council, Pastoral Constitution *Gaudium et Spes*, 16: AAS 58 (1966), 1037; *Catechism of the Catholic Church*, 2464-2487.

money raises ever more pressing questions, which necessarily call for greater transparency and honesty in personal and social activity.

c. **Freedom**

199. *Freedom is the highest sign in man of his being made in the divine image and, consequently, is a sign of the sublime dignity of every human person.*[435] "Freedom is exercised in relationships between human beings. Every human person, created in the image of God, has the natural right to be recognized as a free and responsible being. All owe to each other this duty of respect. The *right to the exercise of freedom*, especially in moral and religious matters, is an inalienable requirement of the dignity of the human person."[436] The meaning of freedom must not be restricted, considering it from a purely individualistic perspective and reducing it to the *arbitrary and uncontrolled exercise* of one's own personal autonomy: "Far from being achieved in total self-sufficiency and the absence of relationships, freedom only truly exists where reciprocal bonds, governed by truth and justice, link people to one another."[437] The understanding of freedom becomes deeper and broader when it is defended, even at the social level, in all of its various dimensions.

200. *The value of freedom, as an expression of the singularity of each human person, is respected when every member of society is permitted to fulfil his personal vocation*; to seek the truth and profess his religious, cultural and political ideas; to express his opinions; to choose his state of life and, as far as possible, his line of work; to pursue initiatives of an economic, social or political nature. This must take place within a "strong juridical framework,"[438] within the limits imposed by the common good and public order, and, in every case, in a manner characterized by responsibility.

On the other hand, *freedom must also be expressed as the capacity to refuse what is morally negative, in whatever guise it may be presented*,[439] as the capacity to distance oneself effectively from everything that could hinder personal, family or social growth. The fullness of freedom consists in the capacity to be in possession of oneself in view of the genuine good, within the context of the universal common good.[440]

d. **Justice**

201. *Justice is a value that accompanies the exercise of the corresponding cardinal moral virtue.*[441] According to its most classic formulation, it "consists in the constant

---

[435] Cf. Second Vatican Ecumenical Council, Pastoral Constitution *Gaudium et Spes*, 17: AAS 58 (1966), 1037-1038; *Catechism of the Catholic Church*, 1705, 1730; Congregation for the Doctrine of the Faith, Instruction *Libertatis Conscientia*, 28: AAS 79 (1987), 565.

[436] *Catechism of the Catholic Church*, 1738.

[437] Cf. Congregation for the Doctrine of the Faith, Instruction *Libertatis Conscientia*, 26: AAS 79 (1987), 564-565.

[438] John Paul II, Encyclical Letter *Centesimus Annus*, 42: AAS 83 (1991), 846. This statement is made in the context of economic initiative, but it appears correct to apply it also to other areas of personal activity.

[439] Cf. John Paul II, Encyclical Letter *Centesimus Annus*, 17: AAS 83 (1991), 814-815.

[440] Cf. John XXIII, Encyclical Letter *Pacem in Terris*: AAS 55 (1963), 289-290.

[441] Cf. Saint Thomas, *Summa Theologiae*, I-II, q. 6: Ed. Leon. 6, 55-63.

and firm will to give their due to God and neighbor."[442] From a subjective point of view, justice is translated into behavior that is *based on the will to recognize the other as a person*, while, from an objective point of view, it constitutes *the decisive criteria of morality in the intersubjective and social sphere.*[443]

The Church's social Magisterium constantly calls for the most classical forms of justice to be respected: *commutative, distributive* and *legal justice.*[444] Ever greater importance has been given to *social justice,*[445] which represents a real development in *general justice*, the justice that regulates social relationships according to the criterion of observance of the *law. Social justice*, a requirement related to the *social question* which today is worldwide in scope, concerns the social, political and economic aspects and, above all, the structural dimension of problems and their respective solutions.[446]

202. *Justice is particularly important in the present-day context, where the individual value of the person, his dignity and his rights — despite proclaimed intentions — are seriously threatened by the widespread tendency to make exclusive use of criteria of utility and ownership.* Justice too, on the basis of these criteria, is considered in a reductionist manner, whereas it acquires a fuller and more authentic meaning in Christian anthropology. Justice, in fact, is not merely a simple human convention, because what is "just" is not first determined by the law but by the profound identity of the human being.[447]

203. *The full truth about man makes it possible to move beyond a contractualistic vision of justice, which is a reductionist vision, and to open up also for justice the new horizon of solidarity and love.* "By itself, justice is not enough. Indeed, it can even betray itself, unless it is open to that deeper power which is love."[448] In fact, the Church's social doctrine places alongside the value of justice that of solidarity, in that it is the privileged way of peace. If peace is the fruit of justice, "today one could say, with the same exactness and the same power of biblical inspiration (cf. *Is* 32:17; *Jas* 3:18): *Opus solidaritatis pax*, peace as the fruit of *solidarity.*"[449] The goal of *peace*, in fact, "will certainly be achieved through the putting into effect of social and international justice, but also through the practice of the virtues which favor togetherness, and which teach us to live in unity, so as to build in unity, by giving and receiving, a new society and a better world."[450]

---

[442] *Catechism of the Catholic Church*, 1807; cf. Saint Thomas Aquinas, *Summa Theologiae*, II-II, q. 58, a. 1: Ed. Leon. 9, 9-10: "iustitia est perpetua et constans voluntas ius suum unicuique tribuendi."
[443] Cf. John XXIII, Encyclical Letter *Pacem in Terris*: AAS 55 (1963), 282-283.
[444] Cf. *Catechism of the Catholic Church*, 2411.
[445] Cf. *Catechism of the Catholic Church*, 1928-1942, 2425-2449, 2832; Pius XI, Encyclical Letter *Divini Redemptoris*: AAS 29 (1937), 92.
[446] Cf. John Paul II, Encyclical Letter *Laborem Exercens*, 2: AAS 73 (1981), 580-583.
[447] Cf. John Paul II, Encyclical Letter *Sollicitudo Rei Socialis*, 40: AAS 80 (1988), 568; cf. *Catechism of the Catholic Church*, 1929.
[448] John Paul II, Message for the 2004 World Day of Peace, 10: AAS 96 (2004), 121.
[449] John Paul II, Encyclical Letter *Sollicitudo Rei Socialis*, 39: AAS 80 (1988), 568.
[450] John Paul II, Encyclical Letter *Sollicitudo Rei Socialis*, 39: AAS 80 (1988), 568.

VIII. THE WAY OF LOVE

204. *Among the virtues in their entirety, and in particular between virtues, social values and love, there exists a deep bond that must be ever more fully recognized.* Love, often restricted to relationships of physical closeness or limited to merely subjective aspects of action on behalf of others, must be reconsidered in its authentic value as the *highest and universal criterion of the whole of social ethics.* Among all paths, even those sought and taken in order to respond to the ever new forms of current *social questions*, the "more excellent way" (cf. *1 Cor* 12:31) is that *marked out by love.*

205. *It is from the inner wellspring of love that the values of truth, freedom and justice are born and grow.* Human life in society is ordered, bears fruits of goodness and responds to human dignity when it is founded on truth; when it is lived in justice, that is, in the effective respect of rights and in the faithful carrying out of corresponding duties; when it is animated by selflessness, which makes the needs and requirements of others seem as one's own and intensifies the communion of spiritual values and the concern for material necessities; when it is brought about in the freedom that befits the dignity of men and women, prompted by their rational nature to accept responsibility for their actions.[451] These values constitute the pillars which give strength and consistency to the edifice of life and deeds: they are values that determine the quality of every social action and institution.

206. *Love presupposes and transcends justice*, which "must find its fulfilment in charity."[452] If justice is "in itself suitable for 'arbitration' between people concerning the reciprocal distribution of objective goods in an equitable manner, love and only love (including that kindly love that we call 'mercy') is capable of restoring man to himself."[453] *Human relationships cannot be governed solely by the measure of justice*: "The experience of the past and of our own time demonstrates that justice alone is not enough, that it can even lead to the negation and destruction of itself . . . It has been precisely historical experience that, among other things, has led to the formulation of the saying: *summum ius, summa iniuria.*"[454] In fact, "in every sphere of interpersonal relationships justice must, *so to speak, be 'corrected' to a considerable extent* by that love which, as St. Paul proclaims, 'is patient and kind' or, in other words, possesses the characteristics of that *merciful love* which is so much of the essence of the Gospel and Christianity."[455]

207. *No legislation, no system of rules or negotiation will ever succeed in persuading men and peoples to live in unity, brotherhood and peace; no line of reasoning will ever be able to surpass the appeal of love.* Only love, in its quality as *"form of the virtues,"*[456] can

---

[451] Cf. John XXIII, Encyclical Letter *Pacem in Terris*: AAS 55 (1963), 265-267.

[452] John Paul II, Message for the 2004 World Day of Peace, 10: AAS 96 (2004), 120.

[453] John Paul II, Encyclical Letter *Dives in Misericordia*, 14: AAS 72 (1980), 1223.

[454] John Paul II, Encyclical Letter *Dives in Misericordia*, 12: AAS 72 (1980), 1216.

[455] John Paul II, Encyclical Letter *Dives in Misericordia*, 14: AAS 72 (1980), 1224; cf. *Catechism of the Catholic Church*, 2212.

[456] Saint Thomas Aquinas, *Summa Theologiae*, II-II, q. 23, a. 8: Ed. Leon. 8, 72; cf. *Catechism of the Catholic Church*, 1827.

animate and shape social interaction, moving it towards peace in the context of a world that is ever more complex. In order that all this may take place, however, it is necessary that care be taken to show love not only in its role of prompting individual deeds but also as a force capable of inspiring new ways of approaching the problems of today's world, of profoundly renewing structures, social organizations, legal systems from within. In this perspective love takes on the characteristic style of *social and political charity*: "Social charity makes us love the common good,"[457] it makes us effectively seek the good of all people, considered not only as individuals or private persons but also in the social dimension that unites them.

208. *Social and political charity is not exhausted in relationships between individuals but spreads into the network formed by these relationships, which is precisely the social and political community; it intervenes in this context seeking the greatest good for the community in its entirety.* In so many aspects the neighbor to be loved is found "*in society,*" such that to love him concretely, assist him in his needs or in his indigence may mean something different than it means on the mere level of relationships between individuals. *To love him on the social level means, depending on the situations, to make use of social mediations to improve his life or to remove social factors that cause his indigence.* It is undoubtedly an act of love, the work of mercy by which one responds *here and now* to a real and impelling need of one's neighbor, but it is an equally indispensable act of love to strive to *organize and structure society* so that one's neighbor will not find himself in poverty, above all when this becomes a situation within which an immense number of people and entire populations must struggle, and when it takes on the proportions of a true *worldwide social issue.*

---

[457] Paul VI, Address to the Food and Agriculture Association on the twenty-fifth anniversary of its foundation (16 November 1970): *Insegnamenti di Paolo VI*, vol. VIII, p. 1153.

PART TWO

". . . the Church's social teaching is itself a valid instrument
of evangelization. As such, it proclaims God and his mystery
of salvation in Christ to every human being,
and for that very reason reveals man to himself.
In this light, and only in this light,
does it concern itself with everything else:
the human rights of the individual,
and in particular of the 'working class,'
the family and education, the duties of the State,
the ordering of national and international society,
economic life, culture, war and peace,
and respect for life from the moment of conception until death."

(*Centesimus Annus*, 54)

CHAPTER FIVE

THE FAMILY,
THE VITAL CELL OF SOCIETY

I. THE FAMILY, THE FIRST NATURAL SOCIETY

209. *The importance and centrality of the family with regard to the person and society is repeatedly underlined by Sacred Scripture.* "It is not good that the man should be alone" (Gen 2:18). From the texts that narrate the creation of man (cf. Gen 1:26-28, 2:7-24) there emerges how — in God's plan — the couple constitutes "the first form of communion between persons."[458] Eve is created like Adam as the one who, in her otherness, completes him (cf. Gen 2:18) in order to form with him "one flesh" (Gen 2:24; cf. Mt 19:5-6).[459] At the same time, both are involved in the work of procreation, which makes them co-workers with the Creator: "Be fruitful and multiply, and fill the earth" (Gen 1:28). The family is presented, in the Creator's plan, as "the *primary place of 'humanization'* for the person and society" and the "cradle of life and love."[460]

210. *It is in the family that one learns the love and faithfulness of the Lord, and the need to respond to these* (cf. Ex 12:25-27, 13:8,14-15; Deut 6:20-25, 13:7-11; 1 Sam 3:13). It is in the family that children learn their first and most important lessons of practical wisdom, to which the virtues are connected (cf. Prov 1:8-9, 4:1-4, 6:20-21; Sir 3:1-16, 7:27-28). Because of all this, the Lord himself is the guarantor of the love and fidelity of married life (cf. Mal 2:14-15).

Jesus was born and lived in a concrete family, accepting all its characteristic features[461] *and he conferred the highest dignity on the institution of marriage*, making it a sacrament of the new covenant (cf. Mt 19:3-9). It is in this new perspective that the couple finds the fullness of its dignity and the family its solid foundation.

211. *Enlightened by the radiance of the biblical message, the Church considers the family as the first natural society, with underived rights that are proper to it, and places it at*

---

[458] Second Vatican Ecumenical Council, Pastoral Constitution *Gaudium et Spes*, 12: AAS 58 (1966), 1034.

[459] Cf. *Catechism of the Catholic Church*, 1605.

[460] John Paul II, Post-Synodal Apostolic Exhortation *Christifideles Laici*, 40: AAS 81 (1989), 469.

[461] The Holy Family is an example of family life: "May Nazareth remind us what the family is, what the communion of love is, its stark and simple beauty, its sacred and inviolable character; may it help us to see how sweet and irreplaceable education in the family is; may it teach us its natural function in the social order. May we finally learn the lesson of work": Paul VI, Address at Nazareth (5 January 1964): AAS 56 (1964), 168.

the center of social life. Relegating the family "to a subordinate or secondary role, excluding it from its rightful position in society, would be to inflict grave harm on the authentic growth of society as a whole."[462] The family, in fact, is born of the intimate communion of life and love founded on the marriage between one man and one woman.[463] It possesses its own specific and original social dimension, in that it is the principal place of interpersonal relationships, *the first and vital cell of society*.[464] The family is a divine institution that stands at the foundation of life of the human person as the prototype of every social order.

a. Importance of the family for the person

212. *The family has central importance in reference to the person.* It is in this cradle of life and love that people are *born* and *grow*; when a child *is conceived*, society receives the gift of a new person who is called "from the innermost depths of self to *communion* with others and to the *giving* of self to others."[465] It is in the family, therefore, that the mutual giving of self on the part of man and woman united in marriage creates an environment of life in which children "develop their potentialities, become aware of their dignity and prepare to face their unique and individual destiny."[466]

In the climate of natural affection which unites the members of a family unit, persons are recognized and learn responsibility in the wholeness of their personhood. "The first and fundamental structure for 'human ecology' is the *family*, in which man receives his first formative ideas about truth and goodness, and learns what it means to love and to be loved, and thus what it actually means to be a person."[467] The obligations of its members, in fact, are not limited by the terms of a contract but derive from the very essence of the family, founded on the irrevocable marriage covenant and given structure in the relationships that arise within it following the generation or adoption of children.

b. Importance of the family for society

213. *The family, the natural community in which human social nature is experienced, makes a unique and irreplaceable contribution to the good of society.* The family unit, in fact, is born from the communion of persons. "'*Communion*' has to do with the personal relationship between the 'I' and the 'thou.' '*Community*' on the other hand transcends this framework and moves towards a 'society,' a 'we.' The family, as a community of persons, is thus the first human 'society.'"[468]

---

462 John Paul II, Letter to Families *Gratissimam Sane*, 17: AAS 86 (1994), 906.
463 Cf. Second Vatican Ecumenical Council, Pastoral Constitution *Gaudium et Spes*, 48: AAS 58 (1966), 1067-1069
464 Cf. Second Vatican Ecumenical Council, Decree *Apostolicam Actuositatem*, 11: AAS 58 (1966), 848.
465 John Paul II, Post-Synodal Apostolic Exhortation *Christifideles Laici*, 40: AAS 81 (1989), 468.
466 John Paul II, Encyclical Letter *Centesimus Annus*, 39: AAS 83 (1991), 841.
467 John Paul II, Encyclical Letter *Centesimus Annus*, 39: AAS 83 (1991), 841.
468 John Paul II, Letter to Families *Gratissimam Sane*, 7: AAS 86 (1994), 875; cf. *Catechism of the Catholic Church*, 2206.

A society built on a family scale is the best guarantee against drifting off course into individualism or collectivism, because within the family the person is always at the center of attention as an end and never as a means. It is patently clear that the good of persons and the proper functioning of society are closely connected "with the healthy state of conjugal and family life."[469] Without families that are strong in their communion and stable in their commitment peoples grow weak. In the family, moral values are taught starting from the very first years of life, the spiritual heritage of the religious community and the cultural legacy of the nation are transmitted. In the family one learns social responsibility and solidarity.[470]

214. *The priority of the family over society and over the State must be affirmed.* The family in fact, at least in its procreative function, is the condition itself for their existence. With regard to other functions that benefit each of its members, it proceeds in importance and value the functions that society and the State are called to perform.[471] The family possesses inviolable rights and finds its legitimization in human nature and not in being recognized by the State. *The family, then, does not exist for society or the State, but society and the State exist for the family.*

Every social model that intends to serve the good of man must not overlook the centrality and social responsibility of the family. In their relationship to the family, society and the State are seriously obligated to observe the principle of subsidiarity. In virtue of this principle, public authorities may not take away from the family tasks which it can accomplish well by itself or in free association with other families; on the other hand, these same authorities have the duty to sustain the family, ensuring that it has all the assistance that it needs to fulfil properly its responsibilities.[472]

II. MARRIAGE, THE FOUNDATION OF THE FAMILY

a. The value of marriage

215. *The family has its foundation in the free choice of the spouses to unite themselves in marriage, in respect for the meaning and values of this institution that does not depend on man but on God himself:* "For the good of the spouses and their offspring as well as of society, this sacred bond no longer depends on human decision alone. For God himself is the author of marriage and has endowed it with various benefits and purposes."[473] Therefore, the institution of marriage — "intimate partnership of life and love . . . established by the Creator and endowed by him with its own proper laws"[474] — is not the result of human conventions or of legislative pre-

---

[469] Second Vatican Ecumenical Council, Pastoral Constitution *Gaudium et Spes*, 47: AAS 58 (1966), 1067; cf. *Catechism of the Catholic Church*, 2210.

[470] Cf. *Catechism of the Catholic Church*, 2224.

[471] Cf. Holy See, *Charter of the Rights of the Family*, Preamble, D-E, Vatican Polyglot Press, Vatican City 1983, p. 6.

[472] Cf. John Paul II, Apostolic Exhortation *Familiaris Consortio*, 45: AAS 74 (1982), 136-137; *Catechism of the Catholic Church*, 2209.

[473] Second Vatican Ecumenical Council, Pastoral Constitution *Gaudium et Spes*, 48: AAS 58 (1966), 1067-1068.

[474] Second Vatican Ecumenical Council, Pastoral Constitution *Gaudium et Spes*, 48: AAS 58 (1966), 1067.

scriptions but acquires its stability from divine disposition.[475] It is an institution born, even in the eyes of society, "from the human act by which the partners mutually surrender themselves to each other,"[476] and is founded on the very nature of that conjugal love which, as a total and exclusive gift of person to person, entails a definitive commitment expressed by mutual, irrevocable and public consent.[477] This commitment means that the relationships among family members are marked also by a sense of justice and, therefore, by respect for mutual rights and duties.

216. *No power can abolish the natural right to marriage or modify its traits and purpose. Marriage in fact is endowed with its own proper, innate and permanent characteristics.* Notwithstanding the numerous changes that have taken place in the course of the centuries in the various cultures and in different social structures and spiritual attitudes, in every culture there exists a certain sense of the dignity of the marriage union, although this is not evident everywhere with the same clarity.[478] This dignity must be respected in its specific characteristics and must be safeguarded against any attempt to undermine it. Society cannot freely legislate with regard to the marriage bond by which the two spouses promise each other fidelity, assistance and acceptance of children, but it is authorized to regulate its civil effects.

217. *The characteristic traits of marriage are: totality,* by which the spouses give themselves to each other mutually in every aspect of their person, physical and spiritual; *unity* which makes them "one flesh" (*Gen* 2:24); *indissolubility* and *fidelity* which the definitive mutual giving of self requires; the *fruitfulness* to which this naturally opens itself.[479] God's wise plan for marriage — a plan accessible to human reason notwithstanding the difficulties arising from "hardness of heart" (cf. *Mt* 19:8; *Mk* 10:5) — cannot be evaluated exclusively in light of the *de facto* behavior and concrete situations that are at divergence with it. A radical denial of God's original plan is found in *polygamy,* "because it is contrary to the equal personal dignity of men and women who in matrimony give themselves with a love that is total and therefore unique and exclusive."[480]

218. *In its "objective" truth, marriage is ordered to the procreation and education of children.*[481] The marriage union, in fact, gives fullness of life to that sincere gift of self, the fruit of which is children, who in turn are a gift for the parents, for the whole family and all of society.[482] *Nonetheless, marriage was not instituted for the sole*

[475] Cf. *Catechism of the Catholic Church*, 1603.
[476] Second Vatican Ecumenical Council, Pastoral Constitution *Gaudium et Spes*, 48: AAS 58 (1966), 1067.
[477] Cf. *Catechism of the Catholic Church*, 1639.
[478] Cf. *Catechism of the Catholic Church*, 1603.
[479] Cf. John Paul II, Apostolic Exhortation *Familiaris Consortio*, 13: AAS 74 (1982), 93-96.
[480] John Paul II, Apostolic Exhortation *Familiaris Consortio*, 19: AAS 74 (1982), 102.
[481] Cf. Second Vatican Ecumenical Council, Pastoral Constitution *Gaudium et Spes*, 48, 50: AAS 58 (1966), 1067-1069, 1070-1072.
[482] Cf. John Paul II, Letter to Families *Gratissimam Sane*, 11: AAS 86 (1994), 883-886.

reason of procreation.[483] Its indissoluble character and its value of communion remain even when children, although greatly desired, do not arrive to complete conjugal life. In this case, the spouses "can give expression to their generosity by adopting abandoned children or performing demanding services for others."[484]

b. The sacrament of marriage

219. *By Christ's institution, the baptized live the inherent human reality of marriage in the supernatural form of a sacrament, a sign and instrument of grace.* The theme of the marriage covenant, as the meaningful expression of the communion of love between God and men and as the symbolic key to understanding the different stages of the great covenant between God and his people, is found throughout salvation history.[485] At the centre of the revelation of the divine plan of love is the gift that God makes to humanity in his Son, Jesus Christ, "the Bridegroom who loves and gives himself as the Savior of humanity, uniting it to himself as his body. He reveals the original truth of marriage, the truth of the 'beginning' (cf. *Gen* 2:24; *Mt* 19:5), and, freeing man from his hardness of heart, he makes man capable of realizing this truth in its entirety."[486] It is in the spousal love of Christ for the Church, which shows its fullness in the offering made on the cross that the sacramentality of marriage originates. The grace of this sacrament conforms the love of the spouses to the love of Christ for the Church. Marriage, as a sacrament, is a covenant in love between a man and a woman.[487]

220. *The sacrament of marriage takes up the human reality of conjugal love in all its implications* and "gives to Christian couples and parents a power and a commitment to live their vocation as lay people and therefore to 'seek the kingdom of God by engaging in temporal affairs and by ordering them according to the plan of God.'"[488] Intimately united to the Church by virtue of the sacrament that makes it a "domestic Church" or a "little Church," the Christian family is called therefore "to be a sign of unity for the world and in this way to exercise its

---

[483] Cf. Second Vatican Ecumenical Council, Pastoral Constitution *Gaudium et Spes*, 50: AAS 58 (1966), 1070-1072.

[484] *Catechism of the Catholic Church*, 2379.

[485] Cf. John Paul II, Apostolic Exhortation *Familiaris Consortio*, 12: AAS 74 (1982), 93: "For this reason the central word of Revelation, 'God loves his people,' is likewise proclaimed through the living and concrete word whereby a man and a woman express their conjugal love. Their bond of love becomes the image and the symbol of the covenant which unites God and his people (cf. *Hos* 2:21; *Jer* 3:6-13; *Is* 54). And the same sin which can harm the conjugal covenant becomes an image of the infidelity of the people to their God: idolatry is prostitution (cf. *Ezek* 16:25), infidelity is adultery, disobedience to the law is abandonment of the spousal love of the Lord. But the infidelity of Israel does not destroy the eternal fidelity of the Lord, and therefore the ever faithful love of God is put forward as the model of the of faithful love which should exist between spouses (cf. *Hos* 3)."

[486] John Paul II, Apostolic Exhortation *Familiaris Consortio*, 13: AAS 74 (1982), 93-94.

[487] Cf. Second Vatican Ecumenical Council, Pastoral Constitution *Gaudium et Spes*, 48: AAS 58 (1966), 1067-1069.

[488] John Paul II, Apostolic Exhortation *Familiaris Consortio*, 47: AAS 74 (1982), 139; the quotation in the text is taken from Second Vatican Ecumenical Council, Dogmatic Constitution *Lumen Gentium*, 31: AAS 57 (1965), 37.

prophetic role by bearing witness to the Kingdom and peace of Christ, towards which the whole world is journeying."[489]

Conjugal charity, which flows from the very charity of Christ, offered through the sacrament, makes Christian spouses witnesses to a new social consciousness inspired by the Gospel and the Paschal Mystery. The natural dimension of their love is constantly purified, strengthened and elevated by sacramental grace. In this manner, besides offering each other mutual help on the path to holiness, Christian spouses become a sign and an instrument of Christ's love in the world. By their very lives they are called to bear witness to and proclaim the religious meaning of marriage, which modern society has ever greater difficulty recognizing, especially as it accepts relativistic perspectives of the natural foundation itself of the institution of marriage.

III. THE SOCIAL SUBJECTIVITY OF THE FAMILY

a. Love and the formation of a community of persons

221. *The family is present as the place where communion — that communion so necessary for a society that is increasingly individualistic — is brought about. It is the place where an authentic community of persons develops and grows,*[490] *thanks to the endless dynamism of love, which is the fundamental dimension of human experience and which finds in the family the privileged place for making itself known.* "Love causes man to find fulfilment through the sincere gift of self. To love means to give and to receive something which can be neither bought nor sold, but only given freely and mutually."[491]

It is thanks to love, the essential reality for defining marriage and the family that every person — man and woman — is recognized, accepted and respected in his dignity. From love arise relationships lived in gratuitousness, which "by respecting and fostering personal dignity in each and every one as the only basis for value . . . takes the form of heartfelt acceptance, encounter and dialogue, disinterested availability, generous service and deep solidarity."[492] The existence of families living this way exposes the failings and contradictions of a society that is for the most part, even if not exclusively, based on efficiency and functionality. By constructing daily a network of interpersonal relationships, both internal and external, the family is instead "the first and irreplaceable school of social life, and example and stimulus for the broader community relationships marked by respect, justice, dialogue and love."[493]

222. *Love is also expressed in the generous attention shown to the elderly who live in families: their presence can take on great value.* They are an example of connections between generations, a resource for the well-being of the family and of the whole of society: "Not only do they show that there are aspects of life — human, cul-

[489] John Paul II, Apostolic Exhortation *Familiaris Consortio*, 48: AAS 74 (1982), 140; cf. *Catechism of the Catholic Church*, 1656-1657, 2204.
[490] Cf. John Paul II, Apostolic Exhortation *Familiaris Consortio*, 18: AAS 74 (1982), 100-101.
[491] John Paul II, Letter to Families *Gratissimam Sane*, 11: AAS 86 (1994), 883.
[492] John Paul II, Apostolic Exhortation *Familiaris Consortio*, 43: AAS 74 (1982), 134.
[493] John Paul II, Apostolic Exhortation *Familiaris Consortio*, 43: AAS 74 (1982), 134.

tural, moral and social values — which cannot be judged in terms of economic efficiency, but they can also make an effective contribution in the work-place and in leadership roles. In short, it is not just a question of doing something for older people, but also of accepting them in a realistic way as partners in shared projects — at the level of thought, dialogue and action."[494] As the Sacred Scripture says: "They still bring forth fruit in old age" (*Ps* 92:15). The elderly constitute and important school of life, capable or transmitting values and traditions, and of fostering the growth of younger generations, who thus learn to seek not only their own good but also that of others. If the elderly are in situations where they experience suffering and dependence, not only do they need health care services and appropriate assistance, but — and above all — they need to be treated with love.

223. *The human being is made for love and cannot live without love.* When it is manifested as the total gift of two persons in their complementarities, love cannot be reduced to emotions or feelings, much less to mere sexual expression. In a society that tends more and more to relativize and trivialize the very experience of love and sexuality, exalting its fleeting aspects and obscuring its fundamental values, it is more urgent than ever to proclaim and bear witness that *the truth* of conjugal love and sexuality exist where there is a full and total gift of persons, with the characteristics of *unity* and *fidelity*.[495] This truth, a source of joy, hope and life, remains impenetrable and unattainable as long as people close themselves off in relativism and scepticism.

224. *Faced with theories that consider gender identity as merely the cultural and social product of the interaction between the community and the individual, independent of personal sexual identity without any reference to the true meaning of sexuality, the Church does not tire of repeating her teaching:* "Everyone, man and woman, should acknowledge and accept his sexual identity. Physical, moral and spiritual *difference* and *complementarities* are oriented towards the goods of marriage and the flourishing of family life. The harmony of the couple and of society depends in part on the way in which the complementarities, needs and mutual support between the sexes are lived out."[496] According to this perspective, it is obligatory that positive law *be conformed* to the natural law, according to which *sexual identity is indispensable*, because it is the objective condition for forming a couple in marriage.

225. *The nature of conjugal love requires the stability of the married relationship and its indissolubility.* The absence of these characteristics compromises the relationship of exclusive and total love that is proper to the marriage bond, bringing great pain to the children and damaging repercussions also on the fabric of society.

[494] John Paul II, Message to the Second World Assembly on Ageing, Madrid (3 April 2002): *L'Osservatore Romano*, English edition, 24 April 2002, p. 6; cf. John Paul II, Apostolic Exhortation *Familiaris Consortio*, 27: *AAS* 74 (1982), 113-114.

[495] Cf. Second Vatican Ecumenical Council, Pastoral Constitution *Gaudium et Spes*, 48: *AAS* 58 (1966), 1067-1069; *Catechism of the Catholic Church*, 1644-1651.

[496] *Catechism of the Catholic Church*, 2333.

The stability and indissolubility of the marriage union must not be entrusted solely to the intention and effort of the individual persons involved. The responsibility for protecting and promoting the family as a fundamental natural institution, precisely in consideration of its vital and essential aspects, falls to the whole of society. The need to confer an institutional character on marriage, basing this on a public act that is socially and legally recognized, arises from the basic requirements of social nature.

The introduction of divorce into civil legislation has fuelled a relativistic vision of the marriage bond and is broadly manifested as it becomes "truly a plague on society."[497] Couples who preserve and develop the value of indissolubility "in a humble and courageous manner . . . perform the role committed to them of being in the world a 'sign' — a small and precious sign, sometimes also subjected to temptation, but always renewed — of the unfailing fidelity with which God and Jesus Christ love each and every human being."[498]

226. *The Church does not abandon those who have remarried after a divorce. She prays for them and encourages them in the difficulties that they encounter in the spiritual life, sustaining them in faith and in hope.* For their part, these persons, insofar as they are baptized, can and indeed must participate in the life of the Church. They are exhorted to listen to the Word of God, to attend the sacrifice of the Mass, to persevere in prayer, to perform acts of charity and take part in community projects for justice and peace, to raise their children in faith, and to nurture a spirit of penitence and works of penance in order to beseech, day after day, the grace of God.

Reconciliation in the sacrament of Penance — which opens the way to the sacrament of the Eucharist — can only be given to those who, after repenting, are sincerely disposed to a new form of life that is no longer in contradiction with the indissolubility of marriage.[499]

Acting in this fashion, the Church professes her fidelity to Christ and to his truth; at the same time she shows a maternal spirit to her children, especially those who, through no fault of their own, have been abandoned by their legitimate spouse. With steadfast trust she believes that even those who have turned away from the Lord's commandment, and continue to live in that state, can obtain from God the grace of conversion and salvation, if they persevere in prayer, penance and charity.[500]

227. De facto *unions, the number of which is progressively increasing, are based on a false conception of an individual's freedom to choose*[501] *and on a completely privatistic vision of marriage and family.* Marriage is not a simple agreement to live together

---

[497] *Catechism of the Catholic Church*, 2385; cf. *Catechism of the Catholic Church*, 1650-1651, 2384.

[498] John Paul II, Apostolic Exhortation *Familiaris Consortio*, 20: AAS 74 (1982), 104.

[499] The respect owed to the sacrament of Marriage, as well as to the married couples themselves, their families and the faith community, forbids pastors regardless of motivation and pretext — even pastoral — from setting up any kind of ceremony for the divorced who wish to remarry. Cf. John Paul II, Apostolic Exhortation *Familiaris Consortio*, 20: AAS 74 (1982), 104.

[500] Cf. John Paul II, Apostolic Exhortation *Familiaris Consortio*, 77, 84: AAS 74 (1982), 175-178, 184-186.

[501] Cf. John Paul II, Letter to Families *Gratissimam Sane*, 14: AAS 86 (1994), 893-896; *Catechism of the Catholic Church*, 2390.

but a relationship with a social dimension that is unique with regard to all other relationships, since the *family* — attending as it does to caring for and educating children — is the principal instrument for making each person grow in an integral manner and integrating him positively into social life.

Making "de facto unions" legally equivalent to the family would discredit the model of the family, which cannot be brought about in a precarious relationship between persons[502] but only in a permanent union originating in marriage, that is, in a covenant between one man and one women, founded on the mutual and free choice that entails full conjugal communion oriented towards procreation.

228. *Connected with de facto unions is the particular problem concerning demands for the legal recognition of unions between homosexual persons*, which is increasingly the topic of public debate. Only an anthropology corresponding to the full truth of the human person can give an appropriate response to this problem with its different aspects on both the societal and ecclesial levels.[503] The light of such anthropology reveals "how incongruous is the demand to accord 'marital' status to unions between persons of the same sex. It is opposed, first of all, by the objective impossibility of making the partnership fruitful through the transmission of life according to the plan inscribed by God in the very structure of the human being. Another obstacle is the absence of the conditions for that interpersonal complementarity between male and female willed by the Creator at both the physical-biological and the eminently psychological levels. It is only in the union of two sexually different persons that the individual can achieve perfection in a synthesis of unity and mutual psychophysical completion."[504]

Homosexual persons are to be fully respected in their human dignity[505] and encouraged to follow God's plan with particular attention in the exercise of chastity.[506] This duty calling for respect does not justify the legitimization of behavior that is not consistent with moral law, even less does it justify the recognition of a right to marriage between persons of the same sex and its being considered equivalent to the family.[507]

"If, from the legal standpoint, marriage between a man and a woman were to be considered just one possible form of marriage, the concept of marriage would

---

[502] Cf. *Catechism of the Catholic Church*, 2390.

[503] Cf. Congregation for the Doctrine of the Faith, Letter on the Pastoral Care of Homosexual Persons (1 October 1986), 1-2: AAS 79 (1987), 543-544.

[504] John Paul II, Address to the Tribunal of the Roman Rota (21 January 1999), 5: *L'Osservatore Romano*, English edition, 10 February 1999, p. 3.

[505] Cf. Congregation for the Doctrine of the Faith, Document on *Some Considerations Concerning the Response to Legislative Proposals on the Non-Discrimination of Homosexual Persons* (23 July 1992): *L'Osservatore Romano*, 24 July 1992, p. 4; cf. Congregation for the Doctrine of the Faith, Declaration *Persona Humana* (29 December 1975), 8: AAS 68 (1976), 84-85.

[506] Cf. *Catechism of the Catholic Church*, 2357-2359.

[507] Cf. John Paul II, Address to Spanish Bishops on their *Ad Limina* Visit (19 February 1998), 4: *L'Osservatore Romano*, English edition, 11 March 1998, p. 5; Pontifical Council for the Family, *Family, Marriage and "De facto Unions"* (26 July 2000), 23, Libreria Editrice Vaticana, Vatican City 2000, pp. 40-43; Congregation for the Doctrine of the Faith, Considerations Regarding Proposals to Give Legal Recognition to Unions Between Homosexual Persons (3 June 2003), Libreria Editrice Vaticana, Vatican City 2003.

undergo a radical transformation, with grave detriment to the common good. By putting homosexual unions on a legal plane analogous to that of marriage and the family, the State acts arbitrarily and in contradiction with its duties."[508]

229. *The solidity of the family nucleus is a decisive resource for the quality of life in society, therefore the civil community cannot remain indifferent to the destabilizing tendencies that threaten its foundations at their very roots.* Although legislation may sometimes tolerate morally unacceptable behavior,[509] *it must never weaken the recognition of indissoluble monogamous marriage as the only authentic form of the family.* It is therefore necessary that the public authorities "resist these tendencies which divide society and are harmful to the dignity, security and welfare of the citizens as individuals, and they must try to ensure that public opinion is not led to undervalue the institutional importance of marriage and the family."[510]

It is the task of the Christian community and of all who have the good of society at heart to reaffirm that "the family constitutes, much more than a mere juridical, social and economic unit, a community of love and solidarity, which is uniquely suited to teach and transmit cultural, ethical, social, spiritual and religious values, essential for the development and well-being of its own members and of society."[511]

b. The family is the sanctuary of life

230. *Conjugal love is by its nature open to the acceptance of life.*[512] The dignity of the human being, called to proclaim the goodness and fruitfulness that come from God, is eminently revealed in the task of procreation: "Human fatherhood and motherhood, while remaining *biologically similar* to that of other living beings in nature, contain in an essential and unique way a *'likeness' to God* which is the basis of the family as a community of human life, as a community of persons united in love (*communio personarum*)."[513]

Procreation expresses the social subjectivity of the family and sets in motion a dynamism of love and solidarity between the generations upon which society is founded. It is necessary to rediscover the social value of that *portion* of the common good inherent in each new human being. Every child "becomes a gift to its brothers, sisters, parents and entire family. *Its life becomes a gift for the very people who were givers of life* and who cannot help but feel its presence, its sharing in their life and its contribution to their common good and to that of the community of the family."[514]

---

[508] Congregation for the Doctrine of the Faith, Considerations Regarding Proposals to Give Legal Recognition to Unions Between Homosexual Persons (3 June 2003), 8, Libreria Editrice Vaticana, Vatican City 2003, p. 9.

[509] Cf. John Paul II, Encyclical Letter *Evangelium Vitae*, 71: AAS 87 (1995), 483; Saint Thomas Aquinas, *Summa Theologiae*, I-II, q. 96, a. 2 ("Utrum ad legem humanam pertineat omnia vitia cohibere"): Ed. Leon. 7, 181.

[510] John Paul II, Apostolic Exhortation *Familiaris Consortio*, 81: AAS 74 (1982), 183.

[511] Holy See, *Charter of the Rights of the Family* (24 November 1983), Preamble, E, Vatican Polyglot Press, Vatican City 1983, p. 6.

[512] Cf. *Catechism of the Catholic Church*, 1652.

[513] John Paul II, Letter to Families *Gratissimam Sane*, 6: AAS 86 (1994), 874; cf. *Catechism of the Catholic Church*, 2366.

[514] John Paul II, Letter to Families *Gratissimam Sane*, 11: AAS 86 (1994), 884.

231. *The family founded on marriage is truly the sanctuary of life,* "the place in which life — the gift of God — can be properly welcomed and protected against the many attacks to which it is exposed, and can develop in accordance with what constitutes authentic human growth."[515] Its role in promoting and building the culture of life [516] against "the possibility of a destructive *'anti-civilization,'* as so many present trends and situations confirm,"[517] is decisive and irreplaceable.

Christian families have then, in virtue of the sacrament received, a particular mission that makes them witnesses and proclaimers of the Gospel of life. This is a commitment which in society takes on the value of true and courageous prophecy. It is for this reason that "serving the *Gospel of life* . . . means that the family, particularly through its membership in family associations, works to ensure that the laws and institutions of the State in no way violate the right to life, from conception to natural death, but rather protect and promote it."[518]

232. *The family contributes to the social good in an eminent fashion through responsible motherhood and fatherhood, the spouses' special participation in God's work of creation.*[519] The weight of this responsibility must not be used as a justification for being selfishly closed but must guide the decisions of the spouses in a generous acceptance of life. "In relation to physical, economic, psychological and social conditions, responsible parenthood is exercised both in the duly pondered and generous decision to have a large family, and in the decision, made for serious reasons and in respect of the moral law, to avoid for a time or even indeterminately a new birth."[520] The motivations that should guide the couple in exercising responsible motherhood and fatherhood originate in the full recognition of their duties towards God, towards themselves, towards the family and towards society in a proper hierarchy of values.

233. *Concerning the "methods" for practising responsible procreation, the first to be rejected as morally illicit are sterilization and abortion.*[521] The latter in particular is a horrendous crime and constitutes a particularly serious moral disorder;[522] far from being a right, it is a sad phenomenon that contributes seriously to spreading a mentality against life, representing a dangerous threat to a just and democratic social coexistence.[523]

515 John Paul II, Encyclical Letter *Centesimus Annus*, 39: AAS 83 (1991), 842.
516 Cf. John Paul II, Encyclical Letter *Evangelium Vitae*, 92: AAS 87 (1995), 505-507.
517 John Paul II, Letter to Families *Gratissimam Sane*, 13: AAS 86 (1994), 891.
518 John Paul II, Encyclical Letter *Evangelium Vitae*, 93: AAS 87 (1995), 507-508.
519 Cf. Second Vatican Ecumenical Council, Pastoral Constitution *Gaudium et Spes*, 50: AAS 58 (1966), 1070-1072; *Catechism of the Catholic Church*, 2367.
520 Paul VI, Encyclical Letter *Humanae Vitae*, 10: AAS 60 (1968), 487; cf. Second Vatican Ecumenical Council, Pastoral Constitution *Gaudium et Spes*, 50: AAS 58 (1966), 1070-1072.
521 Cf. Paul VI, Encyclical Letter *Humanae Vitae*, 14: AAS 60 (1968), 490-491.
522 Cf. Second Vatican Ecumenical Council, Pastoral Constitution *Gaudium et Spes*, 51: AAS 58 (1966), 1072-1073; *Catechism of the Catholic Church*, 2271-2272; John Paul II, Letter to Families *Gratissimam Sane*, 21: AAS 86 (1994), 919-920; John Paul II, Encyclical Letter *Evangelium Vitae*, 58, 59, 61-62: AAS 87 (1995), 466-468, 470-472.
523 Cf. John Paul II, Letter to Families *Gratissimam Sane*, 21: AAS 86 (1994), 919-920; John Paul II, Encyclical Letter *Evangelium Vitae*, 72, 101: AAS 87 (1995), 484-485, 516-518; *Catechism of the Catholic Church*, 2273.

Also to be rejected is recourse to contraceptive methods in their different forms:[524] *this rejection is based on a correct and integral understanding of the person and human sexuality*[525] *and represents a moral call to defend the true development of peoples.*[526] On the other hand, the same reasons of an anthropological order justify recourse to periodic abstinence during times of the woman's fertility.[527] Rejecting contraception and using natural methods for regulating births means choosing to base interpersonal relations between the spouses on mutual respect and total acceptance, with positive consequences also for bringing about a more human order in society.

234. *The judgment concerning the interval of time between births, and that regarding the number of children, belongs to the spouses alone.* This is one of their inalienable rights, to be exercised before God with due consideration of their obligations towards themselves, their children already born, the family and society.[528] The intervention of public authorities within the limits of their competence to provide information and enact suitable measures in the area of demographics must be made in a way that fully respects the persons and the freedom of the couple. Such intervention may never become a substitute for their decisions.[529] All the more must various organizations active in this area refrain from doing the same.

All programmes of economic assistance aimed at financing campaigns of sterilization and contraception, as well as the subordination of economic assistance to such campaigns, are to be morally condemned as affronts to the dignity of the person and the family. The answer to questions connected with population growth must instead by sought in simultaneous respect both of sexual morals and of social ethics, promoting greater justice and authentic solidarity so that dignity is given to life in all circumstances, starting with economic, social and cultural conditions.

235. *The desire to be a mother or a father does not justify any "right to children," whereas the rights of the unborn child are evident. The unborn child must be guaranteed the best possible conditions of existence through the stability of a family founded on marriage, through the complementarities of the two persons, father and mother.*[530] The rapid development of research and its technological application in the area of reproduction poses new and delicate questions that involve society and the norms that regulate human social life.

---

[524] Cf. Second Vatican Ecumenical Council, Pastoral Constitution *Gaudium et Spes*, 51: AAS 58 (1966), 1072-1073; Paul VI, Encyclical Letter *Humanae Vitae*, 14: AAS 60 (1968), 490-491; John Paul II, Apostolic Exhortation *Familiaris Consortio*, 32: AAS 74 (1982), 118-120; *Catechism of the Catholic Church*, 2370; Pius XI, Encyclical Letter *Casti Connubii* (31 December 1930): AAS 22 (1930), 559-561.

[525] Cf. Paul VI, Encyclical Letter *Humanae Vitae*, 7: AAS 60 (1968), 485; John Paul II, Apostolic Exhortation *Familiaris Consortio*, 32: AAS 74 (1982), 118-120.

[526] Cf. Paul VI, Encyclical Letter *Humanae Vitae*, 17: AAS 60 (1968), 493-494.

[527] Cf. Paul VI, Encyclical Letter *Humanae Vitae*, 16: AAS 60 (1968), 491-492; John Paul II, Apostolic Exhortation *Familiaris Consortio*, 32: AAS 74 (1982), 118-120; *Catechism of the Catholic Church*, 2370.

[528] Cf. Second Vatican Ecumenical Council, Pastoral Constitution *Gaudium et Spes*, 50: AAS 58 (1966), 1070-1072; *Catechism of the Catholic Church*, 2368; Paul VI, Encyclical Letter *Populorum Progressio*, 37: AAS 59 (1967), 275-276.

[529] Cf. *Catechism of the Catholic Church*, 2372.

[530] Cf. *Catechism of the Catholic Church*, 2378.

It must be repeated that the ethical unacceptability of all *reproductive techniques* — such as the donation of sperm or ova, surrogate motherhood, heterologous artificial fertilization — that make use of the uterus of another woman or of gametes of persons other than the married couple, injuring the right of the child to be born of one father and one mother who are father and mother both from a biological and from a legal point of view. Equally unacceptable are methods that separate the unitive act from the procreative act by making use of laboratory techniques, such as homologous artificial insemination or fertilization, such that the child comes about more as the result of an act of technology than as the natural fruit of a human act in which there is a full and total giving of the couple.[531] Avoiding recourse to different forms of so-called "assisted procreation" that replace the marriage act means respecting — both in the parents and in the children that they intend to generate — the integral dignity of the human person.[532] On the other hand, those methods that are meant to lend assistance to the conjugal act or to the attainment of its effects are legitimate.[533]

236. *An issue of particular social and cultural significance today, because of its many and serious moral implications, is human cloning. This term refers per se to the reproduction of a biological entity that is genetically identical to the originating organism.* In thought and experimental practice it has taken on different meanings which in turn entail different procedures from the point of view of the techniques employed as well as of the goals sought. The term can be used to refer to the simple laboratory *replication* of cells or of a portion of DNA. But specifically today it is used to refer to the reproduction of individuals at the embryonic stage with methods that are different from those of natural fertilization and in such a way that the new beings are genetically identical to the individual from which they originate. This type of cloning can have a *reproductive* purpose, that of producing human embryos, or a so-called *therapeutic* purpose, tending to use such embryos for scientific research or more specifically for the production of stem cells.

From an ethical point of view, the simple *replication* of normal cells or of a portion of DNA presents no particular ethical problem. Very different, however, is the Magisterium's judgment on cloning understood in the proper sense. Such cloning is contrary to the dignity of human procreation because it takes place in total absence of an act of personal love between spouses, being agamic and asexual reproduction.[534] In the second place, this type of reproduction represents a form of total domination over the reproduced individual on the part of the one reproducing it.[535]

---

[531] Cf. Congregation for the Doctrine of the Faith, Instruction *Donum Vitae* (22 February 1987), II, 2, 3, 5: AAS 80 (1988), 88-89, 92-94; *Catechism of the Catholic Church*, 2376-2377.

[532] Cf. Congregation for the Doctrine of the Faith, Instruction *Donum Vitae* (22 February 1987), II, 7: AAS 80 (1988), 95-96.

[533] Cf. *Catechism of the Catholic Church*, 2375.

[534] Cf. John Paul II, Address to the Pontifical Academy for Life (21 February 2004), 2: *L'Osservatore Romano*, English edition, 3 March 2004, p. 7.

[535] Cf. Pontifical Academy for Life, *Reflections on Cloning*: Libreria Editrice Vaticana, Vatican City 1997; Pontifical Council for Justice and Peace, *The Church and Racism*. Contribution of the Holy See to the World Conference against Racism, Racial Discrimination, Xenophobia and Related Intolerance, 21, Vatican Press, Vatican City 2001, p. 22.

The fact that cloning is used to create embryos from which cells can be removed for therapeutic use does not attenuate its moral gravity, because in order that such cells may be removed the embryo must first be created and then destroyed.[536]

237. *Parents, as ministers of life, must never forget that the spiritual dimension of procreation is to be given greater consideration than any other aspect*: "Fatherhood and motherhood represent a *responsibility which is not simply physical but spiritual in nature;* indeed, through these realities there passes the genealogy of the person, which has its eternal beginning in God and which must lead back to him."[537] Welcoming human life in the unified aspects of its physical and spiritual dimensions, families contribute to the "communion of generations" and in this way provide essential and irreplaceable support for the development of society. For this reason, "the family has a right to assistance by society in the bearing and rearing of children. Those married couples who have a large family have a right to adequate aid and should not be subjected to discrimination."[538]

c. The task of educating

238. *In the work of education, the family forms man in the fullness of his personal dignity according to all his dimensions, including the social dimension.* The family, in fact, constitutes "a community of love and solidarity, which is uniquely suited to teach and transmit cultural, ethical, social, spiritual and religious values, essential for the development and well-being of its own members and of society."[539] By exercising its mission to educate, the family contributes to the common good and constitutes the first school of social virtue, which all societies need.[540] In the family, persons are helped to grow in freedom and responsibility, indispensable prerequisites for any function in society. With education, certain fundamental values are communicated and assimilated.[541]

239. *The family has a completely original and irreplaceable role in raising children.*[542] The parents' love, placing itself at the service of children to draw forth from them

---

[536] Cf. John Paul II, Address to the Eighteenth International Congress of the Transplantation Society (29 August 2000), 8: AAS 92 (2000), 826.

[537] John Paul II, Letter to Families *Gratissimam Sane*, 10: AAS 86 (1994), 881.

[538] Holy See, *Charter of the Rights of the Family*, art. 3 c, Vatican Polyglot Press, Vatican City 1983, p. 9. The United Nations *Universal Declaration of Human Rights* (10 December 1948) affirms that "the family is the natural and fundamental group unit of society and is entitled to protection by society and the State" (article 16,3).

[539] Holy See, *Charter of the Rights of the Family*, Preamble, E, Vatican Polyglot Press, Vatican City 1983, p. 6.

[540] Cf. Second Vatican Ecumenical Council, Declaration *Gravissimum Educationis*, 3: AAS 58 (1966), 731-732; Second Vatican Ecumenical Council, Pastoral Constitution *Gaudium et Spes*, 52: AAS 58 (1966), 1073-1074; John Paul II, Apostolic Exhortation *Familiaris Consortio*, 37, 43: AAS 74 (1982), 127-129; *Catechism of the Catholic Church*, 1653, 2228.

[541] Cf. John Paul II, Apostolic Exhortation *Familiaris Consortio*, 43: AAS 74 (1982), 134-135.

[542] Cf. Second Vatican Ecumenical Council, Declaration *Gravissimum Educationis*, 3: AAS 58 (1966), 731-732; Second Vatican Ecumenical Council, Pastoral Constitution *Gaudium et Spes*, 61: AAS 58 (1966), 1081-1082; Holy See, *Charter of the Rights of the Family*, art. 5, Vatican Polyglot Press, Vatican City 1983, pp. 10-11; *Catechism of the Catholic Church*, 2223. The *Code of Canon Law* devotes canons 793-799 and canon 1136 to this right and duty of parents.

("*e-ducere*") the best that is in them, finds its fullest expression precisely in the task of educating. "As well as being a *source*, the parents' love is also the *animating* principle and therefore the *norm* inspiring and guiding all concrete educational activity, enriching it with the values of kindness, constancy, goodness, service, disinterestedness and self-sacrifice that are the most precious fruit of love."[543]

The right and duty of parents to educate their children is "*essential*, since it is connected with the transmission of human life; it is *original and primary* with regard to the educational role of others, on account of the uniqueness of the loving relationship between parents and children; and it is *irreplaceable and inalienable*, and therefore incapable of being entirely delegated to others or usurped by others."[544] Parents have the duty and right to impart a religious education and moral formation to their children,[545] a right the State cannot annul but which it must respect and promote. This is a primary right that the family may not neglect or delegate.

240. *Parents are the first educators, not the only educators, of their children. It belongs to them, therefore, to exercise with responsibility their educational activity in close and vigilant cooperation with civil and ecclesial agencies.* "Man's community aspect itself — both civil and ecclesial — demands and leads to a broader and more articulated activity resulting from well-ordered collaboration between the various agents of education. All these agents are necessary, even though each can and should play its part in accordance with the special competence and contribution proper to itself."[546] Parents have the right to choose the formative tools that respond to their convictions and to seek those means that will help them best to fulfil their duty as educators, in the spiritual and religious sphere also. Public authorities have the duty to guarantee this right and to ensure the concrete conditions necessary for it to be exercised.[547] In this context, cooperation between the family and scholastic institutions takes on primary importance.

241. *Parents have the right to found and support educational institutions.* Public authorities must see to it that "public subsidies are so allocated that parents are truly free to exercise this right without incurring unjust burdens. Parents should not have to sustain, directly or indirectly, extra charges which would deny or unjustly limit the exercise of this freedom."[548] The refusal to provide public economic support to non-public schools that need assistance and that render a service to civil society is to be considered an injustice. "Whenever the State lays claim to an educational monopoly, it oversteps its rights and offends justice . . . The State cannot without

[543] John Paul II, Apostolic Exhortation *Familiaris Consortio*, 36: AAS 74 (1982), 127.
[544] John Paul II, Apostolic Exhortation *Familiaris Consortio*, 36: AAS 74 (1982), 126; cf. *Catechism of the Catholic Church*, 2221.
[545] Cf. Second Vatican Ecumenical Council, Declaration *Dignitatis Humanae*, 5: AAS 58 (1966), 933; John Paul II, Message for the 1994 World Day of Peace, 5: AAS 86 (1994), 159-160.
[546] John Paul II, Apostolic Exhortation *Familiaris Consortio*, 40: AAS 74 (1982), 131.
[547] Cf. Second Vatican Ecumenical Council, Declaration *Gravissimum Educationis*, 6: AAS 58 (1966), 733-734; *Catechism of the Catholic Church*, 2229.
[548] Holy See, *Charter of the Rights of the Family*, art. 5 b, Vatican Polyglot Press, Vatican City 1983, p. 11; cf. Second Vatican Ecumenical Council, *Dignitatis Humanae*, 5: AAS 58 (1966), 933.

injustice merely tolerate so-called private schools. Such schools render a public service and therefore have a right to financial assistance."[549]

242. *The family has the responsibility to provide an integral education.* Indeed, all true education "is directed towards the formation of the human person in view of his final end and the good of that society to which he belongs and in the duties of which he will, as an adult, have a share."[550] This integrality is ensured when children — with the witness of life and in words — are educated in dialogue, encounter, sociality, legality, solidarity and peace, through the cultivation of the fundamental virtues of justice and charity.[551]

In the education of children, the role of the father and that of the mother are equally necessary.[552] The parents must therefore work together. They must exercise authority with respect and gentleness but also, when necessary, with firmness and vigor: it must be credible, consistent, and wise and always exercised with a view to children's integral good.

243. *Parents have, then, a particular responsibility in the area of sexual education.* It is of fundamental importance for the balanced growth of children that they are taught in an orderly and progressive manner the meaning of sexuality and that they learn to appreciate the human and moral values connected with it. "In view of the close links between the sexual dimension of the person and his or her ethical values, education must bring the children to a knowledge of and respect for moral norms as the necessary and highly valuable guarantee for responsible personal growth in human sexuality."[553] Parents have the obligation to inquire about the methods used for sexual education in educational institutions in order to verify that such an important and delicate topic is dealt with properly.

d. The dignity and rights of children

244. *The Church's social doctrine constantly points out the need to respect the dignity of children.* "In the family, which is a community of persons, special attention must be devoted to the children by developing a profound esteem for their personal dignity, and a great respect and generous concern for their rights. This is true for every child, but it becomes all the more urgent the smaller the child is and the more it is in need of everything, when it is sick, suffering or handicapped."[554]

The rights of children must be legally protected within juridical systems. In the first place, it is necessary that the social value of childhood be publicly recognized in

---

[549] Congregation for the Doctrine of the Faith, Instruction *Libertatis Conscientia*, 94: AAS 79 (1987), 595-596.

[550] Second Vatican Ecumenical Council, Declaration *Gravissimum Educationis*, 1: AAS 58 (1966), 729.

[551] Cf. John Paul II, Apostolic Exhortation *Familiaris Consortio*, 43: AAS 74 (1982), 134-135.

[552] Cf. Second Vatican Ecumenical Council, Pastoral Constitution *Gaudium et Spes*, 52: AAS 58 (1966), 1073-1074.

[553] John Paul II, Apostolic Exhortation *Familiaris Consortio*, 37: AAS 74 (1982), 128; cf. Pontifical Council for the Family, *The Truth and Meaning of Human Sexuality: Guidelines for Education within the Family* (8 December 1995), Libreria Editrice Vaticana 1995.

[554] John Paul II, Apostolic Exhortation *Familiaris Consortio*, 26: AAS 74 (1982), 111-112.

all countries: "No country on earth, no political system can think of its own future otherwise than through the image of these new generations that will receive from their parents the manifold heritage of values, duties and aspirations of the nation to which they belong and of the whole human family."[555] The first right of the child is to "be born in a real family,"[556] a right that has not always been respected and that today is subject to new violations because of developments in genetic technology.

245. *The situation of a vast number of the world's children is far from being satisfactory, due to the lack of favorable conditions for their integral development despite the existence of a specific international juridical instrument for protecting their rights,*[557] *an instrument that is binding on practically all members of the international community.* These are conditions connected with the lack of health care, or adequate food supply, little or no possibility of receiving a minimum of academic formation or inadequate shelter. Moreover, some serious problems remain unsolved: trafficking in children, child labor, the phenomenon of "street children," the use of children in armed conflicts, child marriage, the use of children for commerce in pornographic material, also in the use of the most modern and sophisticated instruments of social communication. It is essential to engage in a battle, at the national and international levels, against the violations of the dignity of boys and girls caused by sexual exploitation, by those caught up in paedophilia, and by every kind of violence directed against these most defenceless of human creatures.[558] These are criminal acts that must be effectively fought with adequate preventive and penal measures by the determined action of the different authorities involved.

IV. THE FAMILY AS ACTIVE PARTICIPANT IN SOCIAL LIFE

a. Solidarity in the family

246. *The social subjectivity of the family, both as a single unit and associated in a group, is expressed as well in the demonstrations of solidarity and sharing not only among families themselves but also in the various forms of participation in social and political life.* This is what happens when the reality of the family is founded on love: being born in love and growing in love, solidarity belongs to the family as a constitutive and structural element.

This is a solidarity that can take on the features of service and attention to those who live in poverty and need, to orphans, the handicapped, the sick, the elderly, to those who are in mourning, to those with doubts, to those who live in

---

[555] John Paul II, Address to the General Assembly of the United Nations
(2 October 1979), 21: AAS 71 (1979), 1159; cf. John Paul II, Message to the Secretary-General of the United Nations on the occasion of the World Summit for Children (22 September 1990): AAS 83 (1991), 358-361.

[556] John Paul II, Address to the Committee of European Journalists for the Rights of the Child (13 January 1979): *L'Osservatore Romano*, English edition, 22 January 1979, p. 5.

[557] Cf. *Convention on the Rights of the Child*, which came into force in 1990 and which the Holy See has ratified.

[558] Cf. John Paul II, Message for the 1996 World Day of Peace, 2-6: AAS 88 (1996), 104-107.

loneliness or who have been abandoned. It is a solidarity that opens itself to acceptance, to guardianship, to adoption; it is able to bring every situation of distress to the attention of institutions so that, according to their specific competence, they can intervene.

247. *Far from being only objects of political action, families can and must become active subjects*, working "to see that the laws and institutions of the State not only do not offend but support and positively defend the rights and duties of the family. Along these lines, families should grow in awareness of being 'protagonists' of what is known as 'family politics' and assume responsibility for transforming society."[559] To this end, family associations must be promoted and strengthened. "Families have the right to form associations with other families and institutions, in order to fulfil the family's role suitably and effectively, as well as to protect the rights, foster the good and represent the interests of the family. On the economic, social, juridical and cultural levels, the rightful role of families and family associations must be recognized in the planning and development of programmes which touch on family life."[560]

b. **The family, economic life and work**

248. *The relationship existing between the family and economic life is particularly significant.* On one hand, in fact, the economy ("*oiko-nomia*," household management) was born from domestic work. The home has been for a long time — and in many regions still is — a place of production and the centre of life. The dynamism of economic life, on the other hand, develops with the initiative of people and is carried out in the manner of concentric circles, in ever broader networks of production and exchange of goods and services that involves families in continuously increasing measure. The family, therefore, must rightfully be seen as an essential agent of economic life, guided not by the market mentality but by the logic of sharing and solidarity among generations.

249. *Family and work are united by a very special relationship.* "The family constitutes one of the most important terms of reference for shaping the social and ethical order of human work."[561] This relationship has its roots in the relation existing between the person and his right to possess the fruit of his labor and concerns not only the individual as a singular person but also *as* a member of a family, understood as a "*domestic society*."[562]

Work is essential insofar as it represents the condition that makes it possible to establish a family, for the means by which the family is maintained are obtained through work. Work also conditions the process of personal development, since a family afflicted by unemployment runs the risk of not fully achieving its end.[563]

---

[559] John Paul II, Apostolic Exhortation *Familiaris Consortio*, 44: AAS 74 (1982), 136; cf. Holy See, *Charter of the Rights of the Family*, art. 9, Vatican Polyglot Press, Vatican City 1983, p. 13.
[560] Holy See, *Charter of the Rights of the Family*, art. 8 a-b, Vatican Polyglot Press, Vatican City 1983, p. 12.
[561] John Paul II, Encyclical Letter *Laborem Exercens*, 10: AAS 73 (1981), 601.
[562] Leo XIII, Encyclical Letter *Rerum Novarum: Acta Leonis XIII*, 11 (1892), 104.
[563] Cf. John Paul II, Encyclical Letter *Laborem Exercens*, 10: AAS 73 (1981), 600-602.

The contribution that the family can make to the reality of work is valuable and, in many instances, irreplaceable. It is a contribution that can be expressed both in economic terms and through the great resources of solidarity that the family possesses and that are often an important support for those within the family who are without work or who are seeking employment. Above all and more fundamentally, it is a contribution that is made by educating to the meaning of work and by offering direction and support for the professional choices made.

250. *In order to protect this relationship between family and work, an element that must be appreciated and safeguarded is that of a family wage,* a wage sufficient to maintain a family and allow it to live decently.[564] Such a wage must also allow for savings that will permit the acquisition of property as a guarantee of freedom. The right to property is closely connected with the existence of families, which protect themselves from need thanks also to savings and to the building up of family property.[565] There can be several different ways to make a family wage a concrete reality. Various forms of important social provisions help to bring it about, for example, family subsidies and other contributions for dependent family members, and also remuneration for the domestic work done in the home by one of the parents.[566]

251. *In the relationship between the family and work, particular attention must be given to the issue of the work of women in the family,* more generally to the recognition of the so-called work of "housekeeping," which also involves the responsibility of men as husbands and fathers. The work of housekeeping, starting with that of the mother, precisely because it is a service directed and devoted to the quality of life, constitutes a type of activity that is eminently personal and personalizing, and that must be socially recognized and valued,[567] also by means of economic compensation in keeping with that of other types of work.[568] At the same time, care must be taken to eliminate all the obstacles that prevent a husband and wife from making free decisions concerning their procreative responsibilities and, in particular, those that do not allow women to carry out their maternal role fully.[569]

---

[564] Cf. Pius XI, Encyclical Letter *Quadragesimo Anno*: AAS 23 (1931), 200; Second Vatican Ecumenical Council, Pastoral Constitution *Gaudium et Spes*, 67: AAS 58 (1966), 1088-1089; John Paul II, Encyclical Letter *Laborem Exercens*, 19: AAS 73 (1981), 625-629.

[565] Cf. Leo XIII, Encyclical Letter *Rerum Novarum*: Acta Leonis XIII, 11 (1892), 105; Pius XI, Encyclical Letter *Quadragesimo Anno*: AAS 23 (1931), 193-194.

[566] Cf. John Paul II, Encyclical Letter *Laborem Exercens*, 19: AAS 73 (1981), 625-629; Holy See, *Charter of the Rights of the Family*, art. 10 a, Vatican Polyglot Press, Vatican City 1983, p. 14.

[567] Cf. Pius XII, Allocution to Women on the Dignity and Mission of Women (21 October 1945): AAS 37 (1945), 284-295; John Paul II, Encyclical Letter *Laborem Exercens*, 19: AAS 73 (1981), 625-629; John Paul II, Apostolic Exhortation *Familiaris Consortio*, 23: AAS 74 (1982), 107-109; Holy See, *Charter of the Rights of the Family*, art. 10 b, Vatican Polyglot Press, Vatican City 1983, p. 14.

[568] Cf. John Paul II, Letter to Families *Gratissimam Sane*, 17: AAS 86 (1994), 903-906.

[569] Cf. John Paul II, Encyclical Letter *Laborem Exercens*, 19: AAS 73 (1981), 625-629; John Paul II, Apostolic Exhortation *Familiaris Consortio*, 23: AAS 74 (1982), 107-109.

V. SOCIETY AT THE SERVICE OF THE FAMILY

252. *The starting point for a correct and constructive relationship between the family and society is the recognition of the subjectivity and the social priority of the family.* Their intimate relationship requires that "society should never fail in its fundamental task of respecting and fostering the family."[570] Society, and in particular State institutions, respecting the priority and "antecedence" of the family, is called to *guarantee and foster the genuine identity of family life* and to avoid and fight all that alters or wounds it. This requires political and legislative action to safeguard family values, from the promotion of intimacy and harmony within families to the respect for unborn life and to the effective freedom of choice in educating children. Therefore, neither society nor the State may absorb, substitute or reduce the social dimension of the family; rather, they must honor it, recognize it, respect it and promote it according to *the principle of subsidiarity.*[571]

253. *Society's service of the family becomes concrete in recognizing, respecting and promoting the rights of the family.*[572] *This means that authentic and effective family policies must be brought about* with specific interventions that are able to meet the needs arising from the rights of the family as such. In this sense, there is a necessary prerequisite, one that is essential and indispensable: the *recognition* — which entails protecting, appreciating and promoting — the identity of the family, *the natural society founded on marriage.* This recognition represents a clear line of demarcation between the family, understood correctly, and all other forms of cohabitation which, by their very nature, deserve neither the name nor the status of family.

254. *The recognition on the part of civil society and the State of the priority of the family over every other community, and even over the reality of the State, means overcoming merely individualistic conceptions and accepting the family dimension as the indispensable cultural and political perspective in the consideration of persons.* This is not offered as an alternative, but rather as a support and defence of the very rights that people have as individuals. This perspective makes it possible to draw up normative criteria for a correct solution to different social problems, because people must not be considered only as individuals but also in relation to the family nucleus to which they belong, the specific values and needs of which must be taken into due account.

---

[570] John Paul II, Apostolic Exhortation *Familiaris Consortio*, 45: AAS 74 (1982), 136.
[571] Cf. *Catechism of the Catholic Church*, 2211.
[572] Cf. John Paul II, Apostolic Exhortation *Familiaris Consortio*, 46: AAS 74 (1982), 137-139.

CHAPTER SIX

HUMAN WORK

I. BIBLICAL ASPECTS

a. **The duty to cultivate and care for the earth**

255. *The Old Testament presents God as the omnipotent Creator* (cf. Gen 2:2; Job 38-41; Ps 104; Ps 147) *who fashions man in his image and invites him to work the soil* (cf. Gen 2:5-6), *and cultivate and care for the garden of Eden in which he has placed him* (cf. Gen 2:15). To the first human couple God entrusts the task of subduing the earth and exercising dominion over every living creature (cf. Gen 1:28). The dominion exercised by man over other living creatures, however, is not to be despotic or reckless; on the contrary he is to "cultivate and care for" (Gen 2:15) the goods created by God. These goods were not created by man, but have been received by him as a precious gift that the Creator has placed under his responsibility. Cultivating the earth means not abandoning it to itself; exercising dominion over it means taking care of it, as a wise king cares for his people and a shepherd his sheep.

In the Creator's plan, created realities, which are good in themselves, exist for man's use. The wonder of the mystery of man's grandeur makes the psalmist exclaim: "What is man that you are mindful of him, and the son of man that you care for him? Yet you have made him little less than god, and crown him with glory and honor. You have given him dominion over the works of your hands; you have put all things under his feet" (Ps 8:5-7).

256. *Work is part of the original state of man and precedes his fall; it is therefore not a punishment or curse.* It becomes toil and pain because of the sin of Adam and Eve, who break their relationship of trust and harmony with God (cf. Gen 3:6-8). The prohibition to eat "of the tree of the knowledge of good and evil" (Gen 2:17) reminds man that he has received everything as a gift and that he continues to be a creature and not the Creator. It was precisely this temptation that prompted the sin of Adam and Eve: "you will be like God" (Gen 3:5). They wanted absolute dominion over all things, without having to submit to the will of the Creator. From that moment, the soil becomes miserly, unrewarding, sordidly hostile (cf. Gen 4:12); only by the sweat of one's brow will it be possible to reap its fruit (cf. Gen 3:17,19). Notwithstanding the sin of our progenitors, however, the Creator's plan, the meaning of His creatures — and among these, man, who is called to cultivate and care for creation — remain unaltered.

257. *Work has a place of honor because it is a source of riches, or at least of the conditions for a decent life, and is, in principle, an effective instrument against poverty* (cf. Pr 10:4). *But one must not succumb to the temptation of making an idol of work, for the ultimate and definitive meaning of life is not to be found in work. Work is essential, but it is God — and not work — who is the origin of life and the final goal of man.* The underlying principle of wisdom in fact is the fear of the Lord. The demand of justice, which stems from it, precedes concerns for profit: "Better is a little with the fear of the Lord than great treasure and trouble with it" (Pr 15:16). "Better is a little with righteousness than great revenues with injustice" (Pr 16:8).

258. *The apex of biblical teaching on work is the commandment of the Sabbath rest.* For man, bound as he is to the necessity of work, this rest opens to the prospect of a fuller freedom, that of the eternal Sabbath (cf. Heb 4:9-10). Rest gives men and women the possibility to remember and experience anew God's work, from Creation to Redemption, to recognize themselves as his work (cf. Eph 2:10), and to give thanks for their lives and for their subsistence to him who is their author.

The memory and the experience of the Sabbath constitute a barrier against becoming slaves to work, whether voluntarily or by force, and against every kind of exploitation, hidden or evident. In fact, the Sabbath rest, besides making it possible for people to participate in the worship of God, was instituted in defence of the poor. Its function is also that of freeing people from the antisocial degeneration of human work. The Sabbath rest can even last a year; this entails the expropriation of the fruits of the earth on behalf of the poor and the suspension of the property rights of landowners: "For six years you shall sow your land and gather in its yield; but the seventh year you shall let it rest and lie fallow, that the poor of your people may eat; and what they leave the wild beasts may eat. You shall do likewise with your vineyard, and with your olive orchard" (Ex 23:10-11). This custom responds to a profound intuition: the accumulation of goods by some can sometimes cause others to be deprived of goods.

b. Jesus, a man of work

259. *In his preaching, Jesus teaches that we should appreciate work.* He himself, having "become like us in all things, devoted most of the years of his life on earth to *manual work* at the carpenter's bench"[573] in the workshop of Joseph (cf. Mt 13:55; Mk 6:3), to whom he was obedient (cf. Lk 2:51). Jesus condemns the behavior of the useless servant, who hides his talent in the ground (cf. Mt 25:14-30) and praises the faithful and prudent servant whom the Master finds hard at work at the duties entrusted to him (cf. Mt 24:46). *He describes his own mission as that of working:* "My Father *is working* still, and I *am working*" (Jn 5:17), and his disciples as workers in the harvest of the Lord, which is the evangelization of humanity (cf. Mt 9:37-38). For these workers, the general principle according to which "the laborer deserves his wages" (Lk 10:7) applies. They are therefore authorized to remain in the houses in which they have been welcomed, eating and drinking what is offered to them (cf. Lk 10:7).

---

[573] John Paul II, Encyclical Letter *Laborem Exercens*, 6: AAS 73 (1981), 591.

260. *In his preaching, Jesus teaches man not to be enslaved by work. Before all else, he must be concerned about his soul; gaining the whole world is not the purpose of his life* (cf. *Mk* 8:36). The treasures of the earth, in fact, are consumed, while those in heaven are imperishable. It is on these latter treasures that men and women must set their hearts (cf. *Mt* 6:19-21). Work, then, should not be a source of anxiety (cf. *Mt* 6:25,31,34). When people are worried and upset about many things, they run the risk of neglecting the Kingdom of God and His righteousness (cf. *Mt* 6:33), which they truly need. Everything else, work included, will find its proper place, meaning and value only if it is oriented to this one thing that is necessary and that will never be taken away (cf. *Lk* 10:40-42).

261. *During his earthly ministry Jesus works tirelessly, accomplishing powerful deeds to free men and women from sickness, suffering and death.* The Sabbath — which the Old Testament had put forth as a day of liberation and which, when observed only formally, lost its authentic significance — is reaffirmed by Jesus in its original meaning: "The Sabbath was made for man, not man for the Sabbath" (*Mk* 2:27). By healing people on this day of rest (cf. *Mt* 12:9-14; *Mk* 3:1-6; *Lk* 6:6-11, 13:10-17, 14:1-6), he wishes to show that the Sabbath is his, because he is truly the Son of God, and that it is the day on which men should dedicate themselves to God and to others. Freeing people from evil, practising brotherhood and sharing: these give to work its noblest meaning, that which allows humanity to set out on the path to the eternal Sabbath, when rest will become the festive celebration to which men and women inwardly aspire. It is precisely in orienting humanity towards this experience of God's Sabbath and of his fellowship of life that work is the inauguration on earth of the new creation.

262. *Human activity aimed at enhancing and transforming the universe can and must unleash the perfections which find their origin and model in the uncreated Word.* In fact, the Pauline and Johannine writings bring to light the Trinitarian dimension of creation, in particular the link that exists between the Son—Word — the *Logos* — and creation (cf. *Jn* 1:3; *1 Cor* 8:6; *Col* 1:15-17). Created in him and through him, redeemed by him, the universe is not a happenstance conglomeration but a "cosmos."[574] It falls to man to discover the order within it and to heed this order, bringing it to fulfilment: "In Jesus Christ the visible world which God created for man — the world that, when sin entered, 'was subjected to futility' (*Rom* 8:20; cf. *ibid.* 8:19-22) — recovers again its original link with the divine source of Wisdom and Love."[575] In this way — that is, bringing to light in ever greater measure "the unsearchable riches of Christ" (*Eph* 3:8), in creation, human work becomes a service raised to the grandeur of God.

263. *Work represents a fundamental dimension of human existence as participation not only in the act of creation but also in that of redemption.* Those who put up with the difficult rigors of work in union with Jesus cooperate, in a certain sense, with the Son of God in his work of redemption and show that they are disciples of Christ bearing

---

[574] John Paul II, Encyclical Letter *Redemptor Hominis*, 1: AAS 71 (1979), 257.
[575] John Paul II, Encyclical Letter *Redemptor Hominis*, 8: AAS 71 (1979), 270.

his cross, every day, in the activity they are called to do. In this perspective, work can be considered a means of sanctification and an enlivening of earthly realities with the Spirit of Christ.[576] Understood in this way, work is an expression of man's full humanity, in his historical condition and his eschatological orientation. Man's free and responsible action reveals his intimate relationship with the Creator and his creative power. At the same time, it is a daily aid in combating the disfigurement of sin, even when it is by the sweat of his brow that man earns his bread.

c. The duty to work

264. *The awareness that "the form of this world is passing away" (1 Cor 7:31) is not an exoneration from being involved in the world, and even less from work (cf. 2 Thes 3:7-15), which is an integral part of the human condition, although not the only purpose of life.* No Christian, in light of the fact that he belongs to a united and fraternal community, should feel that he has the right not to work and to live at the expense of others (cf. *2 Thes* 3:6-12). Rather, all are charged by the Apostle Paul to make it a point of honor to work with their own hands, so as to "be dependent on nobody" (*1 Thes* 4:12), and to practice a solidarity which is also material by sharing the fruits of their labor with "those in need" (*Eph* 4:28). Saint James defends the trampled rights of workers: "Behold, the wages of the laborers who mowed your fields, which you kept back by fraud, cry out; and the cries of the harvesters have reached the ears of the Lord of hosts" (*Jas* 5:4). Believers are to undertake their work in the style of Christ and make it an occasion for Christian witness, commanding "the respect of outsiders" (*1 Thes* 4:12).

265. *The Fathers of the Church do not consider work as an "opus servile" — although the culture of their day maintained precisely that such was the case — but always as an "opus humanum," and they tend to hold all its various expressions in honor.* By means of work, man governs the world with God; together with God he is its lord and accomplishes good things for himself and for others. Idleness is harmful to man's being, whereas activity is good for his body and soul.[577] Christians are called to work not only to provide themselves with bread, but also in acceptance of their poorer neighbors, to whom the Lord has commanded them to give food, drink, clothing, welcome, care and companionship[578] (cf. *Mt* 25:35-36). Every worker, Saint Ambrose contends, is the hand of Christ that continues to create and to do good.[579]

266. *By his work and industriousness, man — who has a share in the divine art and wisdom — makes creation, the cosmos already ordered by the Father, more beautiful.*[580] *He summons the social and community energies that increase the common good,*[581]

---

[576] Cf. *Catechism of the Catholic Church*, 2427; John Paul II, Encyclical Letter *Laborem Exercens*, 27: AAS 73 (1981), 644-647.

[577] Cf. Saint John Chrysostom, *Homily on Acts*, in *Acta Apostolorum Homiliae* 35,3: PG 60, 258.

[578] Cf. Saint Basil, *Regulae Fusius Tractatae* 42: PG 31, 1023-1027; Saint Athanasius, *Life of Saint Antony*, ch. 3: PG 26, 846.

[579] Cf. Saint Ambrose, *De Obitu Valentiniani Consolatio*, 62: PL 16, 1438.

[580] Cf. Saint Irenaeus, *Adversus Haereses*, 5, 32, 2: PL 7, 1210-1211.

[581] Cf. Theodoret of Cyr, *On Providence*, Orationes 5-7: PG 83, 625-686.

above all to the benefit of those who are neediest. Human work, directed to charity as its final goal, becomes an occasion for contemplation, it becomes devout prayer, vigilantly rising towards and in anxious hope of the day that will not end. "In this superior vision, work, a punishment and at the same time a reward of human activity, involves another relationship, the essentially religious one, which has been happily expressed in the Benedictine formula: *ora et labora!* The religious fact confers on human work an enlivening and redeeming spirituality. Such a connection between work and religion reflects the mysterious but real alliance, which intervenes between human action and the providential action of God."[582]

II. THE PROPHETIC VALUE
OF *RERUM NOVARUM*

267. *The course of history is marked by the profound transformation and the exhilarating conquests of work, but also by the exploitation of so many workers and an offence to their dignity. The Industrial Revolution presented for the Church a critical challenge to which her social Magisterium responded forcefully and prophetically, affirming universally valid and perennially relevant principles in support of workers and their rights.*

For centuries the Church's message was addressed to agricultural societies, characterized by regular cyclical rhythms. Now the Gospel had to be preached and lived in a new "*areopagus,*" in the tumult of social events in a more dynamic society, taking into account the complexities of new phenomena of the unimaginable transformations brought about by mechanisation. At the centre of the Church's pastoral concern was the ever urgent *worker question,* that is, the problem of the exploitation of workers brought about by the new industrial organization of labor, capitalistically oriented, and the problem, no less serious, of ideological manipulation — socialist and communist — of the just claims advanced by the world of labor. The reflections and warnings contained in the Encyclical *Rerum Novarum* of Pope Leo XIII are placed in this historical context.

268. *Rerum Novarum is above all a heartfelt defence of the inalienable dignity of workers,* connected with the importance of the right to property, the principle of cooperation among the social classes, the rights of the weak and the poor, the obligations of workers and employers and the right to form associations.

The orientation of ideas expressed in the Encyclical strengthened the commitment to vitalize Christian social life, which was seen in the birth and consolidation of numerous initiatives of high civic profile: groups and centres for social studies, associations, worker organizations, unions, cooperatives, rural banks, insurance groups and assistance organizations. All of this gave great momentum to labor-related legislation for the protection of workers, above all children and women; to instruction and to the improvement of salaries and cleanliness in the work environment.

269. *Starting with Rerum Novarum, the Church has never stopped considering the problems of workers within the context of a social question which has progressively taken on*

---

[582] John Paul II, Address during his Pastoral Visit to Pomezia, Italy (14 September 1979), 3: *L'Osservatore Romano,* English edition, 1 October 1979, p. 4.

worldwide dimensions.[583] The Encyclical *Laborem Exercens* enhances the personalistic vision that characterized previous social documents, indicating the need for a deeper understanding of the meaning and tasks that work entails. It does this in consideration of the fact that "fresh questions and problems are always arising, there are always fresh hopes, but also fresh fears and threats, connected with this basic dimension of human existence: man's life is built up every day from work, from work it derives its specific dignity, but at the same time work contains the unceasing measure of human toil and suffering, and also of the harm and injustice which penetrate deeply into social life within individual nations and on the international level."[584] In fact, work is the "essential key"[585] to the whole social question and is the condition not only for economic development but also for the cultural and moral development of persons, the family, society and the entire human race.

III. THE DIGNITY OF WORK

a. The subjective and objective dimensions of work

270. *Human work has a twofold significance: objective and subjective.* In the *objective sense*, it is the sum of activities, resources, instruments and technologies used by men and women to produce things, to *exercise dominion over the earth*, in the words of the Book of Genesis. In the *subjective sense*, work is the activity of the human person as a dynamic being capable of performing a variety of actions that are part of the work process and that correspond to his personal vocation: "Man has to subdue the earth and dominate it, because as the 'image of God' he is a person, that is to say, a subjective being capable of acting in a planned and rational way, capable of deciding about himself, and with a tendency to self-realization. As a person, man is therefore the subject of work."[586]

Work in the objective sense constitutes the contingent aspect of human activity, which constantly varies in its expressions according to the changing technological, cultural, social and political conditions. *Work in the subjective sense, however, represents its stable dimension,* since it does not depend on what people produce or on the type of activity they undertake, but only and exclusively on their dignity as human beings. This distinction is critical, both for understanding what the ultimate foundation of the value and dignity of work is, and with regard to the difficulties of organizing economic and social systems that respect human rights.

271. *This subjectivity gives to work its particular dignity, which does not allow that it be considered a simple commodity or an impersonal element of the apparatus for productivity.* Cut off from its lesser or greater objective value, work is an essential expression of the person, it is an *"actus personae."* Any form of materialism or economic tenet that tries to reduce the worker to being a mere instrument of production, a simple *labor force* with an exclusively material value, would end up hopelessly dis-

[583] Cf. John Paul II, Encyclical Letter *Laborem Exercens*, 2: AAS 73 (1981), 580-583.
[584] John Paul II, Encyclical Letter *Laborem Exercens*, 1: AAS 73 (1981), 579.
[585] John Paul II, Encyclical Letter *Laborem Exercens*, 3: AAS 73 (1981), 584.
[586] John Paul II, Encyclical Letter *Laborem Exercens*, 6: AAS 73 (1981), 589-590.

torting the essence of work and stripping it of its most noble and basic human finality. *The human person is the measure of the dignity* of work: "In fact there is no doubt that human work has an ethical value of its own, which clearly and directly remains linked to the fact that the one who carries it out is a person."[587]

The subjective dimension of work must take precedence over the objective dimension, because it is the dimension of the person himself who engages in work, determining its quality and consummate value. If this awareness is lacking, or if one chooses not to recognize this truth, work loses its truest and most profound meaning. In such cases — which are unfortunately all too frequent and widespread — work activity and the very technology employed become more important than the person himself and at the same time are transformed into enemies of his dignity.

272. *Human work not only proceeds from the person, but it is also essentially ordered to and has its final goal in the human person.* Independently of its objective content, work must be oriented to the subject who performs it, because the end of work, any work whatsoever, always remains man. Even if one cannot ignore the objective component of work with regard to its quality, this component must nonetheless be subordinated to the self-realization of the person, and therefore to the subjective dimension, thanks to which it is possible to affirm that *work is for man and not man for work.* "It is always man who is the purpose of work, whatever work it is that is done by man — even if the common scale of values rates it as the merest 'service,' as the most monotonous, even the most alienating work."[588]

273. *Human work also has an intrinsic social dimension.* A person's work, in fact, is naturally connected with that of other people. Today "more than ever, work is *work with others* and *work for others.* It is a matter of doing something for someone else."[589] The fruits of work offer occasions for exchange, relationship and encounter. Work, therefore, cannot be properly evaluated if its social nature is not taken into account: "For man's productive effort cannot yield its fruits unless a truly social and organic body exists, unless a social and juridical order watches over the exercise of work, unless the various occupations, being interdependent, cooperate with and mutually complete one another, and, what is still more important, unless mind, material things, and work combine and form as it were a single whole. Therefore, where the social and individual nature of work is neglected, it will be impossible to evaluate work justly and pay it according to justice."[590]

274. *Work is also "an obligation, that is to say, a duty on the part of man."*[591] Man must work, both because the Creator has commanded it and in order to respond to the need to maintain and develop his own humanity. Work is presented as a moral obligation with respect to one's neighbor, which in the first place is one's own family,

---

[587] John Paul II, Encyclical Letter *Laborem Exercens*, 6: AAS 73 (1981), 590.

[588] John Paul II, Encyclical Letter *Laborem Exercens*, 6: AAS 73 (1981), 592; cf. *Catechism of the Catholic Church*, 2428.

[589] John Paul II, Encyclical Letter *Centesimus Annus*, 31: AAS 83 (1991), 832.

[590] Pius XI, Encyclical Letter *Quadragesimo Anno*: AAS 23 (1931), 200.

[591] John Paul II, Encyclical Letter *Laborem Exercens*, 16: AAS 73 (1981), 619.

but also the society to which one belongs, the nation of which one is son or daughter, the entire human family of which one is member. We are heirs of the work of generations and at the same time shapers of the future of all who will live after us.

275. *Work confirms the profound identity of men and women created in the image and likeness of God:* "As man, through his work, becomes more and more the master of the earth, and as he confirms his dominion over the visible world, again through his work, he nevertheless remains in every case and at every phase of this process within the Creator's original ordering. And this ordering remains necessarily and indissolubly linked with the fact that man was created, as male and female, 'in the image of God.'"[592] This describes human activity in the universe: men and women are not its owner, but those to whom it is entrusted, called to reflect in their own manner of working the image of him in whose likeness they are made.

b. The relationship between labor and capital

276. *Work, because of its subjective or personal character, is superior to every other factor connected with productivity; this principle applies, in particular, with regard to capital.* The term "capital" has different meanings today. Sometimes it indicates the material means of production in a given enterprise, sometimes the financial resources employed to bring about production or used in stock market operations. One can also speak of *"human capital"* to refer to human resources, that is, to man himself in his capacity to engage in labor, to make use of knowledge and creativity, to sense the needs of his fellow workers and a mutual understanding with other members of an organization. The term *"social capital"* is also used to indicate the capacity of a collective group to work together, the fruit of investments in a mutually-binding fiduciary trust. This variety of meanings offers further material for reflecting on what the relationship between work and capital may be today.

277. *The Church's social doctrine has not failed to insist on the relationship between labor and capital,* placing in evidence both the priority of the first over the second as well as their complementarities.

Labor has an intrinsic priority over capital. "This principle directly concerns the process of production: in this process labor is always a primary efficient cause, while capital, the whole collection of means of production, remains a mere instrument or instrumental cause. This principle is an evident truth that emerges from the whole of man's historical experience."[593] This "is part of the abiding heritage of the Church's teaching."[594]

There must exist between work and capital a relationship of complementarities: the very logic inherent within the process of production shows that the two must mutually permeate one another and that there is an urgent need to create economic systems in which the opposition between capital and labor is overcome.[595]

---

[592] John Paul II, Encyclical Letter *Laborem Exercens*, 4: AAS 73 (1981), 586.
[593] John Paul II, Encyclical Letter *Laborem Exercens*, 12: AAS 73 (1981), 606.
[594] John Paul II, Encyclical Letter *Laborem Exercens*, 12: AAS 73 (1981), 608.
[595] Cf. John Paul II, Encyclical Letter *Laborem Exercens*, 13: AAS 73 (1981), 608-612.

In times when "capital" and "hired labor," within a less complicated economic system, used to identify with a certain precision not only two elements of production but also and above all two concrete social classes, the Church affirmed that both were in themselves legitimate:[596] "Capital cannot stand without labor, nor labor without capital."[597] This is a truth that applies also today, because "it is altogether false to ascribe either to capital alone or to labor alone what is achieved by the joint work of both; and it is utterly unjust that the one should arrogate unto itself what is being done, denying the effectiveness of the other."[598]

278. *In considering the relationship between labor and capital, above all with regard to the impressive transformations of our modern times, we must maintain that the "principal resource" and the "decisive factor"*[599] *at man's disposal is man himself,* and that "the integral development of the human person through work does not impede but rather promotes the greater productivity and efficiency of work itself."[600] In fact, the world of work is discovering more and more that the value of "human capital" is finding expression in the consciences of workers, in their willingness to create relationships, in their creativity, in their industriousness in promoting themselves, in their ability consciously to face new situations, to work together and to pursue common objectives. These are strictly personal qualities that belong to the subject of work more than to the objective, technical, or operational aspects of work itself. All of this entails a new perspective in the relationship between labor and capital. We can affirm that, contrary to what happened in the former organization of labor in which the subject would end up being less important than the object, than the mechanical process, in our day the subjective dimension of work tends to be more decisive and more important than the objective dimension.

279. *The relationship between labor and capital often shows traits of antagonism that take on new forms with the changing of social and economic contexts.* In the past, the origin of the conflict between capital and labor was found above all "in the fact that the workers put their powers at the disposal of the entrepreneurs, and these, following the principle of maximum profit, tried to establish the lowest possible wages for the work done by the employees."[601] *In our present day, this conflict shows aspects that are new and perhaps more disquieting:* scientific and technological progress and the globalization of markets, of themselves a source of development and progress, expose workers to the risk of being exploited by the mechanisms of the economy and by the unrestrained quest for productivity.[602]

280. *One must not fall into the error of thinking that the process of overcoming the dependence of work on material is of itself capable of overcoming alienation in the work-*

---

[596] Cf. Pius XI, Encyclical Letter *Quadragesimo Anno: AAS* 23 (1931), 194-198.
[597] Leo XIII, Encyclical Letter *Rerum Novarum: Acta Leonis XIII*, 11 (1892), 109.
[598] Pius XI, Encyclical Letter *Quadragesimo Anno: AAS* 23 (1931), 195.
[599] John Paul II, Ecyclical Letter *Centesimus Annus*, 32: *AAS* 83 (1991), 833.
[600] John Paul II, Ecyclical Letter *Centesimus Annus*, 43: *AAS* 83 (1991), 847.
[601] John Paul II, Encyclical Letter *Laborem Exercens*, 11: *AAS* 73 (1981), 604.
[602] Cf. John Paul II, Address to the Pontifical Academy of Social Sciences (6 March 1999), 2: *L'Osservatore Romano*, English edition, 17 March 1999, p. 3.

place or the alienation of labor. The reference here is not only to the many pockets of non-work, concealed work, child labor, underpaid work, exploitation of workers — all of which still persist today — but also to new, much more subtle forms of exploitation of new sources of work, to over-working, to work-as-career that often takes on more importance than other human and necessary aspects, to excessive demands of work that makes family life unstable and sometimes impossible, to a modular structure of work that entails the risk of serious repercussions on the unitary perception of one's own existence and the stability of family relationships. If people are alienated when means and ends are inverted, elements of alienation can also be found in the new contexts of work that is immaterial, light, qualitative more than quantitative, "either through increased sharing in a genuinely supportive community or through increased isolation in a maze of relationships marked by destructive competitiveness and estrangement."[603]

c. **Work, the right to participate**

281. *The relationship between labor and capital also finds expression when workers participate in ownership, management and profits.* This is an all-too-often overlooked requirement and it should be given greater consideration. "On the basis of his work each person is fully entitled to consider himself a part-owner of the great workbench where he is working with everyone else. A way towards that goal could be found by associating labor with the ownership of capital, as far as possible, and by producing a wide range of intermediate bodies with economic, social and cultural purposes. These would be bodies enjoying real autonomy with regard to public authorities, pursuing their specific aims in honest collaboration with each other and in subordination to the demands of the common good. These would be living communities both in form and in substance, as members of each body would be looked upon and treated as persons and encouraged to take an active part in the life of the body."[604] The new ways that work is organized, where knowledge is of greater account than the mere ownership of the means of production, concretely shows that work, because of its subjective character, entails the right to participate. This awareness must be firmly in place in order to evaluate the proper place of work in the process of production and to find ways of participation that are in line with the subjectivity of work in the distinctive circumstances of different concrete situations.[605]

d. **The relationship between labor and private property**

282. *The Church's social Magisterium sees an expression of the relationship between labor and capital also in the institution of private property, in the right to and the use of private property.* The right to private property is subordinated to the principle of the universal destination of goods and must not constitute a reason for impeding the work

---

[603] John Paul II, Encyclical Letter *Centesimus Annus*, 41: AAS 83 (1991), 844.
[604] John Paul II, Encyclical Letter *Laborem Exercens*, 14: AAS 73 (1981), 616.
[605] Cf. Second Vatican Ecumenical Council, Pastoral Constitution *Gaudium et Spes*, 9: AAS 58 (1966), 1031-1032.

or development of others. Property, which is acquired in the first place through work, must be placed at the service of work. This is particularly true regarding the possession of the means of production, but the same principle also concerns the goods proper to the world of finance, technology, knowledge, and personnel.

The means of production "cannot be possessed against labor, they cannot even be possessed for possession's sake."[606] It becomes illegitimate to possess them when property "is not utilized or when it serves to impede the work of others, in an effort to gain a profit which is not the result of the overall expansion of work and the wealth of society, but rather is the result of curbing them or of illicit exploitation, speculation or the breaking of solidarity among working people."[607]

283. *Private and public property, as well as the various mechanisms of the economic system, must be oriented to an economy of service to mankind,* so that they contribute to putting into effect the principle of the universal destination of goods. The issue of ownership and use of new technologies and knowledge — which in our day constitute a particular form of property that is no less important than ownership of land or capital[608] — becomes significant in this perspective. These resources, like all goods, have a *universal destination*; they too must be placed in a context of legal norms and social rules that guarantee that they will be used according to the criteria of justice, equity and respect of human rights. The new discoveries and technologies, thanks to their enormous potential, can make a decisive contribution to the promotion of social progress; but if they remain concentrated in the wealthier countries or in the hands of a small number of powerful groups, they risk becoming sources of unemployment and increasing the gap between developed and underdeveloped areas.

e. Rest from work

284. *Rest from work is a right.*[609] As God "rested on the seventh day from all the work which he had done" (*Gen* 2:2), so too men and women, created in his image, are to enjoy sufficient rest and free time that will allow them to tend to their family, cultural, social and religious life.[610] The institution of the Lord's Day contributes to this.[611] On Sundays and other Holy Days of Obligation, believers must refrain from "engaging in work or activities that hinder the worship owed to God, the joy proper to the Lord's Day, the performance of the works of mercy, and the appropriate relaxation of mind and body."[612] Family needs and service of great importance to society constitute legitimate excuses from the obligation of Sunday rest, but these must not create habits that are prejudicial to religion, family life or health.

[606] John Paul II, Encyclical Letter *Laborem Exercens*, 14: AAS 73 (1981), 613.
[607] John Paul II, Encyclical Letter *Centesimus Annus*, 43: AAS 83 (1991), 847.
[608] Cf. John Paul II, Encyclical Letter *Centesimus Annus*, 32 AAS 83 (1991), 832-833.
[609] Cf. John Paul II, Encyclical Letter *Laborem Exercens*, 19: AAS 73 (1981), 625-629; John Paul II, Encyclical Letter *Centesimus Annus*, 9: AAS 83 (1991), 804.
[610] Cf. Second Vatican Ecumenical Council, Pastoral Constitution *Gaudium et Spes*, 67: AAS 58 (1966), 1088-1089.
[611] Cf. *Catechism of the Catholic Church*, 2184.
[612] *Catechism of the Catholic Church*, 2185.

285. *Sunday is a day that should be made holy by charitable activity, devoting time to family and relatives, as well as to the sick, the infirm and the elderly.* One must not forget the "brethren who have the same needs and the same rights, yet cannot rest from work because of poverty and misery."[613] *Moreover, Sunday is an appropriate time for the reflection, silence, study and meditation that foster the growth of the interior Christian life.* Believers should distinguish themselves on this day too by their moderation, avoiding the excesses and certainly the violence that mass entertainment sometimes occasions.[614] The Lord's Day should always be lived as a day of liberation that allows us to take part in "the festal gathering and the assembly of the firstborn who are enrolled in heaven" (cf. *Heb* 12:22-23), anticipating thus the celebration of the definitive Passover in the glory of heaven.[615]

286. *Public authorities have the duty to ensure that, for reasons of economic productivity, citizens are not denied time for rest and divine worship.* Employers have an analogous obligation regarding their employees.[616] Christians, in respect of religious freedom and of the common good of all, should seek to have Sundays and the Church's Holy Days recognized as legal holidays. "They have to give everyone a public example of prayer, respect and joy, and defend their traditions as a precious contribution to the spiritual life of society."[617] "Every Christian should avoid making unnecessary demands on others that would hinder them from observing the Lord's Day."[618]

IV. THE RIGHT TO WORK

a. Work is necessary

287. *Work is a fundamental right and a good for mankind,*[619] *a useful good, worthy of man because it is an appropriate way for him to give expression to and enhance his human dignity. The Church teaches the value of work not only because it is always something that belongs to the person but also because of its nature as something necessary.*[620] Work is needed to form and maintain a family,[621] to have a right to property,[622] to contribute to the common good of the human family.[623] In considering

---

[613] *Catechism of the Catholic Church*, 2186.
[614] Cf. *Catechism of the Catholic Church*, 2187.
[615] Cf. John Paul II, Apostolic Letter *Dies Domini*, 26: AAS 90 (1998), 729: "In celebrating Sunday, both the 'first' and the 'eighth' day, the Christian is led towards the goal of eternal life."
[616] Cf. Leo XIII, Encyclical Letter *Rerum Novarum: Acta Leonis XIII*, 11 (1892), 110.
[617] *Catechism of the Catholic Church*, 2188.
[618] *Catechism of the Catholic Church*, 2187.
[619] Cf. Second Vatican Ecumenical Council, Pastoral Constitution *Gaudium et Spes*, 26: AAS 58 (1966), 1046-1047; John Paul II, Encyclical Letter *Laborem Exercens*, 9, 18: AAS 73 (1981), 598-600, 622-625; John Paul II, Address to the Pontifical Academy of Social Sciences (25 April 1997), 3: *L'Osservatore Romano*, English edition, 14 May 1997, p. 5; John Paul II, Message for the 1999 World Day of Peace, 8: AAS 91 (1999), 382-383.
[620] Cf. Leo XIII, Encyclical Letter *Rerum Novarum: Acta Leonis XIII*, 11 (1892), 128.
[621] Cf. John Paul II, Encyclical Letter *Laborem Exercens*, 10: AAS 73 (1981), 600-602.
[622] Cf. Leo XIII, Encyclical Letter *Rerum Novarum: Acta Leonis XIII*, 11 (1892), 103; John Paul II, Encyclical Letter *Laborem Exercens*, 14: AAS 73 (1981), 612-616; John Paul II, Encyclical Letter *Centesimus Annus*, 31: AAS 83 (1991), 831-832.
[623] Cf. John Paul II, Encyclical Letter *Laborem Exercens*, 16: AAS 73 (1981), 618-620.

the moral implications that the question of work has for social life, the Church cannot fail to indicate unemployment as a "real social disaster,"[624] above all with regard to the younger generations.

288. *Work is a good belonging to all people and must be made available to all who are capable of engaging in it. "Full employment" therefore remains a mandatory objective for every economic system oriented towards justice and the common good.* A society in which the right to work is thwarted or systematically denied, and in which economic policies do not allow workers to reach satisfactory levels of employment, "cannot be justified from an ethical point of view, nor can that society attain social peace."[625] An important role and, consequently, a particular and grave responsibility in this area falls to "indirect employers,"[626] that is, those subjects — persons or institutions of various types — in a position to direct, at the national or international level, policies concerning labor and the economy.

289. *The planning capacity of a society oriented towards the common good and looking to the future is measured also and above all on the basis of the employment prospects that it is able to offer.* The high level of unemployment, the presence of obsolete educational systems and of persistent difficulties in gaining access to professional formation and the job market represent, especially for many young people, a huge obstacle on the road to human and professional fulfilment. In fact, those who are unemployed or underemployed suffer the profound negative consequences that such a situation creates in a personality and they run the risk of being marginalized within society, of becoming victims of social exclusion.[627] In general, this is the drama that strikes not only young people, but also women, less specialized workers, the persons with disabilities, immigrants, ex-convicts, the illiterate, all those who face greater difficulties in the attempt to find their place in the world of employment.

290. *Maintaining employment depends more and more on one's professional capabilities.*[628] *Instructional and educational systems must not neglect human or technological formation, which are necessary for gainfully fulfilling one's responsibilities.* The ever more widespread necessity of changing jobs many times in one's lifetime makes it imperative that the educational system encourage people to be open to on-going updating and re-training. Young people should be taught to act upon their own initiative, to accept the responsibility of facing with adequate competencies the risks connected with a fluid economic context that is often unpredictable in the way it evolves.[629] Equally indispensable is the task of offering suitable courses of formation for adults seeking re-training and for the unemployed. More generally,

---

[624] John Paul II, Encyclical Letter *Laborem Exercens*, 18: AAS 73 (1981), 623.

[625] John Paul II, Encyclical Letter *Centesimus Annus*, 43: AAS 83 (1991), 848; cf. *Catechism of the Catholic Church*, 2433.

[626] Cf. John Paul II, Encyclical Letter *Laborem Exercens*, 17: AAS 73 (1981), 620-622.

[627] Cf. *Catechism of the Catholic Church*, 2436.

[628] Cf. Second Vatican Ecumenical Council, Pastoral Constitution *Gaudium et Spes*, 66: AAS 58 (1966), 1087-1088.

[629] Cf. John Paul II, Encyclical Letter *Laborem Exercens*, 12: AAS 73 (1981), 605-608.

people need concrete forms of support as they journey in the world of work, starting precisely with formational systems, so that it will be less difficult to cope with periods of change, uncertainty and instability.

b. The role of the State and civil society in promoting the right to work

291. *Employment problems challenge the responsibility of the State, whose duty it is to promote active employment policies*, that is, policies that will encourage the creation of employment opportunities within the national territory, providing the production sector with incentives to this end. The duty of the State does not consist so much in directly guaranteeing the right to work of every citizen, making the whole of economic life very rigid and restricting individual free initiative, as much as in the duty to "sustain business activities by creating conditions which will ensure job opportunities, by stimulating those activities where they are lacking or by supporting them in moments of crisis."[630]

292. *Given the quickly developing global dimensions of economic-financial relationships and of the labor market, there is a need to promote an effective international cooperation among States* by means of treaties, agreements and common plans of action that safeguard the right to work, even in the most critical phases of the economic cycle, at the national and international levels. It is necessary to be aware of the fact that human work is a right upon which the promotion of social justice and civil peace directly depend. Important tasks in this regard fall to international organizations and to labor unions. Joining forces in the most suitable ways, they must strive first of all to create "an ever more tightly knit fabric of juridical norms that protect the work of men, women and youth, ensuring its proper remuneration."[631]

293. *To promote the right to work it is important today, as in the days* of Rerum Novarum, *that there be "an open process by which society organize[s] itself."*[632] Meaningful testimonies and examples of self-organization can be found in the numerous initiatives, business and social, characterized by forms of participation, cooperation and self-management that manifest the joining of energies in solidarity. These are offered to the market as a multifaceted sector of work activity whose mark of distinction is the special attention given to the relational components of the goods produced and of the services rendered in many areas: instruction, health care, basic social services and culture. The initiatives of this so-called "third sector" represent an ever more important opportunity for the development of labor and the economy.

c. The family and the right to work

294. *Work is "a foundation for the formation of family life, which is a natural right and something that man is called to."*[633] It ensures a means of subsistence and serves as

---

[630] John Paul II, Encyclical Letter *Centesimus Annus*, 48: AAS 83 (1991), 853.
[631] Paul VI, Address to the International Labor Organization (10 June 1969), 21: AAS 61 (1969), 500; cf. John Paul II, Address to the International Labor Organization (15 June 1982), 13: AAS 74 (1982), 1004-1005.
[632] John Paul II, Encyclical Letter *Centesimus Annus*, 16: AAS 83 (1991), 813.
[633] John Paul II, Encyclical Letter *Laborem Exercens*, 10: AAS 73 (1981), 600.

a guarantee for raising children.[634] Family and work, so closely interdependent in the experience of the vast majority of people, deserve finally to be considered in a more realistic light, with an attention that seeks to understand them together, without the limits of a strictly private conception of the family or a strictly economic view of work. In this regard, it is necessary that businesses, professional organizations, labor unions and the State promote policies that, from an employment point of view, do not penalize but rather support the family nucleus. In fact, family life and work mutually affect one another in different ways. Travelling great distances to the workplace, working two jobs, physical and psychological fatigue all reduce the time devoted to the family.[635] Situations of unemployment have material and spiritual repercussions on families, just as tensions and family crises have negative influences on attitudes and productivity in the area of work.

d. Women and the right to work

295. *The feminine genius is needed in all expressions in the life of society, therefore the presence of women in the workplace must also be guaranteed.* The first indispensable step in this direction is the concrete possibility of access to professional formation. *The recognition and defence of women's rights in the context of work generally depend on the organization of work, which must take into account the dignity and vocation of women,* whose "true advancement . . . requires that labor should be structured in such a way that women do not have to pay for their advancement by abandoning what is specific to them."[636] This issue is the measure of the *quality of society* and its *effective defence* of women's right to work.

The persistence of many forms of discrimination offensive to the dignity and vocation of women in the area of work is due to a long series of conditioning that penalizes women, who have seen "their prerogatives misrepresented" and themselves "relegated to the margins of society and even reduced to servitude."[637] These difficulties, unfortunately, have not been overcome, as is demonstrated wherever there are situations that demoralize women, making them objects of a very real exploitation. An urgent need to recognize effectively the rights of women in the workplace is seen especially under the aspects of pay, insurance and social security.[638]

e. Child labor

296. *Child labor, in its intolerable forms, constitutes a kind of violence that is less obvious than others but it is not for this reason any less terrible.*[639] This is a violence that,

---

[634] Cf. John Paul II, Encyclical Letter *Laborem Exercens*, 10: AAS 73 (1981), 600-602; John Paul II, Apostolic Exhortation *Familiaris Consortio*, 23: AAS 74 (1982), 107-109.

[635] Cf. Holy See, *Charter of the Rights of the Family*, art. 10, Vatican Polyglot Press, Vatican City 1983, p. 13-14.

[636] John Paul II, Encyclical Letter *Laborem Exercens*, 19: AAS 73 (1981), 628.

[637] John Paul II, *Letter to Women*, 3: AAS 87 (1995), 804.

[638] Cf. John Paul II, Apostolic Exhortation *Familiaris Consortio*, 24: AAS 74 (1982), 109-110.

[639] Cf. John Paul II, Message for the 1996 World Day of Peace, 5: AAS 88 (1996), 106-107.

beyond all political, economic and legal implications, remains essentially a moral problem. Pope Leo XIII issued the warning: "in regard to children, great care should be taken not to place them in workshops and factories until their bodies and minds are sufficiently developed. For, just as very rough weather destroys the buds of spring, so does too early an experience of life's hard toil blight the young promise of a child's faculties, and render any true education impossible."[640] After more than a hundred years, the blight of child labor has not yet been overcome.

Even with the knowledge that, at least for now, in certain countries the contribution made by child labor to family income and the national economy is indispensable, and that in any event certain forms of part-time work can prove beneficial for children themselves, the Church's social doctrine condemns the increase in "the exploitation of children in the workplace in conditions of veritable slavery."[641] This exploitation represents a serious violation of human dignity, with which every person, "no matter how small or how seemingly unimportant in utilitarian terms,"[642] is endowed.

f. Immigration and work

297. *Immigration can be a resource for development rather than an obstacle to it.* In the modern world, where there are still grave inequalities between rich countries and poor countries, and where advances in communications quickly reduce distances, the immigration of people looking for a better life is on the increase. These people come from less privileged areas of the earth and their arrival in developed countries is often perceived as a threat to the high levels of well-being achieved thanks to decades of economic growth. In most cases, however, immigrants fill a labor need which would otherwise remain unfilled in sectors and territories where the local workforce is insufficient or unwilling to engage in the work in question.

298. *Institutions in host countries must keep careful watch to prevent the spread of the temptation to exploit foreign laborers, denying them the same rights enjoyed by nationals, rights that are to be guaranteed to all without discrimination.* Regulating immigration according to criteria of equity and balance[643] is one of the indispensable conditions for ensuring that immigrants are integrated into society with the guarantees required by recognition of their human dignity. Immigrants are to be received as persons and helped, together with their families, to become a part of societal life.[644] In this context, the *right of reuniting families should be respected and promot-*

---

[640] Leo XIII, Encyclical Letter *Rerum Novarum: Acta Leonis XIII*, 11 (1892), 129.

[641] John Paul II, Message for the 1998 World Day of Peace, 6: AAS 90 (1998), 153.

[642] John Paul II, Message to the Secretary-General of the United Nations on the occasion of the World Summit for Children (22 September 1990): AAS 83 (1991), 360.

[643] Cf. John Paul II, Message for the 2001 World Day of Peace, 13: AAS 91 (2001), 241; Pontifical Council "Cor Unum" - Pontifical Council for the Pastoral Care of Migrants and Itinerant People, *Refugees: a Challenge to Solidarity*, 6: Libreria Editrice Vaticana, Vatican City 1992, p. 10.

[644] Cf. *Catechism of the Catholic Church*, 2241.

ed.[645] At the same time, conditions that foster increased work opportunities in people's place of origin are to be promoted as much as possible.[646]

g. The world of agriculture and the right to work

299. *Agricultural labor merits special attention, given the important social, cultural and economic role that it continues to play in the economic systems of many countries, and also considering the many problems that need to be met in the context of an ever more globalized economy as well as its growing significance in safeguarding the natural environment.* "Radical and urgent changes are therefore needed in order to restore to agriculture — and to rural people — their just value as the basis for a healthy economy, within the social community's development as a whole."[647]

The profound and radical changes underway at the social and cultural levels also in agriculture and in the more expansive rural world urgently call for a thorough examination of the meaning of agricultural work in its many different dimensions. This is a challenge of great importance that must be met with agricultural and environmental policies that are capable of overcoming a concept of welfare continuing from the past and of developing new perspectives for modern agriculture that is in a position to play a significant role in social and economic life.

300. *In some countries a redistribution of land as part of sound policies of agrarian reform is indispensable, in order to overcome the obstacles that an unproductive system of latifundium — condemned by the Church's social doctrine*[648] *— places on the path of genuine economic development.* "Developing countries can effectively counter the present process under which land ownership is being concentrated in a few hands if they face up to certain situations that constitute real structural problems, for example legislative deficiencies and delays regarding both recognition of land titles and in relation to the credit market, a lack of concern over agricultural research and training, and neglect of social services and infrastructures in rural areas."[649] Agrarian reform therefore becomes a moral obligation more than a political necessity, since the failure to enact such reform is a hindrance in these countries to the benefits arising from the opening of markets and, generally, from the abundant growth opportunities offered by the current process of globalization.[650]

---

[645] Cf. Holy See, *Charter of the Rights of the Family*, art. 12, Vatican Polyglot Press, Vatican City 1983, p. 14; John Paul II, Apostolic Exhortation *Familiaris Consortio*, 77: AAS 74 (1982), 175-178.

[646] Cf. Second Vatican Ecumenical Council, Pastoral Constitution *Gaudium et Spes*, 66: AAS 58 (1966), 1087-1088; John Paul II, Message for the 1993 World Day of Peace, 3: AAS 85 (1993), 431-433.

[647] John Paul II, Encyclical Letter *Laborem Exercens*, 21: AAS 73 (1981), 634.

[648] Cf Paul VI, Encyclical Letter *Populorum Progressio*, 23: AAS 59 (1967), 268-269.

[649] Pontifical Council for Justice and Peace, *Towards a Better Distribution of Land. The Challenge of Agrarian Reform* (23 November 1997), 13: Libreria Editrice Vaticana, Vatican City 1997, p. 18.

[650] Cf. Pontifical Council for Justice and Peace, *Towards a Better Distribution of Land. The Challenge of Agrarian Reform* (23 November 1997), 35: Libreria Editrice Vaticana, Vatican City 1997, p. 33.

V. THE RIGHTS OF WORKERS

a. The dignity of workers and the respect for their rights

301. *The rights of workers, like all other rights, are based on the nature of the human person and on his transcendent dignity.* The Church's social Magisterium has seen fit to list some of these rights, in the hope that they will be recognized in juridical systems: the right to a just wage;[651] the right to rest;[652] the right "to a working environment and to manufacturing processes which are not harmful to the workers' physical health or to their moral integrity";[653] the right that one's personality in the workplace should be safeguarded "without suffering any affront to one's conscience or personal dignity";[654] the right to appropriate subsidies that are necessary for the subsistence of unemployed workers and their families;[655] the right to a pension and to insurance for old age, sickness, and in case of work-related accidents;[656] the right to social security connected with maternity;[657] the right to assemble and form associations.[658] These rights are often infringed, as is confirmed by the sad fact of workers who are underpaid and without protection or adequate representation. It often happens that work conditions for men, women and children, especially in developing countries, are so inhumane that they are an offence to their dignity and compromise their health.

b. The right to fair remuneration and income distribution

302. *Remuneration is the most important means for achieving justice in work relationships.*[659] The "just wage is the legitimate fruit of work."[660] They commit grave injustice who refuse to pay a just wage or who do not give it in due time and in proportion to the work done (cf. Lv 19:13; Dt 24:14-15; Jas 5:4). A salary is the instrument that permits the laborer to gain access to the goods of the earth. "Remuneration for labor is to be such that man may be furnished the means to cultivate worthily his own material, social, cultural, and spiritual life and that of his dependents, in view of the function and productiveness of each one, the conditions of the factory or workshop, and the common good."[661] The simple agree-

---

[651] Cf. John Paul II, Encyclical Letter *Laborem Exercens*, 19: AAS 73 (1981), 625-629.

[652] Cf. John Paul II, Encyclical Letter *Laborem Exercens*, 19: AAS 73 (1981), 625-629.

[653] John Paul II, Encyclical Letter *Laborem Exercens*, 19: AAS 73 (1981), 629.

[654] John Paul II, Encyclical Letter *Centesimus Annus*, 15: AAS 83 (1991), 812.

[655] Cf. John Paul II, Encyclical Letter *Laborem Exercens*, 18: AAS 73 (1981), 622-625.

[656] Cf. John Paul II, Encyclical Letter *Laborem Exercens*, 19: AAS 73 (1981), 625-629.

[657] Cf. John Paul II, Encyclical Letter *Laborem Exercens*, 19: AAS 73 (1981), 625-629.

[658] Cf. Leo XIII, Encyclical Letter *Rerum Novarum: Acta Leonis XIII*, 11 (1892), 135; Pius XI, Encyclical Letter *Quadragesimo Anno*: AAS 23 (1931), 186; Pius XII, Encyclical Letter *Sertum Laetitiae*: AAS 31 (1939), 643; John XXIII, Encyclical Letter *Pacem in Terris*: AAS 55 (1963), 262-263; Second Vatican Ecumenical Council, Pastoral Constitution *Gaudium et Spes*, 68: AAS 58 (1966), 1089-1090; John Paul II, Encyclical Letter *Laborem Exercens*, 20: AAS 73 (1981), 629-632; John Paul II, Encyclical Letter *Centesimus Annus*, 7: AAS 83 (1991), 801-802.

[659] Cf. John Paul II, Encyclical Letter *Laborem Exercens*, 19: AAS 73 (1981), 625-629.

[660] *Catechism of the Catholic Church*, 2434; cf. Pius XI, Encyclical Letter *Quadragesimo Anno*: AAS 23 (1931), 198-202: "The Just Wage" is the title of Chapter Four (nos. 65-76) of Part Two.

[661] Second Vatican Ecumenical Council, Pastoral Constitution *Gaudium et Spes*, 67: AAS 58 (1966), 1088-1089.

ment between employee and employer with regard to the amount of pay to be received is not sufficient for the agreed-upon salary to qualify as a "just wage," because a just wage "must not be below the level of subsistence" [662] of the worker: natural justice precedes and is above the freedom of the contract.

303. *The economic well-being of a country is not measured exclusively by the quantity of goods it produces but also by taking into account the manner in which they are produced and the level of equity in the distribution of income,* which should allow everyone access to what is necessary for their personal development and perfection. An equitable distribution of income is to be sought on the basis of criteria not merely of commutative justice but also of social justice that is, considering, beyond the objective value of the work rendered, the human dignity of the subjects who perform it. Authentic economic well-being is pursued also by means of suitable *social policies for the redistribution of income* which, taking general conditions into account, look at merit as well as at the need of each citizen.

c. **The right to strike**

304. *The Church's social doctrine recognizes the legitimacy of striking* "when it cannot be avoided, or at least when it is necessary to obtain a proportionate benefit,"[663] when every other method for the resolution of disputes has been ineffectual.[664] Striking, one of the most difficult victories won by labor union associations, may be defined as the collective and concerted refusal on the part of workers to continue rendering their services, for the purpose of obtaining by means of such pressure exerted on their employers, the State or on public opinion either better working conditions or an improvement in their social status. Striking "as a kind of ultimatum"[665] must always be a peaceful method for making demands and fighting for one's rights; it becomes "morally unacceptable when accompanied by violence, or when objectives are included that are not directly linked to working conditions or are contrary to the common good."[666]

VI. SOLIDARITY AMONG WORKERS

a. **The importance of unions**

305. *The Magisterium recognizes the fundamental role played by labor unions, whose existence is connected with the right to form associations or unions to defend the vital interests of workers employed in the various professions.* Unions "grew up from the struggle of the workers — workers in general but especially the industrial workers

---

[662] Leo XIII, Encyclical Letter *Rerum Novarum: Acta Leonis XIII*, 11 (1892), 131.
[663] *Catechism of the Catholic Church*, 2435.
[664] Cf. Second Vatican Ecumenical Council, Pastoral Constitution *Gaudium et Spes*, 68: AAS 58 (1966), 1089-1090; John Paul II, Encyclical Letter *Laborem Exercens*, 20: AAS 73 (1981), 629-632; *Catechism of the Catholic Church*, 2430.
[665] John Paul II, Encyclical Letter *Laborem Exercens*, 20: AAS 73 (1981), 632.
[666] *Catechism of the Catholic Church*, 2435.

— to protect their just rights *vis-à-vis* the entrepreneurs and the owners of the means of production."[667] Such organizations, while pursuing their specific purpose with regard to the common good, are a positive influence for social order and solidarity, and are therefore an *indispensable element of social life*. The recognition of workers' rights has always been a difficult problem to resolve because this recognition takes place within complex historical and institutional processes, and still today it remains incomplete. This makes the practice of authentic solidarity among workers more fitting and necessary than ever.

306. *The Church's social doctrine teaches that relations within the world of work must be marked by cooperation: hatred and attempts to eliminate the other are completely unacceptable.* This is also the case because in every social system both "labor" and "capital" represent indispensable components of the process of production. In light of this understanding, the Church's social doctrine "does not hold that unions are no more than a reflection of the 'class' structure of society and that they are a mouthpiece for a class struggle which inevitably governs social life."[668] *Properly speaking, unions are promoters of the struggle for social justice*, for the rights of workers in their particular professions: "This struggle should be seen as a normal endeavor 'for' the just good . . . not a struggle 'against' others."[669] Being first of all instruments of solidarity and justice, unions may not misuse the tools of contention; because of what they are called to do, they must overcome the temptation of believing that all workers should be union-members, they must be capable of self-regulation and be able to evaluate the consequences that their decisions will have on the common good.[670]

307. *Beyond their function of defending and vindicating, unions have the duty of acting as representatives working for "the proper arrangement of economic life" and of educating the social consciences of workers* so that they will feel that they have an active role, according to their proper capacities and aptitudes, in the whole task of economic and social development and in the attainment of the universal common good.[671] Unions and other forms of labor associations are to work in cooperation with other social entities and are to take an interest in the management of public matters. Union organizations have the duty to exercise influence in the political arena, making it duly sensitive to labor problems and helping it to work so that workers' rights are respected. Unions do not, however, have the character of "political parties" struggling for power, and they should not be forced to submit to the decisions of political parties nor be too closely linked to them. "In such a situation they easily lose contact with their specific role, which is to secure the just rights of workers within the framework of the common good of the whole of society; instead they become *an instrument used for other purposes*."[672]

---

[667] John Paul II, Encyclical Letter *Laborem Exercens*, 20: AAS 73 (1981), 629.
[668] John Paul II, Encyclical Letter *Laborem Exercens*, 20: AAS 73 (1981), 630.
[669] John Paul II, Encyclical Letter *Laborem Exercens*, 20: AAS 73 (1981), 630.
[670] Cf. *Catechism of the Catholic Church*, 2430.
[671] Cf. Second Vatican Ecumenical Council, Pastoral Constitution *Gaudium et Spes*, 68: AAS 58 (1966), 1090.
[672] John Paul II, Encyclical Letter *Laborem Exercens*, 20: AAS 73 (1981), 631.

b. New forms of solidarity

308. *The modern socio-economic context, characterized by ever more rapid processes of economic and financial globalization, prompts unions to engage in renewal. Today, unions are called to act in new ways,*[673] widening the scope of their activity of solidarity so that protection is afforded not only to the traditional categories of workers, but also to workers with *non-standard* or limited-time contracts, employees whose jobs are threatened by business mergers that occur with ever increasing frequency, even at the international level; to those who do not have a job, to immigrants, seasonal workers and those who, because they have not had professional updating, have been dismissed from the labor market and cannot be re-admitted without proper re-training.

Given the changes that have taken place in the world of work, solidarity can be recovered, and perhaps with a firmer foundation in respect to the past, if the effort is made to rediscover the subjective value of work: "there must be continued study of the subject of work and of the subject's living conditions." For this reason, "there is a need for ever new movements of solidarity of the workers and with the workers."[674]

309. *Pursuing "new forms of solidarity,"*[675] *workers' associations must focus their efforts on the acceptance of greater responsibilities* not only in relation to the traditional mechanisms for redistribution but also in relation to the production of wealth and the creation of social, political and cultural conditions which will permit all who are able and willing to work to exercise their right to work in full respect for their dignity as workers. The gradual obsolescence of organizational models based on salaried workers in big business makes it fitting to update the norms and systems of social security that have traditionally protected workers and guaranteed their fundamental rights.

VII. THE "NEW THINGS"
OF THE WORLD OF WORK

a. An epoch-making phase of transition

310. *The phenomenon of globalization is one of the most important causes of the current change in the organization of work. This phenomenon brings about new forms of production where plants are located away from where strategies are decided and far from the markets where the goods are consumed.* There are two primary factors driving this phenomenon: the extraordinary speed of communication no longer limited by space or time, and the relative ease with which merchandise and people are transported from one part of the world to another. This entails a fundamental consequence for processes of production, as property is ever further removed and often

---

[673] Cf. John Paul II, Address to the International Conference for Union Representatives (2 December 1996), 4: *L'Osservatore Romano*, English edition, 11 December 1996, p. 8.

[674] John Paul II, Encyclical Letter *Laborem Exercens*, 8: AAS 73 (1981), 597.

[675] John Paul II, Message to the Participants in the International Symposium on Work (14 Sepember 2001), 4: *L'Osservatore Romano*, English edition, 17 October 2001, p. 3.

indifferent to the social effects of the decisions made. On the other hand, if it is true that globalization is neither good nor bad in itself, but depends on how it is used,[676] it must be affirmed that *a globalization of safeguards, minimum essential rights and equity is necessary.*

311. *One of the most significant characteristics of the new organization of work is the physical fragmentation of the cycle of production, promoted in order to obtain greater efficiency and greater profits.* In this perspective, the traditional space-time coordinates within which the cycle of production formerly took place undergoes an unprecedented tranformation that determines a change in the structure of work itself. All of this has significant consequences for the life of individuals and communities subjected to radical changes both on the level of material conditions and of culture and values. On the worldwide and local levels, this phenomenon presently involves millions of people, independently of their profession, social standing or cultural preparation. The reorganization of time, its standardization and the changes currently underway in the use of space — comparable in extent to the first Industrial Revolution insofar as they involve every sector of production, on every continent, independent of their level of development — are therefore to be considered a crucial challenge, also at the level of ethics and culture, in the area of defining a renewed system for the defence of work.

312. *The globalization of the economy, with the liberalization of markets, the stiffening of competition, the increase of specialized businesses in providing goods and services, requires greater flexibility in the labor market and in organizing and managing production processes.* In making an evaluation in this delicate area, it seems appropriate to lend greater moral, cultural and planning attention to giving direction to social and political activity concerning issues connected with the identity and content of new work, in a market and an economy that are themselves new. In fact, the changes in the labor market are often an effect of the change to which work has been subjected, and not one of its causes.

313. *Work, above all within the economic systems of the more developed countries, is going through a phase that marks the passage from an industrial-type economy to an economy essentially built on services and technological innovations.* In other words, what is happening is that services and activities with a predominant informational content show a much greater rapidity of growth than traditional primary and secondary sectors. This entails far-ranging consequences for organizing the production and exchange of goods, defining job requirements and providing effective social protection.

Thanks to technological innovations, the world of work is being enriched with new professions while others are disappearing. In fact, in the present phase of transition there is a continuous movement of workers from the industrial sector to that of services. As the economic and social models connected with big factories and

---

[676] Cf. John Paul II, Address to the Pontifical Academy of Social Sciences (27 April 2001), 2: *AAS* 93 (2001), 599.

with a homogenous working class lose ground, the employment prospects in the third sector improve. In particular, there is an increase in job activity in the area of personal services, in part-time, temporary and "non-traditional" employment, that is, work that does not fit into a category that would classify the job-holder either as an employee or as self-employed.

314. *The transition currently underway signals the move from dependent work with no prescribed time limit, understood as a stable job, to a series of jobs characterized by many kinds of work activities,* from a world of a unified, definite and recognized concept of work to a universe of jobs where there is great variety, fluidity and a wealth of promises. There are also many questions of concern, especially with regard to the growing uncertainty of work, the persistent presence of structural unemployment and the inadequacy of current systems of social security. The demands of competition, technological innovation and the complexities of financial fluxes must be brought into harmony with the defence of workers and their rights.

This uncertainty and instability involve not only the labor conditions of workers in more developed countries but affect also, and above all, the less advanced economic realities in developing countries and countries with economies in transition. This latter category, besides the complicated problems associated with changing models of the economy and of production, must deal daily with the difficult adjustment required by the current phenomenon of globalization. The situation is particularly dramatic for the world of work, affected by vast and radical cultural and structural changes in contexts that are often without legislative support and lack programmes of professional training and social assistance.

315. *The decentralization of production, which assigns to smaller companies several tasks previously undertaken by larger production interests, gives vitality and new energy to the area of small and medium-sized businesses.* In this way, alongside traditional artisans there emerge new businesses characterized by small production interests at work in modern production sectors or in decentralized activities of larger companies. Many activities that yesterday required the hiring of employees are today carried out in new ways that encourage independent labor and are therefore marked by higher risk and greater responsibility.

Work in small and medium-sized businesses, the work of artisans and independent work can represent an occasion to make the actual work experience more human, both in terms of the possibility of establishing positive personal relationships in smaller-sized communities and in terms of the opportunities for greater initiative and industriousness. In these sectors, however, there are more than just a few cases of unjust treatment, of poorly paid and, above all, uncertain work.

316. *In developing countries, moreover, there has been an expansion in recent years of "informal" and "hidden" economic activities. This represents a promising sign of economic growth and development, but it raises many ethical and legal problems.* In fact, the significant increase in job opportunities in the context of such activities is owed to the lack of specialization in a large segment of the local work force and to disorderly growth in formal economic sectors. Large numbers of people are thus forced to work under seriously distressing conditions and in situations that lack the rules necessary for safeguarding workers' dignity. Levels of productivity, income and living standards are extremely low and often inadequate for guaranteeing to workers and their families the minimum level of subsistence.

b. Social doctrine and the "new things"

317. *Given these impressive "new things" in the world of work, the Church's social doctrine recommends first of all to avoid the error of insisting that the current changes take place in a deterministic manner.* The decisive factor and "referee" of this complex phase of change is *once more the human person*, who must remain the true protagonist of his work. He can and must take on in a creative and responsible fashion the present innovations and re-organizations, so that they lead to the growth of the person, the family, society and the entire human family.[677] Enlightenment for all can be found in the appeal of the *subjective dimension of work*, which according to the teaching of the Church's social doctrine must be given due priority, because human work "proceeds directly from persons created in the image of God and called to prolong the work of creation by subduing the earth."[678]

318. *Mechanistic and economistic interpretations of the activity of production, however prevalent and influential they may be, have been outdated by scientific analysis of the problems connected with work.* More today than in the past, these conceptions are seen to be completely inadequate for interpreting the facts, which everyday demonstrate more and more the meaning of work as a free and creative activity of the human person. Concrete findings should also provide the impetus for the immediate dismissal of theoretical perspectives and restrictive, insufficient operative criteria concerning the present dynamics. These prove to be intrinsically incapable of identifying the broad spectrum of concrete and urgent human needs that go well beyond merely economic categories. The Church is well aware and has always taught that men and women, unlike every other living being, have certain needs that are not restricted merely to "having,"[679] because their nature and vocation are inextricably linked with the Transcendent One. The human person faces the adventure of the transformation of things through work in order to satisfy requirements and needs that are first of all material, but he does so in obedience to an impulse that pushes him ever further beyond the results obtained, to the quest of what will correspond most intimately to his vital inner needs.

319. *The historical forms in which human work is expressed change, but not its permanent requirements, which are summed up in the respect of the inalienable human rights of workers.* Faced with the risk of denying these rights, *new forms of solidarity* must

---

[677] Cf. John Paul II, Encyclical Letter *Laborem Exercens*, 10: AAS 73 (1981), 600-602.
[678] *Catechism of the Catholic Church*, 2427.
[679] Cf. Second Vatican Ecumenical Council, Pastoral Constitution *Gaudium et Spes*, 35: AAS 58 (1966), 1053; Paul VI, Encyclical Letter *Populorum Progressio*, 19: AAS 59 (1967), 266-267; John Paul II, Encyclical Letter *Laborem Exercens*, 20: AAS 73 (1981), 629-632; John Paul II, Encyclical Letter *Sollicitudo Rei Socialis*, 28: AAS 80 (1988), 548-550.

be envisioned and brought about, taking into account the interdependence that unites workers among themselves. The more substantial the changes are, the more decisive the commitment of intellect and will to defend the dignity of work needs to be, in order to strengthen, at different levels, the institutions involved. This perspective makes it possible to orient the current transformations for the best, in the direction — so necessary — of complementarities between the local and the global economic dimensions, the "old" and the "new" economy, technological innovation and the need to safeguard human work, as well as economic growth and development compatible with the environment.

320. *Men and women of science and culture are called to make their particular contribution to solving the vast and complex problems connected with work, which in some areas take on dramatic proportions. This contribution is very important for coming up with the proper solutions.* This is a responsibility that requires that they identify the occasions and risks present in the changes taking place, and above all that they suggest lines of action for guiding change in a way that will be most beneficial to the development of the entire human family. To these men and women falls the important task of reading and interpreting the social phenomena with wisdom and with love of truth, leaving behind concerns imposed by special or personal interests. Their contribution, precisely because it is of a theoretical nature, becomes an essential point of reference for the concrete action prescribed by economic policies.[680]

321. *The present scenarios of profound transformation of human work call even more urgently for an authentically global development in solidarity that is capable of involving every region of the world including those less advantaged.* Regarding these less advantaged regions, the start of a process of wide-ranging development in solidarity not only represents a concrete possibility for creating new job opportunities, but is also seen as a genuine condition for the survival of entire peoples. "Solidarity too must become globalized."[681]

Economic and social imbalances in the world of work must be addressed by restoring a just hierarchy of values and placing the human dignity of workers before all else. "The new realities that are having such a powerful impact on the productive process, such as the globalization of finance, economics, trade and labor, must never violate the dignity and centrality of the human person, nor the freedom and democracy of peoples. If solidarity, participation and the possibility to govern these radical changes are not the solution, they are certainly the necessary ethical guarantee so that individuals and peoples do not become tools but the protagonists of their future. All this can be achieved and, since it is possible, it becomes a duty."[682]

---

[680] Cf. John Paul II, Message to the Participants in the International Symposium on Work (14 September 2001), 5: *L'Osservatore Romano*, English edition, 17 October 2001, p. 3.

[681] John Paul II, Greeting after the Mass for the Jubilee of Workers (1 May 2000), 2: *L'Osservatore Romano*, English edition, 10 May 2000, p. 4.

[682] John Paul II, Homily at the Mass for the Jubilee of Workers (1 May 2000), 3: *L'Osservatore Romano*, English edition, 10 May 2000, p. 5.

322. *There is an ever greater need for a careful consideration of the new situation of work in the present-day context of globalization, in a perspective that values people's natural tendency to establish relationships.* In this regard it must be affirmed that universality is a dimension of human beings, not of things. Technology may be the instrumental cause of globalization, but the universality of the human family is its ultimate cause. For this reason, work too has a universal dimension, insofar as it is based on the relational nature of human beings. Technology, especially electronics, has allowed the relational aspect of work to spread throughout the world, giving to globalization a particularly rapid rhythm. The ultimate foundation of this dynamism is the working person, who is always the subjective — and never the objective — element. Therefore, globalized work too originates in the anthropological foundation of the inherent relational dimension of work. The negative aspects of the globalization of work must not damage the possibility opening up for all people: *that of giving expression to a humanism of work on a planetary scale,* to solidarity in the world of work on this same level, so that working in similar contexts, spread throughout the world and interconnected, people will understand ever better their one, shared vocation.

CHAPTER SEVEN

ECONOMIC LIFE

I. BIBLICAL ASPECTS

a. Man, poverty and riches

323. *In the Old Testament a twofold attitude towards economic goods and riches is found. On one hand, an attitude of appreciation sees the availability of material goods as necessary for life.* Abundance — not wealth or luxury — is sometimes seen as a blessing from God. In Wisdom Literature, poverty is described as a negative consequence of idleness and of a lack of industriousness (cf. *Prov* 10:4), but also as a natural fact (cf. *Prov* 22:2). *On the other hand, economic goods and riches are not in themselves condemned so much as their misuse.* The prophetic tradition condemns fraud, usury, exploitation and gross injustice, especially when directed against the poor (cf. *Is* 58:3-11; *Jer* 7:4-7; *Hos* 4:1-2; *Am* 2:6-7; *Mic* 2:1-2). This tradition, however, although looking upon the poverty of the oppressed, the weak and the indigent as an evil, also sees in the condition of poverty a symbol of the human situation before God, from whom comes every good as a gift to be administered and shared.

324. *Those who recognize their own poverty before God, regardless of their situation in life, receive particular attention from him:* when the poor man seeks, the Lord answers; when he cries out, the Lord listens. The divine promises are addressed to the poor: they will be heirs to the Covenant between God and his people. God's saving intervention will come about through a new David (cf. *Ezek* 34:22-31), who like King David — only more so — will be defender of the poor and promoter of justice; he will establish a new covenant and will write a new law in the hearts of believers (cf. *Jer* 31:31-34).

When sought or accepted with a religious attitude, poverty opens one to recognizing and accepting the order of creation. In this perspective, the "rich man" is the one who places his trust in his possessions rather than in God, he is the man who makes himself strong by the works of his own hands and trusts only in his own strength. Poverty takes on the status of a moral value when it becomes an attitude of humble availability and openness to God, of trust in him. This attitude makes it possible for people to recognize the relativity of economic goods and to treat them as divine gifts to be administered and shared, because God is the first owner of all goods.

325. *Jesus takes up the entire Old Testament tradition even with regard to economic goods, wealth and poverty, and he gives them great clarity and fullness* (cf. *Mt* 6:24, 13:22; *Lk* 6:20-24, 12:15-21; *Rom* 14:6-8; *1 Tim* 4:4). Through the gift of his Spirit and the conversion of hearts, he comes to establish the "Kingdom of God," so that a new manner of social life is made possible, in justice, brotherhood, solidarity and sharing. The Kingdom inaugurated by Christ perfects the original goodness of the created order and of human activity, which were compromised by sin. Freed from evil and being placed once more in communion with God, man is able to continue the work of Jesus, with the help of his Spirit. In this, man is called to render justice to the poor, releasing the oppressed, consoling the afflicted, actively seeking a new social order in which adequate solutions to material poverty are offered and in which the forces thwarting the attempts of the weakest to free themselves from conditions of misery and slavery are more effectively controlled. When this happens, the Kingdom of God is already present on this earth, although it is not of the earth. It is in this Kingdom that the promises of the Prophets find final fulfilment.

326. *In the light of Revelation, economic activity is to be considered and undertaken as a grateful response to the vocation which God holds out for each person.* Man is placed in the garden to till and keep it, making use of it within well specified limits (cf. *Gen* 2:16-17) with a commitment to perfecting it (cf. *Gen* 1:26-30, 2:15-16; *Wis* 9:2-3). Bearing witness to the grandeur and goodness of the Creator, he walks towards the fullness of freedom to which God calls him. Good administration of the gifts received, and of material goods also, is a work of justice towards oneself and towards others. What has been received should be used properly, preserved and increased, as suggested by the parable of the talents (cf. *Mt* 25:14-30; *Lk* 19:12-27).

Economic activity and material progress must be placed at the service of man and society. If people dedicate themselves to these with the faith, hope and love of Christ's disciples, even the economy and progress can be transformed into places of salvation and sanctification. In these areas too it is possible to express a love and a solidarity that are more than human, and to contribute to the growth of a new humanity that anticipates the world to come.[683] Jesus sums up all of revelation in calling the believer to *become rich before God* (cf. *Lk* 12:21). The economy too is useful to this end, when its function as an instrument for the overall growth of man and society, of the human quality of life, is not betrayed.

327. *Faith in Jesus Christ makes it possible to have a correct understanding of social development, in the context of an integral and solidary humanism.* In this regard, the contribution of theological reflection offered by the Church's social Magisterium is very useful: "*Faith in Christ the Redeemer*, while it illuminates from within the nature of development, also guides us in the task of collaboration. In the Letter of St. Paul to the Colossians, we read that Christ is 'the firstborn of all creation,' and that 'all things were created through him' and for him (*Col* 1:15-16). In fact, 'all things hold together in him,' since 'in him all the fullness of God was pleased to dwell, and through him to reconcile to himself all things' (v. 20). A part of this divine plan, which begins from eternity in Christ, the perfect 'image' of the Father, and which culminates in him, 'the firstborn from the dead' (v. 15-18), *in our own*

---

[683] Cf. John Paul II, Encyclical Letter *Laborem Exercens*, 25-27: AAS 73 (1981), 638-647.

history, marked by our personal and collective effort to raise up the human condition and to overcome the obstacles which are continually arising along our way. It thus prepares us to share in the fullness which 'dwells in the Lord' and which he communicates 'to his body, which is the Church' (v. 18; cf. *Eph* 1:22-23). At the same time sin, which is always attempting to trap us and which jeopardizes our human achievements, is conquered and redeemed by the 'reconciliation' accomplished by Christ (cf. *Col* 1:20)."[684]

b. Wealth exists to be shared

328. *Goods, even when legitimately owned, always have a universal destination; any type of improper accumulation is immoral, because it openly contradicts the universal destination assigned to all goods by the Creator.* Christian salvation is an integral liberation of man, which means being freed not only from need but also in respect to possessions. "For the love of money is the root of all evils; it is through this craving that some have wandered away from the faith" (*1 Tim* 6:10). The Fathers of the Church insist more on the need for the conversion and transformation of the consciences of believers than on the need to change the social and political structures of their day. They call on those who work in the economic sphere and who possess goods to consider themselves administrators of the goods that God has entrusted to them.

329. *Riches fulfil their function of service to man when they are destined to produce benefits for others and for society.*[685] "How could we ever do good to our neighbor," asks St. Clement of Alexandria, "if none of us possessed anything?"[686] In the perspective of St. John Chrysostom, riches belong to some people so that they can gain merit by sharing them with others.[687] Wealth is a good that comes from God and is to be used by its owner and made to circulate so that even the needy may enjoy it. Evil is seen in the immoderate attachment to riches and the desire to hoard. St. Basil the Great invites the wealthy to open the doors of their storehouses and he exhorts them: "A great torrent rushes, in thousands of channels, through the fertile land: thus, by a thousand different paths, make your riches reach the homes of the poor."[688] Wealth, explains Saint Basil, is like water that issues forth from the fountain: the greater the frequency with which it is drawn, the purer it is, while it becomes foul if the fountain remains unused.[689] The rich man — Saint Gregory the Great will later say — is only an administrator of what he possesses; giving what is required to the needy is a task that is to be performed with humility because the goods do not belong to the one who distributes them. He who retains riches only for himself is not innocent; giving to those in need means paying a debt.[690]

[684] John Paul II, Encyclical Letter *Sollicitudo Rei Socialis*, 31: AAS 80 (1988), 554-555.

[685] Cf. *The Shepherd of Hermas*, Liber Tertium, Allegory I: PG 2, 954.

[686] Clement of Alexandria, Homily *What Rich Man Will Be Saved?*, 13: PG 9, 618.

[687] Cf. Saint John Chrysostom, *Homiliae XXI de Statuis ad Populum Antiochenum Habitae*, 2, 6-8: PG 49, 41-46.

[688] Saint Basil the Great, *Homilia in Illud Lucae, Destruam Horrea Mea*, 5: PG 31, 271.

[689] Cf. Saint Basil the Great, *Homilia in Illud Lucae, Destruam Horrea Mea*, 5: PG 31, 271.

[690] Cf. Saint Gregory the Great, *Regula Pastoralis*, 3, 21: PL 77, 87. Title of § 21: "Quomodo admonendi qui aliena non appetunt, sed sua retinent; et qui sua tribuentes, aliena tamen rapiunt."

II. MORALITY AND THE ECONOMY

330. *The Church's social doctrine insists on the moral connotations of the economy.* Pope Pius XI, in a passage from the Encyclical *Quadragesimo Anno*, speaks of the relationship between the economy and morality. "Even though economics and moral science employs each its own principles in its own sphere, it is, nevertheless, an error to say that the economic and moral orders are so distinct from and alien to each other that the former depends in no way on the latter. Certainly the laws of economics, as they are termed, being based on the very nature of material things and on the capacities of the human body and mind, determine the limits of what productive human effort cannot, and of what it can attain in the economic field and by what means. Yet it is reason itself that clearly shows, on the basis of the individual and social nature of things and of men, the purpose which God ordained for all economic life. But it is only the moral law which, just as it commands us to seek our supreme and last end in the whole scheme of our activity, so likewise commands us to seek directly in each kind of activity those purposes which we know that nature, or rather God the Author of nature, established for that kind of action, and in orderly relationship to subordinate such immediate purposes to our supreme and last end."[691]

331. *The relation between morality and economics is necessary, indeed intrinsic: economic activity and moral behavior are intimately joined one to the other. The necessary distinction between morality and the economy does not entail the separation of these two spheres but, on the contrary, an important reciprocity.* Just as in the area of morality one must take the reasons and requirements of the economy into account, so too in the area of the economy one must be open to the demands of morality: "In the economic and social realms, too, the dignity and complete vocation of the human person and the welfare of society as a whole are to be respected and promoted. For man is the source, the centre, and the purpose of all economic and social life."[692] Giving the proper and due weight to the interests that belong specifically to the economy does not mean rejecting as irrational all considerations of a meta-economic order. This is so because the purpose of the economy is not found in the economy itself, but rather in its being destined to humanity and society.[693] The economy, in fact, whether on a scientific or practical level, has not been entrusted with the purpose of fulfilling man or of bringing about proper human coexistence. Its task, rather, is partial: the production, distribution and consumption of material goods and services.

332. *The moral dimension of the economy shows that economic efficiency and the promotion of human development in solidarity are not two separate or alternative aims but one indivisible goal.* Morality, which is a necessary part of economic life, is neither opposed to it nor neutral: if it is inspired by justice and solidarity, it represents a factor of social efficiency within the economy itself. The production of goods is a

---

[691] Pius XI, Encyclical Letter *Quadragesimo Anno*: AAS 23 (1931), 190-191.
[692] Second Vatican Ecumenical Council, Pastoral Constitution *Gaudium et Spes*, 63: AAS 58 (1966), 1084.
[693] Cf. *Catechism of the Catholic Church*, 2426.

duty to be undertaken in an efficient manner, otherwise resources are wasted. On the other hand, it would not be acceptable to achieve economic growth at the expense of human beings, entire populations or social groups, condemning them to indigence. The growth of wealth, seen in the availability of goods and services, and the moral demands of an equitable distribution of these must inspire man and society as a whole to practice the essential virtue of solidarity,[694] in order to combat, in a spirit of justice and charity, those "structures of sin"[695] wherever they may be found and which generate and perpetuate poverty, underdevelopment and degradation. These structures are built and strengthened by numerous concrete acts of human selfishness.

333. *If economic activity is to have a moral character, it must be directed to all men and to all peoples.* Everyone has the right to participate in economic life and the duty to contribute, each according to his own capacity, to the progress of his own country and to that of the entire human family.[696] If, to some degree, everyone is responsible for everyone else, then each person also has the duty to commit himself to the economic development of all.[697] This is a duty in solidarity and in justice, but it is also the best way to bring economic progress to all of humanity. When practiced morally, economic activity is therefore service mutually rendered by the production of goods and services that are useful for the growth of each person, and it becomes an opportunity for every individual to embody solidarity and live the vocation of "communion with others for which God created him."[698] The effort to create and carry out social and economic projects that are capable of encouraging a more equitable society and a more human world represents a difficult challenge, but also a stimulating duty for all who work in the economic sector and are involved with the economic sciences.[699]

334. *The economy has as its object the development of wealth and its progressive increase, not only in quantity but also in quality; this is morally correct if it is directed to man's overall development in solidarity and to that of the society in which people live and work.* Development, in fact, cannot be reduced to a mere process of accumulating goods and services. On the contrary, accumulation by itself, even were it for the common good, is not a sufficient condition for bringing about authentic human happiness. In this sense, the Church's social Magisterium warns against the treachery hidden within a development that is only quantitative, for the "*excessive* availability of every kind of material goods for the benefit of certain social groups, easily makes people slaves of 'possession' and of immediate gratification . . . This is the so-called civilization of 'consumption' or 'consumerism.' "[700]

---

[694] Cf. John Paul II, Encyclical Letter *Sollicitudo Rei Socialis*, 40: AAS 80 (1988), 568-569.

[695] John Paul II, Encyclical Letter *Sollicitudo Rei Socialis*, 36: AAS 80 (1988), 561.

[696] Cf. Second Vatican Ecumenical Council, Pastoral Constitution *Gaudium et Spes*, 65: AAS 58 (1966), 1086-1087.

[697] Cf. John Paul II, Encyclical Letter *Sollicitudo Rei Socialis*, 32: AAS 80 (1988), 556-557.

[698] John Paul II, Encyclical Letter *Centesimus Annus*, 41: AAS 83 (1991), 844.

[699] Cf. John Paul II, Message for the 2000 World Day of Peace, 15-16: AAS 92 (2000), 366-367.

[700] John Paul II, Encyclical Letter *Sollicitudo Rei Socialis*, 28: AAS 80 (1988), 548.

335. *In the perspective of an integral and solidary development, it is possible to arrive at a proper appreciation of the moral evaluation that the Church's social doctrine offers in regard to the market economy or, more simply, of the free economy:* "If by 'capitalism' is meant an economic system which recognizes the fundamental and positive role of business, the market, private property and the resulting responsibility for the means of production, as well as free human creativity in the economic sector, then the answer is certainly in the affirmative, even though it would perhaps be more appropriate to speak of a 'business economy,' 'market economy' or simply 'free economy'. But if by 'capitalism' is meant a system in which freedom in the economic sector is not circumscribed within a strong juridical framework which places it at the service of human freedom in its totality, and which sees it as a particular aspect of that freedom, the core of which is ethical and religious, then the reply is certainly negative."[701] In this way a Christian perspective is defined regarding social and political conditions of economic activity, not only its rules but also its moral quality and its meaning.

III. PRIVATE INITIATIVE AND BUSINESS INITIATIVE

336. *The Church's social doctrine considers the freedom of the person in economic matters a fundamental value and an inalienable right to be promoted and defended.* "Everyone has the *right to economic initiative*; everyone should make legitimate use of his talents to contribute to the abundance that will benefit all, and to harvest the just fruits of his labor."[702] This teaching warns against the negative consequences that would arise from weakening or denying the *right of economic initiative*: "Experience shows us that the denial of this right, or its limitation in the name of an alleged 'equality' of everyone in society, diminishes, or in practice absolutely destroys the spirit of initiative, that is to say the *creative subjectivity of the citizen*."[703] From this perspective, free and responsible initiative in the economic sphere can also be defined as an act that reveals the humanity of men and women as creative and relational subjects. Such intiative, then, should be given *ample leeway*. The State has the moral obligation to enforce strict limitations only in cases of incompatibility between the pursuit of common good and the type of economic activity proposed or the way it is undertaken.[704]

337. The creative dimension is an essential component of human activity, even in the area of business, and it is especially manifested in the areas of planning and innovation. "Organizing such a productive effort, planning its duration in time, making sure that it corresponds in a positive way to the demands which it must

[701] John Paul II, Encyclical Letter *Centesimus Annus*, 42: AAS 83 (1991), 845-846.

[702] *Catechism of the Catholic Church*, 2429; cf. Second Vatican Ecumenical Council, Pastoral Constitution *Gaudium et Spes*, 63: AAS 58 (1966), 1084-1085: John Paul II, Encyclical Letter *Centesimus Annus*, 48: AAS 83 (1991), 852-854; John Paul II, Encyclical Letter *Sollicitudo Rei Socialis*, 15: AAS 80 (1988), 528-530; John Paul II, Encyclical Letter *Laborem Exercens*, 17: AAS 73 (1981), 620-622; John XXIII, Encyclical Letter *Mater et Magistra*: AAS 53 (1961), 413-415.

[703] John Paul II, Encyclical Letter *Sollicitudo Rei Socialis*, 15: AAS 80 (1988), 529; cf. *Catechism of the Catholic Church*, 2429.

[704] Cf. John Paul II, Encyclical Letter *Centesimus Annus*, 16: AAS 83 (1991), 813-814.

satisfy, and taking the necessary risks — all this too is a source of wealth in today's society. In this way, the *role of disciplined and creative human work and*, as an essential part of that work, *initiative and entrepreneurial ability* becomes increasingly evident and decisive."[705] At the basis of this teaching we can see the belief that "man's principal resource is man himself. His intelligence enables him to discover the earth's productive potential and the many different ways in which human needs can be satisfied."[706]

a. **Business and its goals**

338. *Businesses should be characterized by their capacity to serve the common good of society through the production of useful goods and services.* In seeking to produce goods and services according to plans aimed at efficiency and at satisfying the interests of the different parties involved, businesses create wealth for all of society, not just for the owners but also for the other subjects involved in their activity. Besides this typically economic function, *businesses also perform a social function, creating opportunities for meeting, cooperating and the enhancement the abilities of the people involved.* In a business undertaking, therefore, the economic dimension is the condition for attaining not only economic goals, but also social and moral goals, which are all pursued together.

A business' objective must be met in economic terms and according to economic criteria, but the authentic values that bring about the concrete development of the person and society must not be neglected. In this personalistic and community vision, "a business cannot be considered only as a 'society of capital goods'; it is also a 'society of persons' in which people participate in different ways and with specific responsibilities, whether they supply the necessary capital for the company's activities or take part in such activities through their labor."[707]

339. *All those involved in a business venture must be mindful that the community in which they work represents a good for everyone and not a structure that permits the satisfaction of someone's merely personal interests.* This awareness alone makes it possible to build an economy that is truly at the service of mankind and to create programmes of real cooperation among the different partners in labor.

A very important and significant example in this regard is found in the activity of so-called cooperative enterprises, small and medium-sized businesses, commercial undertakings featuring hand-made products and family-sized agricultural ventures. The Church's social doctrine has emphasized the contribution that such activities make to enhance the value of work, to the growth of a sense of personal and social responsibility, a democratic life and the human values that are important for the progress of the market and of society.[708]

---

[705] John Paul II, Encyclical Letter *Centesimus Annus*, 32: AAS 83 (1991), 833.
[706] John Paul II, Encyclical Letter *Centesimus Annus*, 32: AAS 83 (1991), 833.
[707] John Paul II, Encyclical Letter *Centesimus Annus*, 43: AAS 83 (1991), 847.
[708] Cf. John XXIII, Encyclical Letter *Mater et Magistra*: AAS 53 (1961), 422-423.

340. *The social doctrine of the Church recognizes the proper role of profit as the first indicator that a business is functioning well:* "when a firm makes a profit, this means that productive factors have been properly employed."[709] But this does not cloud her awareness of the fact that a business may show a profit while not properly serving society.[710] For example, "it is possible for the financial accounts to be in order, and yet for the people — who make up the firm's most valuable asset — to be humiliated and their dignity offended."[711] This is what happens when businesses are part of social and cultural systems marked by the exploitation of people, tending to avoid the obligations of social justice and to violate the rights of workers.

It is essential that within a business the legitimate pursuit of profit should be in harmony with the irrenounceable protection of the dignity of the people who work at different levels in the same company. These two goals are not in the least contrary to one another, since, on the one hand, it would not be realistic to try to guarantee the firm's future without the production of useful goods and services and without making a profit, which is the fruit of the economic activity undertaken. On the other hand, allowing workers to develop themselves fosters increased productivity and efficiency in the very work undertaken. A business enterprise must be a community of solidarity,[712] that is not closed within its own company interests. It must move in the direction of a "social ecology"[713] of work and contribute to the common good also by protecting the natural environment.

341. *Although the quest for equitable profit is acceptable in economic and financial activity, recourse to usury is to be morally condemned:* "Those whose usurious and avaricious dealings lead to the hunger and death of their brethren in the human family indirectly commit homicide, which is imputable to them."[714] This condemnation extends also to international economic relations, especially with regard to the situation in less advanced countries, which must never be made to suffer "abusive if not usurious financial systems."[715] More recently, the Magisterium used strong and clear words against this practice, which is still tragically widespread, describing usury as "a scourge that is also a reality in our time and that has a stranglehold on many peoples' lives."[716]

342. *Businesses today move in economic contexts that are becoming ever broader* and in which national States show limits in their capacity to govern the rapid processes of change that effect international economic and financial relations. This situation leads businesses to *take on new and greater responsibilities with respect to the past.* Never has their role been so decisive with regard to the authentic integral development of humanity in solidarity. Equally decisive in this sense is their level

[709] John Paul II, Encyclical Letter *Centesimus Annus*, 35 AAS 83 (1991), 837.
[710] Cf. *Catechism of the Catholic Church*, 2424.
[711] John Paul II, Encyclical Letter *Centesimus Annus*, 35: AAS 83 (1991), 837.
[712] Cf. John Paul II, Encyclical Letter *Centesimus Annus*, 43: AAS 83 (1991), 846-848.
[713] John Paul II, Encyclical Letter *Centesimus Annus*, 38: AAS 83 (1991), 841.
[714] *Catechism of the Catholic Church*, 2269.
[715] *Catechism of the Catholic Church*, 2438.
[716] John Paul II, Catechesis at General Audience (4 February 2004), 3: *L'Osservatore Romano*, English edition, 11 February 2004, p. 11.

of awareness that "development either becomes shared in common by every part of the world or it undergoes a process of regression even in zones marked by constant progress. This tells us a great deal about the nature of *authentic* development: either all the nations of the world participate, or it will not be true development."[717]

b. Role of business owners and management

343. *Economic initiative is an expression of human intelligence and of the necessity of responding to human needs in a creative and cooperative fashion.* Creativity and cooperation are signs of the authentic concept of business competition: a *"cumpetere,"* that is, a seeking together of the most appropriate solutions for responding in the best way to needs as they emerge. The sense of responsibility that arises from free economic initiative takes not only the form of an *individual virtue* required for individual human growth, but also of a *social virtue* that is necessary for the development of a community in solidarity. "Important virtues are involved in this process, such as diligence, industriousness, prudence in undertaking reasonable risks, reliability and fidelity in interpersonal relationships, as well as courage in carrying out decisions which are difficult and painful but necessary, both for the overall working of a business and in meeting possible set-backs."[718]

344. *The roles of business owners and management have a central importance from the viewpoint of society, because they are at the heart of that network of technical, commercial, financial and cultural bonds that characterizes the modern business reality.* Due to the increasing complexity of business activities, decisions made by companies produce a number of very significant interrelated effects, both in the economic and social spheres. For this reason the exercise of responsibility by business owners and management requires — in addition to specific updating that is the object of continuous efforts — constant reflection on the moral motivations that should guide the personal choices of those to whom these tasks fall.

Business owners and management must not limit themselves to taking into account only the economic objectives of the company, the criteria for economic efficiency and the proper care of "capital" as the sum of the means of production. It is also their precise duty to respect concretely the human dignity of those who work within the company.[719] These workers constitute "the firm's most valuable asset"[720] and the decisive factor of production.[721] In important decisions concerning strategy and finances, in decisions to buy or sell, to resize, close or to merge a site, financial and commercial criteria must not be the only considerations made.

345. *The Church's social doctrine insists on the need for business owners and management to strive to structure work in such a way so as to promote the family, especially mothers, in*

[717] John Paul II, Encyclical Letter *Sollicitudo Rei Socialis*, 17: AAS 80 (1988), 532.
[718] John Paul II, Encyclical Letter *Centesimus Annus*, 32: AAS 83 (1991), 833.
[719] Cf. *Catechism of the Catholic Church*, 2432.
[720] John Paul II, Encyclical Letter *Centesimus Annus*, 35: AAS 83 (1991), 837.
[721] Cf. John Paul II, Encyclical Letter *Centesimus Annus*, 32: AAS 83 (1991), 832-835.

the fulfillment of their duties[722]; *to accede, in light of an integral vision of man and development, to the demand for the quality* "of the goods to be produced and consumed, the quality of the services to be enjoyed, the quality of the environment and of life in general";[723] to invest, when the necessary economic conditions and conditions of political stability are present, in those places and sectors of production that offer individuals and peoples "an opportunity to make good use of their own labor."[724]

IV. ECONOMIC INSTITUTIONS
AT THE SERVICE OF MAN

346. *One of the higher priority issues in economics is the utilization of resources,*[725] *that is, of all those goods and services to which economic subjects — producers and consumers in the private and public spheres — attribute value because of their inherent usefulness in the areas of production and consumption.* Resources in nature are quantitatively scarce, which means that each individual economic subject, as well as each individual society, must necessarily come up with a plan for their utilization in the most rational way possible, following the logic dictated by the "*principle of economizing.*" Both the effective solution of the more general, and fundamental, economic problem of limited means with respect to individual and social — private and public — need, and the overall structural and functional efficiency of the entire economic system depend on this. This efficiency directly involves the responsibility and capacity of the various agents concerned, such as the market, the State and intermediate social bodies.

a. **Role of the free market**

347. *The free market is an institution of social importance because of its capacity to guarantee effective results in the production of goods and services.* Historically, it has shown itself able to initiate and sustain economic development over long periods. There are good reasons to hold that, in many circumstances, "*the free market* is the most efficient instrument for utilizing resources and effectively responding to needs."[726] The Church's social doctrine appreciates the secure advantages that the mechanisms of the free market offer, making it possible as they do to utilize resources better and facilitating the exchange of products. These mechanisms "above all . . . give central place to the person's desires and preferences, which, in a contract, meet the desires and preferences of another person."[727]

A *truly competitive market is an effective instrument for attaining important objectives of justice:* moderating the excessive profits of individual businesses, respond-

---

[722] Cf. John Paul II, Encyclical Letter *Laborem Exercens*, 19: AAS 73 (1981), 625-629.
[723] John Paul II, Encyclical Letter *Centesimus Annus*, 36: AAS 83 (1991), 838.
[724] John Paul II, Encyclical Letter *Centesimus Annus*, 36: AAS 83 (1991), 840.
[725] Concerning the utilization of resources and goods, the Church's social doctrine offers its teaching regarding the universal destination of goods and regarding private property; cf. Chapter Four, Part III of the present document.
[726] John Paul II, Encyclical Letter *Centesimus Annus*, 34: AAS 83 (1991), 835.
[727] John Paul II, Encyclical Letter *Centesimus Annus*, 40: AAS 83 (1991), 843.

ing to consumers' demands, bringing about a more efficient use and conservation of resources, rewarding entrepreneurship and innovation, making information available so that it is really possible to compare and purchase products in an atmosphere of healthy competition.

348. *The free market cannot be judged apart from the ends that it seeks to accomplish and from the values that it transmits on a societal level.* Indeed, the market cannot find in itself the principles for its legitimization; it belongs to the consciences of individuals and to public responsibility to establish a just relationship between means and ends.[728] The *individual profit* of an economic enterprise, although legitimate, must never become the sole objective. Together with this objective there is another, equally fundamental but of a higher order: *social usefulness*, which must be brought about not in contrast to but in keeping with the logic of the market. When the free market carries out the important functions mentioned above it becomes a service to the common good and to integral human development. The inversion of the relationship between means and ends, however, can make it degenerate into an inhuman and alienating institution, with uncontrollable repercussions.

349. *The Church's social doctrine, while recognizing the market as an irreplaceable instrument for regulating the inner workings of the economic system, points out the need for it to be firmly rooted in its ethical objectives, which ensure and at the same time suitably circumscribe the space within which it can operate autonomously.*[729] The idea that the market alone can be entrusted with the task of supplying every category of goods cannot be shared, because such an idea is based on a reductionist vision of the person and society.[730] Faced with the concrete "risk of an 'idolatry' of the market," the Church's social doctrine underlines its limits, which are easily seen in its proven inability to satisfy important human needs, which require goods that "by their nature are not and cannot be mere commodities,"[731] goods that cannot be bought and sold according to the rule of the "exchange of equivalents" and the logic of contracts, which are typical of the market.

350. *The market takes on a significant social function in contemporary society, therefore it is important to identify its most positive potentials and to create the conditions that allow them to be put concretely into effect.* Market operators must be effectively free to compare, evaluate and choose from among various options. Freedom in the economic sector, however, must be regulated by appropriate legal norms so that it will be placed at the service of integral human freedom. "Economic freedom is only one element of human freedom. When it becomes autonomous, when man is seen more as a producer or consumer of goods than as a subject who produces and consumes in order to live, then economic freedom loses its necessary relationship to the human person and ends up by alienating and oppressing him."[732]

---

[728] Cf. John Paul II, Encyclical Letter *Centesimus Annus*, 41: AAS 83 (1991), 843-845.

[729] Cf. Paul VI, Apostolic Letter *Octogesima Adveniens*, 41: AAS 63 (1971), 429-430.

[730] Cf. John Paul II, Encyclical Letter *Centesimus Annus*, 34: AAS 83 (1991), 835-836.

[731] John Paul II, Encyclical Letter *Centesimus Annus*, 40: AAS 83 (1991), 843; cf. *Catechism of the Catholic Church*, 2425.

[732] John Paul II, Encyclical Letter *Centesimus Annus*, 39: AAS 83 (1991), 843.

b. **Action of the State**

351. *The action of the State and of other public authorities must be consistent with the principle of subsidiarity and create situations favorable to the free exercise of economic activity. It must also be inspired by the principle of solidarity and establish limits for the autonomy of the parties in order to defend those who are weaker.*[733] Solidarity without subsidiarity, in fact, can easily degenerate into a "Welfare State," while subsidiarity without solidarity runs the risk of encouraging forms of self-centred localism. In order to respect both of these fundamental principles, the State's intervention in the economic environment must be neither invasive nor absent, but commensurate with society's real needs. "The State has a duty to sustain business activities by creating conditions which will ensure job opportunities, by stimulating those activities where they are lacking or by supporting them in moments of crisis. The State has the further right to intervene when particular monopolies create delays or obstacles to development. In addition to the tasks of harmonizing and guiding development, in exceptional circumstances the State can also exercise a *substitute function*."[734]

352. *The fundamental task of the State in economic matters is that of determining an appropriate juridical framework for regulating economic affairs*, in order to safeguard "the prerequisites of a free economy, which presumes a certain equality between the parties, such that one party would not be so powerful as practically to reduce the other to subservience."[735] Economic activity, above all in a free market context, cannot be conducted in an institutional, juridical or political vacuum. "On the contrary, it presupposes sure guarantees of individual freedom and private property, as well as a stable currency and efficient public services."[736] To fulfil this task, the State must adopt suitable legislation but at the same time it must direct economic and social policies in such a way that it does not become abusively involved in the various market activities, the carrying out of which is and must remain free of authoritarian — or worse, totalitarian — superstructures and constraints.

353. *It is necessary for the market and the State to act in concert, one with the other, and to compliment each other mutually. In fact, the free market can have a beneficial influence on the general public only when the State is organized in such a manner that it defines and gives direction to economic development*, promoting the observation of fair and transparent rules, and making direct interventions — only for the length of time strictly necessary[737] — when the market is not able to obtain the desired efficiency and when it is a question of putting the principle of redistribution into effect. There exist certain sectors in which the market, making use of the mech-

---

[733] Cf. John Paul II, Encyclical Letter *Centesimus Annus*, 15: AAS 83 (1991), 811-813.
[734] John Paul II, Encyclical Letter *Centesimus Annus*, 48: AAS 83 (1991), 853; cf. *Catechism of the Catholic Church*, 2431.
[735] John Paul II, Encyclical Letter *Centesimus Annus*, 15: AAS 83 (1991), 811.
[736] John Paul II, Encyclical Letter *Centesimus Annus*, 48: AAS 83 (1991), 852-853; cf. *Catechism of the Catholic Church*, 2431.
[737] Cf. John Paul II, Encyclical Letter *Centesimus Annus*, 48: AAS 83 (1991), 852-854.

anisms at its disposal, is not able to guarantee an equitable distribution of the goods and services that are essential for the human growth of citizens. In such cases the complementarities of State and market are needed more than ever.

354. *The State can encourage citizens and businesses to promote the common good by enacting an economic policy that fosters the participation of all citizens in the activities of production.* Respect of the principle of subsidiarity must prompt public authorities to seek conditions that encourage the development of individual capacities of initiative, autonomy and personal responsibility in citizens, avoiding any interference which would unduly condition business forces.

With a view to the common good, it is necessary to pursue always and with untiring determination the goal of a proper equilibrium between private freedom and public action, understood both as direct intervention in economic matters and as activity supportive of economic development. In any case, public intervention must be carried out with equity, rationality and effectiveness, and without replacing the action of individuals, which would be contrary to their right to the free exercise of economic initiative. In such cases, the State becomes detrimental to society: a direct intervention that is too extensive ends up depriving citizens of responsibility and creates excessive growth in public agencies guided more by bureaucratic logic than by the goal of satisfying the needs of the person.[738]

355. *Tax revenues and public spending take on crucial economic importance for every civil and political community. The goal to be sought is public financing that is itself capable of becoming an instrument of development and solidarity.* Just, efficient and effective public financing will have very positive effects on the economy, because it will encourage employment growth and sustain business and non-profit activities and help to increase the credibility of the State as the guarantor of systems of social insurance and protection that are designed above all to protect the weakest members of society.

Public spending is directed to the common good when certain fundamental principles are observed: the payment of taxes[739] *as part of the duty of solidarity; a reasonable and fair application of taxes;*[740] *precision and integrity in administering and distributing public resources.*[741] In the redistribution of resources, public spending must observe the principles of solidarity, equality and making use of talents. It must also pay greater attention to families, designating an adequate amount of resources for this purpose.[742]

c. **Role of intermediate bodies**

356. *The social-economic system must be marked by the twofold presence of public and private activity, including private non-profit activity. In this way sundry decision-making*

[738] Cf. John Paul II, Encyclical Letter *Centesimus Annus*, 48: AAS 83 (1991), 852-854.
[739] Cf. Second Vatican Ecumenical Council, Pastoral Constitution *Gaudium et Spes*, 30: AAS 58 (1966), 1049-1050.
[740] Cf. John XXIII, Encyclical Letter *Mater et Magistra*: AAS 53 (1961), 433-434, 438.
[741] Cf. Pius XI, Encyclical Letter *Divini Redemptoris*: AAS 29 (1966), 103-104.
[742] Cf. Pius XII, Radio Message for the fiftieth anniversary of *Rerum Novarum*, 21: AAS 33 (1941), 202; John Paul II, Encyclical Letter *Centesimus Annus*, 49: AAS 83 (1991), 854-856; John Paul II, Apostolic Exhortation *Familiaris Consortio*, 45: AAS 74 (1982), 136-137.

and activity-planning centres come to take shape. The use of certain categories of goods, collective goods and goods meant for common utilization, cannot be dependent on mechanisms of the market,[743] nor does their use fall under the exclusive competence of the State. The State's task relative to these goods is that of making use of all social and economic initiatives promoted by intermediate bodies that produce public effects. Civil society, organized into its intermediate groups, is capable of contributing to the attainment of the common good by placing itself in a relationship of collaboration and effective complementarities with respect to the State and the market. It thus encourages the development of a fitting economic democracy. In this context, State intervention should be characterized by a genuine solidarity, which as such must never be separated from subsidiarity.

357. *Private non-profit organizations have their own specific role to play in the economic sphere. These organizations are marked by the fearless attempt to unite efficiency in production with solidarity.* In general, they are built on agreements of association and manifest a common way of thinking in the members who choose to join. The State is called to respect the nature of these organizations and to make proper use of their various features, putting into practice the fundamental principle of subsidiarity, which requires that the dignity and autonomous responsibility of the "subsidiary" subject be respected and promoted.

d. Savings and consumer goods

358. *Consumers, who in many cases have a broad range of buying power well above the mere subsistence level, exercise significant influence over economic realities by their free decisions regarding whether to put their money into consumer goods or savings.* In fact, the possibility to influence the choices made within the economic sector is in the hands of those who must decide where to place their financial resources. Today more than in the past it is possible to evaluate the available options not only on the basis of the expected return and the relative risk but also by making a value judgment of the investment projects that those resources would finance, in the awareness that "the decision to invest in one place rather than another, in one productive sector rather than another, is always a moral and cultural choice."[744]

359. *Purchasing power must be used in the context of the moral demands of justice and solidarity, and in that of precise social responsibilities.* One must never forget "the duty of charity . . ., that is, the duty to give from one's 'abundance,' and sometimes even out of one's needs, in order to provide what is essential for the life of a poor person."[745] This responsibility gives to consumers the possibility, thanks to the wider circulation of information, of directing the behavior of producers, through preferences — individual and collective — given to the products of certain com-

---

[743] Cf. John Paul II, Encyclical Letter *Centesimus Annus*, 40: AAS 83 (1991), 843.
[744] John Paul II, Encyclical Letter *Centesimus Annus*, 36: AAS 83 (1991), 839-840.
[745] John Paul II, Encyclical Letter *Centesimus Annus*, 36: AAS 83 (1991), 839.

panies rather than to those of others, taking into account not only the price and quality of what is being purchased but also the presence of correct working conditions in the company as well as the level of protection of the natural environment in which it operates.

360. *The phenomenon of consumerism maintains a persistent orientation towards "having" rather than "being."* This confuses the "criteria for correctly distinguishing new and higher forms of satisfying human needs from artificial new needs which hinder the formation of a mature personality."[746] To counteract this phenomenon it is necessary to create "life-styles in which the quest for truth, beauty, goodness and communion with others for the sake of common growth are the factors which determine consumer choices, savings and investments."[747] It is undeniable that ways of life are significantly influenced by different social contexts, for this reason the cultural challenge that consumerism poses today must be met with greater resolve, above all in consideration of future generations, who risk having to live in a natural environment that has been pillaged by an excessive and disordered consumerism.[748]

V. THE "NEW THINGS"
IN THE ECONOMIC SECTOR

a. Globalization: opportunities and risks

361. *Our modern era is marked by the complex phenomenon of economic and financial globalization,* a process that progressively integrates national economies at the level of the exchange of goods and services and of financial transactions. In this process, an ever growing number of those involved in the economic sector is prompted to adopt a more global perspective concerning the choices that they must make with regard to future growth and profits. The new perspective of global society does not simply consist in the presence of economic and financial bonds between national forces at work in different countries, which have moreover always been present, but in the pervasiveness and the absolutely unprecedented nature of the system of relations that is developing. The role of financial markets is becoming ever more decisive and central. Following the liberalization of capital exchange and circulation, these market dimensions have increased enormously and with incredible speed, to the point that agents can "in real time," transfer large quantities of capital from one part of the globe to another. This is a multifaceted reality that is difficult to decipher, since it expands at different levels and is in continuous evolution along paths that cannot easily be predicted.

362. *Globalization gives rise to new hopes while at the same time it poses troubling questions.*[749] *Globalization is able to produce potentially beneficial effects for the whole of humanity.* In the wake of dizzying developments in the field of telecommunica-

---

[746] John Paul II, Encyclical Letter *Centesimus Annus*, 36: AAS 83 (1991), 839.
[747] John Paul II, Encyclical Letter *Centesimus Annus*, 36: AAS 83 (1991), 839.
[748] Cf. John Paul II, Encyclical Letter *Centesimus Annus*, 37: AAS 83 (1991), 840.
[749] Cf. John Paul II, Post-Synodal Apostolic Exhortation *Ecclesia in America*, 20: AAS 91 (1999), 756.

tions, the growth of the system of economic and financial relations has brought about simultaneously a significant reduction in the costs of communications and new communication technologies, and has accelerated the process by which commercial trade and financial transactions are expanding worldwide. In other words, the two phenomena of economic-financial globalization and technological progress have mutually strengthened each other, making the whole process of this present phase of transition extremely rapid.

In analyzing the present context, besides identifying the opportunities now opening up in the era of the global economy, one also comes to see the risks connected with the new dimensions of commercial and financial relations. In fact, there are indications aplenty that point to a trend of *increasing inequalities*, both between advanced countries and developing countries, and within industrialized countries. The growing economic wealth made possible by the processes described above is accompanied by an increase in relative poverty.

363. *Looking after the common good means making use of the new opportunities for the redistribution of wealth among the different areas of the planet, to the benefit of the under-privileged that until now have been excluded or cast to the sidelines of social and economic progress.*[750] "The challenge, in short, is to ensure a globalization in solidarity, a globalization without marginalization."[751] This technological progress itself risks being unfairly distributed among countries. In fact, technological innovations can penetrate and spread within a specific community only if the potential beneficiaries have a minimum level of knowledge and financial resources. It is evident that, because of the great disparities between countries regarding access to technical and scientific knowledge and to the most recent products of technology, the process of globalization ends up increasing rather than decreasing the inequalities between countries in terms of economic and social development. Given the nature of the current dynamics, the free circulation of capital is not of itself sufficient to close the gap between developing countries and the more advanced countries.

364. *Trade represents a fundamental component of international economic relations, making a decisive contribution to the specialization in certain types of production and to the economic growth of different countries.* Today more than ever, international trade — if properly oriented — promotes development and can create new employment possibilities and provide useful resources. The Church's social doctrine has time and again called attention to aberrations in the system of international trade,[752] which often, owing to protectionist policies, discriminates against products coming from poorer countries and hinders the growth of industrial activity in and the transfer of technology to these countries.[753] The continuing deterioration in terms of the exchange of raw materials and the widening of the gap between rich and poor countries has prompted the social Magisterium to point out the impor-

---

[750] Cf. John Paul II, Address to members of the "Centesimus Annus - Pro Pontifice" Foundation (9 May 1998), 2: *L'Osservatore Romano*, English edition, 27 May 1998, p. 6.
[751] John Paul II, Message for the 1998 World Day of Peace, 3: AAS 90 (1998), 150.
[752] Cf. Paul VI, *Populorum Progressio*, 61: AAS 59 (1967), 287.
[753] Cf. John Paul II, Encyclical Letter *Sollicitudo Rei Socialis*, 43: AAS 80 (1988), 574-575.

tance of ethical criteria that should form the basis of international economic relations: the pursuit of the common good and the universal destination of goods; equity in trade relationships; and attention to the rights and needs of the poor in policies concerning trade and international cooperation. Otherwise, "the poor nations remain ever poor while the rich ones become still richer."[754]

365. *An adequate solidarity in the era of globalization requires that human rights be defended.* In this regard, the Magisterium points out that not only the "vision of an effective international public authority at the service of human rights, freedom and peace has not yet been entirely achieved, but there is still in fact much hesitation in the international community about the obligation to respect and implement human rights. This duty touches all fundamental rights, excluding that arbitrary picking and choosing which can lead to rationalizing forms of discrimination and injustice. Likewise, we are witnessing the emergence of an alarming gap between a series of new 'rights' being promoted in advanced societies – the result of new prosperity and new technologies – and other more basic human rights still not being met, especially in situations of underdevelopment. I am thinking here for example about the right to food and drinkable water, to housing and security, to self-determination and independence – which are still far from being guaranteed and realized."[755]

366. *As globalization spreads it must be accompanied by an ever more mature awareness on the part of different organizations of civil society of the new tasks to which they are called on a worldwide level.* Thanks also to resolute action taken by these organizations, it will be possible to place the present process of economic and financial growth taking place on a global scale within a framework that guarantees an effective respect of human rights and of the rights of peoples, as well as an equitable distribution of resources within every country and between different countries: "freedom of trade is fair only when it is in accord with the demands of justice."[756]

Special attention must be given to specific local features and the cultural differences that are threatened by the economic and financial process currently underway: "Globalization must not be a new version of colonialism. It must respect the diversity of cultures which, within the universal harmony of peoples, are life's interpretive keys. In particular, it must not deprive the poor of what remains most precious to them, including their religious beliefs and practices, since genuine religious convictions are the clearest manifestation of human freedom."[757]

367. *In the era of globalization solidarity between generations must be forcefully emphasized*: "Formerly, in many places, solidarity between generations was a natural family attitude; it also became a duty of the community."[758] It is good that such soli-

[754] Paul VI, *Populorum Progressio*, 57: AAS 59 (1967), 285.
[755] John Paul II, Message for the 2003 World Day of Peace, 5: AAS 95 (2003), 343.
[756] Paul VI, *Populorum Progressio*, 59: AAS 59 (1967), 286.
[757] John Paul II, Address to the Pontifical Academy of Social Sciences (27 April 2001), 4: AAS 93 (2001), 600.
[758] John Paul II, Address to the Pontifical Academy of Social Sciences (11 April 2002), 3: *L'Osservatore Romano*, English edition, 24 April 2002, p. 10.

darity continue to be pursued within national political communities, but today the problem exists also for the global political community, in order that globalization will not occur at the expense of the neediest and the weakest. Solidarity between generations requires that global planning take place according to the principle of the universal destination of goods, which makes it morally illicit and economically counterproductive to burden future generations with the costs involved: morally illicit because it would mean avoiding one's own responsibilities; economically counterproductive because correcting failures is more expensive than preventing them. This principle is to be applied above all — although not only — to the earth's resources and to safeguarding creation, the latter of which becomes a particularly delicate issue because of globalization, involving as it does the entire planet understood as a single ecosystem.[759]

b. **The international financial system**

368. *Financial markets are certainly not an innovation of our day: for a long time now, in different forms, they have been seeking to meet the financial needs of the productivity sector. The experience of history teaches that without adequate financial systems, economic growth would not have taken place.* Large-scale investments typical of modern market economies would have been impossible without the fundamental role of mediation played by financial markets, which among other things brought about an appreciation of the positive functions of savings in the overall development of the economic and social system. If the creation of what is called the "global capital market" has brought benefits, thanks to the fact that the greater mobility of capital allows the productivity sector easier access to resources, on the other hand it has also increased the risk of financial crises. The financial sector, which has seen the volume of financial transactions far surpass that of real transactions, runs the risk of developing according to a mentality that has only itself as a point of reference, without being connected to the real foundations of the economy.

369. *A financial economy that is an end unto itself is destined to contradict its goals, since it is no longer in touch with its roots and has lost sight of its constitutive purpose. In other words, it has abandoned its original and essential role of serving the real economy and, ultimately, of contributing to the development of people and the human community.* In light of the extreme imbalance that characterizes the international financial system, the overall picture appears more disconcerting still: the processes of deregulation of financial markets and innovation tend to be consolidated only in certain parts of the world. This is a source of serious ethical concern, since the countries excluded from these processes do not enjoy the benefits brought about but are still exposed to the eventual negative consequences that financial instability can cause for their real economic systems, above all if they are weak or suffering from delayed development.[760]

---

[759] Cf. John Paul II, Address to members of the Italian Christian Workers' Associations (27 April 2002), 4: *L'Osservatore Romano*, English edition, 12 June 2002, p. 11.

[760] Cf. John Paul II, Address to the Pontifical Academy of Social Sciences (25 April 1997), 6: *L'Osservatore Romano*, English edition, 14 May 1997, p. 5.

The sudden acceleration of these processes, such as the enormous increase in the value of the administrative portfolios of financial institutions and the rapid proliferation of new and sophisticated financial instruments, makes it *more urgent than ever to find institutional solutions capable of effectively fostering the stability of the system without reducing its potential and efficiency.* It is therefore indispensable to introduce a normative and regulatory framework that will protect the stability of the system in all its intricate expressions, foster competition among intermediaries and ensure the greatest transparency to the benefit of investors.

c. Role of the international community in an era of a global economy

370. *The loss of centrality on the part of States must coincide with a greater commitment on the part of the international community to exercise a strong guiding role.* In fact, an important consequence of the process of globalization consists in the gradual loss of effectiveness of nation-states in directing the dynamics of national economic-financial systems. The governments of individual countries find their actions in the economic and social spheres ever more strongly conditioned by the expectations of international capital markets and by the ever more pressing requests for credibility coming from the financial world. Because of the new bonds of interdependence among global operators, the traditional defensive measures of States appear to be destined to failure and, in the presence of new areas of competition, the very notion of a national market recedes into the background.

371. *The more the worldwide economic-financial system reaches high levels of organizational and functional complexity, all the more priority must be given to the task of regulating these processes, directing them towards the goal of attaining the common good of the human family. There is the clear need not just for States but for the international community to take on this delicate chore with adequate and effective political and juridical instruments.*

It is therefore indispensable that international economic and financial institutions should be able to identify the most appropriate institutional solutions and formulate the most suitable plans of action aimed at bringing about a change that, if it were to be passively accepted and simply left to itself, would otherwise produce a dramatic situation detrimental above all to the weakest and defenceless classes of the world's population.

In international agencies it is necessary that the interests of the whole human family be equally represented. It is necessary moreover that "in evaluating the consequences of their decisions, these agencies always give sufficient consideration to peoples and countries which have little weight in the international market, but which are burdened by the most acute and desperate needs, and are thus more dependent on support for their development."[761]

372. *The sphere of politics too, just like that of the economy, must be in a position to extend its range of action beyond national boundaries, quickly taking on an operative*

---

[761] John Paul II, Encyclical Letter *Centesimus Annus*, 58: AAS 83 (1991), 864.

worldwide dimension which alone will permit it to direct the processes now underway not only according to economic parameters but also according to moral criteria. The basic goal is to guide economic processes by ensuring that the dignity of man and his complete development as a person are respected, in the context of the common good.[762] Taking on this task entails the responsibility of accelerating the consolidation of existing institutions and the creation of new entities responsible for this.[763] Economic development, in fact, will be lasting only to the extent that it takes place within a clear and defined normative context and within a broad plan for the moral, civil and cultural growth of the entire human family.

d. An integral development in solidarity

373. *One of the fundamental tasks of those actively involved in international economic matters is to achieve for mankind an integral development in solidarity,* that is to say, "it has to promote the good of every person and of the whole person."[764] To achieve this task requires a vision of the economy that, on the international level, guarantees an equitable distribution of resources and that is responsive to awareness of the interdependence — economic, political and cultural — that today unites people definitively among themselves and makes them feel linked by a sole destiny.[765] Social problems increasingly take on a global dimension. No State can face these alone and find a solution. The present generations have direct experience of the need for solidarity and are concretely aware of the necessity to move beyond an individualistic culture.[766] There is an ever wider awareness of the need for models of development that seek to take on the task not only "of raising all peoples to the level currently enjoyed by the richest countries, but rather of building up a more decent life through united labor, of concretely enhancing every individual's dignity and creativity, as well as his capacity to respond to his personal vocation, and thus to God's call."[767]

374. *A more human development in solidarity will also bring benefit to the richer countries themselves.* In these countries "one frequently observes a sort of existential confusion, an inability to live and to experience properly the meaning of life, even though surrounded by an abundance of material possessions. A sense of alienation and loss of their own humanity has made people feel reduced to the role of cogs in the machinery of production and consumption and they find no way to affirm their own dignity as persons made in the image and likeness of God."[768] Rich

---

[762] Cf. Paul VI, Apostolic Letter *Octogesima Adveniens*, 43-44: AAS 63 (1971), 431-433.

[763] Cf. *Catechism of the Catholic Church*, 2440; Paul VI, *Populorum Progressio*, 78: AAS 59 (1967), 295; John Paul II, Encyclical Letter *Sollicitudo Rei Socialis*, 43: AAS 80 (1988), 574-575.

[764] Paul VI, *Populorum Progressio*, 14: AAS 59 (1967), 264.

[765] Cf. *Catechism of the Catholic Church*, 2437-2438.

[766] Cf. John Paul II, Message for the 2000 World Day of Peace, 13-14: AAS 92 (2000), 365-366.

[767] John Paul II, Encyclical Letter *Centesimus Annus*, 29: AAS 83 (1991), 828-829; cf. Paul VI, Encyclical Letter *Populorum Progressio*, 40-42: AAS 59 (1967), 277-278.

[768] John Paul II, Address at General Audience (1 May 1991): *L'Osservatore Romano*, English edition, 6 May 1991, p. 3. Cf. John Paul II, Encyclical Letter *Sollicitudo Rei Socialis*, 9: AAS 80 (1988), 520-523.

countries have shown the ability to create material well-being, but often at the expense of man and the weaker social classes. "One cannot ignore the fact that the frontiers of wealth and poverty intersect within societies themselves, whether developed or developing. In fact, just as social inequalities — even to the point of lives of misery and poverty — exist in rich countries, so, in parallel fashion, in the less developed countries one often sees manifestations of selfishness and a flaunting of wealth which is as disconcerting as it is scandalous."[769]

e. Need for more educational and cultural formation

375. *For the Church's social doctrine, the economy "is only one aspect and one dimension of the whole of human activity.* If economic life is absolutized, if the production and consumption of goods become the centre of social life and society's only value, not subject to any other value, the reason is to be found not so much in the economic system itself as in the fact that the entire socio-cultural system, by ignoring the ethical and religious dimension, has been weakened, and ends up limiting itself to the production of goods and services alone."[770] The life of man, just like the social life of the community, must not be reduced to its materialistic dimension, even if material goods are extremely necessary both for mere survival and for improving the quality of life. "An increased sense of God and increased self-awareness are fundamental to any *full development of human society*."[771]

376. *Faced with the rapid advancement of technological and economic progress, and with the equally rapid transformation of the processes of production and consumption, the Magisterium senses the need to propose a great deal of educational and cultural formation,* for the Church is aware that "to call for an existence which is qualitatively more satisfying is of itself legitimate, but one cannot fail to draw attention to the new responsibilities and dangers connected with this phase of history . . . In singling out new needs and new means to meet them, one must be guided by a comprehensive picture of man which respects all the dimensions of his being and which subordinates his material and instinctive dimensions to his interior and spiritual ones . . . Of itself, an economic system does not possess criteria for correctly distinguishing new and higher forms of satisfying human needs from artificial new needs which hinder the formation of a mature personality. Thus *a great deal of educational and cultural work* is urgently needed, including the education of consumers in the responsible use of their power of choice, the formation of a strong sense of responsibility among producers and among people in the mass media in particular, as well as the necessary intervention by public authorities."[772]

---

[769] John Paul II, Encyclical Letter *Sollicitudo Rei Socialis*, 14: AAS 80 (1988), 526-527.
[770] John Paul II, Encyclical Letter *Centesimus Annus*, 39: AAS 83 (1991), 842.
[771] *Catechism of the Catholic Church*, 2441.
[772] John Paul II, Encyclical Letter *Centesimus Annus*, 36: AAS 83 (1991), 838-839.

CHAPTER EIGHT

THE POLITICAL COMMUNITY

I. BIBLICAL ASPECTS

a. God's dominion

377. *At the beginning of its history, the people of Israel are unlike other peoples in that they have no king, for they recognize the dominion of Yahweh alone. It is God who inter-venes on Israel's behalf through charismatic individuals*, as recorded in the Book of Judges. The people approach the last of these individuals, Samuel, prophet and judge, to ask for a king (cf. *1 Sam* 8:5; 10:18-19). Samuel warns the Israelites about the consequences of a despotic exercise of kingship (cf. *1 Sam* 8:11-18). However, the authority of the king can also be experienced as a gift of Yahweh who comes to the assistance of his people (cf. *1 Sam* 9:16). In the end, Saul is anointed king (cf. *1 Sam* 10:1-2). These events show the tension that brought Israel to understand kingship in a different way than it was understood by neigh-boring peoples. The king, chosen by Yahweh (cf. *Dt* 17:15; *1 Sam* 9:16) and con-secrated by him (cf. *1 Sam* 16:12-13), is seen as God's son (cf. *Ps* 2:7) and is to make God's dominion and plan of salvation visible (cf. *Ps* 72). The king, then, is to be the defender of the weak and the guarantor of justice for the people. The denunciations of the prophets focus precisely on the kings' failure to fulfil these functions (cf. *1 Kg* 21; *Is* 10:1-4; *Am* 2:6-8, 8:4-8; *Mic* 3:1-4).

378. *The prototype of the king chosen by Yahweh is David, whose humble origins are a favorite topic of the biblical account* (cf. *1 Sam* 16:1-13). David is the recipient of the promise (cf. *2 Sam* 7:13-16; *Ps* 89:2-38, 132:11-18), which places him at the beginning of a special kingly tradition, the "messianic" tradition. Notwithstanding all the sins and infidelities of David and his successors, this tradition culminates in Jesus Christ, who is *par excellence* "Yahweh's anointed" (that is, "the Lord's con-secrated one," cf. *1 Sam* 2:35, 24:7,11, 26:9,16; *Ex* 30:22-32), the son of David (cf. *Mt* 1:1-17; *Lk* 3:23-38; *Rom* 1:3).

   The failure of kingship on the historical level does not lead to the disappearance of the ideal of a king who, in fidelity to Yahweh, will govern with wisdom and act in jus-tice. This hope reappears time and again in the Psalms (cf. *Ps* 2, 18, 20, 21, 72). In the messianic oracles, the figure of a king endowed with the Lord's Spirit, full of wisdom and capable of rendering justice to the poor, is awaited in eschatological times (cf. *Is* 11:2-5; *Jer* 23:5-6). As true shepherd of the people of Israel (cf. *Ezek* 34:23-24, 37:24), he will bring peace to the nations (cf. *Zech* 9:9-10). In Wisdom

Literature, the king is presented as the one who renders just judgments and abhors iniquity (cf. *Prov* 16:12), who judges the poor with equity (cf. *Prov* 29:14) and is a friend to those with a pure heart (cf. *Prov* 22:11). There is a gradual unfolding of the proclamation of what the Gospels and other New Testament writings see fulfilled in Jesus of Nazareth, the definitive incarnation of what the Old Testament foretold about the figure of the king.

b. Jesus and political authority

379. *Jesus refuses the oppressive and despotic power wielded by the rulers of the nations* (cf. *Mk* 10:42) *and rejects their pretension in having themselves called benefactors* (cf. *Lk* 22:25), *but he does not directly oppose the authorities of his time.* In his pronouncement on the paying of taxes to Caesar (cf. *Mk* 12:13-17; *Mt* 22:15-22; *Lk* 20:20-26), he affirms that we must give to God what is God's, implicitly condemning every attempt at making temporal power divine or absolute: God alone can demand everything from man. At the same time, temporal power has the right to its due: Jesus does not consider it unjust to pay taxes to Caesar.

Jesus, the promised Messiah, fought against and overcame the temptation of a political messianism, characterized by the subjection of the nations (cf. *Mt* 4:8-11; *Lk* 4:5-8). He is the Son of Man who came "to serve, and to give his life" (*Mk* 10:45; cf. *Mt* 20:24-28: *Lk* 22:24-27). As his disciples are discussing with one another who is the greatest, Jesus teaches them that they must make themselves least and the servants of all (cf. *Mk* 9:33-35), showing to the sons of Zebedee, James and John, who wish to sit at His right hand, the path of the cross (cf. *Mk* 10:35-40; *Mt* 20:20-23).

c. The early Christian communities

380. *Submission, not passive but "for the sake of conscience"* (*Rom* 13:5), *to legitimate authority responds to the order established by God.* Saint Paul defines the relationships and duties that a Christian is to have towards the authorities (cf. *Rom* 13:1-7). He insists on the civic duty to pay taxes: "Pay all of them their dues, taxes to whom taxes are due, revenue to whom revenue is due, fear to whom fear is due, respect to who respect is due" (*Rom* 13:7). The Apostle certainly does not intend to legitimize every authority so much as to help Christians to *"take thought for what is noble in the sight of all"* (*Rom* 12:17), including their relations with the authorities, insofar as the authorities are at the service of God for the good of the person (cf. *Rom* 13:4; *1 Tim* 2:1-2; *Tit* 3:1) and "to execute [God's] wrath on the wrongdoer" (*Rom* 13:4).

Saint Peter exhorts Christians to "be subject for the Lord's sake to every human institution" (*1 Pet* 2:13). The king and his governors have the duty "to punish those who do wrong and to praise those who do right" (*1 Pet* 2:14). This authority of theirs must be "honored" (*1 Pet* 2: 17), that is, recognized, because God demands correct behavior that will *"silence the ignorance of foolish men"* (*1 Pet* 2:15). Freedom must not be used as a pretext for evil but to serve God (cf. *1 Pet* 2:16). It concerns free and responsible obedience to an authority that causes justice to be respected, ensuring the common good.

381. *Praying for rulers, which Saint Paul recommended even as he was being persecuted, implicitly indicates what political authority ought to guarantee: a calm and tranquil life led with piety and dignity* (cf. *1 Tim* 2:1-2). Christians must "be ready for any honest work" (*Tit* 3:1), showing "perfect courtesy towards all" (*Tit* 3:2), in the awareness that they are saved not by their own deeds but by God's mercy. Without "the washing of regeneration and renewal in the Holy Spirit, which he poured out upon us richly through Jesus Christ our Savior" (*Tit* 3:5-6), all people are "foolish, disobedient, led astray, slaves to various passions and pleasures, passing [their] days in malice and envy, hated by men and hating one another" (*Tit* 3:3). We must not forget the miserable state of the human condition marred by sin, but redeemed by God's love.

382. *When human authority goes beyond the limits willed by God, it makes itself a deity and demands absolute submission; it becomes the Beast of the Apocalypse, an image of the power of the imperial persecutor* "drunk with the blood of the saints and the blood of the martyrs of Jesus" (*Rev* 17:6). The Beast is served by the "false prophet" (*Rev* 19:20), who, with beguiling signs, induces people to adore it. This vision is a prophetic indication of the snares used by Satan to rule men, stealing his way into their spirit with lies. But Christ is the Victorious Lamb who, down the course of human history, overcomes every power that would make it absolute. Before such a power, Saint John suggests the resistance of the martyrs; in this way, believers bear witness that corrupt and satanic power is defeated, because it no longer has any authority over them.

383. *The Church proclaims that Christ, the conqueror of death, reigns over the universe that he himself has redeemed. His kingdom includes even the present times and will end only when everything is handed over to the Father and human history is brought to completion in the final judgment* (cf. *1 Cor* 15:20-28). Christ reveals to human authority, always tempted by the desire to dominate, its authentic and complete meaning as service. God is the one Father, and Christ the one Teacher, of all mankind, and all people are brothers and sisters. Sovereignty belongs to God. The Lord, however, "has not willed to reserve to himself all exercise of power. He entrusts to every creature the functions it is capable of performing, according to the capacities of its own nature. This mode of governance ought to be followed in social life. The way God acts in governing the world, which bears witness to such great regard for human freedom, should inspire the wisdom of those who govern human communities. They should behave as ministers of divine providence."[773]

The biblical message provides endless inspiration for Christian reflection on political power, recalling that it comes from God and is an integral part of the order that he created. This order is perceived by the human conscience and, in social life, finds its fulfilment in the truth, justice, freedom and solidarity that bring peace.[774]

---

[773] *Catechism of the Catholic Church*, 1884.
[774] Cf. John XXIII, Encyclical Letter *Pacem in Terris*: AAS 55 (1963), 266-267, 281-291, 301-302; John Paul II, Encyclical Letter *Sollicitudo Rei Socialis*, 39: AAS 80 (1988), 566-568.

II. FOUNDATION AND PURPOSE
OF THE POLITICAL COMMUNITY

a. Political community, the human person and a people

384. *The human person is the foundation and purpose of political life.*[775] Endowed with a rational nature, the human person is responsible for his own choices and able to pursue projects that give meaning to life at the individual and social level. Being open both to the Transcendent and to others is his characteristic and distinguishing trait. Only in relation to the Transcendent and to others does the human person reach the total and complete fulfilment of himself. This means that for the human person, a naturally social and political being, "social life is not something added on"[776] but is part of an essential and indelible dimension.

The political community originates in the nature of persons, whose conscience "*reveals to them and enjoins them to obey*"[777] *the order which God has imprinted in all his creatures*: "a moral and religious order; and it is this order — and not considerations of a purely extraneous, material order — which has the greatest validity in the solution of problems relating to their lives as individuals and as members of society, and problems concerning individual States and their interrelations."[778] This order must be gradually discovered and developed by humanity. The political community, a reality inherent in mankind, exists to achieve an end otherwise unobtainable: the full growth of each of its members, called to cooperate steadfastly for the attainment of the common good,[779] under the impulse of their natural inclinations towards what is true and good.

385. *The political community finds its authentic dimension in its reference to people*: "it is and should in practice be the organic and organizing unity of a real people."[780] The term "a people" does not mean a shapeless multitude, an inert mass to be manipulated and exploited, but a group of persons, each of whom — "at his proper place and in his own way"[781] — is able to form its own opinion on public matters and has the freedom to express its own political sentiments and to bring them to bear positively on the common good. A people "exists in the fullness of the lives of the men and women by whom it is made up, each of whom . . . is a person aware of his own responsibilities and convictions."[782] Those who belong to a political community, although *organically* united among themselves as a people, maintain an irrepressible *autonomy* at the level of personal existence and of the goals to be pursued.

---

[775] Cf. Second Vatican Ecumenical Council, Pastoral Constitution *Gaudium et Spes*, 25: AAS 58 (1966), 1045-1046; *Catechism of the Catholic Church*, 1881; Congregation for the Doctrine of the Faith, *Doctrinal Note on Some Questions Regarding the Participation of Catholics in Political Life* (24 November 2002), 3: Libreria Editrice Vaticana, Vatican City 2002, p. 8.

[776] Second Vatican Ecumenical Council, Pastoral Constitution *Gaudium et Spes*, 25: AAS 58 (1966), 1045.

[777] John XXIII, Encyclical Letter *Pacem in Terris*: AAS 55 (1963), 258.

[778] John XXIII, Encyclical Letter *Mater et Magistra*: AAS 53 (1961), 450.

[779] Cf. Second Vatican Ecumenical Council, Pastoral Constitution *Gaudium et Spes*, 74 AAS 58 (1966), 1095-1097.

[780] Pius XII, Christmas Radio Message of 24 December 1944: AAS 37 (1945), 13.

[781] Pius XII, Christmas Radio Message of 24 December 1944: AAS 37 (1945), 13.

[782] Pius XII, Christmas Radio Message of 24 December 1944: AAS 37 (1945), 13.

386. *The primary characteristic of a people is the sharing of life and values, which is the source of communion on the spiritual and moral level.* "Human society must primarily be considered something pertaining to the spiritual. Through it, in the bright light of truth men should share their knowledge, be able to exercise their rights and fulfil their obligations, be inspired to seek spiritual values, mutually derive genuine pleasure from beauty of whatever order it be, always be readily disposed to pass on to others the best of their own cultural heritage and eagerly strive to make their own the spiritual achievements of others. These benefits not only influence but at the same time give aim and scope to all that has bearing on cultural expressions, economic and social institutions, political movements and forms, laws, and all other structures by which society is outwardly established and constantly developed."[783]

387. *For every people there is in general a corresponding nation, but for various reasons national boundaries do not always coincide with ethnic boundaries.*[784] *Thus the question of minorities arises, which has historically been the cause of more than just a few conflicts. The Magisterium affirms that minorities constitute groups with precise rights and duties, most of all, the right to exist, which* "can be ignored in many ways, including such extreme cases as its denial through overt or indirect forms of genocide."[785] Moreover, minorities have the right to maintain their culture, including their language, and to maintain their religious beliefs, including worship services. In the legitimate quest to have their rights respected, minorities may be driven to seek greater autonomy or even independence; in such delicate circumstances, dialogue and negotiation are the path for attaining peace. In every case, recourse to terrorism is unjustifiable and damages the cause that is being sought. Minorities are also bound by duties, among which, above all, is working for the common good of the State in which they live. In particular, "a minority group has the duty to promote the freedom and dignity of each one of its members and to respect the decisions of each one, even if someone were to decide to adopt the majority culture."[786]

b. Defending and promoting human rights

388. *Considering the human person as the foundation and purpose of the political community means in the first place working to recognize and respect human dignity through defending and promoting fundamental and inalienable human rights:* "In our time the common good is chiefly guaranteed when personal rights and duties are maintained."[787] The rights and duties of the person contain a concise summary of the principal moral and juridical requirements that must preside over the construc-

---

[783] John XXIII, Encyclical Letter *Pacem in Terris*: AAS 55 (1963), 266.
[784] Cf. John XXIII, Encyclical Letter *Pacem in Terris*: AAS 55 (1963), 283.
[785] John Paul II, Message for the 1989 World Day of Peace, 5: AAS 81 (1989), 98.
[786] John Paul II, Message for the 1989 World Day of Peace, 11: AAS 81 (1989), 101.
[787] John XXIII, Encyclical Letter *Pacem in Terris*: AAS 55 (1963), 273; cf. *Catechism of the Catholic Church*, 2237; John Paul II, Message for the 2000 World Day of Peace, 6: AAS 92 (2000), 362; John Paul II, Address to the Fiftieth General Assembly of the United Nations (5 October 1995), 3: *L'Osservatore Romano*, English edition, 11 October 1995, p. 8.

tion of the political community. These requirements constitute an objective norm on which positive law is based and which cannot be ignored by the political community, because both in existential being and in final purpose the human person precedes the political community. Positive law must guarantee that fundamental human needs are met.

389. *The political community pursues the common good when it seeks to create a human environment that offers citizens the possibility of truly exercising their human rights and of fulfilling completely their corresponding duties.* "Experience has taught us that, unless these authorities take suitable action with regard to economic, political and cultural matters, inequalities between citizens tend to become more and more widespread, especially in the modern world, and as a result human rights are rendered totally ineffective and the fulfilment of duties is compromised."[788]

The full attainment of the common good requires that the political community develop a twofold and complementary action that defends and promotes human rights. "It should not happen that certain individuals or social groups derive special advantage from the fact that their rights have received preferential protection. Nor should it happen that governments in seeking to protect these rights, become obstacles to their full expression and free use."[789]

c. Social life based on civil friendship

390. *The profound meaning of civil and political life does not arise immediately from the list of personal rights and duties. Life in society takes on all its significance when it is based on civil friendship and on fraternity.*[790] The sphere of rights, in fact, is that of safeguarded interests, external respect, the protection of material goods and their distribution according to established rules. The sphere of friendship, on the other hand, is that selflessness, detachment from material goods, giving freely and inner acceptance of the needs of others.[791] *Civil friendship*[792] understood in this way is the most genuine actualization of the principle of fraternity, which is inseparable

---

[788] John XXIII, Encyclical Letter *Pacem in Terris*: AAS 55 (1963), 274.

[789] John XXIII, Encyclical Letter *Pacem in Terris*: AAS 55 (1963), 275.

[790] Cf. Saint Thomas Aquinas, *Sententiae Octavi Libri Ethicorum*, VIII, lect. 1: Ed. Leon. 47, 443: "Est enim naturalis amicitia inter eos qui sunt unius gentis ad invicem, inquantum communicant in moribus et convictu. Quartam rationem ponit ibi: *Videtur autem et civitates continere amicitia*. Et dicit quod per amicitiam videntur conservari civitates. Unde legislatores magis student ad amicitiam conservandam inter cives quam etiam ad iustitiam, quam quandoque intermittunt, puta in poenis inferendis, ne dissensio oriatur. Et hoc patet per hoc quod concordia assimulatur amicitiae, quam quidem, scilicet concordiam, legislatores maxime appetunt, contentionem autem civium maxime expellunt, quasi inimicam salutis civitatis. Et quia tota moralis philosophia videtur ordinari ad bonum civile, ut in principio dictum est, pertinet ad moralem considerare de amicitia."

[791] Cf. *Catechism of the Catholic Church*, 2212-2213.

[792] Cf. Saint Thomas Aquinas, *De Regno. Ad Regem Cypri*, I, 10: Ed. Leon. 42, 461: "omnis autem amicitia super aliqua communione firmatur: eos enim qui conueniunt uel per nature originem uel per morum similitudinem uel per cuiuscumque communionem, uidemus amicitia coniungi. . . Non enim conseruatur amore, cum parua uel nulla sit amicitia subiecte multitudinis ad tyrannum, ut prehabitis patet."

from that of freedom and equality.[793] In large part, this principle has not been put into practice in the concrete circumstances of modern political society, above all because of the influence of individualistic and collectivistic ideologies.

391. *A community has solid foundations when it tends toward the integral promotion of the person and of the common good. In such cases, law is defined, respected and lived according to the manner of solidarity and dedication towards one's neighbor.* Justice requires that everyone should be able to enjoy their own goods and rights; this can be considered the minimum measure of love.[794] Social life becomes more human the more it is characterized by efforts to bring about a more mature awareness of the ideal towards which it should be oriented, which is the "civilization of love."[795]

The human being is a person, not just an individual.[796] The term "person" indicates "a nature endowed with intelligence and free will"[797]: he is therefore a reality that is far superior to that of a subject defined by the needs arising solely from his material dimension. The human person, in fact, although participating actively in projects designed to satisfy his needs within the family and within civil and political society, does not find complete self-fulfilment until he moves beyond the mentality of needs and enters into that of gratuitousness and gift, which fully corresponds to his essence and community vocation.

392. *The gospel precept of charity enlightens Christians as to the deepest meaning of political life.* In order to make it truly human, "no better way exists . . . than by fostering an inner sense of justice, benevolence and service for the common good, and by strengthening basic beliefs about the true nature of the political community and about the proper exercise and limits of public authority."[798] The goal which believers must put before themselves is that of *establishing community relationships among people.* The Christian vision of political society places paramount importance on the value of *community,* both as a model for organizing life in society and as a style of everyday living.

III. POLITICAL AUTHORITY

a. The foundation of political authority

393. *The Church has always considered different ways of understanding authority, taking care to defend and propose a model of authority that is founded on the social nature*

---

[793] "Liberty, equality, fraternity" was the motto of the French Revolution. "In the final analysis, these are Christian ideas," John Paul II affirmed during his first visit to France: Homily at Le Bourget (1 June 1980), 5: *AAS* 72 (1980), 720.

[794] Cf. Saint Thomas Aquinas, *Summa Theologiae,* I-II, q. 99: Ed. Leon. 7, 199-205; Saint Thomas Aquinas, *Summa Theologiae,* II-II, q. 23, ad 1um: Ed. Leon. 8, 168.

[795] Paul VI, Message for the 1977 World Day of Peace: *AAS* 68 (1976), 709.

[796] Cf. *Catechism of the Catholic Church,* 2212.

[797] John XXIII, Encyclical Letter *Pacem in Terris*: *AAS* 55 (1963), 259.

[798] Second Vatican Ecumenical Council, Pastoral Constitution *Gaudium et Spes,* 73: *AAS* 58 (1966), 1095.

of the person. "Since God made men social by nature, and since no society can hold together unless some one be over all, directing all to strive earnestly for the common good, every civilized community must have a ruling authority, and this authority, no less than society itself, has its source in nature, and has, consequently, God for its author."[799] *Political authority is therefore necessary*[800] *because of the responsibilities assigned to it. Political authority is and must be a positive and irreplaceable component of civil life.*[801]

394. *Political authority must guarantee an ordered and upright community life without usurping the free activity of individuals and groups but disciplining and orienting this freedom, by respecting and defending the independence of the individual and social subjects, for the attainment of the common good.* Political authority is an instrument of coordination and direction by means of which the many individuals and intermediate bodies must move towards an order in which relationships, institutions and procedures are put at the service of integral human growth. Political authority, in fact, "whether in the community as such or in institutions representing the State, must always be exercised within the limits of morality and on behalf of the dynamically conceived common good, according to a juridical order enjoying legal status. When such is the case citizens are conscience-bound to obey."[802]

395. *The subject of political authority is the people considered in its entirety as those who have sovereignty.* In various forms, this people transfers the exercise of sovereignty to those whom it freely elects as its representatives, but it preserves the prerogative to assert this sovereignty in evaluating the work of those charged with governing and also in replacing them when they do not fulfil their functions satisfactorily. Although this right is operative in every State and in every kind of political regime, a democratic form of government, due to its procedures for verification, allows and guarantees its fullest application.[803] The mere consent of the people is not, however, sufficient for considering "just" the ways in which political authority is exercised.

[799] John XXIII, Encyclical Letter *Pacem in Terris:* AAS 55 (1963), 269; Leo XIII, Encyclical Letter *Immortale Dei*, in *Acta Leonis XIII*, V, 1885, 120.

[800] Cf. *Catechism of the Catholic Church*, 1898; Saint Thomas Aquinas, *De Regno. Ad Regem Cypri*, I, 1: Ed. Leon. 42, 450: "Si igitur naturale est homini quod in societate multorum uiuat, necesse est in omnibus esse aliquid per quod multitudo regatur. Multis enim existentibus hominibus et unoquoque id quod est sibi congruum prouidente, multitudo in diuersa dispergetur nisi etiam esset aliquid de eo quod ad bonum multitudinis pertinet curam habens, sicut et corpus hominis et cuiuslibet animalis deflueret nisi esset aliqua uis regitiua communis in corpore, quae ad bonum commune omnium membrorum intenderet. Quod considerans Salomon dixit: 'Ubi non est gubernator, dissipabitur populus.'"

[801] Cf. *Catechism of the Catholic Church*, 1897; John XXIII, Encyclical Letter *Pacem in Terris:* AAS 55 (1963), 279.

[802] Second Vatican Ecumenical Council, Pastoral Constitution *Gaudium et Spes*, 74: AAS 58 (1966), 1096.

[803] Cf. John Paul II, Encyclical Letter *Centesimus Annus*, 46: AAS 83 (1991), 850-851; John XXIII, Encyclical Letter *Pacem in Terris:* AAS 55 (1963), 271.

b. Authority as moral force

396. *Authority must be guided by the moral law. All of its dignity derives from its being exercised within the context of the moral order,*[804] *"which in turn has God for its first source and final end."*[805] Because of its necessary reference to the moral order, which precedes it and is its basis, and because of its purpose and the people to whom it is directed, authority cannot be understood as a power determined by criteria of a solely sociological or historical character. "There are some indeed who go so far as to deny the existence of a moral order which is transcendent, absolute, universal and equally binding upon all. And where the same law of justice is not adhered to by all, men cannot hope to come to open and full agreement on vital issues."[806] This order "has no existence except in God; cut off from God it must necessarily disintegrate."[807] It is from the moral order that authority derives its power to impose obligations[808] and its moral legitimacy,[809] not from some arbitrary will or from the thirst for power,[810] and it is to translate this order into concrete actions to achieve the common good.[811]

397. *Authority must recognize, respect and promote essential human and moral values.* These are innate and "flow from the very truth of the human being and express and safeguard the dignity of the person; values which no individual, no majority and no State can ever create, modify or destroy."[812] These values do not have their foundation in provisional and changeable "majority" opinions, but must simply be recognized, respected and promoted as elements of an objective moral law, the natural law written in the human heart (cf. *Rom* 2:15), and as the normative point of reference for civil law itself.[813] If, as a result of the tragic clouding of the collective conscience, scepticism were to succeed in casting doubt on the basic principles of the moral law,[814] the legal structure of the State itself would be shaken to its very foundations, being reduced to nothing more than a mechanism for the pragmatic regulation of different and opposing interests.[815]

398. *Authority must enact just laws, that is, laws that correspond to the dignity of the human person and to what is required by right reason.* "Human law is law insofar as it corresponds to right reason and therefore is derived from the eternal law. When,

[804] Cf. Second Vatican Ecumenical Council, Pastoral Constitution *Gaudium et Spes*, 74: AAS 58 (1966), 1095-1097.

[805] John XXIII, Encyclical Letter *Pacem in Terris*: AAS 55 (1963), 270; cf. Pius XII, Christmas Radio Message of 24 December 1944: AAS 37 (1945), 15; *Catechism of the Catholic Church*, 2235.

[806] John XXIII, Encyclical Letter *Mater et Magistra*: AAS 53 (1961), 449-450.

[807] John XXIII, Encyclical Letter *Mater et Magistra*: AAS 53 (1961), 450.

[808] Cf. John XXIII, Encyclical Letter *Pacem in Terris*: AAS 55 (1963), 269-270.

[809] Cf. *Catechism of the Catholic Church*, 1902.

[810] Cf. John XXIII, Encyclical Letter *Pacem in Terris*: AAS 55 (1963), 258-259.

[811] Cf. Pius XII, Encyclical Letter *Summi Pontificatus*: AAS 31 (1939), 432-433.

[812] John Paul II, Encyclical Letter *Evangelium Vitae*, 71: AAS 87 (1995), 483.

[813] Cf. John Paul II, Encyclical Letter *Evangelium Vitae*, 70: AAS 87 (1995), 481-483; John XXIII, Encyclical Letter *Pacem in Terris*: AAS 55 (1963), 258-259, 279-280.

[814] Cf. Pius XII, Encyclical Letter *Summi Pontificatus*: AAS 31 (1939), 423.

[815] Cf. John Paul II, Encyclical Letter *Evangelium Vitae*, 70: AAS 87 (1995), 481-483; John Paul II, Encyclical Letter *Veritatis Splendor*, 97, 99: AAS 85 (1993), 1209-1211; Congregation for the Doctrine of the Faith, *Doctrinal Note on Some Questions Regarding the Participation of Catholics in Political Life* (24 November 2002), 5-6, Libreria Editrice Vaticana, Vatican City 2002, pp. 11-14.

however, a law is contrary to reason, it is called an unjust law; in such a case it ceases to be law and becomes instead an act of violence."[816] Authority that governs according to reason places citizens in a relationship not so much of subjection to another person as of obedience to the moral order and, therefore, to God himself who is its ultimate source.[817] Whoever refuses to obey an authority that is acting in accordance with the moral order "resists what God has appointed" (*Rom* 13:2).[818] Analogously, whenever public authority — which has its foundation in human nature and belongs to the order pre-ordained by God[819] — fails to seek the common good, it abandons its proper purpose and so delegitimizes itself.

c. The right to conscientious objection

399. *Citizens are not obligated in conscience to follow the prescriptions of civil authorities if their precepts are contrary to the demands of the moral order, to the fundamental rights of persons or to the teachings of the Gospel.*[820] Unjust laws pose dramatic problems of conscience for morally upright people: *when they are called to cooperate in morally evil acts they must refuse.*[821] Besides being a moral duty, such a refusal is also a basic human right which, precisely as such, civil law itself is obliged to recognize and protect. "Those who have recourse to conscientious objection must be protected not only from legal penalties but also from any negative effects on the legal, disciplinary, financial and professional plane."[822]

It is a grave duty of conscience not to cooperate, not even formally, in practices which, although permitted by civil legislation, are contrary to the Law of God. Such cooperation in fact can never be justified, not by invoking respect for the freedom of others nor by appealing to the fact that it is foreseen and required by civil law. No one can escape the moral responsibility for actions taken, and all will be judged by God himself based on this responsibility (cf. *Rom* 2:6; 14:12).

d. The right to resist

400. *Recognizing that natural law is the basis for and places limits on positive law means admitting that it is legitimate to resist authority should it violate in a serious or repeated manner the essential principles of natural law.* Saint Thomas Aquinas writes that "one is obliged to obey . . . insofar as it is required by the order of justice."[823] Natural law is therefore the basis of the right to resistance.

[816] Saint Thomas Aquinas, *Summa Theologiae*, I-II, q. 93, a. 3, ad 2um: Ed. Leon. 7, 164: "Lex humana intantum habet rationem legis, inquantum est secundum rationem rectam: et secundum hoc manifestum est quod a lege aeterna derivatur. Inquantum vero a ratione recedit, sic dicitur lex iniqua: et sic non habet rationem legis, sed magis violentiae cuiusdam."

[817] Cf. John XXIII, Encyclical Letter *Pacem in Terris*: AAS 55 (1963), 270.

[818] Cf. *Catechism of the Catholic Church*, 1899-1900.

[819] Cf. Second Vatican Ecumenical Council, Pastoral Constitution *Gaudium et Spes*, 74: AAS 58 (1966), 1095-1097; *Catechism of the Catholic Church*, 1901.

[820] Cf. *Catechism of the Catholic Church*, 2242.

[821] Cf. John Paul II, Encyclical Letter *Evangelium Vitae*, 73: AAS 87 (1995), 486-487.

[822] John Paul II, Encyclical Letter *Evangelium Vitae*, 74: AAS 87 (1995), 488.

[823] Saint Thomas Aquinas, *Summa Theologiae*, II-II, q. 104, a. 6, ad 3um: Ed. Leon. 9, 392: "principibus saecularibus intantum homo oboedire tenetur, inquantum ordo iustitiae requirit."

There can be many different concrete ways this right may be exercised; there are also many different *ends* that may be pursued. Resistance to authority is meant to attest to the validity of a different way of looking at things, whether the intent is to achieve partial change, for example, modifying certain laws, or to fight for a radical change in the situation.

401. *The Church's social doctrine indicates the criteria for exercising the right to resistance:* "Armed resistance to oppression by political authority is not legitimate, unless all the following conditions are met: 1) there is certain, grave and prolonged violation of fundamental rights, 2) all other means of redress have been exhausted, 3) such resistance will not provoke worse disorders, 4) there is well-founded hope of success; and 5) it is impossible reasonably to foresee any better solution."[824] Recourse to arms is seen as an extreme remedy for putting an end to a "manifest, long-standing tyranny which would do great damage to fundamental personal rights and dangerous harm to the common good of the country."[825] The gravity of the danger that recourse to violence entails today makes it preferable in any case that *passive resistance* be practiced, which is "a way more conformable to moral principles and having no less prospects for success."[826]

e. Inflicting punishment

402. *In order to protect the common good, the lawful public authority must exercise the right and the duty to inflict punishments according to the seriousness of the crimes committed.*[827] The State has the twofold responsibility to *discourage* behavior that is harmful to human rights and the fundamental norms of civil life, and to *repair*, through the penal system, the disorder created by criminal activity. In a *State ruled by law* the power to inflict punishment is correctly entrusted to the Courts: "In defining the proper relationships between the legislative, executive and judicial powers, the Constitutions of modern States guarantee the judicial power the necessary independence in the realm of law."[828]

403. *Punishment does not serve merely the purpose of defending the public order and guaranteeing the safety of persons; it becomes as well an instrument for the correction of the offender, a correction that also takes on the moral value of expiation when the guilty party voluntarily accepts his punishment.*[829] There is a twofold purpose here. On the one hand, *encouraging the re-insertion of the condemned person into society*; on the other, *fostering a justice that reconciles*, a justice capable of restoring harmony in social relationships disrupted by the criminal act committed.

---

[824] *Catechism of the Catholic Church*, 2243.

[825] Paul VI, Encyclical Letter *Populorum Progressio*, 31: AAS 59 (1967), 272.

[826] Congregation for the Doctrine of the Faith, Instruction *Libertatis Conscientia*, 79: AAS 79 (1987), 590.

[827] Cf. *Catechism of the Catholic Church*, 2266.

[828] John Paul II, Address to the Italian Association of Judges (31 March 2000), 4: AAS 92 (2000), 633.

[829] Cf. *Catechism of the Catholic Church*, 2266.

In this regard, the activity that prison chaplains are called to undertake is important, not only in the specifically religious dimension of this activity but also in defence of the dignity of those detained. Unfortunately, the conditions under which prisoners serve their time do not always foster respect for their dignity; and often, prisons become places where new crimes are committed. Nonetheless, the environment of penal institutions offers a privileged forum for bearing witness once more to Christian concern for social issues: "I was . . . in prison and you came to me" (Mt 25:35-36).

404. *The activity of offices charged with establishing criminal responsibility, which is always personal in character, must strive to be a meticulous search for truth and must be conducted in full respect for the dignity and rights of the human person;* this means guaranteeing the rights of the guilty as well as those of the innocent. The juridical principle by which punishment cannot be inflicted if a crime has not first been proven must be borne in mind.

In carrying out investigations, the regulation against the use of torture, even in the case of serious crimes, must be strictly observed: "Christ's disciple refuses every recourse to such methods, which nothing could justify and in which the dignity of man is as much debased in his torturer as in the torturer's victim."[830] International juridical instruments concerning human rights correctly indicate a prohibition against torture as a principle which cannot be contravened under any circumstances.

Likewise ruled out is "the use of detention for the sole purpose of trying to obtain significant information for the trial."[831] Moreover, it must be ensured that "trials are conducted swiftly: their excessive length is becoming intolerable for citizens and results in a real injustice."[832]

Officials of the court are especially called to exercise due discretion in their investigations so as not to violate the rights of the accused to confidentiality and in order not to undermine the principle of the presumption of innocence. Since even judges can make mistakes, it is proper that the law provide for suitable compensation for victims of judicial errors.

405. *The Church sees as a sign of hope "a growing public opposition to the death penalty,* even when such a penalty is seen as a kind of 'legitimate defence' on the part of society. Modern society in fact has the means of effectively suppressing crime by rendering criminals harmless without definitively denying them the chance to reform."[833] Whereas, presuming the full ascertainment of the identity and responsibility of the guilty party, the traditional teaching of the Church does not exclude the death penalty "when this is the only practicable way to defend the lives of human beings effectively against the aggressor."[834] Bloodless methods of deter-

---

[830] John Paul II, Address to the International Committee of the Red Cross, Geneva (15 June 1982), 5: *L'Osservatore Romano*, English edition, 26 July 1982, p. 3.
[831] John Paul II, Address to the Italian Association of Judges (31 March 2000), 4: *AAS* 92 (2000), 633.
[832] John Paul II, Address to the Italian Association of Judges (31 March 2000), 4: *AAS* 92 (2000), 633.
[833] John Paul II, Encyclical Letter *Evangelium Vitae*, 27: *AAS* 87 (1995), 432.
[834] *Catechism of the Catholic Church*, 2267.

rence and punishment are preferred as "they better correspond to the concrete conditions of the common good and are more in conformity to the dignity of the human person."[835] The growing number of countries adopting provisions to abolish the death penalty or suspend its application is also proof of the fact that cases in which it is absolutely necessary to execute the offender "are very rare, if not practically non-existent."[836] The growing aversion of public opinion towards the death penalty and the various provisions aimed at abolishing it or suspending its application constitute visible manifestations of a heightened moral awareness.

IV. THE DEMOCRATIC SYSTEM

406. *The Encyclical* Centesimus Annus *contains an explicit and articulate judgment with regard to democracy:* "The Church values the democratic system inasmuch as it ensures the participation of citizens in making political choices, guarantees to the governed the possibility both of electing and holding accountable those who govern them, and of replacing them through peaceful means when appropriate. Thus she cannot encourage the formation of narrow ruling groups which usurp the power of the State for individual interests or for ideological ends. Authentic democracy is possible only in a State ruled by law, and on the basis of a correct conception of the human person. It requires that the necessary conditions be present for the advancement both of the individual through education and formation in true ideals, and of the 'subjectivity' of society through the creation of structures of participation and shared responsibility."[837]

a. **Values and democracy**

407. *An authentic democracy is not merely the result of a formal observation of a set of rules but is the fruit of a convinced acceptance of the values that inspire democratic procedures: the dignity of every human person, the respect of human rights, commitment to the common good as the purpose and guiding criterion for political life.* If there is no general consensus on these values, the deepest meaning of democracy is lost and its stability is compromised.

The Church's social doctrine sees ethical relativism, which maintains that there are no objective or universal criteria for establishing the foundations of a correct hierarchy of values, as one of the greatest threats to modern-day democracies. "Nowadays there is a tendency to claim that agnosticism and skeptical relativism are the philosophy and the basic attitude which correspond to democratic forms of political life. Those who are convinced that they know the truth and firmly adhere to it are considered unreliable from a democratic point of view, since they do not accept that truth is determined by the majority, or that it is subject to variation according to different political trends. It must be observed in this regard that if there is no ultimate truth

---

[835] *Catechism of the Catholic Church*, 2267.
[836] John Paul II, Encyclical Letter *Evangelium Vitae*, 56: AAS 87 (1995), 464; cf. also John Paul II, Message for the 2001 World Day of Peace, 19: AAS 93 (2001), 244, where recourse to the death penalty is described as "unnecessary."
[837] John Paul II, Encyclical Letter *Centesimus Annus*, 46: AAS 83 (1991), 850.

to guide and direct political action, then ideas and convictions can easily be manipulated for reasons of power. As history demonstrates, a democracy without values easily turns into open or thinly disguised totalitarianism."[838] Democracy is fundamentally "a 'system' and as such is a means and not an end. Its 'moral' value is not automatic, but depends on conformity to the moral law to which it, like every other form of human behavior, must be subject: in other words, its morality depends on the morality of the ends which it pursues and of the means which it employs."[839]

b. Institutions and democracy

408. *The Magisterium recognizes the validity of the principle concerning the division of powers in a State*: "it is preferable that each power be balanced by other powers and by other spheres of responsibility which keep it within proper bounds. This is the principle of the 'rule of law,' in which the law is sovereign, and not the arbitrary will of individuals."[840]

In the democratic system, political authority is accountable to the people. Representative bodies must be subjected to effective social control. This control can be carried out above all in free elections which allow the selection and change of representatives. The obligation on the part of those elected to *give an accounting* of their work — which is guaranteed by respecting electoral terms — is a constitutive element of democratic representation.

409. *In their specific areas (drafting laws, governing, setting up systems of checks and balances), elected officials must strive to seek and attain that which will contribute to making civil life proceed well in its overall course.*[841] Those who govern have the obligation to answer to those governed, but this does not in the least imply that representatives are merely passive agents of the electors. The control exercised by the citizens does not in fact exclude the freedom that elected officials must enjoy in order to fulfil their mandate with respect to the objectives to be pursued. These do not depend exclusively on special interests, but in a much greater part on the function of synthesis and mediation that serve the common good, one of the essential and indispensable goals of political authority.

c. Moral components of political representation

410. *Those with political responsibilities must not forget or underestimate the moral dimension of political representation*, which consists in the commitment to share fully in the destiny of the people and to seek solutions to social problems. In this perspective, responsible authority also means authority exercised with those virtues that make it possible to *put power into practice as service* [842] (patience, mod-

---

[838] John Paul II, Encyclical Letter *Centesimus Annus*, 46: AAS 83 (1991), 850.
[839] John Paul II, Encyclical Letter *Evangelium Vitae*, 70: AAS 87 (1995), 482.
[840] John Paul II, Encyclical Letter *Centesimus Annus*, 44: AAS 83 (1991), 848.
[841] Cf. *Catechism of the Catholic Church*, 2236.
[842] Cf. John Paul II, Post-Synodal Apostolic Exhortation *Christifideles Laici*, 42: AAS 81 (1989), 472-476.

esty, moderation, charity, efforts to share), an authority exercised by persons who are able to accept the common good, and not prestige or the gaining of personal advantages, as the true goal of their work.

411. *Among the deformities of the democratic system, political corruption is one of the most serious*[843] *because it betrays at one and the same time both moral principles and the norms of social justice.* It compromises the correct functioning of the State, having a negative influence on the relationship between those who govern and the governed. It causes a growing distrust with respect to public institutions, bringing about a progressive disaffection in the citizens with regard to politics and its representatives, with a resulting weakening of institutions. Corruption radically distorts the role of representative institutions, because they become an arena for political bartering between clients' requests and governmental services. In this way political choices favor the narrow objectives of those who possess the means to influence these choices and are an obstacle to bringing about the common good of all citizens.

412. *As an instrument of the State, public administration at any level — national, regional, community — is oriented towards the service of citizens:* "Being at the service of its citizens, the State is the steward of the people's resources, which it must administer with a view to the common good."[844] *Excessive bureaucratization* is contrary to this vision and arises when "institutions become complex in their organization and pretend to manage every area at hand. In the end they lose their effectiveness as a result of an impersonal functionalism, an overgrown bureaucracy, unjust private interests and an all-too-easy and generalized disengagement from a sense of duty."[845] The role of those working in public administration is not to be conceived as impersonal or bureaucratic, but rather as an act of generous assistance for citizens, undertaken with a spirit of service.

d. Instruments for political participation

413. *Political parties have the task of fostering widespread participation and making public responsibilities accessible to all.* Political parties are called to interpret the aspirations of civil society, orienting them towards the common good,[846] offering citizens the effective possibility of contributing to the formulation of political choices. They must be democratic in their internal structure, and capable of political synthesis and planning.

Another instrument of political participation is the referendum, whereby a form of direct access to political decisions is practiced. The institution of representation in fact does not exclude the possibility of asking citizens directly about the decisions of great importance for social life.

---

[843] Cf. John Paul II, Encyclical Letter *Sollicitudo Rei Socialis*, 44: AAS 80 (1988), 575-577; John Paul II, Encyclical Letter *Centesimus Annus*, 48: AAS 83 (1991), 852-854; John Paul II, Message for the 1999 World Day of Peace, 6: AAS 91 (1991), 381-382.

[844] John Paul II, Message for the 1998 World Day of Peace, 5: AAS 90 (1998), 152.

[845] John Paul II, Post-Synodal Apostolic Exhortation *Christifideles Laici*, 41: AAS 81 (1989), 471-472.

[846] Cf. Second Vatican Ecumenical Council, Pastoral Constitution *Gaudium et Spes*, 75: AAS 58 (1966), 1097-1099.

e. Information and democracy

414. *Information is among the principal instruments of democratic participation.* Participation without an understanding of the situation of the political community, the facts and the proposed solutions to problems is unthinkable. It is necessary to guarantee a real pluralism in this delicate area of social life, ensuring that there are many forms and instruments of information and communications. It is likewise necessary to facilitate conditions of equality in the possession and use of these instruments by means of appropriate laws. Among the obstacles that hinder the full exercise of the right to objectivity in information,[847] special attention must be given to the phenomenon of the news media being controlled by just a few people or groups. This has dangerous effects for the entire democratic system when this phenomenon is accompanied by ever closer ties between governmental activity and the financial and information establishments.

415. *The media must be used to build up and sustain the human community in its different sectors: economic, political, cultural, educational and religious.*[848] "The information provided by the media is at the service of the common good. Society has a right to information based on truth, freedom, justice and solidarity."[849]

The essential question is whether the current information system is contributing to the betterment of the human person; that is, does it make people more spiritually mature, more aware of the dignity of their humanity, more responsible or more open to others, in particular to the neediest and the weakest. A further aspect of great importance is the requisite that new technologies respect legitimate cultural differences.

416. *In the world of the media the intrinsic difficulties of communications are often exacerbated by ideology, the desire for profit and political control, rivalry and conflicts between groups, and other social evils.* Moral values and principles apply also to the media. "The ethical dimension relates not just to the content of communication (the message) and the process of communication (how the communicating is done) but to fundamental structural and systemic issues, often involving large questions of policy bearing upon the distribution of sophisticated technology and product (who shall be information rich and who shall be information poor?)."[850]

In all three areas — the message, the process and structural issues — one fundamental moral principle always applies: the human person and the human community are

---

[847] Cf. John XXIII, Encyclical Letter *Pacem in Terris*: AAS 55 (1963), 260.

[848] Cf. Second Vatican Ecumenical Council, Decree *Inter Mirifica*, 3: AAS 56 (1964), 146; Paul VI, Apostolic Exhortation *Evangelii Nuntiandi*, 45: AAS 68 (1976), 35-36; John Paul II, Encyclical Letter *Redemptoris Missio*, 37: AAS 83 (1991), 282-286; Pontifical Council for Social Communications, *Communio et Progressio*. 126-134: AAS 63 (1971), 638-640; Pontifical Council for Social Communications, *Aetatis Novae*, 11: AAS 84 (1992), 455-456; Pontifical Council for Social Communications, *Ethics in Advertising* (22 February 1997), 4-8: L'Osservatore Romano, English edition, 16 April 1997, pp. I-II.

[849] *Catechism of the Catholic Church*, 2494; cf. Second Vatican Ecumenical Council, Decree *Inter Mirifica*, 11: AAS 56 (1964), 148-149.

[850] Pontifical Council for Social Communications, *Ethics in Communications* (4 June 2000), 20, Libreria Editrice Vaticana, Vatican City 2000, p. 22.

the end and measure of the use of the media. *A second principle is complementary to the first: the good of human beings cannot be attained independently of the common good of the community to which they belong.*[851] It is necessary that citizens participate in the decision-making process concerning media policies. This participation, which is to be public, has to be genuinely representative and not skewed in favor of special interest groups when the media are a money-making venture.[852]

V. THE POLITICAL COMMUNITY AT THE SERVICE OF CIVIL SOCIETY

a. Value of civil society

417. *The political community is established to be of service to civil society, from which it originates.* The Church has contributed to the distinction between the political community and civil society above all by her vision of man, understood as an autonomous, relational being who is open to the Transcendent. This vision is challenged by political ideologies of an individualistic nature and those of a totalitarian character, which tend to absorb civil society into the sphere of the State. The Church's commitment on behalf of social pluralism aims at bringing about a more fitting attainment of the common good and democracy itself, according to the principles of solidarity, subsidiarity and justice.

Civil society is the sum of relationships and resources, cultural and associative, that are relatively independent from the political sphere and the economic sector. "The purpose of civil society is universal, since it concerns the common good, to which each and every citizen has a right in due proportion."[853] This is marked by a planning capacity that aims at fostering a freer and more just social life, in which the various groups of citizens can form associations, working to develop and express their preferences, in order to meet their fundamental needs and defend their legitimate interests.

b. Priority of civil society

418. *The political community and civil society, although mutually connected and interdependent, are not equal in the hierarchy of ends.* The political community is essentially at the service of civil society and, in the final analysis, the persons and groups of which civil society is composed.[854] Civil society, therefore, cannot be considered an extension or a changing component of the political community; rather, it has priority because it is in civil society itself that the political community finds its justification.

The State must provide an adequate legal framework for social subjects to engage freely in their different activities and it must be ready to intervene, when necessary and

---

[851] Cf. Pontifical Council for Social Communications, *Ethics in Communications* (4 June 2000), 22, Libreria Editrice Vaticana, Vatican City 2000, pp. 23-25.

[852] Cf. Pontifical Council for Social Communications, *Ethics in Communications* (4 June 2000), 24, Libreria Editrice Vaticana, Vatican City 2000, pp. 26-28.

[853] Leo XIII, Encyclical Letter *Rerum Novarum: Acta Leonis XIII*, 11 (1892), 134.

[854] Cf. *Catechism of the Catholic Church*, 1910.

with respect for the principle of subsidiarity, so that the interplay between free associations and democratic life may be directed to the common good. Civil society is in fact multifaceted and irregular; it does not lack its ambiguities and contradictions. It is also the arena where different interests clash with one another, with the risk that the stronger will prevail over the weaker.

c. **Application of the principle of subsidiarity**

419. *The political community is responsible for regulating its relations with civil society according to the principle of subsidiarity.*[855] It is essential that the growth of democratic life begin within the fabric of society. The activities of civil society — above all *volunteer organizations* and *cooperative endeavors* in the *private-social* sector, all of which are succinctly known as the "*third sector*," to distinquish from the State and the market — represent the most appropriate ways to develop the social dimension of the person, who finds in these activities the necessary space to express himself fully. The progressive expansion of social initiatives beyond the State-controlled sphere creates new areas for the active presence and direct action of citizens, integrating the functions of the State. This important phenomenon has often come about largely through informal means and has given rise to new and positive ways of exercising personal rights, which have brought about a qualitative enrichment of democratic life.

420. *Cooperation, even in its less structured forms, shows itself to be one of the most effective responses to a mentality of conflict and unlimited competition that seems so prevalent today.* The relationships that are established in a climate of cooperation and solidarity overcome ideological divisions, prompting people to seek out what unites them rather than what divides them.

Many experiences of volunteer work are examples of great value that call people to look upon civil society as a place where it is possible to rebuild a public ethic based on solidarity, concrete cooperation and fraternal dialogue. All are called to look with confidence to the potentialities that thus present themselves and to lend their own personal efforts for the good of the community in general and, in particular, for the good of the weakest and the neediest. In this way, the principle of the "subjectivity of society" is also affirmed.[856]

VI. THE STATE AND RELIGIOUS COMMUNITIES

A. RELIGIOUS FREEDOM, A FUNDAMENTAL HUMAN RIGHT

421. *The Second Vatican Council committed the Catholic Church to the promotion of religious freedom.* The Declaration *Dignitatis Humanae* explains in its subtitle that it intends to proclaim "the right of the person and of communities to social and civil freedom in religious matters." In order that this freedom, willed by God and inscribed in human nature, may be exercised, no obstacle should be placed in its

---

[855] Cf. Pius XI, Encyclical Letter *Quadragesimo Anno*: AAS 23 (1931), 203; *Catechism of the Catholic Church*, 1883-1885.
[856] Cf. John Paul II, Encyclical Letter *Centesimus Annus*, 49: AAS 83 (1991), 855.

way, since "the truth cannot be imposed except by virtue of its own truth."[857] The dignity of the person and the very nature of the quest for God require that all men and women should be free from every constraint in the area of religion.[858] Society and the State must not force a person to act against his conscience or prevent him from acting in conformity with it.[859] Religious freedom is not a moral licence to adhere to error, nor as an implicit right to error.[860]

422. *Freedom of conscience and religion "concerns man both individually and socially."*[861] The right to religious freedom must be recognized in the juridical order and sanctioned as a civil right;[862] nonetheless, it is not of itself an unlimited right. The *just limits* of the exercise of religious freedom must be determined in each social situation with political prudence, according to the requirements of the common good, and ratified by the civil authority through legal norms consistent with the objective moral order. Such norms are required by "the need for the effective safeguarding of the rights of all citizens and for the peaceful settlement of conflicts of rights, also by the need for an adequate care of genuine public peace, which comes about when men live together in good order and in true justice, and finally by the need for a proper guardianship of public morality."[863]

423. *Because of its historical and cultural ties to a nation, a religious community might be given special recognition on the part of the State. Such recognition must in no way create discrimination within the civil or social order for other religious groups.*[864] The vision of the relations between States and religious organizations promoted by the Second Vatican Council corresponds to the requirements of a State ruled by law and to the norms of international law.[865] The Church is well aware that this vision is not shared by all; the right to religious freedom, unfortunately, "is being violated by many States, even to the point that imparting catechesis, having it imparted, and receiving it become punishable offences."[866]

B. The Catholic Church and the Political Community

a. Autonomy and independence

424. *Although the Church and the political community both manifest themselves in visible organizational structures, they are by nature different because of their configuration*

---

[857] Second Vatican Ecumenical Council, Declaration *Dignitatis Humanae*, 1: AAS 58 (1966), 929.

[858] Cf. Second Vatican Ecumenical Council, Declaration *Dignitatis Humanae*, 2: AAS 58 (1966), 930-931; *Catechism of the Catholic Church*, 2106.

[859] Cf. Second Vatican Ecumenical Council, Declaration *Dignitatis Humanae*, 3: AAS 58 (1966), 931-932.

[860] Cf. *Catechism of the Catholic Church*, 2108.

[861] *Catechism of the Catholic Church*, 2105.

[862] Cf. Second Vatican Ecumenical Council, Declaration *Dignitatis Humanae*, 2: AAS 58 (1966), 930-931; *Catechism of the Catholic Church*, 2108.

[863] Second Vatican Ecumenical Council, Declaration *Dignitatis Humanae*, 7: AAS 58 (1966), 935; *Catechism of the Catholic Church*, 2109.

[864] Cf. Second Vatican Ecumenical Council, Declaration *Dignitatis Humanae*, 6: AAS 58 (1966), 933-934; *Catechism of the Catholic Church*, 2107.

[865] Cf. John Paul II, Message for the 1999 World Day of Peace, 5: AAS 91 (1999), 380-381.

[866] John Paul II, Apostolic Exhortation *Catechesi Tradendae*, 14: AAS 71 (1979), 1289.

and because of the ends they pursue. The Second Vatican Council solemnly reaffirmed that, "in their proper spheres, the political community and the Church are mutually independent and self-governing."[867] The Church is organized in ways that are suitable to meet the spiritual needs of the faithful, while the different political communities give rise to relationships and institutions that are at the service of everything that is part of the temporal common good. The autonomy and independence of these two realities is particularly evident with regards to their ends.

The duty to respect religious freedom requires that the political community guarantee the Church the space needed to carry out her mission. For her part, the Church has no particular area of competence concerning the structures of the political community: "The Church respects the *legitimate autonomy of the democratic order* and is not entitled to express preferences for this or that institutional or constitutional solution,"[868] nor does it belong to her to enter into questions of the merit of political programmes, except as concerns their religious or moral implications.

b. Cooperation

425. *The mutual autonomy of the Church and the political community does not entail a separation that excludes cooperation.* Both of them, although by different titles, serve the personal and social vocation of the same human beings. The Church and the political community, in fact, express themselves in organized structures that are not ends in themselves but are intended for the service of man, to help him to exercise his rights fully, those inherent in his reality as a citizen and a Christian, and to fulfil correctly his corresponding duties. The Church and the political community can more effectively render this service "for the good of all if each works better for wholesome mutual cooperation in a way suitable to the circumstances of time and place."[869]

426. *The Church has the right to the legal recognition of her proper identity.* Precisely because her mission embraces all of human reality, the Church, sensing that she is "truly and intimately linked with mankind and its history,"[870] claims the freedom to express her moral judgment on this reality, whenever it may be required to defend the fundamental rights of the person or for the salvation of souls.[871]

The Church therefore seeks: freedom of expression, teaching and evangelization; freedom of public worship; freedom of organization and of her own internal government; freedom of selecting, educating, naming and transferring her ministers; freedom for constructing religious buildings; freedom to acquire and possess sufficient goods for her activity; and freedom to form associations not only

---

[867] Second Vatican Ecumenical Council, Pastoral Constitution *Gaudium et Spes*, 76: AAS 58 (1966), 1099; cf. *Catechism of the Catholic Church*, 2245.
[868] John Paul II, Encyclical Letter *Centesimus Annus*, 47: AAS 83 (1991), 852.
[869] Second Vatican Ecumenical Council, Pastoral Constitution *Gaudium et Spes*, 76: AAS 58 (1966), 1099.
[870] Second Vatican Ecumenical Council, Pastoral Constitution *Gaudium et Spes*, 1: AAS 58 (1966), 1026.
[871] Cf. Code of Canon Law, canon 747, § 2; *Catechism of the Catholic Church*, 2246.

for religious purposes but also for educational, cultural, health care and charitable purposes.[872]

427. *In order to prevent or attenuate possible conflicts between the Church and the political community, the juridical experience of the Church and the State have variously defined stable forms of contact and suitable instruments for guaranteeing harmonious relations.* This experience is an essential reference point for all cases in which the State has the presumption to invade the Church's area of action, impairing the freedom of her activity to the point of openly persecuting her or, vice versa, for cases in which church organizations do not act properly with respect to the State.

---

[872] Cf. John Paul II, Letter to the Heads of State Signing the Final Helsinki Act (1 September 1980), 4: *AAS* 72 (1980), 1256-1258.

CHAPTER NINE

THE INTERNATIONAL COMMUNITY

I. BIBLICAL ASPECTS

a. Unity of the human family

428. *The biblical accounts of creation bring out the unity of the human family and teach that the God of Israel is the Lord of history and of the cosmos.* His action embraces the whole world and the entire human family, for whom his work of creation is destined. God's decision to make man in his image and likeness (cf. Gen 1:26-27) gives the human being a unique dignity that extends to all generations (cf. Gen 5) and throughout the entire earth (cf. Gen 10). *The Book of Genesis indicates moreover that the human being was not created in isolation* but within a context, an integral part of which are those living spaces that ensure his freedom (the garden), various possibilities for food (the trees of the garden), work (the command to cultivate) and above all community (the gift of someone who is like himself) (cf. Gen 2:8-24). Throughout the Old Testament, the conditions that ensure the fullness of human life are the object of a divine blessing. God wants to guarantee that man has what is necessary for his growth, his freedom of self-expression, success in his work, and a wealth of human relationships.

429. *Following the destruction wrought by the flood, God's covenant with Noah (cf. Gen 9:1-17), and in him with all of humanity, shows that God wants to maintain for the human community the blessing of fertility,* the task of subduing creation and the absolute dignity and inviolability of human life that had characterized the first creation. This is God's desire despite the fact that, with sin, the decadence of violence and injustice, which was punished by the flood, had entered creation. The Book of *Genesis* presents with admiration the diversity of peoples, the result of God's creative activity (cf. Gen 10:1-32). At the same time, it denounces man's refusal to accept his condition as creature with the episode of the Tower of Babel (cf. Gen 11,1-9). In the divine plan, all peoples had "one language and the same words" (cf. Gen 11:1), but humanity became divided, turning its back on the Creator (cf. Gen 11:4).

430. *The covenant that God established with Abraham, chosen to be "the father of a multitude of nations" (Gen 17:4), opens the way for the human family to make a return to its Creator.* The history of salvation leads the people of Israel to believe that God's action was restricted to their land. Little by little, however, the conviction grows that God is at work also among other nations (cf. Is 19:18-25). The

Prophets would announce, for the eschatological times, a pilgrimage of the nations to the Lord's temple and an era of peace among the peoples (cf. *Is* 2:2-5, 66:18-23). Israel, scattered in exile, would become definitively aware of its role as a witness to the one God (cf. *Is* 44:6-8), the Lord of the world and of the history of the nations (cf. *Is* 44:24-28).

b. Jesus Christ, prototype and foundation of the new humanity

431. *The Lord Jesus is the prototype and foundation of the new humanity.* In him, the true "likeness of God" (2 *Cor* 4:4), man — who is created in the image of God — finds his fulfilment. In the definitive witness of love that God has made manifest in the cross of Christ, all the barriers of enmity have already been torn down (cf. *Eph* 2:12-18), and for those who live a new life in Christ, racial and cultural differences are no longer causes of division (cf. *Rom* 10:12; *Gal* 3:26-28; *Col* 3:11).

Thanks to the Spirit, the Church is aware of the divine plan of unity that involves the entire human race (cf. *Acts* 17:26), a plan destined to reunite in the mystery of salvation wrought under the saving Lordship of Christ (cf. *Eph* 1:8-10) all of created reality, which is fragmented and scattered. From the day of Pentecost, when the Resurrection is announced to diverse peoples, each of whom understand it in their own language (cf. *Acts* 2:6), the Church fulfils her mission of restoring and bearing witness to the unity lost at Babel. Due to this ecclesial ministry, the human family is called to rediscover its unity and recognize the richness of its differences, in order to attain "full unity in Christ."[873]

c. The universal vocation of Christianity

432. *The Christian message offers a universal vision of the life of men and peoples on earth* [874] *that makes us realize the unity of the human family*.[875] This unity is not to be built on the force of arms, terror or abuse of power; rather, it is the result of that "supreme *model of unity*, which is a reflection of the intimate life of God, one God in three Persons, . . . what we Christians mean by the word '*communion*'";[876] it is an achievement of the *moral and cultural force of freedom*.[877] The Christian message has been decisive for making humanity understand that peoples tend to unite not only because of various forms of organization, politics, economic plans or in the name of an abstract ideological internationalism, but because they freely seek to cooperate, aware "that they are living members of the whole human family."[878] The world community must be presented, over and over again and with

---

[873] Cf. Second Vatican Ecumenical Council, Dogmatic Constitution *Lumen Gentium*, 1: AAS 57 (1965), 5.

[874] Cf. Pius XII, Address to Catholic Jurists on the Communities of States and Peoples (6 December 1953), 2: AAS 45 (1953), 795.

[875] Cf. Second Vatican Ecumenical Council, Pastoral Constitution *Gaudium et Spes*, 42: AAS 58 (1966), 1060-1061.

[876] John Paul II, Encyclical Letter *Sollicitudo Rei Socialis*, 40: AAS 80 (1988), 569.

[877] Cf. John Paul II, Address to the Fiftieth General Assembly of the United Nations (5 October 1995), 12: *L'Osservatore Romano*, English edition, 11 October 1995, p. 9.

[878] John XXIII, Encylical Letter *Pacem in Terris*: AAS 55 (1963), 296.

ever increasing clarity, as the concrete figure of the unity willed by the Creator. "The unity of the human family has always existed, because its members are human beings all equal by virtue of their natural dignity. Hence there will always exist the objective need to promote, in sufficient measure, the *universal* common good, which is the common good of the entire human family."[879]

II. THE FUNDAMENTAL RULES
OF THE INTERNATIONAL COMMUNITY

a. The international community and values

433. *The centrality of the human person and the natural inclination of persons and peoples to establish relationships among themselves are the fundamental elements for building a true international community, the ordering of which must aim at guaranteeing the effective universal common good.*[880] Despite the widespread aspiration to build an authentic international community, the unity of the human family is not yet becoming a reality. This is due to obstacles originating in materialistic and nationalistic ideologies that contradict the values of the person integrally considered in all his various dimensions, material and spiritual, individual and community. In particular, any theory or form whatsoever of racism and racial discrimination is morally unacceptable.[881]

The coexistence among nations is based on the same values that should guide relations among human beings: truth, justice, active solidarity and freedom.[882] The Church's teaching, with regard to the constitutive principles of the international community, requires that relations among peoples and political communities be justly regulated according to the principles of reason, equity, law and negotiation, excluding recourse to violence and war, as well as to forms of discrimination, intimidation and deceit.[883]

434. *International law becomes the guarantor of the international order,*[884] that is of coexistence among political communities that seek individually to promote the common good of their citizens and strive collectively to guarantee that of all peoples,[885] aware that the common good of a nation cannot be separated from the good of the entire human family.[886]

---

[879] John XXIII, Encylical Letter *Pacem in Terris*: AAS 55 (1963), 292.

[880] Cf. *Catechism of the Catholic Church*, 1911.

[881] Cf. Second Vatican Ecumenical Council, Declaration *Nostra Aetate*, 5: AAS 58 (1966), 743-744; John XXIII. Encyclical Letter *Pacem in Terris*: AAS 55 (1963), 268, 281: Paul VI, Encyclical LetteAr *Populorum Progressio*, 63: AAS 59 (1967), 288; Paul VI, Apostolic Letter *Octogesima Adveniens*, 16: AAS 63 (1971), 413; Pontifical Council for Justice and Peace, *The Church and Racism*. Contribution of the Holy See to the World Conference against Racism, Racial Discrimination, Xenophobia and Related Intolerance, Vatican Press, Vatican City 2001.

[882] Cf. John XXIII, Encyclical Letter *Pacem in Terris*: AAS 55 (1963), 279-280.

[883] Cf. Paul VI, Address to the United Nations (4 October 1965), 2: AAS 57 (1965), 879-880.

[884] Cf. Pius XII, Encyclical Letter *Summi Pontificatus*, 29: AAS 31 (1939) 438-439.

[885] Cf. John XXIII, Encyclical Letter *Pacem in Terris*: AAS 55 (1963), 292; John Paul II, Encyclical Letter *Centesimus Annus*, 52: AAS 83 (1991), 857-858.

[886] Cf. John XXIII, Encyclical Letter in *Pacem in Terris*: AAS 55 (1963), 284.

The international community is a juridical community founded on the sovereignty of each member State, without bonds of subordination that deny or limit its independence.[887] Understanding the international community in this way *does not in any way mean relativizing or destroying the different and distinctive characteristics of each people, but encourages their expression.*[888] Valuing these different identities helps to overcome various forms of division that tend to separate peoples and fill them with a self-centredness that has destabilizing effects.

435. *The Magisterium recognizes the importance of national sovereignty, understood above all as an expression of the freedom that must govern relations between States.*[889] Sovereignty represents the subjectivity [890] of a nation, in the political, economic, social and even cultural sense. The cultural dimension takes on particular importance as a source of strength in resisting acts of aggression or forms of domination that have repercussions on a country's freedom. Culture constitutes the guarantee for the preservation of the identity of a people and expresses and promotes its *spiritual sovereignty.*[891]

National sovereignty is not, however, absolute. Nations can freely renounce the exercise of some of their rights in view of a common goal, in the awareness that they form a "family of nations"[892] where mutual trust, support and respect must prevail. In this perspective, special attention should be given to the fact that there is still no international agreement that adequately addresses "the rights of nations,"[893] the preparation of which could profitably deal with questions concerning justice and freedom in today's world.

b. Relations based on harmony between the juridical and moral orders

436. *To bring about and consolidate an international order that effectively guarantees peaceful mutual relations among peoples, the same moral law that governs the life of men must also regulate relations among States:* "a moral law the observance of which should be inculcated and promoted by the public opinion of all the nations and of

---

[887] Cf. Pius XII, *Christmas Radio Message on a Just International Peace* (24 December 1939) 5: AAS 32 (1940) 9-11; Pius XII, *Address to Catholic Jurists on the Community of States and of Peoples* (6 December 1953) 2: AAS 45 (1953), 395-396; John XXIII, Encyclical Letter *Pacem in Terris*: AAS 55 (1963), 289.

[888] Cf. John Paul II, Address to the Fiftieth General Assembly of the United Nations (5 October 1995), 9-10: *L'Osservatore Romano*, English edition, 11 October 1995, p. 9.

[889] Cf. John XXIII, Encyclical Letter *Pacem in Terris*: AAS 55 (1963), 289-290; John Paul II, Address to the Fiftieth General Assembly of the United Nations (5 October 1995), 15: *L'Osservatore Romano*, English edition, 11 October 1995, p. 10.

[890] Cf. John Paul II, Encyclical Letter *Sollicitudo Rei Socialis*, 15: AAS 80 (1988), 528-530.

[891] Cf. John Paul II, Address to UNESCO (2 June 1980), 14: *L'Osservatore Romano*, English edition, 23 June 1980, p. 11.

[892] John Paul II, Address to the Fiftieth General Assembly of the United Nations (5 October 1995), 14: *L'Osservatore Romano*, English edition, 11 October 1995, p. 10; cf. also John Paul II, Address to the Diplomatic Corps (13 January 2001), 8: *L'Osservatore Romano*, English edition, 17 January 2001, p. 2.

[893] John Paul II, Address to the Fiftieth General Assembly of the United Nations (5 October 1995), 6: *L'Osservatore Romano*, English edition, 11 October 1995, p. 8.

all the States with such a unanimity of voice and force that no one would dare to call it into question or to attenuate its binding force."[894] The *universal moral law*, written on the human heart, must be considered effective and indelible as the living expression of the shared conscience of humanity, a "grammar" [895] on which to build the future of the world.

437. *Universal respect of the principles underlying "a legal structure in conformity with the moral order"* [896] *is a necessary condition for the stability of international life.* The quest for such stability has led to the gradual elaboration of a "right of nations"[897] (*"ius gentium"*), which can be considered as "the ancestor of international law."[898] Juridical and theological reflection, firmly based on natural law, has formulated "universal principles which are prior to and superior to the internal law of States,"[899] such as the unity of the human race, the equal dignity of every people, the rejection of war as a means for resolving disputes, the obligation to cooperate for attaining the common good and the need to be faithful to agreements undertaken (*pacta sunt servanda*). This last principle should be especially emphasized in order to avoid "temptation to appeal to the *law of force* rather than to the *force of law*."[900]

438. *To resolve the tensions that arise among different political communities and can compromise the stability of nations and international security, it is indispensable to make use of common rules in a commitment to negotiation and to reject definitively the idea that justice can be sought through recourse to war.*[901] "If war can end without winners or losers in a suicide of humanity, then we must repudiate the logic which leads to it: the idea that the effort to destroy the enemy, confrontation and war itself are factors of progress and historical advancement."[902]

Not only does the Charter of the United Nations ban recourse to force, but it rejects even the threat to use force.[903] This provision arose from the tragic experience of the Second World War. During that conflict the Magisterium did not fail to identify certain indispensable factors for building a renewed international order: the freedom and territorial integrity of each nation, defence of the rights of minorities, an equitable sharing of the earth's resources, the rejection of war and

---

[894] Pius XII Christmas Radio Message (24 December 1941): AAS 34 (1942) 16.

[895] John Paul II, Address to the Fiftieth General Assembly of the United Nations (5 October 1995), 3: *L'Osservatore Romano*, English edition, 11 October 1995, p. 8.

[896] John XXIII, Encyclical Letter *Pacem in Terris*: AAS 55 (1963), 277.

[897] Cf. Pius XII, Encyclical Letter *Summi Pontificatus*: AAS 31 (1939) 438-439; Pius XII, Christmas Radio Message (24 December 1941): AAS 34 (1942) 16-17; John XXIII Encyical Letter *Pacem in Terris*: AAS 55 (1963), 290, 292.

[898] John Paul II, Address to the Diplomatic Corps (12 January 1991), 8: *L'Osservatore Romano*, English edition, 14 January 1991, p. 3.

[899] John Paul II, Message for the 2004 World Day of Peace, 5: AAS 96 (2004), 116.

[900] John Paul II, Message for the 2004 World Day of Peace, 5: AAS 96 (2004), 117; cf. also John Paul II, Message to the Rector of the Pontifical Lateran University (21 March 2002), 6: *L'Osservatore Romano*, 22 March 2002, p. 6.

[901] Cf. John Paul II, Encyclical Letter *Centesimus Annus*, 23: AAS 83 (1991), 820-821.

[902] John Paul II, Encyclical Letter *Centesimus Annus*, 18: AAS 83 (1991), 816.

[903] Cf. Charter of the United Nations (26 June 1945), art. 2.4; John Paul II, Message for the 2004 World Day of Peace, 6: AAS 96 (2004), 117.

an effective plan of disarmament, fidelity to agreements undertaken and an end to religious persecution.[904]

439. *In order to consolidate the primacy of law, the principle of mutual confidence is of the utmost importance.*[905] *In this perspective, normative instruments for the peaceful resolution of controversies must be reformulated so as to strengthen their scope and binding force.* Processes of negotiation, mediation, conciliation and arbitration that are provided for in international law must be supported with the creation of "a totally effective juridical authority in a peaceful world."[906] Progress in this direction will allow the international community to be seen no longer as a simple aggregation of States in various moments of their existence, but as a structure in which conflicts can be peacefully resolved. "As in the internal life of individual States . . . a system of private vendetta and reprisal has given way to the rule of law, so too a similar step forward is now urgently needed in the international community."[907] In short, "international law must ensure that the law of the more powerful does not prevail."[908]

III. THE ORGANIZATION
OF THE INTERNATIONAL COMMUNITY

a. The value of international organizations

440. *The Church is a companion on the journey towards an authentic international "community," which has taken a specific direction with the founding of the United Nations Organization in 1945.* The United Nations "has made a notable contribution to the promotion of respect for human dignity, the freedom of peoples and the requirements of development, thus preparing the cultural and institutional soil for the building of peace."[909] In general, the Church's social doctrine views positively the role of intergovernmental organizations, especially those operating in specific sectors.[910] However, it has reservations when they address problems incorrectly.[911] The Magisterium recommends that the activity of international

---

[904] Cf. Pius XII, Christmas Radio Message (24 December 1941): AAS 34 (1942), 18.

[905] Cf. Pius XII, Christmas Radio Message (24 December 1945): AAS 38 (1946), 22; John XXIII, Encyclical Letter *Pacem in Terris*: AAS 55 (1963), 287-288.

[906] John Paul II, Address to the International Court of Justice, The Hague (13 May 1985), 4: AAS 78 (1986), 520.

[907] John Paul II, Encyclical Letter *Centesimus Annus*, 52: AAS 83 (1991), 858.

[908] John Paul II, Message for the 2004 World Day of Peace, 9: AAS 96 (2004), 120.

[909] John Paul II, Message for the 2004 World Day of Peace, 7: AAS 96 (2004), 118.

[910] Cf. John XIII, Encyclical Letter *Mater et Magistra*: AAS 53 (1961), 426, 439; John Paul II, Address to the 20th General Conference of FAO (12 November 1979), 6: *L'Osservatore Romano*, English edition, 26 November 1979, p. 6; John Paul II, Address to UNESCO (2 June 1980), 5, 8: *L'Osservatore Romano*, English edition, 23 June 1980, pp. 9-10; John Paul II, Address to the Council of Ministers of the Conference on Security and Cooperation in Europe (CSCE) (30 November 1993), 3, 5: *L'Osservatore Romano*, English edition, 8 December 1993, pp. 1-2.

[911] Cf. John Paul II, Message to Nafis Sadik, Secretary General of the 1994 International Conference on Population and Development (18 March 1994): AAS 87 (1995), 191-192; John Paul II, Message to Gertrude Mongella, Secretary General of the United Nations Fourth World Conference on Woman (26 May 1995): *L'Osservatore Romano*, English edition, 31 May 1995, p. 2.

agencies respond to human needs in social life and in areas of particular importance for the peaceful and ordered coexistence of nations and peoples.[912]

441. *Concern for an ordered and peaceful coexistence within the human family prompts the Magisterium to insist on the need to establish* "some universal public authority acknowledged as such by all and endowed with effective power to safeguard, on the behalf of all, security, regard for justice, and respect for rights."[913] In the course of history, despite the changing viewpoints of the different eras, there has been a constant awareness of the need for a similar authority to respond to worldwide problems arising from the quest for the common good: it is essential that such an authority arise from mutual agreement and that it not be imposed, nor must it be understood as a kind of "global super-State."[914]

Political authority exercised at the level of the international community must be regulated by law, ordered to the common good and respectful of the principle of subsidiarity. "The public authority of the world community is not intended to limit the sphere of action of the public authority of the individual political community, much less to take its place. On the contrary, its purpose is to create, on a world basis, an environment in which the public authorities of each political community, their citizens and intermediate associations can carry out their tasks, fulfil their duties and exercise their rights with greater security."[915]

442. *Because of the globalization of problems, it has become more urgent than ever to stimulate international political action that pursues the goals of peace and development through the adoption of coordinated measures.*[916] The Magisterium recognizes that the interdependence among men and nations takes on a moral dimension and is the determining factor for relations in the modern world in the economic, cultural, political and religious sense. In this context it is hoped that there will be a revision of international organizations, a process that "presupposes the overcoming of political rivalries and the renouncing of all desire to manipulate these organizations, which exist solely for the *common good*,"[917] for the purpose of achieving "*a greater degree of international ordering*."[918]

In particular, intergovernmental structures must effectively perform their functions of control and guidance in the economic field because the attainment of the common good has become a goal that is beyond the reach of individual States, even if they are dominant in terms of power, wealth, and political strength.[919] International

[912] Cf. Second Vatican Ecumenical Council, Pastoral Constitution *Gaudium et Spes*, 84: AAS 58 (1966), 1107-1108.
[913] Second Vatican Ecumenical Council, Pastoral Constitution *Gaudium et Spes*, 82: AAS 58 (1966), 1105; cf. John XXIII, Encyclical Letter *Pacem in Terris*: AAS 55 (1963), 293; Paul VI, Encyclical Letter *Populorum Progressio*, 78: AAS 59 (1967), 295.
[914] John Paul II, Message for the 2003 World Day of Peace, 6: AAS 95 (2003), 344.
[915] John XXIII, Encyclical Letter *Pacem in Terris*: AAS 55 (1963), 294-295.
[916] Cf. Paul VI, Encyclical Letter *Populorum Progressio*, 51-55 and 77-79: AAS 59 (1967), 282-284, 295-296.
[917] John Paul II, Encyclical Letter *Sollicitudo Rei Socialis*, 43: AAS 80 (1988), 575.
[918] John Paul II, Encyclical Letter *Sollicitudo Rei Socialis*, 43: AAS 80 (1988), 575; cf. John Paul II, Message for the 2004 World Day of Peace, 7: AAS 96 (2004), 118.
[919] Cf. John Paul II, Encyclical Letter *Centesimus Annus*, 58: AAS 83 (1991), 863-864.

agencies must moreover guarantee the attainment of that equality which is the basis of the right of all to participate in the process of full development, duly respecting legitimate differences.[920]

443. *The Magisterium positively evaluates the associations that have formed in civil society in order to shape public opinion in its awareness of the various aspects of international life*, with particular attention paid to the respect of human rights, as seen in "the number of recently established private associations, some worldwide in membership, almost all of them devoted to monitoring with great care and commendable objectivity what is happening internationally in this sensitive field."[921]

Governments should feel encouraged by such commitments, which seek to put into practice the ideals underlying the international community, "particularly through the practical gestures of solidarity and peace made by the many individuals also involved in *Non-Governmental Organizations and in Movements for human rights*."[922]

b. **The juridical personality of the Holy See**

444. *The Holy See, or Apostolic See,*[923] *enjoys full international subjectivity as a sovereign authority that performs acts which are juridically its own. It exercises an external sovereignty recognized within the context of the international community which reflects that exercised within the Church* and is marked by *organizational unity* and *independence*. The Church makes use of the juridical means necessary or useful for carrying out her mission.

The international activity of the Holy See is manifested objectively under different aspects: the right to active and passive delegation; the exercise of *ius contrahendi* in stipulating treaties; participation in intergovernmental organizations, such as those under the auspices of the United Nations; and mediation initiatives in situations of conflict. This activity aims at offering non-partisan service to the international community, since it seeks no advantage for itself but only the good of the entire human family. In this context, the Holy See particularly avails itself of its own diplomatic personnel.

445. *The diplomatic service of the Holy See, the product of an ancient and proven practice, is an instrument that works not only for the freedom of the Church* ("libertas Ecclesiae") *but also for the defence and promotion of human dignity, as well as for a social order based on the values* of justice, truth, freedom and love. "By an innate right inherent within our spiritual mission itself and advanced by development of historical events over the centuries, we also send our legates to the Supreme Authorities of States in which the Catholic Church has taken root or in which she is present in some way. It is of course true that the purposes of the Church and the State are of different orders, and that both are perfect societies, endowed therefore with their

---

[920] Cf. John Paul II, Encyclical Letter *Sollicitudo Rei Socialis*, 33, 39: AAS 80 (1988), 557-559, 566-568.
[921] John Paul II, Encyclical Letter *Sollicitudo Rei Socialis*, 26: AAS 80 (1988), 544-547.
[922] John Paul II, Message for the 2004 World Day of Peace, 7: AAS 96 (2004), 118.
[923] Cf. *Code of Canon Law*, canon 361.

own means, and are autonomous in their respective spheres of activity. But it is also true that both the one and the other undertake to serve the good of the same common subject, man, called by God to eternal salvation and put on earth so that he might, with the help of grace attain unto salvation through his work, which brings him well-being in the peaceful setting of society."[924] The good of people and human communities is served by a structured dialogue between the Church and civil authorities, which also finds expression in the stipulation of mutual agreements. This dialogue tends to establish or strengthen relations of mutual understanding and cooperation, and also serves to prevent or resolve eventual disputes. Its goal is to contribute to the progress of every people and all humanity in justice and peace.

IV. INTERNATIONAL COOPERATION FOR DEVELOPMENT

a. Cooperation to guarantee the right to development

446. *The solution to the problem of development requires cooperation among individual political communities.* "Political communities condition one another and we can affirm that each one will succeed in its development by contributing to the development of others. For this to happen, understanding and collaboration are essential."[925] It may seem that underdevelopment is impossible to eliminate, as though it were a death sentence, especially considering the fact that it is not only the result of erroneous human choices but also the consequence of "economic, financial and social *mechanisms*"[926] and "structures of sin"[927] that prevent the full development of men and peoples.

These difficulties must nonetheless be met with strong and resolute determination, because development is not only an aspiration but a right [928] *that, like every right, implies a duty.* "Collaboration in the development of the whole person and of every human being is in fact a duty of *all towards all,* and must be shared by the four parts of the world: East and West, North and South."[929] As the Magisterium sees it, the *right to development* is based on the following principles: unity of origin and a shared destiny of the human family; equality between every person and between every community based on human dignity; the universal destination of the goods of the earth; the notion of development in its entirety; and the centrality of the human person and solidarity.

---

[924] Paul VI, Apostolic Letter *Sollicitudo Omnium Ecclesiarum: AAS* 61 (1969), 476.

[925] John XXIII, Encyclical Letter *Mater et Magistra: AAS* 53 (1961), 499; cf. Pius XII, Christmas Radio Message (24 December 1945): *AAS* 38 (1946), 22.

[926] John Paul II, Encyclical Letter *Sollicitudo Rei Socialis,* 16: *AAS* 80 (1988), 531.

[927] John Paul II, Encyclical Letter *Sollicitudo Rei Socialis,* 36-37, 39: *AAS* 80 (1988), 561-564, 567.

[928] Cf. Paul VI, Encyclical Letter *Populorum Progressio,* 22: *AAS* 59 (1967), 268; Paul VI, Apostolic Letter *Octogesima Adveniens,* 43: *AAS* 63 (1971), 431-432; John Paul II, Encyclical Letter *Sollicitudo Rei Socialis,* 32-33: *AAS* 80 (1988), 556-559; John Paul II, Encyclical Letter *Centesimus Annus,* 35: *AAS* 83 (1991), 836-838; cf. also Paul VI, Address to the International Labor Organisation (10 June 1969), 22: *AAS* 61 (1969), 500-501; John Paul II, Address to the Participants in the European Convention on the Church's Social Teaching (20 June 1997), 5: *L'Osservatore Romano,* English edition, 23 July 1997, p. 3; John Paul II, Address to Italian Business and Trade-Union Leaders (2 May 2000), 3: *L'Osservatore Romano,* English edition, 10 May 2000, p. 5.

[929] John Paul II, Encyclical Letter *Sollicitudo Rei Socialis,* 32: *AAS* 80 (1988), 556.

447. *The Church's social doctrine encourages forms of cooperation that are capable of facilitating access to the international market on the part of countries suffering from poverty and underdevelopment.* "Even in recent years it was thought that the poorest countries would develop by isolating themselves from the world market and by depending only on their own resources. Recent experience has shown that countries which did this have suffered stagnation and recession, while the countries which experienced development were those which succeeded in taking part in the general interrelated economic activities at the international level. It seems therefore that the chief problem is that of gaining fair access to the international market, based not on the unilateral principle of the exploitation of the natural resources of these countries but on the proper use of human resources."[930] Among the causes that greatly contribute to underdevelopment and poverty, in addition to the impossibility of acceding to the international market,[931] mention must be made of illiteracy, lack of food security, the absence of structures and services, inadequate measures for guaranteeing basic health care, the lack of safe drinking water and sanitation, corruption, instability of institutions and of political life itself. There is a connection between poverty and, in many countries, the lack of liberty, possibilities for economic initiative and a national administration capable of setting up an adequate system of education and information.

448. *The spirit of international cooperation requires that, beyond the strict market mentality, there should be an awareness of the duty to solidarity, justice and universal charity.*[932] In fact, there exists "*something which is due to man because he is man, by reason of his lofty dignity.*"[933] Cooperation is the path to which the entire international community should be committed, "according to an adequate notion of the common good in relation to the whole human family."[934] Many positive results flow from this; for example, an increase of confidence in the potential of poor people and therefore of poor countries and an equitable distribution of goods.

b. **The fight against poverty**

449. *At the beginning of the New Millennium, the poverty of billions of men and women is* "the one issue that most challenges our human and Christian consciences."[935] Poverty poses a dramatic problem of justice; in its various forms and with its various effects, it is characterized by an unequal growth that does not recognize the "equal right of all people to take their seat 'at the table of the common banquet'."[936] Such poverty makes it impossible to bring about that *full humanism* which the

---

[930] John Paul II, Encyclical Letter *Centesimus Annus*, 33: AAS 83 (1991), 835.
[931] Cf. Paul VI, Encyclical Letter *Populorum Progressio*, 56-61: AAS 59 (1967), 285-287.
[932] Cf. Paul VI, Encyclical Letter *Populorum Progressio*, 44: AAS 59 (1967), 279.
[933] John Paul II, Encyclical Letter *Centesimus Annus*, 34: AAS 83 (1991), 836.
[934] John Paul II, Encyclical Letter *Centesimus Annus*, 58: AAS 83 (1991), 863.
[935] John Paul II, Message for the 2000 World Day of Peace, 14: AAS 92 (2000), 366; cf. John Paul II, Message for the 1993 World Day of Peace, 1: AAS 85 (1993), 429-430.
[936] John Paul II, Encyclical Letter *Sollicitudo Rei Socialis*, 33: AAS 80 (1988), 558; cf. Paul VI, Encyclical Letter *Populorum Progressio*, 47: AAS 59 (1967), 280.

Church hopes for and pursues so that persons and peoples may "be more" [937] and live in conditions that are more human.[938]

The fight against poverty finds a strong motivation in the option or preferential love of the Church for the poor.[939] In the whole of her social teaching the Church never tires of emphasizing certain fundamental principles of this teaching, first and foremost, the *universal destination of goods*.[940] Constantly reaffirming the principle of *solidarity*, the Church's social doctrine demands action to promote "the good of all and of each individual, because we are *all* really responsible for *all*."[941] The principle of solidarity, even in the fight against poverty, must always be appropriately accompanied by that of *subsidiarity*, thanks to which it is possible to foster the spirit of initiative, the fundamental basis of all social and economic development in poor countries.[942] The poor should be seen "not as a problem, but as people who can become the principal builders of a new and more human future for everyone."[943]

c. Foreign debt

450. *The right to development must be taken into account when considering questions related to the debt crisis of many poor countries.*[944] Complex causes of various types lie at the origin of the debt crisis. At the international level there are the fluctuation of exchange rates, financial speculation and economic neo-colonialism; within individual debtor countries there is corruption, poor administration of public monies or the improper utilization of loans received. The greatest sufferings, which can be traced back both to structural questions as well as personal behavior, strike the people of poor and indebted countries who are not responsible for this situation. The international community cannot ignore this fact; while reaffirming the principle that debts must be repaid, ways must be found that do not compromise the "fundamental right of peoples to subsistence and progress."[945]

---

[937] Paul VI, Encyclical Letter *Populorum Progressio*, 6: AAS 59 (1967), 260; cf. John Paul II, Encyclical Letter *Sollicitudo Rei Socialis*, 28: AAS 80 (1988), 548-550.

[938] Cf. Paul VI, Encyclical Letter *Populorum Progressio*, 20-21: AAS 59 (1967), 267-268.

[939] Cf. John Paul II, Address to the Third General Conference of Latin American Bishops, Puebla, Mexico (28 January 1979), I/8: AAS 71 (1979), 194-195.

[940] Cf. Paul VI, Encyclical Letter *Populorum Progressio*, 22: AAS 59 (1967), 268.

[941] John Paul II, Encyclical Letter *Sollicitudo Rei Socialis*, 38: AAS 80 (1988), 566.

[942] Cf. Paul VI, Encyclical Letter *Populorum Progressio*, 55: AAS 59 (1967), 284; John Paul II, Encyclical Letter *Sollicitudo Rei Socialis*, 44: AAS 80 (1988), 575-577.

[943] John Paul II, Message for the World Day of Peace 2000, 14: AAS 92 (2000), 366.

[944] Cf. John Paul II, Apostolic Letter *Tertio Millennio Adveniente*, 51: AAS 87 (1995), 36; John Paul II, Message for the 1998 World Day of Peace, 4: AAS 90 (1998), 151-152; John Paul II, Address to the Conference of the Inter-Parliamentarian Union (30 November 1998): *Insegnamenti di Giovanni Paolo II*, XXI, 2 (1998), 1162-1163; John Paul II, Message for the 1999 World Day of Peace, 9: AAS 91 (1999), 383-384.

[945] John Paul II, Encyclical Letter *Centesimus Annus*, 35: AAS 83 (1991), 838; cf. also the document *At the Service of the Human Community: an Ethical Approach to the International Debt Question*, published by the Pontifical Commission "Iustitia et Pax" (27 December 1986), Vatican City 1986.

CHAPTER TEN

SAFEGUARDING THE ENVIRONMENT

I. BIBLICAL ASPECTS

451. *The living experience of the divine presence in history is the foundation of the faith of the people of God*: "We were Pharaoh's slaves in Egypt, and the Lord brought us out of Egypt with a mighty hand" (*Deut* 6:21). A look at history permits one to have an overview of the past and discover God at work from the very beginning: "A wandering Aramean was my father" (*Deut* 26:5); of his people God can say: "I took your father Abraham from beyond the river" (*Josh* 24:3). This reflection permits us to look to the future with hope, sustained by the promise and the covenant that God continually renews.

The faith of Israel is lived out in the space and time of this world, perceived not as a hostile environment, nor as an evil from which one must be freed, but rather as the gift itself of God, as the place and plan that he entrusts to the responsible management and activity of man. Nature, the work of God's creative action, is not a dangerous adversary. It is God who made all things, and with regard to each created reality "God saw that it was good" (cf. *Gen* 1:4,10,12,18,21,25). At the summit of this creation, which "was very good" (*Gen* 1:31), God placed man. Only man and woman, among all creatures, were made by God "in his own image" (*Gen* 1,27). The Lord entrusted all of creation to their responsibility, charging them to care for its harmony and development (Cf. *Gen* 1:26-30). This special bond with God explains the privileged position of the first human couple in the order of creation.

452. *The relationship of man with the world is a constitutive part of his human identity. This relationship is in turn the result of another still deeper relationship between man and God.* The Lord has made the human person to be a partner with him in dialogue. Only in dialogue with God does the human being find his truth, from which he draws inspiration and norms to make plans for the future of the world, which is the *garden* that God has given him to keep and till (cf. *Gen* 2:15). Not even sin could remove this duty, although it weighed down this exalted work with pain and suffering (cf. *Gen* 3:17-19).

Creation is always an object of praise in Israel's prayer: "O Lord, how manifold are your works! In wisdom have you made them all" (*Ps* 104:24). Salvation is perceived as a *new creation* that re-establishes that harmony and potential for growth that sin had compromised: "I create new heavens and a new earth" (*Is* 65:17) — says the Lord — in which "the wilderness becomes a fruitful field . . . and righteousness [will] abide in the fruitful field . . . My people will abide in a peaceful habitation" (*Is* 32:15-18).

453. *The definitive salvation that God offers to all humanity through his own Son does not come about outside of this world. While wounded by sin, the world is destined to undergo a radical purification* (cf. 2 Pet 3:10) that will make it a renewed world (cf. Is 65:17, 66:22; Rev 21:1), finally becoming the place where "righteousness dwells" (2 Pet 3:13).

In his public ministry, Jesus makes use of natural elements. Not only is he a knowledgeable interpreter of nature, speaking of it in images and parables, but he also dominates it (cf. the episode of the calming of the storm in Mt 14:22-33; Mk 6:45-52; Lc 8:22-25; Jn 6:16-21). The Lord puts nature at the service of his plan of redemption. He asks his disciples to look at things, at the seasons and at people with the trust of children who know that they will never be abandoned by a provident Father (cf. Lk 11:11-13). *Far from being enslaved by things, the disciple of Jesus must know how to use them in order to bring about sharing and brotherhood* (cf. Lk 16:9-13).

454. *The entrance of Jesus Christ into the history of the world reaches its culmination in the Paschal Mystery, where nature itself takes part in the drama of the rejection of the Son of God and in the victory of his Resurrection* (cf. Mt 27:45,51, 28:2). Crossing through death and grafting onto it the new splendor of the Resurrection, Jesus inaugurates a new world in which everything is subjected to him (cf. 1 Cor 15:20-28) and he creates anew those relationships of order and harmony that sin had destroyed. Knowledge of the imbalances existing between man and nature should be accompanied by an awareness that in Jesus the reconciliation of man and the world with God — such that every human being, aware of divine love, can find anew the peace that was lost — has been brought about. "Therefore, if any one is in Christ, he is a new creation; the old has passed away, behold, the new has come" (2 Cor 5:17). Nature, which was created in the Word is, by the same Word made flesh, reconciled to God and given new peace (cf. Col 1:15-20).

455. *Not only is the inner man made whole once more, but his entire nature as a corporeal being is touched by the redeeming power of Christ. The whole of creation participates in the renewal flowing from the Lord's Paschal Mystery,* although it still awaits full liberation from corruption, groaning in travail (cf. Rom 8:19-23), in expectation of giving birth to "a new heaven and a new earth" (Rev 21:1) that are the gift of the end of time, the fulfilment of salvation. In the meantime, nothing stands outside this salvation. Whatever his condition of life may be, the Christian is called to serve Christ, to live according to his Spirit, guided by love, the principle of a new life, that brings the world and man back to their original destiny: "whether . . . the world or life or death or the present or the future, all are yours; and you are Christ's, and Christ is God's" (1 Cor 3:22-23).

II. MAN AND THE UNIVERSE OF CREATED THINGS

456. *The biblical vision inspires the behavior of Christians in relation to their use of the earth, and also with regard to the advances of science and technology.* The Second Vatican Council affirmed that man "judges rightly that by his intellect he surpasses the material universe, for he shares in the light of the divine mind."[946] The Council Fathers recognized the progress made thanks to the tireless application of human genius down the centuries, whether in the empirical sciences, the technological disciplines or the liberal arts.[947] Today, "especially with the help of science and technology, man has extended his mastery over nearly the whole of nature and continues to do so."[948]

For man, "created in God's image, received a mandate to subject to himself the earth and all that it contains, and to govern the world with justice and holiness, a mandate to relate himself and the totality of things to him who was to be acknowledged as the Lord and Creator of all. Thus, by the subjection of all things to man, the name of God would be wonderful in all the earth. [The Council teaches that] throughout the course of the centuries, men have labored to better the circumstances of their lives through a monumental amount of individual and collective effort. To believers, this point is settled: considered in itself, this human activity accords with God's will."[949]

457. *The results of science and technology are, in themselves, positive.* "Far from thinking that works produced by man's own talent and energy are in opposition to God's power, and that the rational creature exists as a kind of rival to the Creator, Christians are convinced that the triumphs of the human race are a sign of God's grace and the flowering of His own mysterious design."[950] The Council Fathers also emphasize the fact that "the greater man's power becomes, the farther his individual and community responsibility extends,"[951] and that every human activity is to correspond, according to the design and will of God, to humanity's true good.[952] In this regard, the Magisterium has repeatedly emphasized that the Catholic Church is in no way opposed to progress,[953] rather she considers "science and technology are a wonderful product of a God-given human creativity, since they have provided us with wonderful possibilities, and we all gratefully benefit from them."[954] For this reason, "as people who believe in God, who saw that nature which he had created was 'good,' we rejoice in the technological and economic progress which people, using their intelligence, have managed to make."[955]

---

[946] Second Vatican Ecumenical Council, Pastoral Constitution *Gaudium et Spes*, 15: AAS 58 (1966), 1036.

[947] Cf. Second Vatican Ecumenical Council, Pastoral Constitution *Gaudium et Spes*, 15: AAS 58 (1966), 1036.

[948] Second Vatican Ecumenical Council, Pastoral Constitution *Gaudium et Spes*, 33: AAS 58 (1966), 1052.

[949] Second Vatican Ecumenical Council, Pastoral Constitution *Gaudium et Spes*, 34: AAS 58 (1966), 1052.

[950] Second Vatican Ecumenical Council, Pastoral Constitution *Gaudium et Spes*, 34: AAS 58 (1966), 1053.

[951] Second Vatican Ecumenical Council, Pastoral Constitution *Gaudium et Spes*, 34: AAS 58 (1966), 1053.

[952] Cf. Second Vatican Ecumenical Council, Pastoral Constitution *Gaudium et Spes*, 35: AAS 58 (1966), 1053.

[953] Cf. John Paul II, Address given at Mercy Maternity Hospital, Melbourne (28 November 1986): *L'Osservatore Romano*, English edition, 9 December 1986, p. 13.

[954] John Paul II, Meeting with scientists and representatives of the United Nations University, Hiroshima (25 February 1981), 3: AAS 73 (1981), 422.

[955] John Paul II, Meeting with employees of the Olivetti workshops in Ivrea, Italy (19 March 1990), 5: *L'Osservatore Romano*, English edition, 26 March 1990, p. 7.

458. *The Magisterium's considerations regarding science and technology in general can also be applied to the environment and agriculture.* The Church appreciates "the advantages that result — and can still result — from the study and applications of molecular biology, supplemented by other disciplines such as genetics and its technological application in agriculture and industry."[956] In fact, technology "could be a priceless tool in solving many serious problems, in the first place those of hunger and disease, through the production of more advanced and vigorous strainsof plants, and through the production of valuable medicines."[957] It is important, however, to repeat the concept of "proper application," for "we know that this potential is not neutral: it can be used either for man's progress or for his degradation."[958] For this reason, "it is necessary to maintain an attitude of prudence and attentively sift out the *nature, end and means* of the various forms of applied technology."[959] Scientists, therefore, must "truly use their research and technical skill in the service of humanity,"[960] being able to subordinate them "to moral principles and values, which respect and realize in its fullness the dignity of man."[961]

459. *A central point of reference for every scientific and technological application is respect for men and women, which must also be accompanied by a necessary attitude of respect for other living creatures.* Even when thought is given to making some change in them, "one must take into account the *nature of each being* and of its *mutual connection* in an ordered system."[962] In this sense, the formidable possibilities of biological research raise grave concerns, in that "we are not yet in a position to assess the biological disturbance that could result from indiscriminate genetic manipulation and from the unscrupulous development of new forms of plant and animal life, to say nothing of unacceptable experimentation regarding the origins of human life itself."[963] In fact, "it is now clear that the application of these discoveries in the fields of industry and agriculture have produced harmful long-term effects. This has led to the painful realization that we cannot interfere in one area of the ecosystem without paying due attention both to the consequences of such interference in other areas and to the well-being of future generations."[964]

---

[956] John Paul II, Address to the Pontifical Academy of Sciences (3 October 1981), 3: *L'Osservatore Romano*, English edition, 12 October 1981, p. 4.

[957] John Paul II, Address to the participants in a convention sponsored by the National Academy of Sciences, for the bicentenary of its foundation (21 September 1982), 4: *L'Osservatore Romano*, English edition, 4 October 1982, p. 3.

[958] John Paul II, Meeting with scientists and representatives of the United Nations University, Hiroshima (25 February 1981), 3: AAS 73 (1981), 422.

[959] John Paul II, Meeting with employees of the Olivetti workshops in Ivrea, Italy (19 March 1990), 4: *L'Osservatore Romano*, English edition, 26 March 1990, p. 7.

[960] John Paul II, Homily during Mass at the Victorian Racing Club, Melbourne (26 November 1986), 11: *Insegnamenti di Giovanni Paolo II*, IX, 2 (1986), 1730.

[961] John Paul II, Address to the Pontifical Academy of Sciences (23 October 1982), 6: *Insegnamenti di Giovanni Paolo II*, V, 3 (1982), 892-893.

[962] John Paul II, Encyclical Letter *Sollicitudo Rei Socialis*, 34: AAS 80 (1988), 559.

[963] John Paul II, Message for the 1990 World Day of Peace, 7: AAS 82 (1990), 151.

[964] John Paul II, Message for the 1990 World Day of Peace, 6: AAS 82 (1990), 150.

460. *Man, then, must never forget that "his capacity to transform and in a certain sense create the world through his own work . . . is always based on God's prior and original gift of the things that are."*[965] He must not "make arbitrary use of the earth, subjecting it without restraint to his will, as though it did not have its own requisites and a prior God-given purpose, which man can indeed develop but must not betray."[966] When he acts in this way, "instead of carrying out his role as a co-operator with God in the work of creation, man sets himself up in place of God and thus ends up provoking a rebellion on the part of nature, which is more tyrannized than governed by him."[967]

If man intervenes in nature without abusing it or damaging it, we can say that he "intervenes not in order to modify nature but to foster its development in its own life, that of the creation that God intended. While working in this obviously delicate area, the researcher adheres to the design of God. God willed that man be the king of creation."[968] In the end, it is God himself who offers to men and women the honor of cooperating with the full force of their intelligence in the work of creation.

III. THE CRISIS IN THE RELATIONSHIP BETWEEN MAN AND THE ENVIRONMENT

461. *The biblical message and the Church's Magisterium represent the essential reference points for evaluating the problems found in the relationship between man and the environment.*[969] The underlying cause of these problems can be seen in man's pretension of exercising unconditional dominion over things, heedless of any moral considerations which, on the contrary, must distinguish all human activity.

The tendency towards an "ill-considered"[970] *exploitation of the resources of creation is the result of a long historical and cultural process.* "The modern era has witnessed man's growing capacity for transformative intervention. The aspect of the conquest and exploitation of resources has become predominant and invasive, and today it has even reached the point of threatening the environment's hospitable aspect: the environment as 'resource' risks threatening the environment as 'home'. Because of the powerful means of transformation offered by technological civilization, it sometimes seems that the balance between man and the environment has reached a critical point."[971]

462. *Nature appears as an instrument in the hands of man, a reality that he must constantly manipulate, especially by means of technology.* A reductionistic conception

---

[965] John Paul II, Encyclical Letter *Centesimus Annus*, 37: AAS 83 (1991), 840.

[966] John Paul II, Encyclical Letter *Centesimus Annus*, 37: AAS 83 (1991), 840.

[967] John Paul II, Encyclical Letter *Centesimus Annus*, 37: AAS 83 (1991), 840.

[968] John Paul II, Address to the 35th General Assembly of the World Medical Association (29 October 1983): *L'Osservatore Romano*, English edition, 5 December 1986, p. 11.

[969] Cf. Paul VI, Apostolic Letter *Octogesima Adveniens*, 21: AAS 63 (1971), 416-417.

[970] Paul VI, Apostolic Letter *Octogesimo Adveniens*, 21: AAS 63 (1971), 417.

[971] John Paul II, Address to participants in a convention on "The Environment and Health" (24 March 1997), 2: *L'Osservatore Romano*, English edition, 9 April 1997, p. 2.

quickly spread, starting from the presupposition — which was seen to be erroneous — that an infinite quantity of energy and resources are available, that it is possible to renew them quickly, and that the negative effects of the exploitation of the natural order can be easily absorbed. This reductionistic conception views the natural world in mechanistic terms and sees development in terms of consumerism. Primacy is given to doing and having rather than to being, and this causes serious forms of human alienation.[972]

Such attitudes do not arise from scientific and technological research but from scientism and technocratic ideologies that tend to condition such research. The advances of science and technology do not eliminate the need for transcendence and are not of themselves the cause of the exasperated secularization that leads to nihilism. With the progress of science and technology, questions as to their meaning increase and give rise to an ever greater need to respect the transcendent dimension of the human person and creation itself.

463. *A correct understanding of the environment prevents the utilitarian reduction of nature to a mere object to be manipulated and exploited. At the same time, it must not absolutize nature and place it above the dignity of the human person himself.* In this latter case, one can go so far as to divinize nature or the earth, as can readily be seen in certain ecological movements that seek to gain an internationally guaranteed institutional status for their beliefs.[973]

The Magisterium finds the motivation for its opposition to a concept of the environment based on ecocentrism and on biocentrism in the fact that "it is being proposed that the ontological and axiological difference between men and other living beings be eliminated, since the biosphere is considered a biotic unity of undifferentiated value. Thus man's superior responsibility can be eliminated in favor of an egalitarian consideration of the 'dignity' of all living beings."[974]

464. *A vision of man and things that is sundered from any reference to the transcendent has led to the rejection of the concept of creation and to the attribution of a completely independent existence to man and nature.* The bonds that unite the world to God have thus been broken. This rupture has also resulted in separating man from the world and, more radically, has impoverished man's very identity. Human beings find themselves thinking that they are foreign to the environmental context in which they live. The consequences resulting from this are all too clear: "it is the relationship man has with God that determines his relationship with his fellow men and with his environment. This is why Christian culture has always recognized the creatures that surround man as also gifts of God to be nurtured and safeguarded with a sense of gratitude to the Creator. Benedictine and Franciscan spir-

---

[972] Cf. John Paul II, Encyclical Letter *Sollicitudo Rei Socialis*, 28: AAS 80 (1988), 548-550.

[973] Cf., for example, Pontifical Council for Culture - Pontifical Council for Interreligious Dialogue, *Jesus Christ the Bearer of the Water of Life. A Christian Reflection on the "New Age,"* Libreria Editrice Vaticana, Vatican City 2003, p. 33.

[974] John Paul II, Address to participants in a convention on "The Environment and Health" (24 March 1997), 5: *L'Osservatore Romano*, English edition, 9 April 1997, p. 2.

ituality in particular has witnessed to this sort of kinship of man with his creaturely environment, fostering in him an attitude of respect for every reality of the surrounding world."[975] There is a need to place ever greater emphasis on the intimate connection between environmental ecology and "*human ecology.*"[976]

465. *The Magisterium underscores human responsibility for the preservation of a sound and healthy environment for all.*[977] "If humanity today succeeds in combining the new scientific capacities with a strong ethical dimension, it will certainly be able to promote the environment as a home and a resource for man and for all men, and will be able to eliminate the causes of pollution and to guarantee adequate conditions of hygiene and health for small groups as well as for vast human settlements. Technology that pollutes can also cleanse, production that amasses can also distribute justly, on condition that the ethic of respect for life and human dignity, for the rights of today's generations and those to come, prevails."[978]

IV. A COMMON RESPONSIBILITY

a. The environment, a collective good

466. *Care for the environment represents a challenge for all of humanity. It is a matter of a common and universal duty, that of respecting a common good,*[979] destined for all, by preventing anyone from using "with impunity the different categories of beings, whether living or inanimate — animals, plants, the natural elements — simply as one wishes, according to one's own economic needs."[980] It is a responsibility that must mature on the basis of the global dimension of the present ecological crisis and the consequent necessity to meet it on a worldwide level, since all beings are interdependent in the universal order established by the Creator. "One must take into account the nature of each being and of its mutual connection in an ordered system, which is precisely the 'cosmos.'"[981]

This perspective takes on a particular importance when one considers, in the context of the close relationships that bind the various parts of the ecosystem, *the environmental value of biodiversity,* which must be handled with a sense of responsibility and adequately protected, because it constitutes an extraordinary richness for all of humanity. In this regard, each person can easily recognize, for example, the importance of the Amazon, "one of the world's most precious natural regions because of its bio-diversity which makes it vital for the environmental balance of the entire planet."[982] *Forests* help maintain the essential natural balance necessary

[975] John Paul II, Address to participants in a convention on "The Environment and Health" (24 March 1997), 4: *L'Osservatore Romano*, English edition, 9 April 1997, p. 2.

[976] John Paul II, Encyclical Letter *Centesimus Annus*, 38: AAS 83 (1991), 841.

[977] Cf. John Paul II, Encyclical Letter *Sollicitudo Rei Socialis*, 34: AAS 80 (1988), 559-560.

[978] John Paul II, Address to participants in a convention on "The Environment and Health" (24 March 1997), 5: *L'Osservatore Romano*, English edition, 9 April 1997, p. 2.

[979] Cf. John Paul II, Encyclcal Letter Centesimus Annus, 40: AAS 83 (1991), 843.

[980] John Paul II, Encyclical Letter *Sollicitudo Rei Socialis*, 34: AAS 80 (1988), 559.

[981] John Paul II, Encyclical Letter *Sollicitudo Rei Socialis*, 34: AAS 80 (1988), 559.

[982] John Paul II, Apostolic Exhortation *Ecclesia in America*, 25: AAS 91 (1999) 760.

for life.[983] Their destruction also through the inconsiderate and malicious setting of fires, accelerates the processes of desertification with risky consequences for water reserves and compromises the lives of many indigenous peoples and the well-being of future generations. All individuals as well as institutional subjects must feel the commitment to protect the heritage of forests and, where necessary, promote adequate programs of reforestation.

467. *Responsibility for the environment, the common heritage of mankind, extends not only to present needs but also to those of the future.* "We have inherited from past generations, and we have benefited from the work of our contemporaries: for this reason we have obligations towards all, and we cannot refuse to interest ourselves in those who will come after us, to enlarge the human family."[984] *This is a responsibility that present generations have towards those of the future,*[985] a responsibility that also concerns individual States and the international community.

468. *Responsibility for the environment should also find adequate expression on a juridical level.* It is important that the international community draw up uniform rules that will allow States to exercise more effective control over the various activities that have negative effects on the environment and to protect ecosystems by preventing the risk of accidents. "The State should also actively endeavor within its own territory to prevent destruction of the atmosphere and biosphere, by carefully monitoring, among other things, the impact of new technological or scientific advances . . . [and] ensuring that its citizens are not exposed to dangerous pollutants or toxic wastes."[986]

The juridical content of *"the right to a safe and healthy natural environment"*[987] is gradually taking form, stimulated by the concern shown by public opinion to disciplining the use of created goods according to the demands of the common good and a common desire to punish those who pollute. But juridical measures by themselves are not sufficient.[988] They must be accompanied by a growing sense of responsibility as well as an effective change of mentality and lifestyle.

469. *The authorities called to make decisions concerning health and environmental risks sometimes find themselves facing a situation in which available scientific data are contradictory or quantitatively scarce. It may then be appropriate to base evaluations on the "precautionary principle," which does not mean applying rules but certain guidelines aimed at managing the situation of uncertainty.* This shows the need for making temporary decisions that may be modified on the basis of new facts that eventually become known. Such decisions must be proportional with respect to provisions

---

[983] Cf. John Paul II, Homily in Val Visdende (Italy) for the votive feast of St. John Gualberto (12 July 1987): Insegnamenti di Giovanni Paolo II, X, 3 (1987) 67.

[984] Paul II, Encyclical Letter *Populorum Progressio*, 17: AAS 59 (1967), 266.

[985] Cf. John Paul II, Encyclical Letter *Centesimus Annus*, 37: AAS 83 (1991), 840.

[986] John Paul II, Message for the 1990 World Day of Peace, 9: AAS 82 (1990), 152.

[987] John Paul II, *Address to the European Commission and Court of Human Rights*, Strasbourg (8 October 1988), 5: AAS 81 (1989), 685; cf. John Paul II, Message for the 1999 World Day of Peace, 10: AAS 91 (1999), 384-385.

[988] Cf. John Paul II, Message for the 1999 World Day of Peace, 10: AAS 91 (1999), 384-385.

already taken for other risks. Prudent policies, based on the precautionary principle require that decisions be based on a comparison of the risks and benefits foreseen for the various possible alternatives, including the decision not to intervene. This precautionary approach is connected with the need to encourage every effort for acquiring more thorough knowledge, in the full awareness that science is not able to come to quick conclusions about the absence of risk. The circumstances of uncertainty and provisional solutions make it particularly important that the decision-making process be transparent.

470. *Programs of economic development must carefully consider "the need to respect the integrity and the cycles of nature"*[989] *because natural resources are limited and some are not renewable.* The present rhythm of exploitation is seriously compromising the availability of some natural resources for both the present and the future.[990] Solutions to the ecological problem require that economic activity respect the environment to a greater degree, reconciling the needs of economic development with those of environmental protection. *Every economic activity making use of natural resources must also be concerned with safeguarding the environment and should foresee the costs involved*, which are "an essential element of the actual cost of economic activity."[991] In this context, one considers relations between human activity and *climate change* which, given their extreme complexity, must be opportunely and constantly monitored at the scientific, political and juridical, national and international levels. The climate is a good that must be protected and reminds consumers and those engaged in industrial activity to develop a greater sense of responsibility for their behavior.[992]

An economy respectful of the environment will not have the maximization of profits as its only objective, because environmental protection cannot be assured solely on the basis of financial calculations of costs and benefits. The environment is one of those goods that cannot be adequately safeguarded or promoted by market forces.[993] Every country, in particular developed countries, must be aware of the urgent obligation to reconsider the way that natural goods are being used. Seeking innovative ways to reduce the environmental impact of production and consumption of goods should be effectively encouraged.

Particular attention will have to be reserved for the complex issues surrounding *energy resources*.[994] Non-renewable resources, which highly industrialized and recently industrialized countries draw from, must be put at the service of all humanity. From a moral perspective based on equity and intergenerational solidarity, it will also be necessary to continue, through the contribution of the scientific community, to identify new sources of energy, develop alternative sources

---

[989] John Paul II, Encyclical Letter *Sollicitudo Rei Socialis*, 26: AAS 80 (1988), 546.

[990] Cf. John Paul II, Encyclical Letter *Sollicitudo Rei Socialis,* 34: AAS 80 (1988), 559-560.

[991] John Paul II, Address to the Twenty-Fifth General Conference of FAO (16 November 1989), 8: AAS 82 (1990), 673.

[992] Cf. John Paul II, Address to a study group of the Pontifical Academy of Sciences (6 November 1987): *Insegnamenti di Giovanni Paolo II*, X, 3 (1987) 1018-1020.

[993] Cf. John Paul II, Encyclical Letter *Centesimus Annus*, 40: AAS 83 (1991), 843.

[994] Cf. John Paul II, Address to the participants at the Plenary Assembly of the Pontifical Academy of Sciences (28 October 1994): *Insegnamenti di Giovanni Paolo II*, XVII, 2 (1994) 567-568.

and increase the security levels of nuclear energy.[995] The use of energy, in the context of its relationship to development and the environment, calls for the political responsibility of States, the international community and economic actors. Such responsibility must be illuminated and guided by continual reference to the universal common good.

471. *The relationship of indigenous peoples to their lands and resources deserves particular attention, since it is a fundamental expression of their identity.*[996] Due to powerful agro-industrial interests or the powerful processes of assimilation and urbanization, many of these peoples have already lost or risk losing the lands on which they live,[997] lands tied to the very meaning of their existence.[998] The rights of indigenous peoples must be appropriately protected.[999] These peoples offer an example of a life lived in harmony with the environment that they have come to know well and to preserve.[1000] Their extraordinary experience, which is an irreplaceable resource for all humanity, runs the risk of being lost together with the environment from which they originate.

b. **The use of biotechnology**

472. *In recent years pressing questions have been raised with regard to the use of new forms of biotechnology in the areas of agriculture, animal farming, medicine and environmental protection. The new possibilities offered by current biological and biogenetic techniques are a source of hope and enthusiasm on the one hand, and of alarm and hostility on the other.* The application of various types of biotechnology, their acceptability from a moral point of view, their consequences for human health and their impact on the environment and the economy are the subject of thorough study and heated debate. These are controversial questions that involve scientists and researchers, politicians and legislators, economists and environmentalists, as well as producers and consumers. Christians are not indifferent to these problems, for they are aware of the importance of the values at stake.[1001]

[995] Cf. John Paul II, Address to the participants at a Symposium on physics (18 December 1992): *Insegnamenti di Giovanni Paolo II*, V, 3 (1982), 1631-1634.

[996] Cf. John Paul II, Address to the Indigenous Peoples of the Amazon, Manaus (10 July 1980): *AAS* 72 (1980), 960-961.

[997] Cf. John Paul II, Homily at the Liturgy of the Word with the Indigenous Peoples of the Peruvian Amazon Valley (5 February 1985), 4: *AAS* 77 (1985), 897-898; cf. also Pontifical Council for Justice and Peace, *Towards a Better Distribution of Land. The Challenge of Agrarian Reform* (23 November 1997), 11, Libreria Editrice Vaticana, Vatican City 1997, p. 17.

[998] Cf. John Paul II, Address to the Indigenous Peoples of Australia (29 November 1986), 4: *AAS* 79 (1987), 974-975.

[999] Cf. John Paul II, Address to the Indigenous Peoples of Guatemala (7 March 1983), 4: *AAS* 75 (1983), 742-743; John Paul II, Address to the Indigenous Peoples of Canada (18 September 1984), 7-8: *AAS* 77 (1988), 421-422; John Paul II, Address to the Indigenous Peoples of Ecuador (31 January 1985), II,1: *AAS* 77 (1985), 861; John Paul II, Address to the Indigenous Peoples of Australia (29 November 1986), 10: *AAS* 79 (1987), 976-977.

[1000] Cf. John Paul II, Address to the Indigenous Peoples of Australia (29 November 1986), 4: *AAS* 79 (1987), 974-975; John Paul II, Address to Native Americans (14 September 1987), 4: *L'Osservatore Romano*, English edition, 21 September 1987, p. 21.

[1001] Cf. Pontifical Academy for Life, *Animal and Plant Biotechnology: New Frontiers and New Responsibilities*, Libreria Editrice Vaticana, Vatican City 1999.

473. *The Christian vision of creation makes a positive judgment on the acceptability of human intervention in nature, which also includes other living beings, and at the same time makes a strong appeal for responsibility.*[1002] In effect, nature is not a sacred or divine reality that man must leave alone. Rather, it is a gift offered by the Creator to the human community, entrusted to the intelligence and moral responsibility of men and women. For this reason the human person does not commit an illicit act when, out of respect for the order, beauty and usefulness of individual living beings and their function in the ecosystem, he intervenes by modifying some of their characteristics or properties. Human interventions that damage living beings or the natural environment deserve condemnation, while those that improve them are praiseworthy. *The acceptability of the use of biological and biogenetic techniques is only one part of the ethical problem:* as with every human behavior, it is also necessary to evaluate accurately the real benefits as well as the possible consequences in terms of risks. In the realm of technological-scientific interventions that have forceful and widespread impact on living organisms, with the possibility of significant long-term repercussions, it is unacceptable to act lightly or irresponsibly.

474. *Modern biotechnologies have powerful social, economic and political impact locally, nationally and internationally. They need to be evaluated according to the ethical criteria that must always guide human activities and relations in the social, economic and political spheres.*[1003] *Above all the criteria of justice and solidarity must be taken into account.* Individuals and groups who engage in research and the commercialization of the field of biotechnology must especially abide by these criteria. In any event, one must avoid falling into the error of believing that only the spreading of the benefits connected with the new techniques of biotechnology can solve the urgent problems of poverty and underdevelopment that still afflict so many countries on the planet.

475. *In a spirit of international solidarity, various measures can be taken in relation to the use of new biotechnologies.* In the first place, *equitable commercial exchange, without the burden of unjust stipulations,* is to be facilitated. Promoting the development of the most disadvantaged peoples, however, will not be authentic or effective if it is reduced to the simple exchange of products. It is indispensable to foster *the development of a necessary scientific and technological autonomy* on the part of these same peoples, promoting *the exchange of scientific and technological knowledge and the transfer of technologies to developing countries.*

476. *Solidarity also means appealing to the responsibility of developing countries, and in particular of their political leaders, for promoting trade policies that are favorable to their peoples and the exchange of technology that can improve the conditions of their food supply and health.* In such countries, there must be an increase in research investment, with special attention to the particular characteristics and needs of their territory and population, above all by bearing in mind that some research in the area of

---

[1002] Cf. John Paul II, Address to the Pontifical Academy of Sciences (23 October 1982), 6: *Insegnamenti di Giovanni Paolo II*, V, 3 (1982), 892-893.

[1003] Cf. John Paul II, Address to the Pontifical Academy of Sciences (3 October 1981): AAS 73 (1981), 668-672.

biotechnology, which may be potentially beneficial, requires relatively modest investments. To this end it would be useful to establish national agencies responsible for protecting the common good by means of careful risk management.

477. *Scientists and technicians involved in the field of biotechnology are called to work intelligently and with perseverance in seeking the best solutions to the serious and urgent problems of food supply and health care.* They must not forget that their activity concerns material — both living and inanimate — that belongs to the patrimony of humanity and is destined also to future generations. For believers, it is a question of a gift received from the Creator and entrusted to human intelligence and freedom, which are themselves also gifts from heaven. It is hoped that scientists employ their energies and abilities in research characterized by enthusiasm and guided by a clear and honest conscience.[1004]

478. *Entrepreneurs and directors of public agencies involved in the research, production and selling of products derived from new biotechnologies must take into account not only legitimate profit but also the common good.* This principle, which holds true for every type of economic activity, becomes particularly important for activities that deal with the food supply, medicine, health care and the environment. By their decisions, entrepreneurs and public agency directors involved in this sector can guide developments in the area of biotechnologies towards very promising ends as far as concerns the fight against hunger, especially in poorer countries, the fight against disease and the fight to safeguard the ecosystem, the common patrimony of all.

479. *Politicians, legislators and public administrators are responsible for evaluating the potentials benefits and possible risks connected with the use of biotechnologies.* It is not desirable for their decisions, at the national or international level, to be dictated by pressure from special interest groups. Public authorities must also encourage a correctly informed public opinion and make decisions that are best-suited to the common good.

480. *Leaders in the information sector also have an important task, which must be undertaken with prudence and objectivity.* Society expects information that is complete and objective, which helps citizens to form a correct opinion concerning biotechnological products, above all because this is something that directly concerns them as possible consumers. The temptation to fall into superficial information, fuelled by over enthusiasm or unjustified alarmism, must be avoided.

c. **The environment and the sharing of goods**

481. *As regards the ecological question, the social doctrine of the Church reminds us that the goods of the earth were created by God to be used wisely by all.* They must be

---

[1004] Cf. John Paul II, Address to the Pontifical Academy of Sciences (23 October 1982): *Insegnamenti di Giovanni Paolo II*, V, 3 (1982), 889-893. John Paul II, Address to the participants in a convention sponsored by the National Academy of Sciences, for the bicentenary of its foundation (21 September 1982): *Insegnamenti di Giovanni Paolo II*, V, 3 (1982), 511-515.

shared equitably, in accordance with justice and charity. This is essentially a question of preventing the injustice of hoarding resources: greediness, be it individual or collective, is contrary to the order of creation.[1005] Modern ecological problems are of a planetary dimension and can be effectively resolved only through international cooperation capable of guaranteeing greater coordination in the use of the earth's resources.

482. *The environmental crisis and poverty are connected by a complex and dramatic set of causes that can be resolved by the principle of the universal destination of goods, which offers a fundamental moral and cultural orientation.* The present environmental crisis affects those who are poorest in a particular way, whether they live in those lands subject to erosion and desertification, are involved in armed conflicts or subject to forced immigration, or because they do not have the economic and technological means to protect themselves from other calamities.

Countless numbers of these poor people live in polluted suburbs of large cities, in make-shift residences or in huge complexes of crumbling and unsafe houses (*slums, bidonvilles, barrios, favelas*). In cases where it is necessary to relocate them, in order not to heap suffering upon suffering, adequate information needs to be given beforehand, with choices of decent housing offered, and the people directly involved must be part of the process.

It is moreover necessary to keep in mind the situation of those countries that are penalized by unfair international trade regulations and countries whith a scarcity of capital goods, often aggravated by the burden of the foreign debt. In such cases hunger and poverty make it virtually impossible to avoid an intense and excessive exploitation of the environment.

483. *The close link that exists between the development of the poorest countries, demographic changes and a sustainable use of the environment must not become a pretext for political and economic choices that are at variance with the dignity of the human person.* In developed countries there is a "drop in the birth-rates, with repercussions on the aging of the population, unable even to renew itself biologically."[1006] The situation is different in the developing countries where demographic changes are increasing. Although it is true that an uneven distribution of the population and of available resources creates obstacles to development and a sustainable use of the environment, it must nonetheless be recognized that demographic growth is fully compatible with an integral and shared development.[1007] "There is widespread agreement that a population policy is only one part of an overall development strategy. Accordingly, it is important that any discussion of population policies should keep in mind the actual and projected development of nations and regions. At the same time, it is impossible to leave out of account the very nature of what is meant by the term 'development.' All development worthy of the name

---

[1005] Cf. Second Vatican Ecumenical Council, Pastoral Constitution *Gaudium et Spes*, 69: *AAS* 58 (1966), 1090-1092; Paul VI, Encyclical Letter *Populorum Progressio*, 22: *AAS* 59 (1967), 268.

[1006] John Paul II, Encyclical Letter *Sollicitudo Rei Socialis*, 25: *AAS* 80 (1988), 543; cf. John Paul II, Encyclical Letter *Evangelium Vitae*, 16: *AAS* 87 (1995), 418.

[1007] John Paul II, Encyclical Letter *Sollicitudo Rei Socialis*, 25: *AAS* 80 (1988), 543-544.

must be integral, that is, it must be directed to the true good of every person and of the whole person."[1008]

484. *The principle of the universal destination of goods also applies naturally to water, considered in the Sacred Scriptures as a symbol of purification* (cf. Ps 51:4; Jn 13:8) *and of life* (cf. Jn 3:5; Gal 3:27). "As a gift from God, water is a vital element essential to survival; thus, everyone has a right to it."[1009] Satisfying the needs of all, especially of those who live in poverty, must guide the use of water and the services connected with it. Inadequate access to safe drinking water affects the well-being of a huge number of people and is often the cause of disease, suffering, conflicts, poverty and even death. For a suitable solution to this problem, it "must be set in context in order to establish moral criteria based precisely on the value of life and the respect for the rights and dignity of all human beings."[1010]

485. By its very nature water cannot be treated as just another commodity among many, and it must be used rationally and in solidarity with others. The distribution of water is traditionally among the responsibilities that fall to public agencies, since water is considered a public good. If water distribution is entrusted to the private sector it should still be considered a public good. *The right to water,*[1011] as all human rights, finds its basis in human dignity and not in any kind of merely quantitative assessment that considers water as a merely economic good. Without water, life is threatened. Therefore, the right to safe drinking water is a universal and inalienable right.

d. New lifestyles

486. *Serious ecological problems call for an effective change of mentality leading to the adoption of new lifestyles,*[1012] "in which the quest for truth, beauty, goodness and communion with others for the sake of the common good are the factors that determine consumer choices, savings and investments."[1013] These lifestyles should be inspired by sobriety, temperance, and self-discipline at both the individual and social levels. There is a need to break with the logic of mere consumption and promote forms of agricultural and industrial production that respect the order of creation and satisfy the basic human needs of all. These atti-

---

[1008] John Paul II, Message to Nafis Sadik, Secretary General of the 1994 International Conference on Population and Development (18 March 1994), 3: *AAS* 87 (1995), 191.

[1009] John Paul II, Message to Cardinal Geraldo Majella Agnelo on the occasion of the 2004 Brotherhood Campaign of the Brazilian Bishops' Conference (19 January 2004): *L'Osservatore Romano*, English edition, 17 March 2004, p. 3.

[1010] John Paul II, Message to Cardinal Geraldo Majella Agnelo on the occasion of the 2004 Brotherhood Campaign of the Brazilian Bishops' Conference (19 January 2004): *L'Osservatore Romano*, English edition, 17 March 2004, p. 3.

[1011] Cf. John Paul II, John Paul II, Message for the 2003 World Day of Peace, 5: *AAS* 95 (2003), 343; Pontifical Council for Justice and Peace, *Water, an Essential Element for Life*. A Contribution of the Delegation of the Holy See on the occasion of the 3rd World Water Forum, Kyoto, 16-23 March 2003.

[1012] Cf. John Paul II, Encyclical Letter *Centesimus Annus,* 36: *AAS* 83 (1991), 838-840.

[1013] John Paul II, Encyclical Letter *Centesimus Annus,* 36: *AAS* 83 (1991), 839.

tudes, sustained by a renewed awareness of the interdependence of all the inhabitants of the earth, will contribute to eliminating the numerous causes of ecological disasters as well as guaranteeing the ability to respond quickly when such disasters strike peoples and territories.[1014] The ecological question must not be faced solely because of the frightening prospects that environmental destruction represents; rather it must above all become a strong motivation for an authentic solidarity of worldwide dimensions.

487. *The attitude that must characterize the way man acts in relation to creation is essentially one of gratitude and appreciation; the world, in fact, reveals the mystery of God who created and sustains it.* If the relationship with God is placed aside, nature is stripped of its profound meaning and impoverished. If on the other hand, nature is rediscovered in its creaturely dimension, channels of communication with it can be established, its rich and symbolic meaning can be understood, allowing us to enter into its realm of *mystery*. This realm opens the path of man to God, Creator of heaven and earth. *The world presents itself before man's eyes as evidence of God*, the place where his creative, providential and redemptive power unfolds.

[1014] Cf. John Paul II, Address to the UN Center, Nairobi, Kenya (18 August 1985), 5: *AAS* 78 (1986), 92.

CHAPTER ELEVEN

THE PROMOTION OF PEACE

I. BIBLICAL ASPECTS

488. *Before being God's gift to man and a human project in conformity with the divine plan, peace is in the first place a basic attribute of God*: "the Lord is peace" (*Jdg* 6:24). Creation, which is a reflection of the divine glory, aspires to peace. God created all that exists, and all of creation forms a harmonious whole that is good in its every part (cf. *Gen* 1:4,10,18,21,25,31). Peace is founded on the primary relationship that exists between every human being and God himself, a relationship marked by righteousness (cf. *Gen* 17:1). Following upon the voluntary act by which man altered the divine order, the world experienced the shedding of blood and division. Violence made its appearance in interpersonal relationships (cf. *Gen* 4:1-16) and in social relationships (cf. *Gen* 11:1-9). Peace and violence cannot dwell together, and where there is violence, God cannot be present (cf. *1 Chr* 22:8-9).

489. *In biblical revelation, peace is much more than the simple absence of war; it represents the fullness of life* (cf. *Mal* 2:5). Far from being the work of human hands, it is one of the greatest gifts that God offers to all men and women, and it involves obedience to the divine plan. Peace is the effect of the blessing that God bestows upon his people: "The Lord lift up his countenance upon you, and give you peace" (*Num* 6:26). This peace produces fruitfulness (*Is* 48:19), well-being (cf. *Is* 48:18), prosperity (cf. *Is* 54:13), absence of fear (cf. *Lev* 26:6) and profound joy (cf. *Pr* 12:20).

490. *Peace is the goal of life in society, as is made extraordinarily clear in the messianic vision of peace: when all peoples will go up to the Lord's house, and he will teach them his ways and they will walk along the ways of peace* (cf. *Is* 2:2-5). A new world of peace that embraces all of nature is the promise of the messianic age (cf. *Is* 11:6-9), and the Messiah himself is called "Prince of peace" (*Is* 9:5). Wherever his peace reigns, wherever it is present even in part, no longer will anyone be able to make the people of God fearful (cf. *Zeph* 3:13). It is then that peace will be lasting, because when the king rules according to God's justice, righteousness flourishes and peace abounds "till the moon be no more" (*Ps* 72:7). God longs to give peace to his people: "he will speak of peace to his people, to his saints, to those who turn to him in their hearts" (*Ps* 85:9). Listening to what God has to say to his people about peace, the Psalmist hears these words: "Steadfast love and faithfulness will meet; righteousness and peace will kiss" (*Ps* 85:11).

491. *The promise of peace that runs through the entire Old Testament finds its fulfillment in the very person of Jesus.* Peace, in fact, is the messianic attribute *par excellence*, in which all other beneficial effects of salvation are included. The Hebrew word "*shalom*" expresses this fullness of meaning in its etymological sense of "*completeness*" (cf. *Is* 9:5ff; *Mic* 5:1-4). The kingdom of the Messiah is precisely the kingdom of peace (cf. *Job* 25:2; *Ps* 29:11; 37:11; 72:3,7; 85:9,11; 119:165; 125:5, 128:6; 147:14; *Song* 8:10; *Is* 26:3,12; 32:17f.; 52:7; 54:10; 57:19; 60:17; 66:12; *Hag* 2:9; *Zech* 9:10; *et al.*). Jesus "is our peace" (*Eph 2:14*). He has broken down the dividing wall of hostility among people, reconciling them with God (cf. *Eph* 2:14-16). This is the very effective simplicity with which Saint Paul indicates the radical motivation spurring Christians to undertake a life and a mission of peace.

On the eve of his death, Jesus speaks of his loving relation with the Father and the unifying power that this love bestows upon his disciples. It is a farewell discourse which reveals the profound meaning of his life and can be considered a summary of all his teaching. The gift of peace is the seal on his spiritual testament: "Peace I leave with you; my peace I give to you; not as the world gives do I give to you" (*Jn* 14:27). The words of the Risen Lord will not be any different; every time that he meets his disciples they receive from him the greeting and gift of peace: "Peace be with you" (*Lk* 24:36; *Jn* 20:19,21,26).

492. *The peace of Christ is in the first place reconciliation with the Father, which is brought about by the ministry Jesus entrusted to his disciples and which begins with the proclamation of peace:* "Whatever house you enter, first say, 'Peace be to this house!'" (*Lk* 10:5; cf. *Rom* 1:7). *Peace is then reconciliation with one's brothers and sisters*, for in the prayer that Jesus taught us, the "Our Father," the forgiveness that we ask of God is linked to the forgiveness that we grant to our brothers and sisters: "Forgive us our debts as we also have forgiven our debtors" (*Mt* 6:12). With this twofold reconciliation Christians can become peacemakers and therefore participate in the Kingdom of God, in accordance with what Jesus himself proclaims in the Beatitudes: "Blessed are the peacemakers, for they shall be called children of God" (*Mt* 5:9).

493. *Working for peace can never be separated from announcing the Gospel, which is in fact the "good news of peace"* (*Acts* 10:36; cf. *Eph* 6:15) *addressed to all men and women.* At the centre of "the gospel of peace" (*Eph* 6:15) remains the mystery of the cross, because peace is born of Christ's sacrifice (cf. *Is* 53:5) — "Upon him was the chastisement that made us whole, and with his stripes we were healed." The crucified Jesus has overcome divisions, re-establishing peace and reconciliation, precisely through the cross, "thereby bringing the hostility to an end" (*Eph* 2:16) and bringing the salvation of the Resurrection to mankind.

II. PEACE: THE FRUIT OF JUSTICE AND LOVE

494. *Peace is a value*[1015] *and a universal duty*[1016] *founded on a rational and moral order of society that has its roots in God himself,* "the first source of being, the essen-

---

[1015] Cf. John Paul II, Message for the 1986 World Day of Peace, 1: AAS 78 (1986), 278-279.
[1016] Cf. Paul VI, Message for the 1969 World Day of Peace: AAS 60 (1968), 771; John Paul II, Message for the 2004 World Day of Peace, 4: AAS 96 (2004), 116.

tial truth and the supreme good."[1017] *Peace is not merely the absence of war, nor can it be reduced solely to the maintenance of a balance of power between enemies.*[1018] *Rather it is founded on a correct understanding of the human person*[1019] *and requires the establishment of an order based on justice and charity.*

Peace is the fruit of justice,[1020] (cf. Is 32:17) understood in the broad sense as the respect for the equilibrium of every dimension of the human person. Peace is threatened when man is not given all that is due him as a human person, when his dignity is not respected and when civil life is not directed to the common good. The defence and promotion of human rights is essential for the building up of a peaceful society and the integral development of individuals, peoples and nations.[1021]

Peace is also the fruit of love. "True and lasting peace is more a matter of love than of justice, because the function of justice is merely to do away with obstacles to peace: the injury done or the damage caused. Peace itself, however, is an act and results only from love."[1022]

495. *Peace is built up day after day in the pursuit of an order willed by God* [1023] *and can flourish only when all recognize that everyone is responsible for promoting it.*[1024] To prevent conflicts and violence, it is absolutely necessary that peace begin to take root as a value rooted deep within the heart of every person. In this way it can spread to families and to the different associations within society until the whole of the political community is involved.[1025] In a climate permeated with harmony and respect for justice, an authentic culture of peace[1026] can grow and can even pervade the entire international community. Peace is, consequently, the fruit of "that harmony structured into human society by its Divine Founder and which must be actualized by men as they aspire for ever greater justice."[1027] Such an ideal of peace "cannot be obtained on earth unless the welfare of man is safeguarded and people freely and trustingly share with one another the riches of their minds and their talents."[1028]

[1017] John Paul II, Message for the 1982 World Day of Peace 4: AAS 74 (1982), 328.

[1018] Cf. Second Vatican Ecumenical Council, Pastoral Constitution *Gaudium et Spes*, 78: AAS 58 (1966), 1101-1102.

[1019] Cf. John Paul II, Encyclical Letter *Centesimus Annus*, 51: AAS 83 (1991), 856-857.

[1020] Cf. Paul VI, Message for the 1972 World Day of Peace: AAS 63 (1971), 868.

[1021] Cf. Paul VI, Message for the 1969 World Day of Peace: AAS 60 (1968) 772; John Paul II, Message for the 1999 World Day of Peace, 12: AAS 91 (1999), 386-387.

[1022] Pius XI, Encyclical Letter *Ubi Arcano*: AAS 14 (1922), 686. In the Encyclical, reference is made to Saint Thomas Aquinas, *Summa Theologiae*, II-II, q. 29, a. 3, ad 3um: Ed. Leon. 8, 238; cf. Second Vatican Ecumenical Council, Pastoral Constitution *Gaudium et Spes*, 78: AAS 58 (1966), 1101-1102.

[1023] Cf. Paul VI, Encylical Letter *Populorum Progressio*, 76: AAS 59 (1967), 294-295.

[1024] Cf. Paul VI, Message for the 1974 World Day of Peace: AAS 65 (1973), 672.

[1025] Cf. *Catechism of the Catholic Church*, 2317.

[1026] John Paul II, Address to the Diplomatic Corps (13 January 1997), 3: *L'Osservatore Romano*, English edition, 15 January 1997, pp. 6-7.

[1027] Second Vatican Ecumenical Council, Pastoral Constitution *Gaudium et Spes*, 78: AAS 58 (1966), 1101; cf. *Catechism of the Catholic Church*, 2304.

[1028] Second Vatican Ecumenical Council, Pastoral Constitution *Gaudium et Spes*, 78: AAS 58 (1966), 1101.

496. *Violence is never a proper response.* With the conviction of her faith in Christ and with the awareness of her mission, the Church proclaims "that violence is evil, that violence is unacceptable as a solution to problems, that violence is unworthy of man. Violence is a lie, for it goes against the truth of our faith, the truth of our humanity. Violence destroys what it claims to defend: the dignity, the life, the freedom of human beings."[1029]

The contemporary world too needs the witness of unarmed prophets, who are often the objects of ridicule.[1030] "Those who renounce violence and bloodshed and, in order to safeguard human rights, make use of those means of defence available to the weakest, bear witness to evangelical charity, provided they do so without harming the rights and obligations of other men and societies. They bear legitimate witness to the gravity of the physical and moral risk of recourse to violence, with all its destruction and death."[1031]

III. THE FAILURE OF PEACE: WAR

497. *The Magisterium condemns "the savagery of war"*[1032] *and asks that war be considered in a new way.*[1033] In fact, "it is hardly possible to imagine that in an atomic era, war could be used as an instrument of justice."[1034] War is a "scourge"[1035] and is never an appropriate way to resolve problems that arise between nations, *"it has never been and it will never be,"*[1036] because it creates new and still more complicated conflicts.[1037] When it erupts, war becomes an "unnecessary massacre,"[1038] an "adventure without return"[1039] that compromises humanity's present and threatens its future. *"Nothing is lost by peace; everything may be lost by war."*[1040] The damage caused by an armed conflict is not only material but also moral.[1041] In the end, war is "the failure of all true humanism,"[1042] "it is always a

---

[1029] John Paul II, Address at Drogheda, Ireland (29 September 1979), 9: *AAS* 71 (1979), 1081; cf. Paul VI, Apostolic Exhortation *Evangelii Nuntiandi*, 37: *AAS* 68 (1976), 29.

[1030] Cf. John Paul II, Address to the Pontifical Academy of Sciences (12 November 1983), 5: *AAS* 76 (1984), 398-399.

[1031] *Catechism of the Catholic Church*, 2306.

[1032] Second Vatican Ecumenical Council, Pastoral Constitution *Gaudium et Spes,* 77: *AAS* 58 (1966), 1100; cf. *Catechism of the Catholic Church*, 2307-2317.

[1033] Cf. Second Vatican Ecumenical Council, Pastoral Constitution *Gaudium et Spes,*80: *AAS* 58 (1966), 1103-1104.

[1034] John XXIII, Encyclical Letter *Pacem in Terris*: *AAS* 55 (1963), 291.

[1035] Leo XIII, Address to the College of Cardinals: *Acta Leonis XIII*, 19 (1899), 270-272.

[1036] John Paul II, Meeting with Officials of the Roman Vicariate (17 January 1991): *L'Osservatore Romano*, English edition, 21 January 1991, p. 1; cf. John Paul II, Address to the Latin-Rite Bishops of the Arabian Peninsula (1 October 1990), 4: *AAS* 83 (1991), 475.

[1037] Cf. Paul VI, Address to Cardinals (24 June 1965): *AAS* 57 (1965) 643-644.

[1038] Benedict XV, Appeal to the Leaders of the Warring Nations (1 August 1917): *AAS* 9 (1917), 423.

[1039] John Paul II, Prayer for peace during General Audience (16 January 1991): *Insegnamenti di Giovanni Paolo II*, XIV, 1 (1991), 121.

[1040] Pius XII, Radio Message (24 August 1939): *AAS* 31 (1939) 334; John Paul II, Message for the 1993 World Day of Peace, 4: *AAS* 85 (1993), 433-434; cf. John XXIII, Encyclical Letter *Pacem in Terris*: *AAS* 55 (1963), 288.

[1041] Cf. Second Vatican Ecumenical Council, Pastoral Constitution *Gaudium et Spes* 79: *AAS* 58 (1966), 1102-1103.

[1042] John Paul II, Message for the 1999 World Day of Peace, 11: *AAS* 91 (1999), 385.

defeat for humanity":[1043] "never again some peoples against others, never again! . . . no more war, no more war!"[1044]

498. *Seeking alternative solutions to war for resolving international conflicts has taken on tremendous urgency today*, since "the terrifying power of the means of destruction — to which even medium and small-sized countries have access — and the ever closer links between the peoples of the whole world make it very difficult or practically impossible to limit the consequences of a conflict."[1045] It is therefore essential to seek out the causes underlying bellicose conflicts, especially those connected with structural situations of injustice, poverty and exploitation, which require intervention so that they may be removed. "For this reason, another name for peace is *development*. Just as there is a collective responsibility for avoiding war, so too there is a collective responsibility for promoting development."[1046]

499. *States do not always possess adequate means to provide effectively for their own defence, from this derives the need and importance of international and regional organizations*, which should be in a position to work together to resolve conflicts and promote peace, re-establishing relationships of mutual trust that make recourse to war unthinkable.[1047] "There is reason to hope . . . that by meeting and negotiating, men may come to discover better the bonds that unite them together, deriving from the human nature which they have in common; and that they may also come to discover that one of the most profound requirements of their common nature is this: that between them and their respective peoples it is not fear which should reign but love, a love which tends to express itself in a collaboration that is loyal, manifold in form and productive of many benefits."[1048]

a. Legitimate defense

500. *A war of aggression is intrinsically immoral. In the tragic case where such a war breaks out, leaders of the State that has been attacked have the right and the duty to organize a defence even using the force of arms.*[1049] To be licit, the use of force must correspond to certain strict conditions: "the damage inflicted by the aggressor on the nation or community of nations must be lasting, grave and certain; all other means of putting an end to it must have been shown to be impractical or ineffective; there must be serious prospects of success; the use of arms must not produce evils and disorders graver than the evil to be eliminated. The power of modern means of destruction weighs very heavily in evaluating this condition. These are the traditional elements enumerated in what is called the 'just war' doctrine. The

---

[1043] John Paul II, Address to the Diplomatic Corps (13 January 2003), 4: *L'Osservatore Romano*, English edition, 15 January 2003, p. 3.

[1044] Paul VI, Address to the General Assembly of the United Nations (4 October 1965), 5: AAS 57 (1965), 881.

[1045] John Paul II, Encyclical Letter *Centesimus Annus*, 51: AAS 83 (1991), 857.

[1046] John Paul II, Encyclical Letter *Centesimus Annus*, 52: AAS 83 (1991), 858.

[1047] Cf. John XXIII, Encyclical Letter *Pacem in Terris*: AAS 55 (1963), 288-289.

[1048] John XXIII, Encyclical Letter *Pacem in Terris*: AAS 55 (1963), 291.

[1049] Cf. *Catechism of the Catholic Church*, 2265.

evaluation of these conditions for moral legitimacy belongs to the prudential judgment of those who have responsibility for the common good."[1050]

If this responsibility justifies the possession of sufficient means to exercise this right to defence, States still have the obligation to do everything possible "to ensure that the conditions of peace exist, not only within their own territory but throughout the world."[1051] It is important to remember that "it is one thing to wage a war of self-defence; it is quite another to seek to impose domination on another nation. The possession of war potential does not justify the use of force for political or military objectives. Nor does the mere fact that war has unfortunately broken out mean that all is fair between the warring parties."[1052]

501. *The Charter of the United Nations, born from the tragedy of the Second World War with the intention of preserving future generations from the scourge of war, is based on a generalized prohibition of a recourse to force to resolve disputes between States, with the exception of two cases: legitimate defence and measures taken by the Security Council within the area of its responsibilities for maintaining peace.* In every case, exercising the right to self-defence must respect "the traditional limits of *necessity* and *proportionality*."[1053]

Therefore, engaging in a preventive war without clear proof that an attack is imminent cannot fail to raise serious moral and juridical questions. International legitimacy for the use of armed force, on the basis of rigorous assessment and with well-founded motivations, can only be given by the decision of a competent body that identifies specific situations as threats to peace and authorizes an intrusion into the sphere of autonomy usually reserved to a State.

b. Defending peace

502. *The requirements of legitimate defence justify the existence in States of armed forces, the activity of which should be at the service of peace. Those who defend the security and freedom of a country, in such a spirit, make an authentic contribution to peace.*[1054] Everyone who serves in the armed forces is concretely called to defend good, truth and justice in the world. Many are those who, in such circumstances, have sacrificed their lives for these values and in defence of innocent lives. Very significant in this regard is the increasing number of military personnel serving in multinational forces on humanitarian or peace-keeping missions promoted by the United Nations.[1055]

503. *Every member of the armed forces is morally obliged to resist orders that call for perpetrating crimes against the law of nations and the universal principles of this*

[1050] *Catechism of the Catholic Church*, 2309.
[1051] Pontifical Council for Justice and Peace, *The International Arms Trade*. An ethical reflection (1 May 1994), ch. 1, 6: Libreria Editrice Vaticana, Vatican City 1994, p. 13.
[1052] Second Vatican Ecumenical Council, Pastoral Constitution *Gaudium et Spes*, 79: AAS 58 (1966), 1103.
[1053] John Paul II, Message for the 2004 World Day of Peace, 6: AAS 96 (2004), 117.
[1054] Cf. Second Vatican Ecumenical Council, Pastoral Constitution *Gaudium et Spes*, 79: AAS 58 (1966), 1102-1103; *Catechism of the Catholic Church*, 2310.
[1055] Cf. John Paul II, Message to the Third International Meeting of Military Ordinaries (11 March 1994), 4: AAS 87 (1995), 74.

law.[1056] Military personnel remain fully responsible for the acts they commit in violation of the rights of individuals and peoples, or of the norms of international humanitarian law. Such acts cannot be justified by claiming obedience to the orders of superiors.

Conscientious objectors who, out of principle, refuse military service in those cases where it is obligatory because their conscience rejects any kind of recourse to the use of force or because they are opposed to the participation in a particular conflict, must be open to accepting alternative forms of service. "It seems just that laws should make humane provision for the case of conscientious objectors who refuse to carry arms, provided they accept some other form of community service."[1057]

c. The duty to protect the innocent

504. *The right to use force for purposes of legitimate defence is associated with the duty to protect and help innocent victims who are not able to defend themselves from acts of aggression.* In modern conflicts, which are often within a State, *the precepts of international humanitarian law must be fully respected.* Far too often, the civilian population is hit and at times even becomes a target of war. In some cases, they are brutally massacred or taken from their homes and land by forced transfers, under the guise of "ethnic cleansing,"[1058] which is always unacceptable. In such tragic circumstances, humanitarian aid must reach the civilian population and must never be used to influence those receiving it; the good of the human person must take precedence over the interests of the parties to the conflict.

505. *The principle of humanity inscribed in the conscience of every person and all peoples includes the obligation to protect civil populations from the effects of war.* "That minimum protection of the dignity of every person, guaranteed by international humanitarian law, is all too often violated in the name of military or political demands which should never prevail over the value of the human person. Today we are aware of the need to find a new consensus on humanitarian principles and to reinforce their foundation to prevent the recurrence of atrocities and abuse."[1059]

A particular category of war victim is formed by *refugees*, forced by combat to flee the places where they habitually live and to seek refuge in foreign countries. The Church is close to them not only with her pastoral presence and material support, but also with her commitment to defend their human dignity: "Concern for refugees must lead us to reaffirm and highlight universally recognized human rights, and to ask that the effective recognition of these rights be guaranteed to refugees."[1060]

[1056] Cf. *Catechism of the Catholic Church*, 2313.

[1057] Second Vatican Ecumenical Council, Pastoral Constitution *Gaudium et Spes*, 79: AAS 58 (1966), 1103; cf. *Catechism of the Catholic Church*, 2311.

[1058] John Paul II, Sunday Angelus (7 March 1993), 4: *L'Osservatore Romano*, English edition, 10 March 1993, p. 1; John Paul II, Address to the OSCE Council of Ministers (30 November 1993), 4: AAS 86 (1994), 751.

[1059] John Paul II, Address at General Audience (11 August 1999), 5: *L'Osservatore Romano*, English edition, 25 August 1999, p. 6.

[1060] John Paul II, 1990 Message for Lent, 3: *L'Osservatore Romano*, English edition, 12 February 1990, p. 5.

506. *Attempts to eliminate entire national, ethnic, religious or linguistic groups are crimes against God and humanity itself, and those responsible for such crimes must answer for them before justice.*[1061] The twentieth century bears the tragic mark of different genocides: from that of the Armenians to that of the Ukrainians, from that of the Cambodians to those perpetrated in Africa and in the Balkans. Among these, the Holocaust of the Jewish people, the Shoah, stands out: "the days of the *Shoah* marked a true night of history, with unimaginable crimes against God and humanity."[1062]

The international community as a whole has the moral obligation to intervene on behalf of those groups whose very survival is threatened or whose basic human rights are seriously violated. As members of an international community, States cannot remain indifferent; on the contrary, if all other available means should prove ineffective, it is "legitimate and even obligatory to take concrete measures to disarm the aggressor."[1063] The principle of national sovereignty cannot be claimed as a motive for preventing an intervention in defence of innocent victims.[1064] The measures adopted must be carried out in full respect of international law and the fundamental principle of equality among States.

There is also present within the international community an *International Criminal Court* to punish those responsible for particularly serious acts such as genocide, crimes against humanity, war crimes and crimes of aggression. The Magisterium has not failed to encourage this initiative time and again.[1065]

d. Measures against those who threaten peace

507. *Sanctions, in the forms prescribed by the contemporary international order, seek to correct the behavior of the government of a country that violates the rules of peaceful and ordered international coexistence or that practices serious forms of oppression with regard to its population.* The purpose of these sanctions must be clearly defined and the measures adopted must from time to time be objectively evaluated by the competent bodies of the international community as to their effectiveness and their real impact on the civilian population. *The true objective of such measures is open to the way to negotiation and dialogue. Sanctions must never be used as a means*

[1061] Cf. John Paul II, Message for the 1999 World Day of Peace, 7: AAS 91 (1999), 382; John Paul II, Message for the 2000 World Day of Peace, 7: AAS 92 (2000), 362.

[1062] John Paul II, Address at the *Regina Coeli* (18 April 1993), 3: *L'Osservatore Romano,* English edition, 21 April 1993, p. 12; cf. Commission for Religious Relations with Judaism, *We Remember. A Reflection on the Shoah* (16 March 1998), Libreria Editrice Vaticana, Vatican City 1998.

[1063] John Paul II, Message for the 2000 World Day of Peace, 11: AAS 92 (2000), 363.

[1064] Cf. John Paul II, Address to the Diplomatic Corps (16 January 1993), 13: *L'Osservatore Romano,* English edition, 20 January 1993, p. 9; cf. John Paul II, Address to the International Conference on Nutrition sponsored by FAO and WHO (5 December 1992), 3: AAS 85 (1993), 922-923; John Paul II, Message for the 2004 World Day of Peace, 9: AAS 96 (2004), 120.

[1065] Cf. John Paul II, Sunday Angelus (14 June 1998): *L'Osservatore Romano,* English edition, 17 June 1998, p. 1; John Paul II, Address to participants in the World Congress on Pastoral Promotion of Human Rights (4 July 1998), 5: *L'Osservatore Romano,* English edition, 29 July 1998, p. 8; John Paul II, Message for the 1999 World Day of Peace, 7: AAS 91 (1999), 382; cf. also Pius XII, Address at the Sixth International Congress of Criminal Law (3 October 1953): AAS 45 (1953), 730-744.

for the direct punishment of an entire population: it is not licit that entire populations, and above all their most vulnerable members, be made to suffer because of such sanctions. *Economic sanctions in particular are an instrument to be used with great discernment and must be subjected to strict legal and ethical criteria.*[1066] An *economic embargo* must be of limited duration and cannot be justified when the resulting effects are indiscriminate.

e. Disarmament

508. *The Church's social teaching proposes the goal of "general, balanced and controlled disarmament."*[1067] *The enormous increase in arms represents a grave threat to stability and peace. The principle of sufficiency, by virtue of which each State may possess only the means necessary for its legitimate defence, must be applied both by States that buy arms and by those that produce and furnish them.*[1068] Any excessive stockpiling or indiscriminate trading in arms cannot be morally justified. Such phenomena must also be evaluated in light of international norms regarding the non-proliferation, production, trade and use of different types of arms. Arms can never be treated like other goods exchanged on international or domestic markets.[1069]

Moreover, the Magisterium has made a moral evaluation of the phenomenon of *deterrence*. "The *accumulation of arms* strikes many as a paradoxically suitable way of deterring potential adversaries from war. They see it as the most effective means of ensuring peace among nations. This method of deterrence gives rise to strong moral reservations. The *arms race* does not ensure peace. Far from eliminating the causes of war, it risks aggravating them."[1070] Policies of nuclear deterrence, typical of the Cold War period, must be replaced with concrete measures of disarmament based on dialogue and multilateral negotiations.

509. *Arms of mass destruction — whether biological, chemical or nuclear — represent a particularly serious threat. Those who possess them have an enormous responsibility before God and all of humanity.*[1071] The principle of the non-proliferation of nuclear arms, together with measures of nuclear disarmament and the prohibition of nuclear tests, are intimately interconnected objectives that must be met as soon as possible by means of effective controls at the international level.[1072] The ban on the development, production, stockpiling and use of chemical and biological

---

[1066] Cf. John Paul II, Address to the Diplomatic Corps (9 January 1995), 7: *L'Osservatore Romano*, English edition, 11 January 1995, p. 6.

[1067] John Paul II, Message for the fortieth anniversary of the United Nations (14 October 1985), 6: *L'Osservatore Romano*, English edition, 14 November 1985, p. 4.

[1068] Cf. Pontifical Council for Justice and Peace, *The International Arms Trade. An ethical reflection* (1 May 1994), ch. 1, 9-11, Libreria Editrice Vaticana, Vatican City 1994, p. 14.

[1069] Cf. *Catechism of the Catholic Church*, 2316; John Paul II, Address to the World of Work, Verona, Italy (17 April 1988), 6: *Insegnamenti di Giovanni Paolo II*, XI, 1 (1988), 940.

[1070] *Catechism of the Catholic Church*, 2315.

[1071] Cf. Second Vatican Ecumenical Council, Pastoral Constitution *Gaudium et Spes*, 80: AAS 58 (1966), 1104; *Catechism of the Catholic Church*, 2314; John Paul II, Message for the 1986 World Day of Peace, 2: AAS 78 (1986), 280.

[1072] Cf. John Paul II, Address to the Diplomatic Corps (13 January 1996), 7: *L'Osservatore Romano*, English edition, 17 January 1996, p. 2.

weapons as well as the provisions that require their destruction, complete the international regulatory norms aimed at banning such baleful weapons,[1073] the use of which is explicitly condemned by the Magisterium: "Any act of war aimed indiscriminately at the destruction of entire cities or extensive areas along with their population is a crime against God and man himself. It merits unequivocal and unhesitating condemnation."[1074]

510. *Disarmament must include the banning of weapons that inflict excessively traumatic injury or that strike indiscriminately. This includes anti-personnel landmines, a type of small arm that is inhumanly insidious because it continues to cause harm even long after the cessation of hostilities.* States that produce them, sell them and continue to use them are responsible for seriously delaying the total elimination of these death-dealing weapons.[1075] *The international community must continue its committed efforts aimed at mine-clearance,* fostering effective cooperation — including education and technical training — with those countries that do not have adequate means to clear their territory of mines with all due urgency and that are not able to offer the necessary assistance to victims of mines.

511. *Appropriate measures are needed to control the production, sale, importation and exportation of small arms and light weapons, armaments that facilitate many outbreaks of violence to occur.* The sale and trafficking of such weapons constitute a serious threat to peace: these arms kill and are used for the most part in internal and regional conflicts; their ready availability increases both the risk of new conflicts and the intensity of those already underway. The position of States that apply severe controls on the international transfer of heavy arms while they never, or only very rarely, restrict the sale and trafficking of small arms and light weapons is an unacceptable contradiction. It is indispensable and urgent that Governments adopt appropriate measures to control the production, stockpiling, sale and trafficking of such arms[1076] in order to stop their growing proliferation, in large part among groups of combatants that are not part of the military forces of a State.

512. *The use of children and adolescents as soldiers in armed conflicts — despite the fact that their young age should bar them from being recruited — must be condemned.* Obliged by force to take part in combat or choosing to do so on their own initiative without being fully aware of the consequences, these children are not only deprived of an education and a normal childhood, they are also trained to kill. This constitutes an intolerable crime. The use of child soldiers in combat forces of any kind must be stopped and, at the same time, every possible assistance must be given to the care, education and rehabilitation of those children who have been involved in combat.[1077]

[1073] The Holy See is a party to juridical instruments dealing with nuclear, biological and chemical weapons in order to support such initiatives of the international community.

[1074] Second Vatican Ecumenical Council, Pastoral Constitution *Gaudium et Spes*, 80: AAS 58 (1966), 1104.

[1075] Cf. John Paul II, Message for the 1999 World Day of Peace, 11: AAS 91 (1999), 385-386.

[1076] Cf. John Paul II, Message for the 1999 World Day of Peace, 11: AAS 91 (1999), 385-386.

[1077] Cf. John Paul II, Message for the 1999 World Day of Peace, 11: AAS 91 (1999), 385-386.

f. The condemnation of terrorism

513. *Terrorism is one of the most brutal forms of violence traumatizing the international community today; it sows hatred, death, and an urge for revenge and reprisal.*[1078] From being a subversive strategy typical of certain extremist organizations, aimed at the destruction of material goods or the killing of people, terrorism has now become a shadowy network of political collusion. It can also make use of sophisticated technology, often has immense financial resources at its disposal and is involved in large-scale planning, striking completely innocent people who become chance victims of terrorist actions.[1079] The targets of terrorist attacks are generally places of daily life and not military objectives in the context of a declared war. Terrorism acts and strikes under the veil of darkness, with no regard for any of the rules by which men have always sought to set limits to conflicts, for example through international humanitarian law; "in many cases, terrorist methods are regarded as new strategies of war."[1080] Nor must we overlook the causes that can lead to such unacceptable forms of making demands. The fight against terrorism presupposes the moral duty to help create those conditions that will prevent it from arising or developing.

514. *Terrorism is to be condemned in the most absolute terms. It shows complete contempt for human life and can never be justified, since the human person is always an end and never a means.* Acts of terrorism strike at the heart of human dignity and are an offence against all humanity; *"there exists, therefore, a right to defend oneself from terrorism."*[1081] However, this right cannot be exercised in the absence of moral and legal norms, because the struggle against terrorists must be carried out with respect for human rights and for the principles of a State ruled by law.[1082] The identification of the guilty party must be duly proven, because criminal responsibility is always personal, and therefore cannot be extended to the religions, nations or ethnic groups to which the terrorists belong. International cooperation in the fight against terrorist activity "cannot be limited solely to repressive and punitive operations. It is essential that the use of force, even when necessary, be accompanied by a *courageous and lucid analysis of the reasons behind terrorist attacks.*"[1083] Also needed is a particular commitment on the *"political and educational levels"*[1084] in order to resolve, with courage and determination, the problems that in certain dramatic circumstances can foster terrorism: "the recruitment of terrorists in fact is easier in situations where rights are trampled and injustices are tolerated over a long period of time."[1085]

[1078] Cf. *Catechism of the Catholic Church*, 2297.
[1079] Cf. John Paul II, Message for the 2002 World Day of Peace, 4: *AAS* 94 (2002), 134.
[1080] Second Vatican Ecumenical Council, Pastoral Constitution *Gaudium et Spes*, 79: *AAS* 58 (1966), 1102.
[1081] John Paul II, Message for the 2002 World Day of Peace, 5: *AAS* 94 (2002), 134.
[1082] Cf. John Paul II, Message for the 2004 World Day of Peace, 8: *AAS* 96 (2004), 119.
[1083] John Paul II, Message for the 2004 World Day of Peace, 8: *AAS* 96 (2004), 119.
[1084] John Paul II, Message for the 2004 World Day of Peace, 8: *AAS* 96 (2004), 119.
[1085] John Paul II, Message for the 2002 World Day of Peace, 5: *AAS* 94 (2002), 134.

515. *It is a profanation and a blasphemy to declare oneself a terrorist in God's name.*[1086] In such cases, God, and not only man, is exploited by a person who claims to possess the totality of God's truth rather than one who seeks to be possessed by the truth. To define as "martyrs" those who die while carrying out terrorist attacks distorts the concept of martyrdom, which is the witness of a person who gives himself up to death rather than deny God and his love. Martyrdom cannot be the act of a person who kills in the name of God.

No religion may tolerate terrorism and much less preach it.[1087] Rather, religions must work together to remove the causes of terrorism and promote friendship among peoples.[1088]

IV. THE CONTRIBUTION OF THE CHURCH TO PEACE

516. *The promotion of peace in the world is an integral part of the Church's mission of continuing Christ's work of redemption on earth.* In fact, the Church is, in Christ, a " 'sacrament' or sign and instrument of peace in the world and for the world."[1089] The promotion of true peace is an expression of Christian faith in the love that God has for every human being. From a liberating faith in God's love there arises a new vision of the world and a new way of approaching others, whether the other is an individual or an entire people. It is a faith that transforms and renews life, inspired by the peace that Christ left to his disciples (cf. *Jn* 14:27). Moved solely by this faith, the Church intends to promote the unity of Christians and a fruitful cooperation with believers of other religions. Differences of religion must not be a cause of conflict; the shared quest for peace on the part of all believers is a vital source of unity among peoples.[1090] The Church calls on individuals, peoples, States and nations to share her concern for re-establishing and consolidating peace, placing particular emphasis on the important role of international law.[1091]

517. *The Church teaches that true peace is made possible only through forgiveness and reconciliation.*[1092] It is not easy to forgive when faced with the consequences of war and conflict because violence, especially when it leads "to the very depths of inhumanity and suffering,"[1093] leaves behind a heavy burden of pain. This pain can only be eased by a deep, faithful and courageous reflection on the part of all parties, a reflection capable of facing present difficulties with an attitude that has

---

[1086] Cf. John Paul II, Address to Representatives from the World of Culture, Art and Science, Astana, Kazakhstan (24 September 2001), 5: *L'Osservatore Romano*, English edition, 26 September 2001, p. 7.

[1087] Cf. John Paul II, Message for the 2002 World Day of Peace, 7: AAS 95 (2002), 135-136.

[1088] Cf. "Decalogue of Assisi for Peace," 1, in the letter addressed by John Paul II to Heads of State and of Government on 24 February 2002: *L'Osservatore Romano*, English edition, 6 March 2002, p. 12.

[1089] John Paul II, Message for the 2000 World Day of Peace, 20: AAS 92 (2000), 369.

[1090] John Paul II, Message for the 1988 World Day of Peace, 3: AAS 80 (1988), 282-284.

[1091] Cf. John Paul II, Message for the 2004 World Day of Peace, 9: AAS 96 (2004), 120.

[1092] Cf. John Paul II Message for the 2002 World Day of Peace, 9: AAS 94 (2002), 136-137; John Paul II, Message for the 2004 World Day of Peace, 10: AAS 96 (2004), 121.

[1093] John Paul II, Letter on the occasion of the fiftieth anniversary of the outbreak of the Second World War (27 August 1989), 2: *L'Osservatore Romano*, English edition, 4 September 1989, p. 1.

been purified by repentance. The weight of the past, which cannot be forgotten, can be accepted only when mutual forgiveness is offered and received; this is a long and difficult process, but one that is not impossible.[1094]

518. *Mutual forgiveness must not eliminate the need for justice and still less does it block the path that leads to truth. On the contrary, justice and truth represent the concrete requisites for reconciliation.* Initiatives aimed at establishing international judicial bodies are therefore appropriate. In virtue of the principle of universal jurisdiction and guided by suitable procedural norms that respect the rights of the accused and of the victims, such bodies are able to ascertain the truth about crimes perpetrated during armed conflicts.[1095] However, in order to re-establish relationships of mutual acceptance between divided peoples in the name of reconciliation, it is necessary to go beyond the determination of criminal behavior, both of commission and omission, and the procedures for seeking reparation.[1096] It is necessary, moreover, to promote respect for *the right to peace*. This right "encourages the building of a society in which structures of power give way to structures of cooperation, with a view to the common good."[1097]

519. *It is through prayer that the Church engages in the battle for peace.* Prayer opens the heart not only to a deep relationship with God but also to an encounter with others marked by respect, understanding, esteem and love.[1098] Prayer instils courage and lends support to all "true friends of peace,"[1099] those who love peace and strive to promote it in the various circumstances in which they live. Liturgical prayer is "the summit towards which the action of the Church tends and, at the same time, the source from which she draws her strength."[1100] In particular, the Eucharistic celebration, "the source and summit of the Christian life,"[1101] is a limitless wellspring for all authentic Christian commitment to peace.[1102]

[1094] Cf. John Paul II, Message for the 1997 World Day of Peace, 3 and 4: *AAS* 89 (1997), 193.
[1095] Cf. Pius XII, Address to the Sixth International Congress on Criminal Law (3 October 1953): *AAS* 65 (1953) 730-744; John Paul II, Address to the Diplomatic Corps (13 January 1997), 4: *L'Osservatore Romano*, English edition, 15 January 1997, p. 7. John Paul II, Message for the 1999 World Day of Peace, 7: *AAS* 91 (1999), 382.
[1096] Cf. John Paul II, Message for the 1997 World Day of Peace, 3, 4, 6: *AAS* 89 (1997), 193, 196-197.
[1097] John Paul II, Message for the 1999 World Day of Peace, 11: *AAS* 91 (1999), 385.
[1098] Cf. John Paul II, Message for the 1992 World Day of Peace, 4: *AAS* 84 (1992), 323-324.
[1099] Paul VI, Message for the 1968 World Day of Peace: *AAS* 59 (1967), 1098.
[1100] Second Vatican Ecumenical Council, Constitution *Sacrosanctum Concilium*, 10: *AAS* 56 (1964), 102.
[1101] Second Vatican Ecumenical Council, Constitution *Lumen Gentium*, 11: *AAS* 57 (1965), 15.
[1102] The eucharistic celebration begins with a greeting of peace, the greeting of Christ to his disciples. The *Gloria* is a prayer for peace for all the people of God on the earth. Prayer for peace is made through the anaphora at Mass: an appeal for the peace and unity of the Church, for the peace of the entire family of God in this life, for the advancement of peace and salvation in the world. During the communion rite the Church prays that the Lord will "grant us peace in our day" and remembers Christ's gift that consists of his peace, invoking "the peace and unity of his Kingdom." Before communion, the entire assembly exchanges a sign of peace and the assembly prays that the Lamb of God, who takes away the sins of the world will "grant us peace." The eucharistic celebration concludes with the assembly being dismissed in the peace of Christ. There are many prayers that invoke peace for the world. In these, peace is sometimes associated with justice, for example, as in the opening prayer for the Eighth Sunday in Ordinary Time, in which the Church asks God to guide the course of world events in justice and peace, according to his will.

520. The *World Days of Peace* are particularly intense moments of prayer for peace and for the commitment to build a world of peace. Pope Paul VI instituted these Days to dedicate to "thoughts and resolutions of Peace a special observance on the first day of the civil year."[1103] *The Papal Messages on these annual occasions represent a rich source for the renewal and development of the Church's social doctrine* and show the Church's constant pastoral activity aimed at the promotion of peace. "Peace expresses itself only in peace, a peace which is not separate from the demands of justice, but which is fostered by personal sacrifice, clemency, mercy and love."[1104]

[1103] Paul VI, Message for the 1968 World Day of Peace: *AAS* 59 (1967), 1100.
[1104] Paul VI, Message for the 1976 World Day of Peace: *AAS* 67 (1975), 671.

PART THREE

"As far as the Church is concerned, the social message
of the Gospel must not be considered a theory,
but above all else a basis and a motivation for action."

(*Centesimus Annus*, 57)

CHAPTER TWELVE

SOCIAL DOCTRINE AND ECCLESIAL ACTION

I. PASTORAL ACTION IN THE SOCIAL FIELD

a. Social doctrine and the inculturation of faith

521. *Aware of the power of Christianity to renew even cultural and social realities,*[1105] *the Church offers the contribution of her teaching to the building up of the human community by bringing out the social significance of the Gospel.*[1106] At the end of the nineteenth century, the Church's Magisterium systematically addressed the pressing social questions of the time, creating "a lasting paradigm for the Church. The Church, in fact, has something to say about specific human situations, individual, and communal, national and international. She formulates a genuine doctrine for these situations, a *corpus* which enables her to analyze social realities, to make judgments about them and to indicate directions to be taken for the just resolution of the problems involved."[1107] The intervention of Pope Leo XIII in the social and political reality of his time with the Encyclical *Rerum Novarum* "gave the Church 'citizenship status' as it were, amid the changing realities of public life, and this standing would be more fully confirmed later on."[1108]

522. *In her social doctrine the Church offers above all an integral vision of man and a complete understanding of his personal and social dimensions.* Christian anthropology reveals the inviolable dignity of every person and places the realities of work, economics and politics into an original perspective that sheds light on authentic human values while at the same time inspiring and sustaining the task of Christian witness in the varied areas of personal, cultural and social life. Thanks to the "first fruits of the Spirit" (*Rom* 8:23), Christians become "capable of discharging the new law of love (cf. *Rom* 8:1-11). Through this Spirit, who is 'the pledge of our inheritance' (*Eph* 1:14), the whole man is renewed from within, even to the achievement of 'the redemption of the body' (*Rom* 8:23)."[1109] In this sense the Church's social doctrine shows how the moral basis of all social action consists in the human development of the person and identifies the norm for

---

[1105] Cf. Congregation for the Clergy, *General Directory for Catechesis*, 18, Libreria Editrice Vaticana, Vatican City 1997, pp. 21-22.

[1106] Cf. John Paul II, Encyclical Letter *Redemptoris Missio*, 11: AAS 83 (1991), 259-260.

[1107] John Paul II, Encyclical Letter *Centesimus Annus*, 5: AAS 83 (1991), 799.

[1108] John Paul II, Encyclical Letter *Centesimus Annus*, 5: AAS 83 (1991), 799.

[1109] Second Vatican Ecumenical Council, Pastoral Constitution *Gaudium et Spes*, 22: AAS 58 (1966), 1043.

social action corresponding to humanity's true good and as efforts aimed at creating the conditions that will allow every person to satisfy his integral vocation.

523. *This Christian anthropology gives life to and supports the pastoral task of inculturation of the faith, which aims at an interior renewal, through the power of the Gospel, of modern man's criteria of judgment, the values underlying his decisions, the way he thinks and the models after which his life is patterned.* "Through inculturation the Church, for her part, becomes a more intelligible sign of what she is and a more effective instrument of mission."[1110] The contemporary world is marked by a rift between the Gospel and culture, by a secularized vision of salvation that tends to reduce even Christianity to "merely human wisdom, a pseudo-science of well-being."[1111] The Church is aware that she must take "*a giant step forward* in her evangelization effort, and enter into *a new stage of history* in her missionary dynamism."[1112] The Church's social doctrine is situated within this pastoral vision: "The 'new evangelization,' which the modern world urgently needs, . . . must include among its essential elements *a proclamation of the Church's social doctrine.*"[1113]

b. Social doctrine and social pastoral activity

524. *The Church's social teaching is the indispensable reference point that determines the nature, modality, articulation and development of pastoral activity in the social field.* It is the expression of the ministry of social evangelization, aimed at enlightening, stimulating and supporting the integral promotion of the human person through the practice of Christian liberation in its earthly and transcendent dimension. The Church exists and is at work within history. She interacts with the society and culture of her time in order to fulfil her mission of announcing the newness of the Christian message to all people, in the concrete circumstances of their difficulties, struggles and challenges. She does so in such a way that faith enlightens them so that they can understand the truth that "true liberation consists in opening oneself to the love of Christ."[1114] The Church's social pastoral ministry is the living and concrete expression of the full awareness of her evangelizing mission in the social, economic, cultural and political realities of the world.

525. *The social message of the Gospel must guide the Church in her twofold pastoral activity: that of helping men and women to discover the truth and to choose the path that they will follow, and that of encouraging Christians to bear witness with a spirit of service to the Gospel in the field of social activity.* "Today more than ever the Word of God will be unable to be proclaimed and heard unless it is accompanied by the witness of the power of the Holy Spirit, working within the action of Christians in the service of their brothers and sisters, at the points in which their existence and

[1110] John Paul II, Encyclical Letter *Redemptoris Missio*, 52: AAS 83 (1991), 300; cf. Paul VI, Apostolic Exhortation *Evangelii Nuntiandi*, 20: AAS 68 (1976), 18-19.
[1111] John Paul II, Encyclical Letter *Redemptoris Missio*, 11: AAS 83 (1991), 259-260.
[1112] John Paul II, Post-Synodal Apostolic Exhortation *Christifideles Laici*, 35: AAS 81 (1989), 458.
[1113] John Paul II, Encyclical Letter *Centesimus Annus*, 5: AAS 83 (1991), 800.
[1114] John Paul II; Encyclical Letter *Redemptoris Missio*, 11: AAS 83 (1991), 259.

their future are at stake."[1115] The need for a new evangelization helps the Church to understand that "today more than ever . . . her social message will gain credibility more immediately from the *witness of action* than as a result of its internal logic and consistency."[1116]

526. *The Church's social doctrine provides the fundamental criteria for pastoral action in the area of social activity: proclaiming the Gospel; plac-ing the Gospel message in the context of social realities; planning actions aimed at the renewal of these realities; and conforming them to the demands of Christian morality.* A new evangelization of society requires first of all the proclamation of the Gospel: God saves every person and the whole person in Jesus Christ. It is this proclamation that reveals man to himself and that must become the principle for interpreting social realities. In proclaiming the Gospel, the social dimension is an essential and unavoidable but not the only dimension. It is a dimension that must reveal the unlimited possibilities of Christian salvation, even if it is not possible in time to conform social realities perfectly and definitively to the Gospel. No results attained, not even the most spectacular, can escape the limits of human freedom and the eschatological tension of every created reality.[1117]

527. *Above all, the pastoral activity of the Church in the social sector must bear witness to the truth of the human person.* Christian anthropology permits a discernment of social problems that will never find an adequate solution if the transcendent character of the human person, fully revealed in faith, is not safeguarded.[1118] *The social action of Christians must be inspired by the fundamental principle of the centrality of the human person.*[1119] The need to promote the integral identity of the human person prompts Christians to propose those eminent values that govern every well-ordered and productive human society: truth, justice, love and freedom.[1120] Pastoral activity in the social field must seek to ensure that the renewal of public life is linked to an effective respect for these values. In this way, the Church's multifaceted evangelical witness seeks to promote the awareness of the good of each person and of all people as an unlimited resource for the development of every aspect of life in society.

c. Social doctrine and formation

528. *The Church's social doctrine is an indispensable reference point for a totally integrated Christian formation.* The insistence of the Magisterium in proposing this doctrine as a source of inspiration for the apostolate and for social action comes from the conviction that it constitutes an extraordinary resource for formation;

[1115] Paul VI, Apostolic Letter *Octogesima Adveniens,* 51: AAS 63 (1971), 440.
[1116] John Paul II, Encyclical Letter *Centesimus Annus,* 57: AAS 83 (1991), 862.
[1117] Cf. John Paul II, Encyclical Letter *Sollicitudo Rei Socialis,* 48: AAS 80 (1988), 583-584.
[1118] Cf. Second Vatican Ecumenical Council, Pastoral Constitution *Gaudium et Spes,* 76: AAS 58 (1966), 1099-1100.
[1119] Cf. John XXIII, Encyclical Letter *Mater et Magistra*: AAS 53 (1961), 453; John Paul II, Encyclical Letter *Centesimus Annus* 54: AAS 83 (1991), 859-860.
[1120] Cf. John XXIII, Encyclical Letter *Pacem in Terris*: AAS 55 (1963), 265-266.

"this is especially true for the lay faithful who have responsibilities in various fields of social and public life. Above all, it is indispensable that they have a more exact knowledge . . . of the *Church's social doctrine*."[1121] This doctrinal patrimony is neither taught nor known sufficiently, which is part of the reason for its failure to be suitably reflected in concrete behavior.

529. *The formative value of the Church's social doctrine should receive more attention in catechesis.*[1122] Catechesis is the systematic teaching of Christian doctrine in its entirety, with a view to initiating believers into the fullness of Gospel life.[1123] The ultimate aim of catechesis "is to put people not only in touch but in communion, in intimacy, with Jesus Christ."[1124] In this way, it becomes possible to recognize the action of the Holy Spirit, from whom comes the gift of new life in Christ.[1125] Seen in this light, in its service of educating to the faith, the concern of catechesis *must not fail* "to clarify properly realities such as man's activity for his integral liberation, the search for a society with greater solidarity and fraternity, the fight for justice and the building of peace."[1126] In order to do so, the fullness of the social Magisterium must be presented: its history, its content and its methodology. Direct contact with the texts of the social encyclicals, read within an ecclesial context, enriches its reception and application, thanks to the contribution of the different areas of competency and professions represented within the community.

530. *In the context of catechesis above all it is important that the teaching of the Church's social doctrine be directed towards motivating action for the evangelization and humanization of temporal realities.* Through this doctrine, in fact, the Church expresses a theoretical and practical knowledge that gives support to the commitment of transforming social life, helping it to conform ever more fully to the divine plan. Social catechesis aims at the formation of men and women who, in their respect for the moral order, are lovers of true freedom, people who "will form their own judgments in the light of truth, direct their activities with a sense of responsibility, and strive for what is true and just in willing cooperation with others."[1127] *The witness of a Christian life has an extraordinary formative value*: "In particular *the life of holiness* which is resplendent in so many members of the People of God, humble and often unseen, constitutes the simplest and most attractive way to perceive at once the beauty of truth, the liberating force of God's love, and the value of unconditional fidelity to all the demands of the Lord's law, even in the most difficult circumstances."[1128]

[1121] Cf. John Paul II, Post-Synodal Apostolic Exhortation *Christifideles Laici*, 60: AAS 81 (1989), 511.

[1122] Cf. Congregation for the Clergy, *General Directory for Catechesis*, 30, Libreria Editrice Vaticana, Vatican City 1997, pp. 30-32.

[1123] Cf. John Paul II, Apostolic Exhortation *Catechesi Tradendae*, 18: AAS 71 (1979), 1291-1292.

[1124] John Paul II, Apostolic Exhortation *Catechesi Tradendae*, 5: AAS 71 (1979), 1281.

[1125] Cf. Congregation for the Clergy, *General Directory for Catechesis*, 54, Libreria Editrice Vaticana, Vatican City 1997, p. 54.

[1126] John Paul II, Apostolic Exhortation *Catechesi Tradendae*, 29: AAS 71 (1979), 1301-1302; cf. also Congregation for the Clergy, *General Directory for Catechesis*, 17, Libreria Editrice Vaticana, Vatican City 1997, p. 21.

[1127] Second Vatican Ecumenical Council, Declaration *Dignitatis Humanae*, 8: AAS 58 (1966), 935.

[1128] John Paul II, Encyclical Letter *Veritatis Splendoris*, 107: AAS 85 (1993), 1217.

531. *The Church's social doctrine must be the basis of an intense and constant work of formation, especially of the lay faithful. Such a formation should take into account their obligations in civil society.* "It belongs to the layman, without waiting passively for orders and directives, to take the initiative freely and to infuse a Christian spirit into the mentality, customs, laws and structures of the community in which they live."[1129] *The first level* of the formation of lay Christians should be to help them to become capable of meeting their daily activities effectively in the cultural, social, economic and political spheres and to develop in them a sense of duty that is at the service of the common good.[1130] A *second level* concerns the formation of a political conscience in order to prepare lay Christians to exercise political power. "Those with a talent for the difficult yet noble art of politics, or whose talents in this matter can be developed, should prepare themselves for it, and forgetting their own convenience and material interests, they should engage in political activity."[1131]

532. *Catholic educational institutions can and indeed must carry out a precious formative service, dedicating themselves in a particular way to the inculturation of the Christian message, that is to say, to the productive encounter between the Gospel and the various branches of knowledge.* The Church's social doctrine is a necessary means for an efficacious Christian education towards love, justice and peace, as well as for a conscious maturation of moral and social duties in the various cultural and professional fields.

The "Social Weeks" of Catholics that the Magisterium has always encouraged are important examples of formational opportunities. They represent privileged moments for the expression and growth of the lay faithful, who are then capable of making their specific high-level contribution to the temporal order. Various countries find that these *Weeks* are veritable *cultural laboratories* for the exchange of reflections and experiences, the study of emerging problems and the identification of new operative approaches.

533. *No less important is the commitment to use the Church's social doctrine in the formation of priests and candidates to the priesthood who, in the context of their preparation for ministry, must develop a thorough knowledge of the Church's teaching and her pastoral concerns in the social sphere as well as a keen interest in the social issues of their day.* The Congregation for Catholic Education has published a document, *Guidelines for the Study and Teaching of the Church's Social Doctrine in the Formation of Priests*,[1132] which gives specific indications and recommendations for a correct and appropriate plan of studies for this teaching.

d. Promoting dialogue

534. *The Church's social doctrine is a privileged instrument of dialogue between Christian communities and the civil and political community.* It is an appropriate tool for promot-

---

[1129] Paul VI, Encyclical Letter *Populorum Progressio*, 81: AAS 59 (1967), 296-297.
[1130] Cf. Second Vatican Ecumenical Council, Pastoral Constitution *Gaudium et Spes*, 75: AAS 58 (1966), 1097-1098.
[1131] Second Vatican Ecumenical Council, Pastoral Constitution *Gaudium et Spes*, 75: AAS 58 (1966), 1098.
[1132] 30 December 1988, Vatican Polyglot Press, Rome 1988.

ing and cultivating attitudes of authentic and productive cooperation in ways adapted to the circumstances. The commitment of civil and political authorities, called to serve the personal and social vocation of mankind according to their own areas of competence and with the means available to them, can find in the social teaching of the Church an important support and a rich source of inspiration.

535. *The social teaching of the Church is also fertile soil for dialogue and collaboration in the ecumenical sphere.* This is already happening in various places on a broad scale concerning the defence of the dignity of the human person, the promotion of peace, the concrete and effective struggle against the miseries of today's world, such as hunger and poverty, illiteracy, the unequal distribution of the goods of the earth and the lack of housing. This multifaceted cooperation increases awareness that all are brothers and sisters in Christ, and makes the journey along the path of ecumenism easier.

536. *In the common tradition of the Old Testament, the Catholic Church is able to engage in dialogue with her Jewish brothers and sisters, which she does also through her social doctrine, in order to build together a future of justice and peace for all people, as sons and daughters of the one God.* This common spiritual heritage fosters mutual knowledge and reciprocal esteem,[1133] on the basis of which broader agreement can be reached concerning the elimination of all forms of discrimination and the defence of human dignity.

537. *The Church's social doctrine is also characterized by a constant call to dialogue among all members of the world's religions* so that together they will be able to seek the most appropriate forms of cooperation. Religion has an important role to play in the pursuit of peace, which depends on a common commitment to the integral development of the human person.[1134] In the spirit of the *meetings for prayer held in Assisi,*[1135] the Church continues to invite believers of other religions to dialogue and encourage everywhere effective witness to those values shared by the entire human family.

e. The subjects of social pastoral activity

538. *The entire people of God has a role to play as the Church fulfils her mission.* In various ways and through every member according to the gifts and the manner of acting proper to each vocation, the people of God must respond to the *duty* to proclaim and bear witness to the Gospel (cf. *1 Cor* 9:16), in the awareness that *"missionary activity is a matter for all Christians."*[1136]

    Pastoral work in the social sector is also meant for all Christians, who are called to become active subjects in bearing witness to this social doctrine and to be fully part of the solid tradition of the "fruitful activity of many millions of people, who,

[1133] Cf. Second Vatican Ecumenical Council, Declaration *Nostra Aetate*, 4: AAS 58 (1966), 742-743.
[1134] Cf. John Paul II, Encyclical Letter *Sollicitudo Rei Socialis*, 32: AAS 80 (1988), 556-557.
[1135] 27 October 1986; 24 January 2002.
[1136] John Paul II, Encyclical Letter *Redemptoris Missio*, 2: AAS 83 (1991), 250.

spurred on by the social Magisterium, have sought to make that teaching the inspiration for their involvement in the world."[1137] Acting either as individuals or together with others in various groups, associations and organizations, Christians of today represent "a *great movement for the defence of the human person* and the safeguarding of human dignity."[1138]

539. *In the particular Church, the primary responsibility for the pastoral commitment to evangelize social realities falls to the Bishop,* assisted by priests, religious men and women, and the laity. With special reference to local realities, the Bishop is responsible for promoting the teaching and diffusion of the Church's social doctrine, which he should do through appropriate institutions.

The pastoral action of the Bishop is realized through the ministry of priests, who participate in the Bishop's mission of teaching, sanctifying and governing the Christian community. Through suitable formation programmes, the priest should make known the social teaching of the Church and foster in the members of his community an awareness of their right and duty to be active subjects of this doctrine. Through the celebration of the sacraments, especially Eucharist and Reconciliation, the priest helps the faithful to live their social commitment as a fruit of the mystery of salvation. He should animate pastoral action in the social field, giving particular attention to the formation and spiritual accompaniment of lay Christians engaged in social and political life. The priest who carries out pastoral service in various ecclesial associations, especially those dedicated to the social apostolate, has the duty to promote the growth of such groups through the proper teaching of social doctrine.

540. *This pastoral work in the social sector also includes the work of consecrated persons according to their particular charism. Their shining witness, especially in situations of great poverty, represents a reminder to all people of the values of holiness and generous service to one's neighbor.* The total gift of self made by men and women religious is offered to the contemplation of everyone as an eloquent and prophetic sign of the Church's social doctrine. Placing themselves totally at the service of the mystery of Christ's love for mankind and the world, religious anticipate and show by their very lives some of the traits of the new humanity that this social doctrine seeks to encourage. In chastity, poverty and obedience, consecrated persons place themselves at the service of pastoral charity, especially by prayer, thanks to which they contemplate God's plan for the world and beg the Lord to open the heart of all persons to welcome within themselves the gift of a new humanity, the price of Christ's sacrifice.

II. SOCIAL DOCTRINE
AND THE COMMITMENT OF THE LAY FAITHFUL

a. **The lay faithful**

541. *The essential characteristic of the lay faithful who work in the Lord's vineyard (cf. Mt 20:1-16) is the secular nature of their Christian discipleship, which is carried out pre-*

[1137] John Paul II, Encyclical Letter *Centesimus Annus*, 3: AAS 83 (1991), 795.
[1138] John Paul II, Encyclical Letter *Centesimus Annus*, 3: AAS 83 (1991), 796.

cisely in the world. "It belongs to the laity to seek the kingdom of God by engaging in temporal affairs and directing them according to God's will."[1139] By Baptism, the laity are incorporated into Christ and are made participants in his life and mission according to their specific identity. "The term 'laity' is here understood to mean all the faithful except those in Holy Orders and those who belong to a religious state approved by the Church. That is, the faithful who, by Baptism are incorporated into Christ, are placed in the People of God and in their own way share the priestly, prophetic and kingly office of Christ, and to the best of their ability carry on the mission of the whole Christian people in the Church and in the world."[1140]

542. *The identity of the lay faithful is born in and nourished by the sacraments of* Baptism, Confirmation and the Eucharist. Baptism conforms the person to Christ, Son of the Father, first-born of every creature, sent to all as Teacher and Redeemer. Confirmation configures the individual to Christ, sent to give new life to creation and to every being through the outpouring of his Spirit. The Eucharist makes the believer a participant in the unique and perfect sacrifice that Christ offered to the Father, in his own flesh, for the salvation of the world.

Lay Catholics are disciples of Christ starting with the sacraments, that is, by virtue of what God has wrought in them, marking them with the very image of his Son Jesus Christ. It is from this divine gift of grace, and not from human concession, that is born the threefold *"munus"* (*gift and duty*) that characterizes the lay person as *prophet, priest and king,* according to his secular nature.

543. *It is the proper duty of the lay faithful to proclaim the Gospel with an exemplary witness of life rooted in Christ and lived in temporal realities*: the family; professional commitment in the world of work, culture, science and research; the exercise of social, economic and political responsibilities. All secular human realities — both personal and social, including various environments and historical situations, as well as structures and institutions — are the context in which the lay Christian lives and works. These realities are places where God's love is received; the commitment of the lay faithful must correspond to this vision and is to be considered an expression of evangelical charity; "for the lay faithful to be present and active in the world is not only an anthropological and sociological reality, but in a specific way, a theological and ecclesiological reality as well."[1141]

544. *The witness of the lay faithful is born from the gift of grace, recognized, nurtured and brought to maturity.*[1142] This motivation makes their commitment in the world significant and is opposed to the characteristics of action that are proper to atheistic humanism, which lack an ultimate basis and are circumscribed within purely temporal limits. The eschatological perspective is the key that allows a correct

---

[1139] Second Vatican Ecumenical Council, Dogmatic Constitution *Lumen Gentium,* 31: AAS 57 (1965), 37.
[1140] Second Vatican Ecumenical Council, Dogmatic Constitution *Lumen Gentium,* 31: AAS 57 (1965), 37.
[1141] John Paul II, Post-Synodal Apostolic Exhortation *Christifideles Laici,* 15: AAS 81 (1989), 415.
[1142] Cf. John Paul II, Post-Synodal Apostolic Exhortation *Christifideles Laici,* 24: AAS 81 (1989), 433-435.

understanding of human realities. From the standpoint of definitive goods, the lay faithful are able to engage in earthly activity according to the criteria of authenticity. Standards of living and greater economic productivity are not the only valid indicators for measuring the total fulfilment of the human person in this life, and they are of even less value when considering the life to come, "for man's horizons are not bounded only by the temporal order; living on the level of human history, he preserves the integrity of his eternal destiny."[1143]

b. Spirituality of the lay faithful

545. *The lay faithful are called to cultivate an authentic lay spirituality by which they are reborn as new men and women, both sanctified and sanctifiers, immersed in the mystery of God and inserted in society.* Such a spirituality will build up the world according to Jesus' Spirit. It will make people capable of looking beyond history, without separating themselves from it, of cultivating a passionate love for God without looking away from their bothers and sisters, whom they are able to see as the Lord sees them and love as the Lord loves them. This spirituality precludes both an *intimist spiritualism* and a *social activism*, expressing itself instead in a life-giving synthesis that bestows unity, meaning and hope on an existence that for so many different reasons is contradictory and fragmented. Prompted by such a spirituality, the lay faithful are able to contribute "to the sanctification of the world, as from within like leaven, by fulfilling their own particular duties. Thus, especially by the witness of their own life . . . they must manifest Christ to others."[1144]

546. *The lay faithful must strengthen their spiritual and moral lives, becoming ever more competent in carrying out their social duties.* A deepening of interior motivations and the acquisition of a style appropriate for their work in the social and political spheres are the results of a dynamic and ongoing formation directed above all to the attainment of harmony between life, in all its complexity, and faith. In the experience of believers, in fact, "there cannot be two parallel lives in their existence: on the one hand, the so-called 'spiritual' life, with its values and demands; and on the other, the so-called 'secular' life, that is, life in a family, at work, in social relationships, in the responsibilities of public life and in culture."[1145]

Bringing faith and life together requires following the path judiciously indicated by the haracteristic elements of Christian living: the Word of God as a reference point; the liturgical celebration of the Christian Mystery; personal prayer; the authentic experience of Church enhanced by the particular formational services of discerning spiritual guides; the exercise of the social virtues and a persevering commitment to cultural and professional formation.

[1143] Second Vatican Ecumenical Council, Pastoral Constitution *Gaudium et Spes*, 76: AAS 58 (1966), 1099.

[1144] Second Vatican Ecumenical Council, Dogmatic Constitution *Lumen Gentium*, 31: AAS 57 (1965), 37-38.

[1145] John Paul II, Post-Synodal Apostolic Exhortation *Christifidelis Laici*, 59: AAS 81 (1989), 509.

c. Acting with prudence

547. *The lay faithful should act according to the dictates of prudence, the virtue that makes it possible to discern the true good in every circumstance and to choose the right means for achieving it. Thanks to this virtue, moral principles are applied correctly to particular cases.* We can identify three distinct moments as prudence is exercised to clarify and evaluate situations, to inspire decisions and to prompt action. The first moment is seen in the *reflection and consultation* by which the question is studied and the necessary opinions sought. The second moment is that of *evaluation*, as the reality is *analyzed and judged* in the light of God's plan. The third moment, that of *decision*, is based on the preceding steps and makes it possible to choose between the different actions that may be taken.

548. *Prudence makes it possible to make decisions that are consistent, and to make them with realism and a sense of responsibility for the consequences of one's action.* The rather widespread opinion that equates prudence with shrewdness, with utilitarian calculations, with diffidence or with timidity or indecision, is far from the correct understanding of this virtue. It is a characteristic of practical reason and offers assistance in deciding *with wisdom and courage* the course of action that should be followed, becoming the *measure* of the other virtues. Prudence affirms the good as a duty and shows in what manner the person should accomplish it.[1146] In the final analysis, it is a virtue that requires the mature exercise of thought and responsibility in an objective understanding of a specific situation and in making decisions according to a correct will.[1147]

d. Social doctrine and lay associations

549. *The Church's social doctrine must become an integral part of the ongoing formation of the lay faithful. Experience shows that this formative work is usually possible*

[1146] Cf. *Catechism of the Catholic Church*, 1806.

[1147] The exercise of prudence calls for a progressive formation in order to acquire the necessary qualities: *"memory"* as the capacity to remember one's own past experience with objectivity, without falsification (cf. Saint Thomas Aquinas *Summa Theologiae*, II-II, q. 49, a. 1: Ed. Leon. 8, 367); *"docilitas"* (docility) that allows one to learn from others and to profit from their experience on the basis of an authentic love for truth (cf. Saint Thomas Aquinas *Summa Theologiae*, II-II, q. 49, a. 3: Ed. Leon. 8, 368-369); *"solertia"* (diligence), that is, the ability to face the unexpected with objectivity in order to turn every situation to the service of good, overcoming the temptation of intemperance, injustice, and cowardice (cf. Saint Thomas Aquinas *Summa Theologiae*, II-II, q. 49, a. 4: Ed. Leon. 8, 369-370). These cognitive dispositions permit the development of the necessary conditions for the moment of decision: *"providencia"* (foresight), which is the capacity of weighing the efficacy of a given conduct for the attainment of a moral end (cf. Saint Thomas Aquinas *Summa Theologiae*, II-II, q. 49, a. 6: Ed. Leon. 8, 371) and *"circumspectio"* (circumspection), or the capacity of weighing the circumstances that contribute to the creation of the situation in which a given action will be carried out (cf. Saint Thomas Aquinas *Summa Theologiae*, II-II, q. 49, a. 7: Ed. Leon. 8, 372). In the social context, prudence can be specified under two particular forms: *"regnative"* prudence, that is, the capacity to order all things for the greatest good of society (cf. Saint Thomas Aquinas *Summa Theologiae*, II-II, q. 50, a. 1: Ed. Leon. 8, 374), and *"political"* prudence, which leads citizens to obey, carrying out the indications of authority (cf. Saint Thomas Aquinas *Summa Theologiae*, II-II, q. 50, a. 2: Ed. Leon. 8, 375), without compromising their dignity as a human person (cf. Saint Thomas Aquinas *Summa Theologiae*, II-II, qq. 47-56: Ed. Leon. 8, 348-406).

within lay ecclesial associations that respond to precise "criteria of ecclesiality."[1148] *"Groups, associations and movements* also have their place in the formation of the lay faithful. In fact they have the possibility, each with its own method, of offering a formation through a deeply shared experience in the apostolic life, as well as having the opportunity to integrate, to make concrete and specific the formation that their members receive from other persons and communities."[1149] The Church's social doctrine sustains and sheds light on the role of associations, movements and lay groups that are committed to the Christian renewal of the various sectors of the temporal order.[1150] "Church communion, already present and at work in the activities of the individual, finds its specific expression in the lay faithful working together in groups, that is, in activities done with others in the course of their responsible participation in the life and mission of the Church."[1151]

550. *The Church's social doctrine is extremely important for ecclesial associations that have pastoral action within society as their objective.* These associations represent a privileged point of reference in that their presence in the life of society is characterized by their nature as ecclesial bodies; this shows the importance and value of prayer, reflection and dialogue for addressing and improving social realities. One must keep in mind the distinction, in each case, "between the activities of Christians, acting individually or collectively in their own name as citizens guided by the dictates of a Christian conscience, and their activity acting along with their pastors in the name of the Church."[1152]

The various specialized associations that gather people together in the name of their Christian vocation and mission within a particular professional or cultural field have a precious role to play in forming mature Christians. For example, a Catholic association of doctors forms those who belong to it through the exercise of discernment with regard to the many problems that medical science, biology and other sciences place before the professional competence of doctors, as well as before their personal conscience and faith. The same could be also said of Catholic associations of teachers, legal professionals, businessmen and women, workers, as well as Catholic sports associations and ecological associations and so forth. In this context, the Church's social doctrine shows that it is an effective means for forming individual consciences and a country's culture.

e. Service in the various sectors of social life

551. *The presence of the laity in social life is characterized by service, the sign and expression of love, which is seen in the areas of the family, culture, work, economics and politics according to specific aspects.* Complying with the different demands of their

---

[1148] Cf. John Paul II, Post-Synodal Apostolic Exhortation *Christifideles Laici*, 30: AAS 81 (1989), 446-448.

[1149] John Paul II, Post-Synodal Apostolic Exhortation *Christifideles Laici*, 62: AAS 81 (1989), 516-517.

[1150] Cf. John XXIII, Encyclical Letter *Mater et Magistra*: AAS 53 (1961) 455.

[1151] John Paul II, Post-Synodal Apostolic Exhortation *Christifideles laici*, 29: AAS 81 (1989), 443.

[1152] Second Vatican Ecumenical Council, Pastoral Constitution *Gaudium et Spes*, 76: AAS 58 (1966), 1099.

particular area of work, lay men and women express the truth of their faith and, at the same time, the truth of the Church's social doctrine, which fully becomes a reality when it is lived concretely in order to resolve social problems. In fact, the credibility of this social doctrine comes more immediately from the witness of action than from its internal consistency or logic.[1153]

Having entered into The Third Millennium of the Christian era, the lay faithful will open themselves, through their witness, to all people with whom they will take on the burden of the most pressing calls of our time. "Drawn from the treasures of the teaching of the Church, the proposals of this Council are intended for all men, whether they believe in God or whether they do not explicitly acknowledge him; they are intended to help them to a keener awareness of their own destiny, to make the work conform better to the surpassing dignity of man, to strive for a more deeply rooted sense of universal brotherhood and to meet the pressing appeals of our times with a generous and common effort of love."[1154]

1. Service to the human person

552. *Among the areas of the social commitment of the laity, service to the human person emerges as a priority.* Promoting the dignity of every person, the most precious possession of men and women, is the "essential task, in a certain sense, the central and unifying task of the service which the Church, and the lay faithful in her, are called to render to the human family."[1155]

The first form in which this task is undertaken consists in the commitment and efforts to renew oneself interiorly, because human history is not governed by an impersonal determinism but by a plurality of subjects whose free acts shape the social order. Social institutions do not of themselves guarantee, as if automatically, the common good; the internal "renewal of the Christian spirit"[1156] *must precede* the commitment to improve society "according to the mind of the Church on the firmly established basis of social justice and social charity."[1157]

It is from the conversion of hearts that there arises concern for others, loved as brothers or sisters. This concern helps us to understand the obligation and commitment to heal institutions, structures and conditions of life that are contrary to human dignity. The laity must therefore *work at the same time for the conversion of hearts and the improvement of structures*, taking historical situations into account and using legitimate means so that the dignity of every man and woman will be truly respected and promoted within institutions.

553. *Promoting human dignity implies above all affirming the inviolability of the right to life, from conception to natural death*, the first among all rights and the condition for

---

[1153] Cf. John XXIII, Encyclical Letter *Mater et Magistra*: AAS 53 (1961) 454; John Paul II, Encyclical Letter *Centesimus Annus*, 57: AAS 83 (1991), 862-863.

[1154] Second Vatican Ecumenical Council, Pastoral Constitution *Gaudium et Spes*, 91: AAS 58 (1966), 1113.

[1155] John Paul II, Post-Synodal Apostolic Exhortation *Christifideles Laici*, 37: AAS 81 (1989), 460.

[1156] Pius XI, Encyclical Letter *Quadragesimo Anno*: AAS 23 (1931), 218.

[1157] Pius XI, Encyclical Letter *Quadragesimo Anno*: AAS 23 (1931), 218.

all other rights of the person.[1158] Respect for personal dignity requires, moreover, that *the religious dimension of the person be recognized*. "This is not simply a requirement 'concerning matters of faith,' but a requirement that finds itself inextricably bound up with the very reality of the individual."[1159] The effective recognition of the *right to freedom of conscience and religious freedom* is one of the highest goods and one of the most serious duties of every people that truly wishes to ensure the good of the individual and of society.[1160] In the present cultural context, there is a particularly urgent need to *defend marriage and the family*, which can be adequately met only if one is convinced of the unique and singular value of these two realities for an authentic development of human society.[1161]

2. Service in culture

554. *Culture must represent a privileged area for the presence and commitment of the Church and individual Christians.* The Second Vatican Council sees the separation of Christian faith and daily life as one of the most serious errors of our day.[1162] Without a metaphysical perspective, the loss of a longing for God in self-serving narcissism and the varied means found in a consumeristic lifestyle; the primacy given to technology and scientific research as ends in themselves; the emphasis placed on appearance, the quest for an image, communication techniques: all of these phenomena must be understood in their cultural aspects and placed in relation to the central issue of the human person, of integral human growth, of the human capacity to communicate and relate with other people, and of the constant human search for an answer to the great questions that run throughout life. It must be kept in mind that "culture is that through which man, as man, becomes more man, 'is' more, has more access to 'being.'"[1163]

555. *Fostering a social and political culture inspired by the Gospel must be an area of particular importance for the lay faithful.* Recent history has shown the weakness and radical failure of commonly held cultural perspectives that prevailed for a long time, especially on the social and political levels. In this area, particularly in the decades following the Second World War, Catholics in different countries have been involved at high levels, which shows with ever greater clarity today the consistency of their inspiration and of their heritage of values. The social and political involvement of Catholics, in fact, has never been limited to the mere transformation of structures, because this involvement takes place at the foundations of a culture that receives and listens to the reasoning made by faith and

---

[1158] Cf. Congregation for the Doctrine of the Faith, Instruction *Donum Vitae*, (22 February 1987): AAS 80 (1988) 70-102.

[1159] John Paul II, Post-Synodal Apostolic Exhortation *Christifideles Laici*, 39: AAS 81 (1989), 466.

[1160] Cf. John Paul II, Post-Synodal Apostolic Exhortation *Christifideles Laici*, 39: AAS 81 (1989), 466.

[1161] Cf. John Paul II, Post-Synodal Apostolic Exhortation *Familiaris Consortio*, 42-48: AAS 74 (1982), 134-140.

[1162] Cf. Second Vatican Ecumenical Council, Pastoral Constitution *Gaudium et Spes*, 43: AAS 58 (1966), 1062.

[1163] John Paul II, Address to UNESCO (2 June 1980), 7: *L'Osservatore Romano*, English edition, 23 June 1980, p. 9.

morality, including them as the basis and goal of concrete planning. When this awareness is lacking, Catholics themselves are condemned to cultural dispersion and their proposals are rendered insufficient and limited. An urgent priority today is also found in the need to present the patrimony of Catholic tradition, its values and content, and the entire spiritual, intellectual and moral heritage of Catholicism, in culturally up-to-date terms. Faith in Jesus Christ, who described himself as "the way and the truth and the life" (*Jn* 14:6), prompts Christians to commit themselves with firm and ever new resolve to building a social and political culture inspired by the Gospel.[1164]

556. *The integral perfection of the person and the good of the whole of society are the essential ends of culture;*[1165] *the ethical dimension of culture is therefore a priority in the social action of the laity.* Failure to pay attention to this dimension easily transforms culture into an instrument that impoverishes humanity. A culture can become sterile and headed for decadence when it "becomes inward looking, and tries to perpetuate obsolete ways of living by rejecting any exchange or debate with regard to the truth about man."[1166] The formation of a culture capable of enriching men and women requires on the contrary the involvement of the whole person, who, in the cultural sphere, expresses his creativity, his intelligence, his knowledge of the world and of human persons; someone moreover who puts to good use his capacity for self-control, personal sacrifice, solidarity and readiness to promote the common good.[1167]

557. *The social and political involvement of the lay faithful in the area of culture moves today in specific directions. The first is that of seeking to guarantee the right of each person to a human and civil culture* "in harmony with the dignity of the human person, without distinction of race, sex, nation, religion, or social circumstances."[1168] This right implies the right of families and persons to free and open schools; freedom of access to the means of social communication together with the avoidance of all forms of monopolies and ideological control of this field; freedom of research, sharing one's thoughts, debate and discussion. At the root of the poverty of so many peoples are also various forms of cultural deprivation and the failure to recognize cultural rights. The commitment to the education and formation of the person has always represented the first concern of Christian social action.

558. *The second challenge for Christian commitment concerns the content of culture, that is, truth.* The question of truth is essential for culture because "it remains each man's

[1164] Cf. Congregation for the Doctrine of the Faith, *Doctrinal Note on Some Questions Regarding the Participation of Catholics in Political Life* (24 November 2002), 7: Libreria Editrice Vaticana, Vatican City 2002, p. 15.
[1165] Cf. Second Vatican Ecumenical Council, Pastoral Constitution *Gaudium et Spes*, 59: AAS 58 (1966), 1079-1080.
[1166] John Paul II, Encyclical Letter *Centesimus Annus*, 50: AAS 83 (1991), 856.
[1167] Cf. John Paul II, Address to UNESCO (2 June 1980), 11: *L'Osservatore Romano*, English edition, 23 June 1980, p. 10.
[1168] Second Vatican Ecumenical Council, Pastoral Constitution *Gaudium et Spes*, 60: AAS 58 (1966), 1081.

duty to retain an understanding of the whole human person in which the values of intellect, will, conscience and fraternity are pre-eminent."[1169] A correct anthropology is the criterion for shedding light on and verifying every historical form of culture. The Christian commitment in the field of culture is opposed to all reductionistic and ideological perspectives of man and life. The dynamism of openness to the truth is guaranteed above all by the fact that "different cultures are basically different ways of facing the question of the meaning of personal existence."[1170]

559. *Christians must work so that the full value of the religious dimension of culture is seen. This is a very important and urgent task for the quality of human life, at both the individual and social levels.* The question arising from the mystery of life and referring to the greater mystery of God is in fact at the centre of every culture; when it is eliminated, culture and the moral life of nations are corrupted.[1171] The authentic religious dimension is an essential part of man and allows him to open his diverse activities to the horizon in which they find meaning and direction. Human religiosity or spirituality is manifested in the forms taken on by a culture, to which it gives vitality and inspiration. The countless works of art of every period bear witness to this. When the religious dimension of the person or of a people is denied, culture itself starts to die off, sometimes disappearing completely.

560. *In the promotion of an authentic culture, the laity will place great importance on mass media, examining above all the contents of the countless choices that people make.* These choices, while varying from group to group and from individual to individual, all have a moral weight and should be evaluated in this light. In order to choose correctly, one must know the norms of the moral order and apply them faithfully.[1172] The Church offers a long tradition of wisdom, rooted in divine Revelation and human reflection,[1173] the theological orientation of which provides an important corrective function to both "the 'atheistic' solution which deprives man of one of his basic dimensions, namely the spiritual one, and to permissive and consumerist solutions, which under various pretexts seek to convince man that he is free from every law and from God himself."[1174] Rather than judging the means of social communication, this tradition is placed at their service: "The Church's culture of *wisdom* can save the media culture of information from becoming a meaningless accumulation of facts."[1175]

561. *The lay faithful will look upon the media as possible and powerful instruments of solidarity*: "Solidarity is a consequence of genuine and right communication and the free circulation of ideas that further knowledge and respect for oth-

---

[1169] Second Vatican Ecumenical Council, Pastoral Constitution *Gaudium et Spes*, 61: AAS 58 (1966), 1082.

[1170] John Paul II, Encyclical Letter *Centesimus Annus*, 24: AAS 83 (1991), 822.

[1171] Cf. John Paul II, Encyclical Letter *Centesimus Annus*, 24: AAS 83 (1991), 821-822.

[1172] Cf. Second Vatican Ecumenical Council, Decree *Inter Mirifica*, 4: AAS 56 (1964), 146.

[1173] Cf. John Paul II, Encyclical Letter *Fides et Ratio*, 36-48: AAS 91 (1999), 33-34.

[1174] John Paul II, Encyclical Letter *Centesimus Annus*, 55: AAS 83 (1991), 861.

[1175] John Paul II, Message for the 1999 World Day of Social Communications, 3: *L'Osservatore Romano*, English edition, 3 February 1999, pp. 1-2.

ers."[1176] This is not the case if the media are used to build and sustain economic systems that serve greed and covetousness. Faced with grave injustices, the decision to ignore completely certain aspects of human suffering reflects an indefensible selectivity.[1177] *Communication structures and policies, and the distribution of technology are factors that help to make some people "information rich" and others "information poor" at a time when prosperity, and even survival, depend on information.* In this way, the media often contribute to the injustices and imbalances that give rise to the very suffering that they report. Communications and information technology, along with training in its use, must aim at eliminating such injustices and imbalances.

562. *Professionals in the field of media are not the only people with ethical duties. Those who make use of the media also have obligations. Media operators who try to meet their responsibilities deserve audiences who are aware of their own responsibilities.* The first duty of media users is to be discerning and selective. Parents, families and the Church have precise responsibilities they cannot renounce. For those who work, in various capacities, in the area of social communications, the warning of St. Paul rings out loud and clear: "Therefore, putting away falsehood, let every one speak the truth with his neighbor, for we are members one of another . . . Let no evil talk come out of your mouths, but only such as is good for edifying, as fits the occasion, that it may impart grace to those who hear" (*Eph* 4:25, 29). Serving the human person through the building up of a human community based on solidarity, justice and love, and spreading the truth about human life and its final fulfilment in God remain at the heart of ethics in the media.[1178] In the light of faith, human communication can be seen as a journey from Babel to Pentecost, or rather, as the personal and social commitment to overcome the collapse of communication (cf. *Gen* 11:4-8), opening people to the gift of tongues (cf. *Acts* 2:5-11), to communication as restored by the power of the Spirit sent by the Son.

3. Service in the economy

563. *Faced with the complexity of today's economic context, the laity will be guided in their action by the principles of the social Magisterium.* It is necessary that these principles be known and accepted in the area of economic activity itself; when they are ignored, above all the principle of the centrality of the human person, the quality of this activity is compromised.[1179]

The commitment of Christians will also be translated into an effort of cultural reflection aimed at *a discernment of the current models of economic and social development.* Reducing the question of development to an exclusively technical

[1176] *Catechism of the Catholic Church*, 2495.
[1177] Cf. Pontifical Council for Social Communications, *Ethics in Communications* (4 June 2000), 14, Libreria Editrice Vaticana, Vatican City 2000, pp. 14-16.
[1178] Cf. Pontifical Council for Social Communications, *Ethics in Communications*, 4 June 2000, 33, Libreria Editrice Vaticana, Vatican City 2000, p. 40.
[1179] Cf. Congregation for the Doctrine of the Faith, *Doctrinal Note on Some Questions Regarding the Participation of Catholics in Political Life* (24 November 2002), 3: Libreria Editrice Vaticana, Vatican City 2002, p. 8.

problem would deprive it of its true content, which instead concerns "the dignity of individuals and peoples."[1180]

564. *Economists, those working in this field and political leaders must sense the urgency of rethinking the economy,* considering, on the one hand, the dramatic material poverty of billions of people and, on the other, the fact that "present economic, social and cultural structures are ill-equipped to meet the demands of genuine development."[1181] The legitimate requirements of economic efficiency need to be better harmonized with those of political participation and social justice. Concretely, this means that solidarity must be made an integral part of the networks of economic, political and social interdependence that the current process of globalization tends to consolidate.[1182] In this effort of rethinking, well organized and destined to have an effect on the way economic realities are seen, associations of a Christian inspiration active in the economic field — organizations of workers, business leaders and economists — have a precious role to play.

4. Service in politics

565. *For the lay faithful, political involvement is a worthy and demanding expression of the Christian commitment of service to others.*[1183] The pursuit of the common good in a spirit of service, the development of justice with particular attention to situations of poverty and suffering, respect for the autonomy of earthly realities, the principle of subsidiarity, the promotion of dialogue and peace in the context of solidarity: these are the criteria that must inspire the Christian laity in their political activity. All believers, insofar as they possess rights and duties as citizens, are obligated to respect these guiding principles. Special attention must be paid to their observance by those who occupy institutional positions dealing with the complex problems of the public domain, whether in local administrations or national and international institutions.

566. *The tasks accompanying responsibilities in social and political institutions demand a strict and articulated commitment that is able to demonstrate clearly the absolute necessity of the moral dimension in social and political life through thoughtful contributions to the political debate, planning and the chosen actions.* Inadequate attention to the moral dimension leads to the dehumanization of life in society and of social and political institutions, thereby consolidating "structures of sin":[1184] "Living and acting in conformity with one's own conscience on questions of politics is not slavish acceptance of positions alien to politics or some kind of confessionalism, but rather the way in which Christians offer their concrete contribution so that, through political life, society will become more just and more consistent with the dignity of the human person."[1185]

[1180] John Paul II, Encyclical Letter *Sollicitudo Rei Socialis*, 41: AAS 80 (1988), 570.
[1181] John Paul II, Message for the 2000 World Day of Peace, 14: AAS 92 (2000), 366.
[1182] Cf. John Paul II, Message for the 2000 World Day of Peace, 17: AAS 92 (2000), 367-368.
[1183] Cf. Paul VI, Apostolic Letter *Octogesima Adveniens*, 46: AAS 63 (1971), 433-436.
[1184] Cf. John Paul II, Encyclical Letter *Sollicitudo Rei Socialis*, 36: AAS 80 (1988), 561-563.
[1185] Congregation for the Doctrine of the Faith, *Doctrinal Note on Some Questions Regarding the Participation of Catholics in Political Life* (24 November 2002), 6: Libreria Editrice Vaticana, Vatican City 2002, p. 13.

567. *In the context of the laity's political commitment, particular attention must be given to preparing believers to exercise the power that will be theirs, especially when they are entrusted with such duties by their fellow citizens in accordance with democratic rules.* They must show appreciation for the democratic system "inasmuch as it ensures the participation of citizens in making political choices, guarantees to the governed the possibility both of electing and holding accountable those who govern them, and of replacing them through peaceful means when appropriate."[1186] They must also reject all secret organizations that seek to influence or subvert the functioning of legitimate institutions. The exercise of authority must take on the character of service to be carried out always in the context of moral law for the attainment of the common good.[1187] Those who exercise political authority must see to it that the energies of all citizens are directed towards the common good; and they are to do so not in an authoritarian style but by making use of moral power sustained in freedom.

568. *The lay faithful are called to identify steps that can be taken in concrete political situations in order to put into practice the principles and values proper to life in society. This calls for a method of discernment,*[1188] at both the personal and community levels, structured around certain key elements: knowledge of the situations, analyzed with the help of the social sciences and other appropriate tools; systematic reflection on these realities in the light of the unchanging message of the Gospel and the Church's social teaching; identification of choices aimed at assuring that the situation will evolve positively. When reality is the subject of careful attention and proper interpretation, concrete and effective choices can be made. However, an absolute value must never be attributed to these choices because no problem can be solved once and for all. "Christian faith has never presumed to impose a rigid framework on social and political questions, conscious that the historical dimension requires men and women to live in imperfect situations, which are also susceptible to rapid change."[1189]

569. *A characteristic context for the exercise of discernment can be found in the functioning of the democratic system, understood by many today in agnostic and relativistic terms that lead to the belief that truth is something determined by the majority and conditioned by political considerations.*[1190] In such circumstances, discernment is particularly demanding when it is exercised with regard to the objectivity and accuracy of information, scientific research and economic decisions that affect the life of the poorest people. It is likewise demanding when dealing with realities that involve fundamental and unavoidable moral duties, such as the sacredness of life,

[1186] John Paul II, Encyclical Letter *Centesimus Annus*, 46: AAS 83 (1991), 850.
[1187] Cf. Second Vatican Ecumenical Council, Pastoral Constitution *Gaudium et Spes*, 74: AAS 58 (1966), 1095-1097.
[1188] Cf. Congregation for Catholic Education, *Guidelines for the Study and Teaching of the Church's Social Doctrine in the Formation of Priests*, 8, Vatican Polyglot Press, Rome 1988, pp. 13-14.
[1189] Congregation for the Doctrine of the Faith, *Doctrinal Note on Some Questions Regarding the Participation of Catholics in Political Life* (24 November 2002), 7: Libreria Editrice Vaticana, Vatican City 2002, pp. 15-16.
[1190] Cf. John Paul II, *Centesimus Annus*, 46: AAS 83 (1991), 850-851.

the indissolubility of marriage, the promotion of the family founded on marriage between a man and a woman.

In such situations certain fundamental criteria are useful: the distinction and, simultaneously, the connection between the legal order and the moral order; fidelity to one's own identity and, at the same time, the willingness to engage in dialogue with all people; the need, in the social judgment and activity of Christians, to refer to the observance of three inseparable values — *natural values*, with respect for the legitimate autonomy of temporal realities; *moral values*, promoting an awareness of the intrinsic ethical dimension of every social and political issue; *supernatural values*, in order to fulfil one's duty in the spirit of the Gospel of Jesus Christ.

570. *When — concerning areas or realities that involve fundamental ethical duties — legislative or political choices contrary to Christian principles and values are proposed or made, the Magisterium teaches that "a well-formed Christian conscience does not permit one to vote for a political programme or an individual law which contradicts the fundamental contents of faith and morals."*[1191] In cases where it is not possible to avoid the implementation of such political programmes or to block or abrogate such laws, the Magisterium teaches that a parliamentary representative, whose personal absolute opposition to these programmes or laws is clear and known to all, may legitimately support proposals aimed at *limiting the damage* caused by such programmes or laws and at diminishing their negative effects on the level of culture and public morality. In this regard, a typical example of such a case would be a law permitting abortion.[1192] The representative's vote, in any case, cannot be interpreted as support of an unjust law but only as a contribution to reducing the negative consequences of a legislative provision, the responsibility for which lies entirely with those who have brought it into being.

Faced with the many situations involving fundamental and indispensable moral duties, it must be remembered that Christian witness is to be considered a fundamental obligation that can even lead to the sacrificing of one's life, to martyrdom in the name of love and human dignity.[1193] The history of the past twenty centuries, as well as that of the last century, is filled with martyrs for Christian truth, witnesses to the faith, hope and love founded on the Gospel. Martyrdom is the witness of one who has been personally conformed to Jesus crucified, expressed in the supreme form of shedding one's blood according to the teaching of the Gospel: if "a grain of wheat falls into the earth and dies . . . it bears much fruit" (Jn 12:24).

571. *The political commitment of Catholics is often placed in the context of the "autonomy" of the State, that is, the distinction between the political and religious spheres.*[1194]

[1191] Congregation for the Doctrine of the Faith, *Doctrinal Note on Some Questions Regarding the Participation of Catholics in Political Life* (24 November 2002), 4: Libreria Editrice Vaticana, Vatican City 2002, p. 9.

[1192] Cf. John Paul II, Encyclical Letter *Evangelium Vitae*, 73: AAS 87 (1995), 486-487.

[1193] Cf. John Paul II, Post-Synodal Exhortation, *Christifideles Laici*, 39: AAS 81 (1989), 466-468.

[1194] Cf. Second Vatican Ecumenical Council, Pastoral Constitution *Gaudium et Spes*, 76: AAS 58 (1966), 1099-1100.

This distinction "is a value that has been attained and recognized by the Catholic Church and belongs to the inheritance of contemporary civilization."[1195] Catholic moral doctrine, however, clearly rejects the prospects of an autonomy that is understood as independence from the moral law: "Such 'autonomy' refers first of all to the attitude of the person who respects the truths that derive from natural knowledge regarding man's life in society, even if such truths may also be taught by a specific religion, because truth is one."[1196] A sincere quest for the truth, using legitimate means to promote and defend the moral truths concerning social life — justice, freedom, respect for life and for other human rights — is a right and duty of all members of a social and political community.

When the Church's Magisterium intervenes in issues concerning social and political life, it does not fail to observe the requirements of a correctly understood autonomy, for "the Church's Magisterium does not wish to exercise political power or eliminate the freedom of opinion of Catholics regarding contingent questions. Instead, it intends — as is its proper function — to instruct and illuminate the consciences of the faithful, particularly those involved in political life, so that their actions may always serve the integral promotion of the human person and the common good. The social doctrine of the Church is not an intrusion into the government of individual countries. It is a question of the lay Catholic's duty to be morally coherent, found within one's conscience, which is one and indivisible."[1197]

572. The principle of autonomy involves respect for every religious confession on the part of the State, which "assures the free exercise of ritual, spiritual, cultural and charitable activities by communities of believers. In a pluralistic society, secularity is a place for communication between the different spiritual traditions and the nation."[1198] Unfortunately, even in democratic societies, there still remain expressions of secular intolerance that are hostile to granting any kind of political or cultural relevance to religious faiths. Such intolerance seeks to exclude the activity of Christians from the social and political spheres because Christians strive to uphold the truths taught by the Church and are obedient to the moral duty to act in accordance with their conscience. These attitudes even go so far, and radically so, as to deny the basis of a natural morality. This denial, which is the harbinger of a moral anarchy with the obvious consequence of the stronger prevailing over the weaker, cannot be accepted in any form by legitimate pluralism, since it undermines the very foundations of human society. In the light of this state of affairs, "the marginalization of Christianity . . . would not bode well for the future

---

[1195] Congregation for the Doctrine of the Faith, *Doctrinal Note on Some Questions Regarding the Participation of Catholics in Political Life* (24 November 2002), 6: Libreria Editrice Vaticana, Vatican City 2002, p. 11.

[1196] Congregation for the Doctrine of the Faith, *Doctrinal Note on Some Questions Regarding the Participation of Catholics in Political Life* (24 November 2002), 6: Libreria Editrice Vaticana, Vatican City 2002, p. 12.

[1197] Congregation for the Doctrine of the Faith, *Doctrinal Note on Some Questions Regarding the Participation of Catholics in Political Life* (24 November 2002), 6: Libreria Editrice Vaticana, Vatican City 2002, pp. 12-13.

[1198] John Paul II, Address to the Diplomatic Corps (12 January 2004), 3: *L'Osservatore Romano*, English edition, 21 January 2004, p. 3.

of society or for consensus among peoples; indeed, it would threaten the very spiritual and cultural foundations of civilization."[1199]

573. *A particular area for discernment on the part of the lay faithful concerns the choice of political instruments, that is, membership in a party or in other types of political participation. A choice must be made that is consistent with values, taking into account actual circumstances.* In every case, whatever choice is made must be rooted in charity and tend towards the attainment of the common good.[1200] It is difficult for the concerns of the Christian faith to be adequately met in one sole political entity; to claim that one party or political coalition responds completely to the demands of faith or of Christian life would give rise to dangerous errors. Christians cannot find one party that fully corresponds to the ethical demands arising from faith and from membership in the Church. Their adherence to a political alliance will never be ideological but always critical; in this way the party and its political platform will be prompted to be ever more conscientious in attaining the true common good, including the spiritual end of the human person.[1201]

574. *The distinction that must be made on the one hand between the demands of faith and socio-political options, and on the other hand between the choices made by individual Christians and the Christian community as such, means that membership in a party or in a political alliance should be considered a personal decision, legitimate at least within the limits of those parties and positions that are not incompatible with Christian faith and values.*[1202] However, the choice of a party, a political alliance, the persons to whom public life is to be entrusted, while involving the conscience of each person, can never be an *exclusively* individual choice. "It is up to the Christian community to analyze with objectivity the situation which is proper to their own country, to shed on it the light of the Gospel's inalterable words and to draw principles of reflection, norms of judgment and directives for action from the social teaching of the Church."[1203] In any case, "no one is permitted to identify the authority of the Church exclusively with his own opinion";[1204] believers should rather "try to guide each other by sincere dialogue in a spirit of mutual charity and with anxious interest above all in the common good."[1205]

[1199] Congregation for the Doctrine of the Faith, *Doctrinal Note on Some Questions Regarding the Participation of Catholics in Political Life* (24 November 2002), 6: Libreria Editrice Vaticana, Vatican City 2002, p. 14.

[1200] Cf. Paul VI, Apostolic Letter *Octogesima Adveniens*, 46: AAS 63 (1971), 433-435.

[1201] Cf. Paul VI, Apostolic Letter *Octogesima Adveniens*, 46: AAS 63 (1971), 433-435.

[1202] Cf. Paul VI, Apostolic Letter *Octogesima Adveniens*, 50: AAS 63 (1971), 439-440.

[1203] Paul VI, Apostolic Letter *Octogesima Adveniens*, 4: AAS 63 (1971), 403-404.

[1204] Second Vatican Ecumenical Council, Pastoral Constitution *Gaudium et Spes*, 43: AAS 58 (1966), 1063.

[1205] Second Vatican Ecumenical Council, Pastoral Constitution *Gaudium et Spes*, 43: AAS 58 (1966), 1063.

CONCLUSION

FOR A CIVILIZATION OF LOVE

a. The help that the Church offers to modern man

575. *In modern society, people are increasingly experiencing a new need for meaning.* "Man will always yearn to know, at least in an obscure way, what is the meaning of his life, of his activity, of his death."[1206] It is difficult to meet the demands of building the future in a new context of an even more complex and interdependent international relations that are also less and less ordered and peaceful. Life and death seem to be solely in the hands of a scientific and technological progress that is moving faster than man's ability to establish its ultimate goals and evaluate its costs. Many phenomena indicate instead that "the increasing sense of dissatisfaction with worldly goods which is making itself felt among citizens of the wealthier nations is rapidly destroying the treasured illusion of an earthly paradise. People are also becoming more and more conscious of their rights as human beings, rights that are universal and inviolable, and they are aspiring to more just and more human relations."[1207]

576. *To these basic questions about the meaning and purpose of human life the Church responds with the proclamation of the Gospel of Christ, which liberates the dignity of the human person from changing opinions and ensures the freedom of men and women as no human law can do.* The Second Vatican Council indicated that the mission of the Church in the contemporary world consists in helping every human being to discover in God the ultimate meaning of his existence. The Church knows well that "God alone, whom she serves, can satisfy the deepest cravings of the human heart, for the world and what it has to offer can never fully satisfy it."[1208] Only God, who created man in his image and redeemed him from sin, can offer a fully adequate answer through the Revelation wrought in his Son made man. The Gospel, in fact, "announces and proclaims the freedom of the sons of God, it rejects all bondage resulting from sin; it scrupulously respects the dignity of conscience and its freedom of choice; it never ceases to encourage the employment of human talents in the service of God and of man, and finally, it commends everyone to the charitable love of all."[1209]

[1206] Second Vatican Ecumenical Council, Pastoral Constitution *Gaudium et Spes*, 41: AAS 58 (1966), 1059.

[1207] John XXIII, Encyclical Letter *Mater et Magistra*: AAS 53 (1961), 451.

[1208] Second Vatican Ecumenical Council, Pastoral Constitution *Gaudium et Spes*, 41: AAS 58 (1966), 1059.

[1209] Second Vatican Ecumenical Council, Pastoral Constitution *Gaudium et Spes*, 41: AAS 58 (1966), 1059-1060.

b. Starting over from faith in Christ

577. *Faith in God and in Jesus Christ sheds light on the moral principles that are "the sole and irreplaceable foundation of that stability and tranquillity, of that internal and external order, private and public, that alone can generate and safeguard the prosperity of States."*[1210] Life in society must be based on the divine plan because "the theological dimension is needed both for interpreting and solving present-day problems in human society."[1211] In the presence of serious forms of exploitation and social injustice, there is "an ever more widespread and acute sense of *the need for a radical* personal and social *renewal* capable of ensuring justice, solidarity, honesty and openness. Certainly, there is a long and difficult road ahead; bringing about such a renewal will require enormous effort, especially on account of the number and gravity of the causes giving rise to and aggravating the situations of injustice present in the world today. But, as history and personal experience show, it is not difficult to discover at the bottom of these situations causes which are properly 'cultural,' linked to particular ways of looking at man, society and the world. Indeed, at the heart of the *issue of culture* we find the *moral sense*, which is in turn rooted and fulfilled in the religious sense."[1212] As for "the social question," we must not be seduced by "the naive expectation that, faced with the great challenges of our time, we shall find some magic formula. No, we shall not be saved by a formula but by a Person and the assurance that he gives us: *I am with you!* It is not therefore a matter of inventing a 'new programme'. The programme already exists: it is the plan found in the Gospel and in the living Tradition, it is the same as ever. Ultimately, it has its centre in Christ himself, who is to be known loved and imitated, so that in him we may live the life of the Trinity, and with him transform history until its fulfilment in the heavenly Jerusalem."[1213]

c. A solid hope

578. *The Church teaches men and women that God offers them the real possibility of overcoming evil and attaining good.* The Lord has redeemed mankind "*bought with a price*" (*1 Cor* 6:20). The meaning and basis of the Christian commitment in the world are founded on this certainty, which *gives rise to hope* despite the sin that deeply marks human history. The divine promise guarantees that the world *does not remain closed in upon itself but is open to the Kingdom of God*. The Church knows the effects of "the mystery of lawlessness" (*2 Thes* 2:7), but she also knows that "there exist in the human person sufficient qualities and energies, a fundamental 'goodness' (cf. *Gen* 1:31), because he is the image of the Creator, placed under the redemptive influence of Christ, who 'united himself in some fashion with every man,' and because the efficacious action of the Holy Spirit 'fills the earth' (*Wis* 1:7)."[1214]

[1210] Pius XII, Encyclical Letter *Summi Pontificatus: AAS* 31 (1939), 425.

[1211] John Paul II, Encyclical Letter *Centesimus Annus*, 55: *AAS* 83 (1991), 860-861.

[1212] John Paul II, Encyclical Letter *Veritatis Splendor*, 98: *AAS* 85 (1993), 1210; cf. John Paul II, Encyclical Letter *Centesimus Annus*, 24: *AAS* 83 (1991), 821-822.

[1213] John Paul II, Apostolic Letter *Novo Millennio Ineunte*, 29: *AAS* 93 (2001), 285.

[1214] John Paul II, Encyclical Letter *Sollicitudo Rei Socialis*, 47: *AAS* 80 (1988), 580.

579. *Christian hope lends great energy to commitment in the social field, because it generates confidence in the possibility of building a better world, even if there will never exist "a paradise of earth."*[1215] Christians, particularly the laity, are urged to act in such a way that "the power of the Gospel might shine forth in their daily social and family life. They conduct themselves as children of the promise and thus strong in faith and hope they make the most of the present (cf. *Eph* 5:16; *Col* 4:5), and with patience await the glory that is to come (cf. *Rom* 8:25). Let them not, then, hide this hope in the depths of their hearts, but let them express it by a continual conversion and by wrestling 'against the world-rulers of this darkness, against the spiritual forces of wickedness' (*Eph* 6:12)."[1216] The religious motivation behind such a commitment may not be shared by all, but the moral convictions that arise from it represent a point of encounter between Christians and all people of good will.

d. Building the "civilization of love"

580. *The immediate purpose of the Church's social doctrine is to propose the principles and values that can sustain a society worthy of the human person. Among these principles, solidarity includes all the others in a certain way.* It represents "one of the fundamental principles of the Christian view of social and political organization."[1217]

Light is shed on this principle by the primacy of love, "the distinguishing mark of Christ's disciples (cf. *Jn* 13:35)."[1218] Jesus teaches us that "the fundamental law of human perfection, and consequently of the transformation of the world, is the new commandment of love"[1219] (cf. *Mt* 22:40, *Jn* 15:12; *Col* 3:14; *Jas* 2:8). Personal behavior is fully human when it is born of love, manifests love and is ordered to love. This truth also applies in the social sphere; Christians must be deeply convinced witnesses of this, and they are to show by their lives how love is the only force (cf. *1 Cor* 12:31-14:1) that can lead to personal and social perfection, allowing society to make progress towards the good.

581. *Love must be present in and permeate every social relationship.*[1220] This holds true especially for those who are responsible for the good of peoples. They "must earnestly cherish in themselves, and try to rouse in others, charity, the mistress and the queen of virtues. For, the happy results we all long for must be chiefly brought about by the plenteous outpouring of charity; of that true Christian charity which is the fulfilling of the whole Gospel law, which is always ready to sacrifice itself for the sake of others, and is man's surest antidote against worldly pride and immoderate love of self."[1221] This love may be called "social char-

---

[1215] John XXIII, Encyclical Letter *Mater et Magistra*: AAS 53 (1961), 541.

[1216] Second Vatican Ecumenical Council, Dogmatic Constitution *Lumen Gentium*, 35: AAS 57 (1965), 40.

[1217] John Paul II, Encyclical Letter *Centesimus Annus*, 10: AAS 83 (1991), 805-806.

[1218] John Paul II, Encyclical Letter *Sollicitudo Rei Socialis*, 40: AAS 80 (1988), 568.

[1219] Second Vatican Ecumenical Council, Pastoral Constitution *Gaudium et Spes*, 38: AAS 58 (1966), 1055-1056; cf. Second Vatican Ecumenical Council, Dogmatic Constitution *Lumen Gentium*, 42: AAS 57 (1965), 47-48; *Catechism of the Catholic Church*, 826.

[1220] Cf. *Catechism of the Catholic Church*, 1889.

[1221] Leo XIII, Encyclical Letter *Rerum Novarum*: Acta Leonis XIII, 11 (1892), 143; cf. Benedict XV, Encyclical Letter *Pacem Dei*: AAS 12 (1920), 215.

ity"[1222] or "political charity"[1223] and must embrace the entire human race.[1224] "Social love"[1225] is the antithesis of egoism and individualism. Without absolutizing social life, as happens with short-sighted perspectives limiting themselves to sociological interpretations, it must not be forgotten that the integral development of the person and social growth mutually influence each other. Selfishness, therefore, is the most insidious enemy of an ordered society. History shows how hearts are devastated when men and women are incapable of recognizing other values or other effective realities apart from material goods, the obsessive quest for which suffocates and blocks their ability to give of themselves.

582. *In order to make society more human, more worthy of the human person, love in social life — political, economic and cultural — must be given renewed value, becoming the constant and highest norm for all activity.* "If justice is in itself suitable for 'arbitration' between people concerning the reciprocal distribution of objective goods in an equitable manner, love and only love (including that kindly love we call 'mercy') is capable of restoring man to himself."[1226] Human relationships cannot be governed solely according to the measure of justice. "Christians know that love is the reason for God's entering into relationship with man. And it is love which he awaits as man's response. Consequently, love is also *the loftiest and most noble form of relationship possible* between human beings. Love must thus enliven every sector of human life and extend to the international order. Only a humanity in which there reigns the 'civilization of love' will be able to enjoy authentic and lasting peace."[1227] In this regard, the Magisterium highly recommends solidarity because it is capable of guaranteeing the common good and fostering integral human development: love "makes one see in neighbor another self."[1228]

583. *Only love can completely transform the human person.*[1229] Such a transformation does not mean eliminating the earthly dimension in a disembodied spirituality.[1230] Those who think they can live the supernatural virtue of love without taking into account its corresponding natural foundations, which include duties of

---

[1222] Cf. Saint Thomas Aquinas, QD *De caritate*, a. 9, c; Pius XI, Encyclical Letter *Quadragesimo Anno*: AAS 23 (1931), 206-207; John XXIII, Encyclical Letter *Mater et Magistra*: AAS 53 (1961) 410; Paul VI, Address to FAO (16 November 1970), 11: AAS 62 (1970), 837-838; John Paul II, Address to the Members of the Pontifical Commission "Iustitia et Pax" (9 February 1980), 7: AAS 72 (1980), 187.

[1223] Cf. Paul VI, Apostolic Letter *Octogesima Adveniens*, 46: AAS 63 (1971), 433-435.

[1224] Cf. Second Vatican Ecumenical Council, Decree *Apostolicam Actuositatem*, 8: AAS 58 (1966), 844-845; Paul VI, Encyclical Letter *Populorum Progressio*, 44: AAS 59 (1967), 279; John Paul II, Post-Synodal Apostolic Exhortation *Christifideles Laici*, 42: AAS 81 (1989), 472-476; *Catechsim of the Catholic Church*, 1939.

[1225] John Paul II, Encyclical Letter *Redemptor Hominis*, 15: AAS 71 (1979), 288.

[1226] John Paul II, Encyclical Letter *Dives in Misericordia*, 14: AAS 72 (1980), 1223.

[1227] John Paul II, Message for the 2004 World Day of Peace, 10: AAS 96 (2004), 121; cf. John Paul II, Encyclical Letter *Dives in Misericordia*, 14: AAS 72 (1980), 1224; *Catechism of the Catholic Church*, 2212.

[1228] Saint John Chrysostom, *Homilia De Perfecta Caritate*, 1, 2: PG 56, 281-282.

[1229] Cf. John Paul II, Apostolic Letter *Novo Millennio Ineunte*, 49-51: AAS 93 (2001), 302-304.

[1230] Cf. John Paul II, Encyclical Letter *Centesimus Annus*, 5: AAS 83 (1991), 798-800.

justice, deceive themselves. "Charity is the greatest social commandment. It respects others and their rights. It requires the practice of justice and it alone makes us capable of it. Charity inspires a life of self-giving: 'Whoever seeks to gain his life will lose it, but whoever loses his life will preserve it' (*Lk* 17:33)."[1231] Nor can love find its full expression solely in the earthly dimension of human relationships and social relations, because it is in relation to God that it finds its full effectiveness. "In the evening of this life, I shall appear before you with empty hands, for I do not ask you, Lord, to count my works. All our justice is blemished in your eyes. I wish, then, to be clothed in your own *justice* and to receive from your *love* the eternal possession of *yourself*."[1232]

[1231] *Catechism of the Catholic Church*, 1889.
[1232] Saint Thérèse of the Child Jesus, Act of Offering in *Story of a Soul*, tr. John Clarke (Washington, D.C.: ICS 1981, p. 277), as quoted in *Catechism of the Catholic Church*, 2011.

INDEX OF REFERENCES

The second column refers to paragraph numbers of the Compendium.
An asterisk following the number indicates that the reference is found in a note.

SACRED SCRIPTURE

Old Testament

Genesis

1:4,10,12,18,21,25	113, 451
1:4,10,12,18,21,25,31	488
1:26	149
1:26-27	26, 36, 428
1:26-28	209
1:26,28-30	149
1:26-30	64, 326, 451
1:27	108, 110, 451
1:28	36, 111, 209, 255
1:28-29	171
1:31	451, 578
2:2	255, 284
2:5-6	255
2:7	108
2:7-24	209
2:8-24	428
2:15	255, 452
2:15-16	326
2:16-17	136, 326
2:17	256
2:18	209
2:19-20	113
2:20	110
2:20.23	149
2:23	110

2:24	209, 217, 219
3:1-24	27
3:5	256
3:6-8	256
3:12	116
3:17-19	452
3:17,19	256
4:1-16	488
4:2-16	116
4:12	256
5	428
9:1-17	429
9:5	112
10	428
10:1-32	429
11:1	429
11:1-9	429, 488
11:4	429
11:4-8	562
17:1	488
17:4	430

Exodus

3:7-8	21
3:14	21
12:25-27	210
13:8,14-15	210
19-24	22
20:13	112
23	24*
23:10-11	258
30:22-32	378
33:11	13

Second Letter to the Thessalonians

2:7	578
3:6-12	264
3:7-15	264

First Letter to Timothy

2:1-2	380, 381
2:4-5	121
4:4	325
6:10	328

Second Letter to Timothy

4:2-5	2

Letter to Titus

3:1	380, 381
3:2	381
3:3	381
3:5-6	381

Letter to the Hebrews

4:9-10	258
10:23	39
12:22-23	285
13:20	1

Letter of James

1:17	12
1:22	70
2:1-9	145
2:8	580
3:18	102, 203
5:1-6	184
5:4	264, 302

First Letter of Peter

1:18-19	1
2:13	380
2:14	380
2:15	380
2:17	380

Second Letter of Peter

3:10	453
3:13	56, 82, 453

First Letter of John

1:8	120
3:16	196
4:8	54
4:10	30, 39
4:11-12	32

Revelation

17:6	382
19:20	382
21:1	453, 455
21:3	60

Ecumenical Councils

(cited according to DS [Denziger-Schönmetzer], except for Second Vatican Council)

Lateran Council IV

800	127*

First Vatican Ecumenical Council

3002	127*
3005	141
3022	127*
3025	127*

Second Vatican Ecumenical Council

Sacrosanctum Concilium

10	519

Inter Mirifica

3	415*
4	560*
11	415*

Lumen Gentium

1	19*, 49, 431
5	49
9	33*
11	519
12	79
31	11, 83*, 220*, 541, 545

Papal Documents

Pope John XXIII

Enc. Letter *Mater et Magistra*
(15 May 1961)

84*, 87*, 94*, 95,
107*, 160*, 164*,
166*, 167*, 176*,
178*, 185*, 189*,
192*, 194*, 336*,
339*, 355*, 384, 396,
440*, 446, 527*, 549*,
551*, 575, 579, 581*

Enc. Letter *Pacem in Terris*
(11 April 1963)

84*, 87*, 94, 95*, 95,
145*, 149*, 153*, 153,
155*, 156*, 156, 164*,
165*, 190*, 197*,
198*, 200*, 201*,
205*, 301*, 383*, 384,
386, 387*, 388, 389,
391, 393, 393*, 395*,
396, 396*, 397*, 398*,
414*, 432, 433*, 434*,
435*, 437, 437*, 439*,
441*, 441, 497, 497*,
499*, 499, 527*

Pope Paul VI

Enc. Letter *Populorum Progressio*
(26 March 1967)

	98, 98*, 102
6	449
13	61, 81, 197*
14	373
17	194*, 467
19	318*
20	449
21	98, 449
22	172, 177*, 446*, 449*, 481*
23	158, 177*, 300*
31	401
35	198*

37	234*
40	198*, 373*
41	373*
42	82, 98, 373*
43	145*
44	145*, 448*, 581*
47	449*
48	194*
51	442*
52	442*
53	442*
54	442*
55	442*, 449*
56	447*
57	364, 447*
58	447*
59	366, 447*
60	447*
61	364*, 447*
63	433*
76	98, 495*
77	98, 442*
78	98, 372*, 441*, 442*
79	98, 442*
80	98
81	83*, 531

Enc. Letter *Humanae Vitae*
(25 July 1968)

7	233*
10	232
14	233*
16	233*
17	233*

Ap. Letter *Sollicitudo Omnium Ecclesiarum*
(29 June 1969)

445

Ap. Letter *Octogesima Adveniens*
(14 May 1971)

	100, 100*
3	80*
4	11*, 80*, 81*, 574
5	80*

11	53*
13	58*
14	62, 82, 105*, 126
15	581
17	155, 158*, 168*

Ap. Exhort. *Catechesi Tradendae*
(16 October 1979)

5	529
14	423
18	529*
29	529

Enc. Letter *Dives in Misericordia*
(30 November 1980)

12	206
14	206, 582

Enc. Letter *Laborem Exercens*
(14 September 1981)

	72, 101*, 269
1	269
2	201*, 269*
3	72*, 87*, 269
4	275
6	259, 270, 271, 272
8	193*, 308
9	287*
10	249, 249*, 287*, 294, 294*, 317*
11	279
12	277, 290*
13	277*
14	177, 189*, 192*, 281, 282, 287*
15	192*
16	274, 287*
17	288*, 336*
18	287*, 287, 301*
19	172, 250*, 251*, 284*, 295, 301*, 301, 302*, 345*
20	301*, 304*, 304, 305, 306, 307, 318*
21	299
22	148

25	326*
26	326*
27	263*, 326*

Ap. Exhort. *Familiaris Consortio*
(22 November 1982)

12	219*
13	217*, 219
18	221*
19	217
20	225
23	251*, 294*
24	295*
26	244
27	222*
32	233*
36	239
37	238*, 243
40	240
42	553*
43	221, 238*, 242*, 553*
44	247, 553*
45	214*, 252, 355*, 553*
46	253*, 553*
47	220, 553*
48	220, 553*
77	226*, 298*
81	229
84	226*

Ap. Exhort. *Reconciliatio et Paenitentia*
(2 December 1985)

2	116
10	121
15	116
16	117, 118, 193*

Enc. Letter *Redemptoris Mater*
(25 March 1987)

37	59

Enc. Letter *Sollicitudo Rei Socialis*
(30 December 1987)

	72, 102, 102*
1	60*, 87*, 104, 162*
3	85*, 85
9	374*

17	200*
18	438
21	157*
23	438*
24	558, 559*, 577*
29	373
31	171, 176, 273, 287*
32	179, 278, 283*, 337, 343, 344*
33	344*, 447
34	347, 349*, 448
35	179, 189*, 340, 344, 446*, 450
36	345, 358, 359, 360, 376, 486*, 486
37	360*, 460, 467*
38	340, 464
39	212, 231, 350, 375
40	347, 349, 356*, 466*, 470*
41	47, 170*, 181*, 280, 333, 348*
42	200, 335
43	278, 282, 288, 338, 340*
44	191*, 408
45	191*
46	86*, 190*, 395*, 406, 407, 567, 569*
47	155, 158, 191*, 424
48	185*, 186*, 187, 188*, 291, 336*, 351, 352, 353*, 354*, 411*
49	185*, 355*, 420*
50	556
51	494*, 498
52	434*, 439, 498
53	60*, 81*, 82*
54	60*, 61, 67, 69, 78, 159*, 527*
55	9*, 560, 577
56	90, 90*
57	193*, 525, 551*
58	371, 442*, 448
59	73, 76, 78

60	90

**Enc. Letter *Veritatis Splendor*
(6 August 1993)**

13	75*
27	70*
34	135*
35	136
44	138*
48	127
50	75*, 140*
51	142
61	139
64	70*
79	75*
80	155*
86	138
87	143*
97	22, 397*
98	577
99	138*, 397*
107	530
110	70*

**Motu Proprio *Socialium Scientiarum*
(1 January 1994)**

	78*

**Ap. Letter *Gratissimam Sane*
(2 February 1994)**

6	111*, 230
7	213
8	111*
10	237
11	218*, 221, 230
13	231
14	111*, 227*
16	111*
17	211, 251*
19	111*
20	111*
21	233*

**Ap. Letter *Tertio Millennio Adveniente*
(10 November 1994)**

13	25*
51	182*, 450*

Message for the 1992 World Day of Peace

4	519*

Message for the 1993 World Day of Peace

1	449*
3	298*
4	497*

Message for the 1994 World Day of Peace

5	239*

Message for the 1996 World Day of Peace

2-6	245*
5	296*

Message for the 1997 World Day of Peace

3	517*, 518*
4	517*, 518*
6	518*

Message for the 1998 World Day of Peace

2	154
3	363
4	450*
5	412
6	296

Message for the 1999 World Day of Peace

3	153, 154
5	423*
6	411*
7	506*, 518*
8	287*
9	450*
10	468*
11	497, 510*, 511*, 512*, 518
12	494*

Message for the 2000 World Day of Peace

6	388*

7	506*
11	506
13	373*
14	373*, 449, 564
15-16	333*
17	564*
20	516

Message for the 2001 World Day of Peace

13	298*
19	405*

Message for the 2002 World Day of Peace

4	513*
5	514
7	515*
9	517*

Message for the 2003 World Day of Peace

5	365, 485*,
6	441

Message for the 2004 World Day of Peace

4	494*
5	437
6	438*, 501
7	440, 442*, 443
8	514*, 514
9	439, 506*, 516*
10	203, 206, 517*, 582

1990 Message for Lent

3	505

Message for the 23rd World Day of Social Communications (1999)

3	560

Speeches, Letters and others Messages

2 December 1978
71
13 January 1979
244

1 May 1991
        374
19 May 1991
        63*
5 December 1992
        506*
16 January 1993
        506*
7 March 1993
        504
18 April 1993
        506
30 November 1993
        440*, 504*
11 March 1994
        502*
18 March 1994
        440*, 483
28 October 1994
        470*
9 January 1995
        507*
26 May 1995
        440*
9 July 1995
        147
5 October 1995
        145*, 152*, 157, 388*,
        432*, 434*, 435*, 435,
        436
13 January 1996
        509*
2 December 1996
        308*
13 January 1997
        495*, 518*
24 March 1997
        461, 463, 464, 465
25 April 1997
        287*, 369*
20 June 1997
        446*
19 February 1998
        228*
9 May 1998
        363*

14 June 1998
        506*
4 July 1998
        506*
30 November 1998
        450*
21 January 1999
        228
6 March 1999
        279*
11 August 1999
        505
31 March 2000
        402, 404
1 May 2000
        321
2 May 2000
        446*
29 August 2000
        236*
13 January 2001
        435*
27 April 2001
        310*, 366
14 September 2001
        309, 320*
24 September 2001
        515*
24 February 2002
        515*
21 March 2002
        437*
3 April 2002
        222
11 April 2002
        367
27 April 2002
        367*
13 January 2003
        497
5 January 2004
        148
7 January 2004
        484
12 January 2004
        572

4 February 2004
                341
21 February 2004
                236*

Church Documents

Catechism of the Catholic Church

1914	189*	2210	213*
1915	189*	2211	252*
1916	189*	2212	206*, 390*, 391*, 582*
1917	189*, 191*	2213	390*
1928	201*	2221	239*
1929	201*, 202*	2223	239*
1930	153*, 201*	2224	213*
1931	105*, 201*	2228	238*
1932	201*	2229	240*
1933	201*	2235	132*, 396*
1934	144*, 201*	2236	409*
1935	201*	2237	388*
1936	201*	2241	298*
1937	201*	2242	399*
1938	201*	2243	401
1939	193*, 201*,581*	2244	47*, 51*
1940	193*, 201*	2245	50*, 424*,
1941	193*, 194*, 201*	2246	426*
1942	193*, 201*	2258	112*
1955	140*	2259	112*
1956	140*	2260	112*
1957	141*	2261	112*
1958	141	2265	500*
1959	142*	2266	402*, 403*
1960	141*	2267	405
1970	20*	2269	341
2011	583*	2271	233*
2034	79*	2272	233*
2037	80*	2273	233*
2039	83*	2297	513*
2062	22	2304	495*
2070	22	2306	496
2105	422	2307	497*
2106	421*	2308	497*
2107	423*	2309	497*, 500
2108	421*, 422*	2310	497*, 502*
2109	422*	2311	497*, 503*
2184	284*	2312	497*
2185	284	2313	497*, 503*
2186	285	2314	497*, 509*
2187	285*, 286	2315	497*, 508
2188	286	2316	497*, 508*
2204	220*	2317	495*, 497*
2206	213*	2333	224
2209	214*	2334	111*

Congregations

Congregation for the Clergy

Church Writers

References
from International Law

ANALYTICAL INDEX

AUTHORITY - AUTHORITIES

AUTONOMY (*see also* AUTONOMY OF THE STATE)

AUTONOMY OF THE STATE

AWARENESS

CHURCH

CITIZEN - CITIZENSHIP

COMMUNITY (see also CIVIL COMMUNITY, POLITICAL COMMUNITY, CHRISTIAN COMMUNITY, FAMILY COMMUNITY, INTERNATIONAL COMMUNITY, SOCIAL COMMUNITY)

CREATOR (*see also* **CREATION**)

CREATURE - CREATED BEING

CREDIT

CRIME - CRIMINAL

CUSTOM - CUSTOMARY

DEMOCRACY - DEMOCRATIC - DEMOCRATIZATION

DEVELOPMENT

DIRECTIVES

DISARM - DISARMAMENT

DISCERNMENT

ECONOMY - ECONOMIC

EPISCOPAL CONFERENCE - *see* **BISHOPS' CONFERENCE**

EQUAL - EQUALITY

EQUITY

FACTORIES - *see* **BUSINESS**

FAILINGS (*see also* **INFIDELITY**)

FAITH

FALLOW

FALSEHOOD - *see* LIE

FAMILY (*see also* FAMILY COMMUNITY)

FRATERNAL - FRATERNITY - BROTHERHOOD

FREE - FREEDOM (see also FREE TIME)

GLOBAL

GLOBAL COMMUNITY - *see* INTERNATIONAL COMMUNITY

GRATUITOUS - GRATUITOUSNESS

GROUPS

HUNGER

IDEOLOGY - IDEOLOGICAL

Scientific and technocratic ideologies, 462

Ideological control and social communications, 557

Christian commitment and ideological visions, 558

ILLITERACY

Illiteracy, poverty and the Church, 5

Illiteracy, underdevelopment and poverty, 447

Illiteracy and ecumenical cooperation, 535

IMBALANCE - DISPARITY (*see also* INEQUALITY)

Social doctrine, denunciation and imbalances, 81

The common good and disparities, 167

State intervention and serious social imbalances, 188

Imbalances in the world of work, 321

Imbalances between man and nature, 454

IMMIGRATION - EMIGRATION - IMMIGRANTS

Octogesima Adveniens and emigration, 100

Unemployment and immigration, 289

Immigration, a resource for development, 297

Regulating immigration, 298

Globalisation, unions and immigrants, 308

IMMORAL - *see* MORAL

IMPOVERISHMENT - *see* POVERTY

INCOME

Distribution of income and justice, 303

Informal economic activities and low incomes, 316

INCORPORATED

The laity, incorporated into Christ by baptism, 541

INCULTURATION

Christian anthropology and inculturation, 523

Educational institutions and inculturation, 532

INDIVIDUAL PERSON

Sin, free act of an individual person, 117

What is true for the individual is also true for peoples, 157

The individual person and development, 168

INDUSTRIOUSNESS

Labor, human capital and industriousness, 278

Independent work and industriousness, 315

INDUSTRY - INDUSTRIAL

The industrial revolution and the labor question, 88

Rerum Novarum and industrial workers, 89

Quadragesimo Anno and industrialization, 91

Pope John XXIII and the industrial revolution, 94

Octogesima Adveniens and post-industrial society, 100

New methods and industrialized nations, 179

The Church and the industrial revolution, 267

Unions and the struggle of industrial workers, 305

New types of work and the first industrial revolution, 311

Passage of work from industry to services, 313

INSTRUCT - INSTRUCTION

INSURANCE

INTERDEPENDENCE

KINGDOM

LABOR (*see also* WORK)

LOVE (*see also* CHARITY)

MAGISTERIUM - see SOCIAL DOCTRINE

MAN - MANKIND - MEN - PEOPLE - MAN AND WOMAN - MEN AND WOMEN

MARGINALIZATION - MARGINAL-IZED

MARKET

NATIONALISTIC

The international community and nationalistic ideologies, 433

NATURAL LAW - NATURAL MORAL LAW

The Ten Commandments and natural law, 22

Human action and natural law, 37

Social relationships and natural law, 53

Natural law and creatures of God, 53

Doctrinal principles and natural law, 89

Pope Pius XII and natural law, 93

Natural moral law, 140

Natural law, rights and duties of the person, 140

Universality of natural moral law, 142

Human society, natural law and duties, 156

Right to use goods and natural law, 172

Natural law and sexual identity, 224

Work, family life and natural law, 294

Human values and natural law, 397

The right to resistance and natural law, 400

International law and natural law, 437

NATURE - NATURAL (*see also* NATURAL LAW)

Civilization and man's place in nature, 14, 15

Religiosity and rational nature of the person, 15

Relation between nature, technology and morality, 16

Rights inherent within the nature of the person, 22

Task of ordering created nature, 36

Fruits of nature and the Kingdom of Christ, 57

Moral truths and human nature, 70

Nature of the Church's social doctrine, 72, 73

Human nature, source of social doctrine, 75, 77

Doctrinal weight, social teaching and nature, 80

Social doctrine and obligations of a secular nature, 83

Universal values and human nature, 85

Sollicitudo Rei Socialis and the nature of development, 102

Relation between God and man and human nature, 110

Man, a social being by his very nature, 110

Original sin and human nature, 115

Jesus Christ, human nature and the nature of God, 122

Man, as a speck of nature, 128

Man, spirit and matter, one nature, 129

Reason belongs to human nature, 140

Civil law and consequences of concrete nature, 142

Freedom and common nature, 142

Human nature and relational subjectivity, 149

Society, contract and human nature, 149*

A society that responds to human nature, 151

Depriving people of rights and doing violence to their nature, 153

Nature of the principle of the common use of goods, 172

Men, rational nature and responsibility, 205

The family and legitimisation of human nature, 214

Marriage and the nature of conjugal love, 215, 225, 230, 237, 253

Work and its social and individual nature, 273

Workers' rights and nature of the person, 301

Human nature and relation with the Transcendent, 318

Faith in Christ and the nature of development, 327, 342

NEGOTIATION

NEIGHBOR

NIHILISM

NORM - NORMATIVE

OBLIGATION - see DUTY

OLD AGE (see also ELDERLY, AGING)

ORDER

ORGANISM

ORGANIZATION - ORGANIZE

PENAL INSTITUTIONS

PEOPLE - PEOPLES (*see also* MAN, PERSON, POPULATION)

POLITICS - POLITICAL - POLITICIANS (*see also* POLITICAL COMMUNITY)

PROCREATION

PRODUCTION - PRODUCT - PRODUCTIVITY

PROFESSION - PROFESSIONAL - PROFESSIONALITY

PROFIT

PROGRESS

PROMOTION

RACE - RACISM

REARING CHILDREN (*see also* EDU-CATE)

REASON

RECONCILIATION

REST (*see also* **FALLOW**)

REVOLUTION

RIGHTS

SOLIDARITY

SON - see CHILDREN

SON OF GOD - see JESUS CHRIST

SOUL

VENTURE - see BUSINESS

VERIFICATION

VIOLENCE

God and spiral of violence, 43

Social doctrine and sin of violence, 81

Deprivation of human rights and violence, 153

Forms of child labor and violence, 296

Unjust laws, act of violence, 398

Recourse to violence and passive resistance, 401

Creation, sin and violence, 429

International community and recourse to violence, 433

Violence, interpersonal and social relations, 488

God, peace and violence, 488

Violence, 496

Recourse to violence, destruction and death, 496

Light weapons and manifestations of violence, 511

Terrorism, a brutal form of violence, 513

Violence, inhumanity and suffering, 517

VIRTUE

Humanism and the cultivation of virtues, 19

Solidarity as a moral and social virtue, 193, 194*

Solidarity as a Christian virtue, 196*

Social principles and exercise of virtues, 197

Justice and corresponding cardinal virtue, 201

Peace, justice and practice of virtues, 203

Bond between virtues, social values and love, 204

Children, the family and virtue, 210

The family, first school of social virtues, 238

Education and cultivation of virtues, 242

Riches and the virtue of solidarity, 332

Economic initiative as a virtue, 343

Authority, virtue and power as service, 410

The laity and exercise of social virtues, 546

The laity and prudence as a virtue, 547, 548

Charity, mistress and queen of virtues, 581

Supernatural virtues of love and justice, 583

VOCATION

The Church, vocation of man and communion, 3, 63

The *Compendium* and the vocation proper to different charisms, 10

The Church, the world and innermost vocation, 18

Vocation of the human race to unity, 19

Trinitarian love and vocation, 34

Christian revelation and vocation, 35, 36

Man's ultimate vocation, 41

Person, vocation and the created universe, 47

The Church, the political community the vocation of human beings, 50, 425

The Church and man's definitive vocation, 51

Man, vocation and the divine plan, 60

Social doctrine and the vocation of man, 61

Life in society and vocation, 62

Social doctrine and earthly vocation, 72

Interdisciplinary dialogue and vocation, 78

Social teaching and vocation, 83

The laity, secular character and vocation, 83

Laborem Exercens, work and vocation, 101

WAGE - *see* SALARY

WAR

WATER

WEALTH - RICHES - RICH - ENRICH

WORKER

Cultural causes and injustices in the world, 577

Divine promise, the world and the Kingdom of God, 578, 579

WORLD COMMUNITY - *see* **INTERNATIONAL COMMUNITY**

WORLD DAY OF PEACE

Pope Paul VI and the World Day of Peace, 99

The World Days of Peace, 520

YOUNG - YOUTH

The Ten Commandments and the rich young man, 22

Mit Brennender Sorge and young people, 92

Octogesima Adveniens and the conditions of young people, 100

Rights of nations and younger generations, 157

Nations and the growth of younger generations, 222

Unemployment and the younger generations, 287

Formation, the job market and young people, 289

Young people and risks within the economic context, 290

International organizations and the work of youth, 292

COVER ART

Allegory of Good Government; fresco by Ambrogio Lorenzetti, 1338-39, Palazzo Pubblico, Siena, Italy. Artwork provided by Scala/Art Resource, NY. Used with permission. All rights reserved.

The allegory begins with the biblical figure of Wisdom, represented on the top left of the back cover as a crowned woman holding a large scale. Two figures are perfectly balanced on the plates of the scale, one representing distributive justice and the other commutative justice. Between these two figures is a large image of Justice personified, dressed in splendid garments. Above this personification is the inscription: "*Diligete justitiam qui judicatis terram*" ("Choose justice, you who govern the earth"), the opening verse of the Book of Wisdom, placed as a word of caution to the City Council that used to meet in this room of the Palazzo Pubblico. Beneath the figure of Justice there is another feminine figure holding in her lap a plane (to smooth out the ambitious) on which the word "Concordia" is written. The significance is very clear: from the Wisdom of God descends human Justice in all its forms, and from Justice there comes Concord or harmony in the life of the city.

From Concord, there is a procession of citizens of different social conditions (seen in the different characteristic manners of dress): artisans and professionals, a priest, a soldier, members of the nobility, and public officials. The procession moves towards an elevated platform where seven people are seated, six of whom are women with their names written above them; they are the virtues *Pax, Fortitudo, Prudentia, Magnanimitas, Temperantia,* and *Justitia*. In the middle is a dignified old man with a scepter in his right hand who represents the City of Siena; above his head are the traditional figures of the theological virtues *Fides, Caritas,* and *Spes*.

Read in reverse order, one understands that prosperity and activity in the areas of work, artisanry and education—represented on the adjacent wall of the same room in a fresco by Lorenzetti that describes the *Effects of Good Government*—are the mature fruits of a civic life guided by the Virtues cultivated in harmony among citizens, a Concord that in turn arises from the Justice administered by those who govern, which in turn is drawn directly from divine Wisdom.

Created for the seat of government of a free republic, these frescoes offer a typically Christian vision of a world whose external order results from an internal order that men and women receive as a gift, but that must also be chosen with responsibility. They are images of both the spiritual transparence and the concrete social situation of the thinkers of the period, with their sure faith in God, the principle of all truth and every form of social life and organization.

VATICAN PRESS